HANDBOOK OF RESEARCH ON TECHNO-ENTREPRENEURSHIP

Handbook of Research on Techno-Entrepreneurship

Edited by

François Thérin

Associate Professor, Grenoble Ecole de Management, France

Edward Elgar
Cheltenham, UK • Northampton, MA, USA

Published by
Edward Elgar Publishing Limited
Glensanda House
Montpellier Parade
Cheltenham
Glos GL50 1UA
UK

Edward Elgar Publishing, Inc.
William Pratt House
9 Dewey Court
Northampton
Massachusetts 01060
USA

A catalogue record for this book
is available from the British Library

Library of Congress Cataloguing in Publication Data

Handbook of research on techno-entrepreneurship / edited by François Thérin.
   p.   cm. — (Elgar original reference)
Includes bibliographical references and index.
1. High technology industries—Management.   2. Technological innnovations
—Management.   3. Entrepreneurship.   I. Thérin, François.

HD62.37.H35 2007
658.4'21—dc22

                                                                    2006026362

ISBN 978 1 84542 286 8 (cased)

Printed and bound in Great Britain by MPG Books Ltd, Bodmin, Cornwall

Contents

v

PART 4 INDUSTRY SPECIFICS: E-ENTREPRENEURSHIP

PART 5 INDUSTRY SPECIFICS: BIOTECHNOLOGIES

Contributors

Khairul Akmaliah Adham, Faculty of Economics and Business, Universiti Kebangsaan Malaysia, 43600 Bangi Selangor, Malaysia, ka@pkrisc.cc.ukm.my

Edward L. Bayham, EXPLOR Bioventures, Saint Louis, MO, USA

Michael Bernasconi, CERAM Sophia-Antipolis, France

Sylvie Blanco, Grenoble Ecole de Management, France

Robert Calcaterra, Nidus Center for Scientific Enterprise, Saint Louis, MO, USA

Ana Rosa del Águila-Obra, University of Málaga, Spain, anarosa@uma.es

Nicola Dellepiane, Department of Production Systems and Managerial Economics, Polytechnic School of Engineering, University of Turin, Italy, nicola @lep.polito.it

Behrend Freese, Deutsche Telekom AG, Laboratories Innovation Development, Berlin, Germany, behrend.freese@telekom.de

David L. Hawk, New Jersey Institute of Technology, University Heights, Newark, NJ, USA

Dianne I. Isabelle, Eric Sprott School of Business, Carleton University & National Research Council of Canada, Ottawa, Canada

Dominique Jolly, CERAM Sophia-Antipolis, France

Jerome A. Katz, Saint Louis University, MO, USA

Thomas Keil, York University, Schulich School of Business, Toronto, Ontario, Canada, tkeil@schulich.yorku.ca

Tobias Kollmann, Chair for E-Business and E-Entrepreneurship, University of Duisburg-Essen, Campus Essen, Germany, Tobias.Kollmann@icb.uni-due.de

Christian Lendner, Lindner-Professor for Entrepreneurship, University of Applied Sciences Deggendorf, Germany, christian.lendner@fh-deggendorf.de

Lalit Manral, Columbia Business School, Columbia University, New York, NY, USA, lm663@columbia.edu

Rory O'Shea, Sloan School of Management, Massachusetts Institute of Technology, Cambridge, MA, USA, roshea@mit.edu

Antonio Padilla-Meléndez, University of Málaga, Spain, apm@uma.es

Annaleena Parhankangas, Helsinki University of Technology, P.O.Box 5500, 02015 TKK, Finland

Igor Prodan, Regional Technological Centre Zasavje, Grajska pot 10, 1430 Hrastnik, SI-Slovenia, igor.prodan@guest.arnes.si

Mohd Fuaad Said, Faculty of Economics and Management, Universiti Putra Malaysia, 43400 UPM Serdang Selangor, Malaysia, fuaad@econ.upm.edu.my

Christian Serarols-Tarres, Universidad Autónoma de Barcelona, Spain, christian.serarols@uab.es

Thorsten Teichert, University of Hamburg, Institute for Retailing and Marketing, Hamburg, Germany, teichert@econ.uni-hamburg.de

Helena Yli-Renko, Lloyd Greif Center for Entrepreneurial Studies, Marshall School of Business, University of Southern California, Los Angeles, CA, USA, hylirenko@marshall.usc.edu

Joseph Zahner, Saint Louis University, MO, USA

Introduction

Techno-entrepreneurship is a recent field which has its roots in the now established field of entrepreneurship. Its aim is to study the specificities of entrepreneurial activities in technology-intensive environments. Why is that important? Techno-entrepreneurship combines the risk factors associated with entrepreneuring with the ones due to the highly uncertain nature of technologies development. This 'squared risk' is a real challenge for new high-tech ventures.

As an emerging field, it was important to consolidate the early writings and this is the aim of the present Handbook. Since the inception of this project almost three years ago, it has been decided to be as open as possible in terms of contributions to allow any researchers to feel that they are working in techno-entreprenurship to contribute to the Handbook. The result is a diverse yet focused collection of contributions: diverse as it ranges from questioning the reality of the field to the study of processes of techno-entrepreneurship, including the role of clusters, incubators and technology transfers and to applications in two of the most techno-entrepreneurial industries of the moment: biotechnology and electronic commerce.

The first part of the Handbook is dedicated to the foundations of the field. The first contribution, by Sylvie Blanco, shows that the concept of technological opportunity recognition is important to resolving part of the uncertainty related to techno-entrepreneurship. Igor Prodan, in Chapter 2, builds a model of technological entrepreneurship in the perspective of regional development by emphasizing key characteristics derived from the literature in entrepreneurship and technology policy. To end this part, Helena Yli-Renko casts light on exchange relationships in entrepreneurship research by mapping the various streams of research on the external relationships of entrepreneurs and entrepreneurial firms in a high-tech context.

The second part focuses on the specific underlying processes in techno-entrepreneurship. Diane Isabelle studies the commercialization of science and technology and the supporting mechanisms. Annaleena Parhankangas and David L. Hawk, using evidence from five new-to-the-world technologies studied over three decades, discuss the balance between exploration and exploitation for high-tech ventures. Behrend Freese, Thomas Keil and Thorsten Teichert focus on radical innovation and how corporate venture capital can help to adress the challenges it presents. Finally, Khairul Akmaliah Adham and Mohd Fuaad Said highlight the importance of mentoring in the pre-seeding phase in the case of Malaysian high-tech entrepreneurs.

The third part of the volume is dedicated to incubators and technology transfers. Christian Lendner explores the growing phenomenon of business incubators in universities to help technology transfers and influence on start-ups. Rory O'Shea develops a conceptual framework of university spin-off activities and suggests that university heads and policy makers can encourage and develop university entrepreneurship by using a comprehensive systems approach for the identification, protection and commercialization of university intellectual property. To close this part, Michael Bernasconi and Dominique Jolly present spin-off activities in the case of Sophia-Antipolis, one of the first technopoles in

France, and trace the history of the development of the techno park and the characteristics of its different phases of development.

The fourth part focuses on the specificities of techno-entrepreneurship in e-business with three contributions. Tobias Kollmann describes what is e-entrepreneurship, positions the net economy among the other economies and shows that the electronic value chain and the value-oriented processing of information serve as the starting point for every net economy venture. Antonio Padilla-Meléndez, Christian Serarols-Tarres and Ana Rosa del Águila-Obra study the profiles of e-entrepreneurs in terms of demographics and motivations in the case of Spain. Finally, Lalit Manral focuses on virtual alliances in the Internet context and presents their dynamics compared to traditional alliances.

The fifth and last part of the volume is dedicated to another industry replete with techno-entrepreneurship: the biotech industry. Edward L. Bayham, Jerome A. Katz, Robert Calcaterra and Joseph Zahner make an in-depth study of the St Louis BioBelt and its success factors and present factors complementary to the earlier chapter on Sophia Antipolis. Finally Nicola Dellepiane studies the strategies of small business in the part of the biotech industry dedicated to DNA–RNA.

After reading one or several of these contributions, the reader will realize how vast and yet mostly unexplored the field of techno-entrepreneurship is. There is a definite need for the exploitation of existing findings and their integration into readable frameworks and for the exploration of the numerous aspects of entrepreneuring in technology-intensive industries. As the high-tech of today is the commodity of tomorrow and as the start-ups of today are the multinationals of tomorrow, no doubt this field will become of interest in the near future to more and more researchers, policy makers and practitioners.

PART 1

FOUNDATIONS OF THE FIELD

1 How techno-entrepreneurs build a potentially exciting future?

Sylvie Blanco

Summary

Technology-based entrepreneurship is assumed to be one of the most important sources of economic value creation and development in Europe. Major incentives and means have been implemented to foster, secure and accelerate the creation and the early growth of high-tech new ventures – whatever their origin. However, despite years of experience, the problem of predicting potential growth and profits of future businesses remains highly uncertain. Actually, techno-entrepreneurship seems to entail both high potential future profits and high uncertainty. A major question concerns the possibility to prove, at least partly, the future value of an opportunity before its realization. This calls for a better understanding of the concept of technological opportunity seen as an anticipated profitable business so as to enable researchers and practitioners to develop procedural knowledge. This chapter proposes to learn from successful techno-entrepreneurs about the way they represent their opportunity early before its concretization so that both procedural and declarative basic knowledge may be identified.

Introduction

Techno-entrepreneurs aim at creating and capturing economic value through the exploration and exploitation of new technology-based solutions. To do so, they have to find their way in an existing world in order to (re)create a new one where they will be able to reap the benefit of their idea and vision. This process, which mainly belongs to opportunity recognition, raises an important issue about the ability to match current and future technologies, market needs and resources in a vision of a future business opportunity which is recognized as exciting by external actors. The ability to recognize business opportunities is one of the first and major skills an entrepreneur should acquire as it will dramatically shape the future of his venture. However, our understanding of this achievement remains vague and hardly actionable to support practitioners. To our view, despite a thorough understanding of the opportunity recognition process, its determinants of success and failure, quite an important lack of understanding remains as to appropriate anticipative approaches. Two questions remain without a satisfying answer: what does reliable knowledge about the future consist of? How to gather and produce such knowledge in an effective manner?

Actually, as in the managerial literature, the entrepreneurship literature assumes that entrepreneurs are able to anticipate and to build a credible vision of their future business. Mostly, two series of parameters explain these abilities: willingness to bear uncertainty and specific cognitive abilities starting with alertness. Techno-entrepreneurs would be more willing to bear uncertainty and more knowledgable about overcoming this difficulty than non-entrepreneurs. Their alertness provides them with the ability to detect and exploit early signs of change and then to tell plausible stories about their future business. Besides, they know how to build precise plans according to detailed objectives, thus taking into account the potential impact of anticipated risks and problems. They formulate a plan for execution, that is to say a series of actions and events in order to capture the opportunity they have in mind. These tasks allow them to detect exciting future businesses and to motivate their potential partners so that they may gain access to the required resources to launch their business platform. Finally, opportunity recognition means both gathering knowledge and conceptualizing future business value. The way these tasks are achieved and combined is crucial to building trust, leveraging external resources and attracting a higher level of investment, of customers and of partners. However, so far, we do not know about the principles and procedures allowing us to gather knowledge about the future and to conceptualize the opportunity as it may concretize. That is why we propose to learn from three successful but different experiences of technological opportunity recognition and to analyse them as anticipation mechanisms.

Technological Opportunity Recognition as Anticipation in the Light of Uncertainty

1.1   Technological opportunity recognition
In his landmark work on capitalism evolution and transformation, Schumpeter (1934) put the emphasis on entrepreneurs as those who, in opposition to traditional capitalists (who exploit existing resources, fields and activities), engage in new activities or ventures that did not exist before. He emphasized how entrepreneurs explore new opportunities in order to build a new world order while deconstructing the old one, thus allowing capitalism to constantly reinvent itself. Hence, entrepreneurship can be defined as an activity and a process involving the discovery, creation and exploitation of opportunities in order to create value thanks to the introduction of new goods, services, processes and organizations.

As argued by Shane and Venkataraman (2000) and Van der Ven and Wakkee (2004), a major topic of entrepreneurship research lies in the way individuals recognize opportunities for business creation. This is one of the first critical abilities in the early stages of the business development process, 'which begins with the realisation of the idea whereby one or more founders take concrete action to set up a commercial enterprise. The process is said to be concluded when a business platform has been established' (Klofsten, 1997). Entrepreneurs are those people who sense, create and respond to change regarding a possible opportunity for profit. Different approaches have been and are still adopted to understand this phenomenon. We can distinguish three main streams of thinking about the nature of an opportunity (Davidsson, 2004): the objective approach suggesting that opportunities do exist in the environment so that analysing key parameters would allow detecting and picking them up – like 'mushrooms'; the subjective objective approach focusing on the ability of a few people to practise this picking, depending on individual characteristics; and the subjective creative approach where the opportunity is built in the mind of the entrepreneurs using partly creative thinking, taking into account external conditions and taking for granted that the opportunity validity will never be fully proven beforehand but afterwards.

Currently, technology-based entrepreneurship means that technology is at the core and origin of the new venture thanks to its potential to accomplish new performance through innovation. Many authors on entrepreneurship have recently paid attention to the concept of innovative opportunities (Gaglio, 1997; Hills and Shrader, 1998; De Koning, 1999; Singh, 1999; Ardichvili et al., 2003). They agree on the fact that it is a social construct based on an initial idea and depending on individuals' value, cognitive behaviours, knowledge, connections to the external environment and motivations. Introducing technology in the scope of entrepreneurship brings in more novelty, new eventualities related to R&D power and assets as well as specific constraints and contexts. As soon as technology is involved, entrepreneurship consists in bringing important changes into the market compared to the more traditional entrepreneurship. Something new or significantly different will be created and exploited and its shape depends both on entrepreneurs' subjective thinking and on environmental conditions. Our position is typically to adopt the subjective creative approach to entrepreneurship.

The process of opportunity recognition starts with the sensing of a need or a possibility for change and action and ends with an innovative solution in which future potential economic value is clear enough and externally recognized. To achieve this, information and knowledge should have been gathered in order to answer key issues regarding (a) how well market needs and technology-based solutions are matched so that one can believe in the 'truth' of a market potential with a limited sense of doubt; (b) how feasible this view is through a path of actions taking place in a malleable and not fully determined environment on which the course of actions will exert a predictable and mastered impact; and (c) how exciting this plausible future may be according to possible options, potential impact and probable consequences for stakeholders.

Opportunities emerge from an idea transformed into a conceptual vision, itself refined and validated through information gathering and concept creation (De Koning, 1999). These two different activities are achieved under very heterogeneous conditions from one situation to the other. For instance, the innovation can consist in transferring existing technological elements from one industry to another, offering new ways to do existing business or to meet existing or potential needs, answering to new market drivers triggered by dominant actors in the industry. However, techno-entrepreneurs do have to pay attention to the problem of matching technology-based solutions with market current and future needs, expectations and constraints. It implies that entrepreneurs have to gather information on the users' wills and constraints regarding the innovative solution and to interpret this information to gain access to a potential market. This refers essentially to the search for information for which entrepreneurs would have specific skills, different from those of managers (Kaish and Gilad, 1991).

However, as in the innovation process, techno-entrepreneurs will have to undergo a series of other activities, including thinking, imagining, incubating, demonstrating, promoting and sustaining (Jolly, 1997). They will extend their resources and knowledge about technology, market and managerial skills through their external networks, thus deploying their absorptive capacity (Cohen and Levinthal, 1990). Because of the novelty of the situation, the high level of uncertainty and the subjective creative characteristics of the opportunity recognition process, it is admitted that action is central to most theories of entrepreneurship and depends concomitantly on various elements, such as knowledge, motivations and (arguably) a stimulus. 'Because action takes place over time, and the future is unknowable,

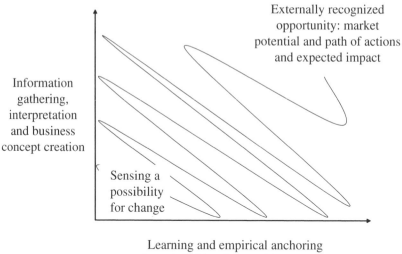

Figure 1.1   Opportunity recognition as a learning process

action is inherently uncertain. This uncertainty is further enhanced by the novelty intrinsic to entrepreneurial actions, such as the creation of new products, new services, new ventures, etc.' (McMullen and Shepherd, 2006). Action may depend on both available knowledge and willingness to gain deeper understanding. It might be directed at extending knowledge about the market, the technology and the available resources, currently and in the future, or at establishing concrete elements such as partnering. Concurrently, techno-entrepreneurs have to create and validate the plausibility of a new business concept. They would use either storytelling or clockbuilding (Collins and Porras, 1994) to draft and redraft their vision linking the past to the present and the future. Hence, the maturation of the initial idea consists in both anchoring it into reality through creative connections and external recognition and enriching it so that it becomes a complete solution upon which to create a profitable venture. Figure 1.1 represents the opportunity recognition process according to these elements. This process is like a continuum of random steps and heuristic rules applied by entrepreneurs, as suggested by Baron (2006), ranging from systematic information search methods to very subjective and interpretive approaches. Building a viable technology-based opportunity is as much a process of experimentation through actions and interactions as one only of systematic information search and analysis through well-known decision tools. These diverse activities may take place anywhere at any time, mainly in the mind of the entrepreneur. Such a statement raises many questions: should specific anticipation or future-oriented methods be implemented? Are these methods useful, relevant and practicable and, if so, under which conditions? For what purpose and when should they be implemented? Which one to implement, in connection with which other one? For which outcome: a probable, an actual, a plausible or a possible representation of the future? Undoubtedly, some procedural knowledge about how entrepreneurs carry out their anticipations might be helpful for newcomers. It should be part of their human capital and more precisely their procedural knowledge (Davidsson, 2004). This implies going further into understanding the existing knowledge about information gathering and concept creation procedures applied by techno-entrepreneurs.

1.2 Information gathering and concept creation in the opportunity recognition process

In the entrepreneurship literature, information search appears to be an important task aimed at reducing the perceived uncertainty of all the stakeholders involved in a given opportunity. Facing a high level of perceived uncertainty, many studies, among them Kaish and Gilad (1991), discuss entrepreneurs' cognitive peculiarities, with their demonstration of perceptual differences and biases. Most authors and practitioners agree on the information to be gathered. Information needs match the three dimensions of the opportunity and are correlated to the level of perceived uncertainty. On the technological dimension, since most techno-entrepreneurs build on non-proven technologies with regard to their industrial diffusion, they face specific technological risks, ranging from technical feasibility to compatibility with the target applications and the context of implementation. Technology-driven new businesses most often build on technology development activities although this may be triggered by market needs. They can be integrated into different paths with increased difficulties and uncertainties: technological evolution, new combination of existing technologies or technological revolution. Technological uncertainty and risk depends on many factors, including the R&D stage, the level of accumulated knowledge and experience, the industrialization of the process, the availability of appropriate raw materials, the degree of integration and interdependence with other technologies within a technical system and the different technical options within the technology or in competitive technologies. Furthermore, in all these situations, problems of technical feasibility and compatibility might be hard to solve since technical requirements may not be known until the technology application is clearly identified. Also, another main technological challenge may be the upscaling from laboratory production to full production. This type of uncertainty is most often handled by scientists and R&D people. It is specific to techno-entrepreneurs in comparison to other entrepreneurs who have also to remain aware of technology evolution and potential discontinuities as potential opportunities and/or threats.

On the market dimension, techno-entrepreneurs have to match technological opportunities with market opportunities throughout the technology development process. They have to do so in order to develop appropriate applications, services and/or products in a way that will create value which the firm will be able to capture. Market uncertainty is about the eventuality that a new technology-based application may meet neither the customer's expectations nor a profitable market. Sometimes, these mismatches are hidden by a few potentially interested customers, namely the pioneers. They may reveal themselves as technological gatekeepers gathering scientific information and free-riding on what is proposed, but with significantly different expectations from those of willing customers, backed by purchasing power. Often, techno-entrepreneurs need to decide which technological options and applications to develop without much reliable information about customers' future expectations and behaviours as these latter are most often even unaware of the existence of a potential new solution. Market uncertainty in that case is an order of magnitude higher. Indeed, the realization of projected and/or potential markets will often be the consequence of how and when the technology will prove itself. Further, facing a more volatile market with shorter product life cycles makes it still more uncertain. Hence, risk for techno-entrepreneurs is not only technological but also market-related. Various options are possible when it comes to finding a path from technology to market in the lower level of uncertainty where customers are already known.

However, these recommendations sound hardly practicable as the information may not exist and be available in the context of technology-based opportunity recognition. Entrepreneurs often cannot even conceive the forms of what they will gather during their venture and thus will build, learn and adapt their trajectory while walking it. At least, information search should take into account some basic principles of uncertainty reduction. Uncertainty is referred to as situations within which people perceive their environments as not predictable thus being unable to decide and to act. A lot of attention has been devoted to uncertainty by researchers in management and entrepreneurship (McMullen and Shepherd, 2006). They noticed that uncertainty can be detrimental to entrepreneurial action because personal characteristics would not allow people to overcome problems such as not perceiving the need or possibility for action, not knowing what to do and thus not being willing to act. However, our purpose is to deal with techno-entrepreneurs, that is to say the people who are able and willing to act and to bear uncertainty. They have to gather complementary information about the propensity of each of the conditioning events of the potential opportunity to occur so that evaluation and decision are made possible. This statement suggests that people are able to judge or to evaluate a cue or a future event, to build an appropriate response and to anticipate its potential impact. These three points match the three levels of perceived uncertainty proposed by Milliken (1987): state uncertainty when the future environment is not predictable; effect uncertainty when the impact of a change is not predictable; and response uncertainty when the choice of options is not clear or their likely consequences are not predictable.

In the case of technology-based opportunities, the uncertainty view allows us to refine the concept: state uncertainty refers notably to the state of the future market: it requires that the entrepreneur identify a possibility for action by forging a belief about a potential change in the market, 'a conviction that certain things are true', qualified by a 'sense of doubt'; this potential change can be assimilated to a possible event. Effect uncertainty may refer to the potential actions and reactions of actors in the market. Different options might coexist without it being possible to know, beforehand, which one will turn out to be true. Response uncertainty implies that the entrepreneur build or create a path of actions matching the past, the present and the future, explaining how to cope with a breach in innovation continuity and identifying the possible impact of a given response.

At this stage, it is worth adding some new comments. Currently, the potential market seems to be knowable up to an acceptable sense of doubt; that is to say, facts and numbers may not be true or false. This amounts to information equivocality. The knowledge of what to do, referring to the path of actions, may rely on known patterns of innovation (Baron, 2006) which may guide information search activities but also information analysis and knowledge creation. This approach might be assimilated to reasoning by analogy or case base reasoning. This raises a series of new questions to be explored if we are willing to produce procedural knowledge about technology-based opportunity recognition: which items are at the core of certain things to be gathered and interpreted? How to select and validate them, according to which criteria? Which patterns may be coherently connected to new situations of innovation and entrepreneurship (Baron)? How to connect these patterns to new situations: is it through adjustment or combination of patterns? Is there room for subjectivity and creativity? Is the output the creation of one or various representations of the opportunity, including, for instance, optional paths?

Concept creation is the other major activity of the entrepreneur in the opportunity recognition process. In a situation of equivocality, techno-entrepreneurs might then also proceed through sensemaking. Sensemaking is instigated in situations within which current and expected states generate discrepancy, thus triggering the need for meaning and for a plausible sense of the future. 'Explicit efforts at sensemaking tend to occur when the current state of the world is perceived to be different from the expected state of the world, or when there is no obvious way to engage the world' (Weick, 1995). The idea that sensemaking is focused on equivocality gives primacy to the search for meaning as a way to deal with uncertainty. Thus we expect to find explicit efforts at sensemaking whenever the current state-of-the-art is perceived to be different from the expected state of the world. This is what may characterize techno-entrepreneurship. When the situation feels 'different', this circumstance is experienced as a situation of discrepancy, breakdown, surprise, disconfirmation, opportunity or interruption. Diverse as these situations may seem, they share the properties that, in every case, an expectation of continuity is breached, ongoing organized collective action becomes disorganized, efforts are made to construct a plausible sense of what is happening and this sense of plausibility normalizes the breach, restores the expectation and enables projects to continue. The core of sensemaking lies in the interplay of action and interpretation. Entrepreneurs are thrown into a continuing, unknowable, unpredictable streaming of experience in search of answers to the question 'What's the story?' but also 'How to make it happen?' Plausible stories animate and gain their validity from subsequent activity.

This proposal advocates a search for plausibility rather than probability. It is the redrafting of an emerging story so that it becomes more comprehensive, not a matter of accuracy, even though entrepreneurs may hold the opposite opinion. It requires resilience in the face of criticism. However, the entrepreneur is aware that he will never get *the* story! Mills (2003) found that stories tend to be seen as plausible when they tap into a continuing sense of the current climate, are consistent with other data, facilitate projects, reduce equivocality, provide an aura of accuracy (reflect the views of a consultant with a strong track record) and offer a potentially exciting future. He adds that taking action generates new data and creates opportunities for dialogue, bargaining, negotiation and persuasion that enrich the sense of what is going on. Finally, entrepreneurs have to design a virtual path that links what exists at present, happened in the past and will be done and realized in the future. In that sense, they put the world in order through sensemaking activities (Weick, 1995), using storytelling but also plan building, as suggested by Collins and Porras (1994).

This overview on information search and concept creation within the scope of the opportunity recognition process reveals a lack of explicit reference to anticipation approaches in management as they are hardly evoked. However, it allows us to identify a preliminary series of heuristic rules that might be applied by techno-entrepreneurs. They are listed in Table 1.1.

These heuristic rules may generate some conflicts with managerial practices and academic theories. More specifically, the idea that sensemaking is driven by plausibility rather that accuracy (Weick, 1995) conflicts with academic theories and managerial practices assuming that the accuracy of managers' perceptions determine the effectiveness of

Table 1.1   Types of heuristic rules in opportunity recognition

Heuristic rules	Possible concretization of the heuristic rule
Knowledge accumulation	Structure: apply known patterns of innovation/entrepreneurship Mastered sense of doubt
Generation of new knowledge	Dialogue, bargaining, negotiation, persuasion Design virtual paths linking the past, the present and the future Storytelling/clockbuilding
Accuracy	Information validated by external points of view from renowned people Resilience in the face of criticism
Plausibility	Ongoing sense of current climate Consistency with other data Facilitating current projects Reduce equivocality

outcomes. This may explain why some scholars propose that the key problem for an organization is not to assess scarce data accurately, but to interpret an abundance of data into 'actionable knowledge' (Bettis and Prahalad, 1995). A major problem is that the potential assessment of this type of human capital in the form of procedural knowledge is quite difficult as it is embedded in factual knowledge and actions. 'Beyond indirect assessment through associated variables, direct assessment includes: direct test of knowledge of facts, self-perception or other informant perception of potentially relevant knowledge of facts, value rareness and non-imitability, direct assessment of hypothetical or simulated procedural knowledge (computer simulation, verbal protocol, assessment center technique), self-perception of other informant perception of potentially relevant skills' (Davidsson, 2004). In this context, we suggest implementing an inductive learning approach through the detailed analysis of concrete situations: that is to say, of true business plans realized for the creation of high-tech new ventures. In each case, we systematically track anticipative items about the future opportunity but we also identify the embedded procedural elements evoking anticipation. As a result, we will analyse which knowledge, both declarative and procedural, is perceived as determinant by entrepreneurs for the acquisition of external recognition and resources to launch their business platform effectively. Nevertheless, this approach requires a robust conceptual framework to allow us a rigorous scanning of empirical data and more precisely of the anticipation approaches and principles lagging behind the sparse heuristic rules we have detected in the literature.

1.3   Identifying embedded procedural knowledge about anticipation

Admittedly, we can assert that techno-entrepreneurs use heuristic rules to build their anticipations about future events and the way they will capture potential new businesses. Before entering into the observation of how successful entrepreneurs proceed, we need to identify the main streams of anticipation on which these heuristic rules may be based.

Anticipation holds a paradoxical status in the mind of both practitioners and researchers. Most of them evoke this notion but hardly define it. Actually, different words are used in different contexts referring to different approaches and objects (knowledge, methods and processes, state of mind and so on). Forecast, foresight, scenario, roadmap and vision are all related to the future but finally amount to sparse knowledge about anticipation with almost no connections. For instance, 'managerial foresight is the ability to predict how managers' actions can create a competitive advantage. They notice that in all theories of competitive advantage, it is implicitly assumed that managers have some degree of foresight about the emergence of an advantage. It is clear that managers must have some foresight that their actions may create an advantage' (Ahuja et al., 2005). In the resource-based view of strategic management, researchers assume that managers are able to understand their resources' future value and complementarities with pre-existing capabilities. In finance, it is assumed that the evolution of shares' value can be a signal of future changes. Surely, some heuristic rules are embedded in these abilities, but they are not easily observable. Finally, on the one hand, it is taken for granted that managers do acquire information for anticipation purpose even though they are not aware of their procedural knowledge (Wilensky, 1967; Ansoff, 1975), they gather information that might be useful in the future (O'Reilly, 1980) with or without relying on existing methods. On the other hand, it is admitted that most of the time they do not succeed both because of the intrinsic complexity and uncertainty of the task and because of individuals' weaknesses and cognitive limitations. As a consequence, the implementation of specific devices to anticipate in the face of uncertainty and turbulence is recommended in order to improve anticipative abilities of people and organizations (Hedberg and Jonsson, 1978). Most of the time, these devices are referred to as business or technological intelligence systems. However, they are hardly connected to the entrepreneurship literature and practice, even though the opposite is the case in the field of innovation.

Basically, anticipation is *to know and to act before an event occurs*. Hence, anticipation is intrinsically related to the concepts of events and time, raising issues of knowledge and action. Conceptually, anticipation can be about knowing before acting, acting to know, acting to trigger events and shape the future, acting to react to events (for instance to contain its development, to allow resilience and swift restoration or to halt its development). Moreover, anticipation is most often evoked in contexts of significant changes. Ansoff, who is one of the first authors on strategy to introduce the notion of strategic surprise, insisted on the necessity to produce knowledge about anticipation. He questioned the strategic planning stream and formulated the concept of weak signals as another way to encompass the future. In that vein, we can now differentiate three main streams of research and practice as regards anticipation. They are synthesized in Table 1.2.

The Type I approach deals with extrapolation of past trends, evolution, continuation or reproduction of successful recipes, taking into account some variable parameters such as seasons in sales forecasts for mass consumption. It is related to evolutionary approaches of the future. The Type II approach of anticipation refers mainly to scenarios where important but already experienced changes may occur. This is based on the expertise and visions of a few 'experts' and leads to some sophisticated potential stories. Technology or product roadmaps enter into this category of anticipation. Type III anticipation systems are based more on sensemaking (Weick, 1995) which consists of making sense of pieces of information such as weak signals (Ansoff, 1975). It refers to situations which have never been experienced before. However, all these approaches have their own limits, the most important perhaps being that they are hardly connected to decision making and action, their feasibility and conditions of validity are difficult to handle, they are not future-oriented enough and cognitive biases may have a much more important impact than expected. Finally, their relevance is not so obvious.

Table 1.2   Synthesis of the main anticipation streams of research and practice in management

	Type I approach	Type II approach	Type III approach
Nature of change	Familiar and recurring	Predictable phenomenon	Unexpected events, novel and unpredictable
Anticipation modes	Clear enough probable future: optimize execution through long-term planning	Alternate or range of possible futures: prepare to be in position to make appropriate choices	Ambiguous and imaginary futures: recreate plausible futures to capture early signs of changes
Basic methods	Extrapolate past trends, plan and execute to achieve good positioning	Experts' foresight and choice, hypothesis, options and simulation	Scan, sense and respond to early signs of change: experiment, learn and decide

Table 1.3   Parameters determining anticipating approaches

Parameters	Description
Level of environmental uncertainty	Trends, phenomenon, surprises
Objectives of anticipating	Shape or adapt, react or trigger, gain external recognition
Time horizon	Short, mid- or long-term
Scope and nature of required knowledge	Width, accuracy, plausibility, dynamics
Organizational means and approach	Episodic or continual

Finally, the main point is that anticipation is somehow a matter of uncertainty reduction and tolerance to ambiguity. As a consequence, it results in the creation of cognitive futures which may be of three different types: the probable future, the plausible future and the possible one. All these futures are connected to the current but evolving situation. They leave room for some residual uncertainty as to their realization (Courtney, 2001). He classifies four levels of residual uncertainty which might be related to the sense of doubt mentioned earlier: *clear enough, alternate futures, range of futures and truly ambiguous future.* This diversity of outcomes reveals that there are different ways to cope with anticipation, thus suggesting that each approach has its own features, relevance and practicability within specified environments. Techno-entrepreneurs might rely on one or another of these approaches according to the parameters identified in Table 1.3.

Finally, anticipation can be viewed as matching knowledge needs about the future and information-processing capabilities, including human cognitive abilities and organizational means. The way these capabilities and needs are matched might resemble a heuristic process of continually updating and deepening plausible interpretations of what is the context, what problem defines it and what remedies it contains. For instance, in the earliest stages of innovation, when the unexpected may give off only weak signals of trouble, individual and collective attention may be paid more to this kind of information. Rather

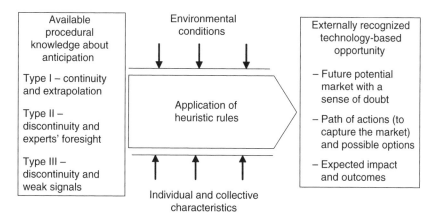

Figure 1.2   Conceptual framework: anticipation and heuristic rules for opportunity recognition

than focusing on the content of anticipation or on the design of sophisticated tools, it seems appropriate to wonder about the production of contextualized procedural knowledge to support managers and entrepreneurs while facing or leading major changes like technological innovation. The conceptual framework presented in Figure 1.2 aims at explaining the relationships between opportunities, heuristic rules and anticipation approaches.

This methodological approach, which is qualitative and inductive, allows us to avoid the obstacles of interviewing entrepreneurs who might not be aware of the way they proceed, thus rationalizing what they have carried out *a posteriori*. To do so, we rely on business plans aimed at launching a business platform and obtaining resources for that purpose. We try to cover the heterogeneity of entrepreneurial situations through two cases which differ regarding both the origin of the venture and their underlying innovation patterns. The first case is called AAT. Initially, the innovation is customer-driven and the context is a spin-off from a Danish SME; customer drivers are supposed to evolve over time thanks to technological progress and the technology might then be used within new industries. LUM is the second case. Initially, the innovation process follows a technology-push model in the context of a public French R&D centre spin-off. More precisely, thanks to the new technology, legal pressures will make the market drivers evolve and the new technology will necessarily be adopted by all the actors of a worldwide mass market, namely electric bulbs. The third case is WEEN. Initially, the innovation follows a diversification model where an existing technology which used high-tech environments may be implemented in more low-tech industries, such as agricultural equipment, so that a new market could be created provided that regulations evolve.

Cases of Opportunity Recognition as Heuristics of Anticipation

2.1   AAT: from customers' dissatisfaction to technological innovation
AAT stands for Advanced Actuator Technology which is the project of creation of a new venture commercializing piezoelectric actuators. It is the story of the improvement of an

existing technology thanks to which existing customers' technical problems are solved. In the long term, these new piezoactuators could enter existing markets within established industries, replacing old technologies or creating new applications. The challenge of this new venture lies in the ability to enter the rocketing worldwide microsystems market with major applications in the automotive, telecommunication, computer, optics and medical industries. There are more and more examples of new ventures growing rapidly by disseminating their micro-technology in many diverse fields of applications.

The initiative was launched by a researcher, working in a Danish SME. He has spent years with his team developing a new process based on the high-quality raw materials of the SME. Taking advantage of a high degree of autonomy, he entered into a R&D partnership with a major industrial actor in the automotive industry. Providing customers with prototypes allowed him to prove the technology's potential capacity to solve major difficulties at his customer's R&D department. At the same time, many other fields of applications had been explored through a market survey but also through collaborative experimentations and informal dialogues. The potential new applications based on his technology are numerous, representing as a whole a fast growing huge market. The Danish SME's top executives are not willing to handle this business development internally and prefer to enter into a spin-off process. In this context, a business plan has been written to convince financial partners.

The objective of the AAT team is to become a European market leader within two years in designing and manufacturing advanced piezoelectric actuators and then to expand worldwide within five to ten years. The future event which is anticipated is the replacement of the old bulk or multilayer piezoactuators technologies by stacked multilayer piezoactuators which are more effective according to existing market drivers. Moreover, these multilayer piezoactuators could trigger the creation of new high-tech niche markets with specific applications such as ultrasonic motors for optical lenses. The future potential market of AAT is described as a combination of four major applications in use within many industrial fields including the automotive, aircraft, optics and lasers, industrial automation, telecoms and computers industries. The four main applications of the technology are actuators for valves, for micro-positioning, for ultrasonic motors and for vibration damping. Hence, the range of options for business development is wide. Given the high technical performance of the AAT solution, the target applications are those requiring high performance and potential medium to high volumes. These applications and customers are already identified and intrinsically known as the AAT team already work with them through R&D contracts. AAT will keep on scanning for new ideas on applications while commercializing the existing ones.

All the target fields of applications will emerge and be transformed rapidly into concrete markets with growing turnovers, at a rate depending mainly on promotion by AAT. The impact of promotion may entail some commercialization delays, however limited. AAT assumes that, as soon as a dominant actor adopts the new technology, other actors will follow. This is the accepted innovation diffusion model for most applications of micro-technologies. The market within the next three years is estimated at about 7500 thousand USD, with 34 employees and a turnover growth rate at about +50 per cent per year. The AAT team has completed its business plan, including an action plan describing their path of actions with potential adjustments in case of unanticipated problems such as the inability to solve new technical problems within new industries. The future vision

Table 1.4   Information gathering about AAT's future market

Potential market	Main descriptive items
Future market/ market evolution	Current market and growth rate
	Emergence of new markets based on the interest of many professional contacts in AAT new know-how
	Pressure of the automotive industry for less polluting diesel motors
	Increasing demand for improved actuators by current industrial partners
	Dissatisfaction of most market industrial actors with past solutions (lack of reliability and high cost)
	Commercial activity started and performance of AAT proved with prototypes
	Key relationships with important customers since it takes several years to develop specific prototypes, with important investment by these customers
	Unlimited scope of applications
Technological solution	Improved performance demonstrated to customers
	Prototypes and tooling effective
	Past experience and recognition by external partners of expertise
	Experimental manufacturing for a limited number of customers highly appreciated
	Invitation to participate in European projects and active participation in diverse projects as an expert
	Difficulties in reacting and coping with AAT new performance for customers
	Uncertainties about mass production capabilities in the short term at least
Future matching between needs and solution	Potential to meet individual customers' requirements (technical features) with low disadvantages
	Strong match between improved performance and market trends/needs/drivers
	Need for promotion to raise potential customers' awareness
	No change in distribution channels: already known by AAT and customers

is built by sticking to the model of development of an emerging technology-based market, namely micro-systems. This model is mainly 'application-based'. It consists in identifying and developing as many industrial applications of the same technology as possible. The success of this kind of business depends equally on technology, market and human abilities to convince partners and customers. It is a matter of creative ideas that should be rapidly implemented in close relations with customers. Table 1.4 gives a detailed view of the main items which have been gathered about the future potential market.

Even though anticipation approaches do not seem to be implemented consciously, we can identify a few mechanisms in the AAT presentation:

1. The team's intrinsic knowledge and renowned expertise allows the team to be credible in presenting the technologies of the future and in explaining how it will expand across markets and applications. Reference is systematically made to the field of microsystems;
2. Concrete field experience in the market, the competition, the technologies and the regulations allows anticipation of the way the different known actors will behave; this is a kind of storytelling helping to make it plausible;

3. Active experimentation with key customers and intrinsic knowledge about customers' objectives, problems and expectations makes it possible to anticipate their future expectations, behaviours and problems; information about their perception of the opportunity and its recognition is being gathered, in the form of weak signals;
4. Statistical forecasts, examination of past trends and customers' expectations and analysis of the market drivers for change (technical difficulties, customers' new requirements and externally created new drivers) enable AAT leaders to explain the reasons for change, thus reinforcing what has been sensed earlier. They also provide readers with accurate quantitative market figures, at least for existing markets;
5. Generation of new knowledge about the future emerges from testing creative ideas directly with potential customers who share their understanding and would suggest new orientations. Attention is paid to weak signals emitted by potential customers so that changing the industrial and commercial focus rapidly is made possible.

AAT's founder relies on the three main approaches of anticipation. However, the dominant one seems to be of type III, where creativity, ability to detect early signs of changes and to make sense of them are key skills. The two other approaches are implemented as ways to reinforce the accuracy and the plausibility of the initial intuition through the use of either known patterns of innovation in the micro-systems industry or specialists' analysis of trends and market evolution. The sense of doubt concerns mainly the choice of priority in applications, which is compensated by optional but plausible paths of actions. All these options lead to the same expected outcome, which is exciting, as it is a 'born-international' venture on high-growth rate markets.

2.2   Case 2: LUM

LUM deals with a technological breakthrough in the field of advanced substrates for micro-optics and micro-electronics applications using laser diodes (for DVD, high definition printing), Leds (for white light displays), hyperfrequence transistors (for telecoms and defence), UV detectors (for environment and healthcare). The entrepreneurial project has been launched by three internationally renowned researchers from a French public research centre. One of them used to be the successful leader of another high-tech business venture as CEO and business developer. After years of pure technological research, the team has managed to improve drastically the technical performance of existing materials, thanks to a new fabrication process. Their experience and their worldwide scientific network allowed them to set up industrial partnerships with major potential customers amongst the biggest companies in the world. They have developed a technical process in their research laboratory to provide their partners with prototypes in order to obtain their industrial qualification. As the results are very encouraging, the team formulate the willingness to exploit this technological knowledge through the creation of a new venture.

The three researchers are internationally renowned for their expertise in their scientific area. When they state that the current technology has reached its limits in performance, the whole scientific community agrees. Thanks to its network of colleagues and some technological scanning, the team is also very knowledgable about potential new technologies and their stage of maturation. They argue why their technology is better and more advanced than any others with worldwide credibility. Currently, diverse technology roadmaps are elaborated, but LUM's is the most widespread and accepted. It states the total replacement of the old technology within ten years to provide high performance to customers. The accuracy of their expectations is reinforced by concrete realizations in other fields of activities. The higher performance of their technology has been proved through experimentation by potential customers.

The positive feedback from some key customers has been completed by a market study to assess the size of the potential market but also to gain more knowledge about customers' future expectations and behaviours. An external company specializing in high-tech marketing in the field of micro-electronics carried out the work whose results confirm the high potential mass market which will emerge within eight to ten years, depending on environmental and political factors. In between, three important markets will emerge and grow, in turn: market 'A' will be innovation-driven and will mature within three to four years; market 'B' will emerge thanks to low cost solutions within five to six years and market 'C' will emerge once the first two have proved to be efficient. The driver will consist of new regulations. The technological roadmap matches perfectly future market expectations as regards the initial new material, then the ability to produce high volume at low cost (process innovation) and finally the ability to diffuse widely to all potential users (technology life cycle adoption). The main sense of doubt lies in the industrial process, the scaling up of production and the ability to reduce costs dramatically. The team is very confident about its ability to remain ahead of the technological competition and to manage a high-growth spin-off developing and manufacturing advanced technologies.

The action path matches exactly the product roadmap. It has been established in order to cope with the specific time to market of each market segment. It calls for both evolution and revolution. It divides into three sub-paths: creation of a complete supply chain, collaborative R&D and partnerships, and implementation of huge manufacturing facilities.

Nevertheless, and despite the expertise-based projection on which the business plan is based, it is worth noting that intermediary businesses have been identified as necessary steps to reach the final target. They allow the leaders to gather complementary and unavailable information and knowledge about initial assumptions regarding customers and technologies. It appears that the building of the future business is achieved step by step or, more precisely, market by market. Each step implies industrial partnerships fine-tuning the technology and commercializing the substrates through planned and controlled technical experimentation (prototyping for materials qualification by customers). The planning of these businesses is spread over three to eight years in close conjunction with market drivers (innovation, cost reduction and regulations). The future impact of these parameters is analysed through analogies with other industries in order to work out future markets' features and figures. Finally, another element that has to be taken into account for future exploitation is the creation of a network of qualified suppliers which has been conceptualized according to known patterns of industrial networks.

LUM's anticipation is strongly anchored in their experts' technology foresight. It suffers little uncertainty as regards the future long-term environment and the drivers of change. Nevertheless, this clear and reliable view seems to be much more uncertain in the short and mid-term. It requires the use of complementary sensemaking approaches and many more action-learning activities with more options to handle in parallel.

2.3   Case 3: WEEN

WEEN is the project of two engineers and a scientist to create a new venture and a new market, namely electronic systems for quality control in the agricultural industry. It is potentially the main field of applications but a diversification into transportation security and logistics flows is possible in the longer term. More precisely, the engineers specialize in acoustic sonar detectors for submarines and work as the founders and leaders of a small engineering society. They have met several times a renowned expert in entomology, working for a French public R&D centre whose team has developed a database referencing insects and the specific noise they make while eating. In the course of informal discussions, the two engineers discovered a potential innovative opportunity in the storage of cereals through combining knowledge about insects' noises while eating and acoustic technologies implemented in submarines. The idea is to improve drastically the detection of insects in cereals so that the use of chemicals is reduced, the loss of cereals is avoided and the quality of products is improved. This could also contribute to a better image for customers willing to focus on quality as a competitive advantage. A spin-off process from the R&D centre is under way.

The future business of WEEN is mainly based on the creative abilities of the team to identify and to solve existing technical problems in quality control within three years and to trigger a major change in the European quality standard for cereals. Once these discontinuous events are realized, continuity starts again. Here, they aim at creating a new high-tech market in a low-tech industry. Once the early development of this market has been achieved, it will follow the evolution of the existing industry. Such an innovation pattern is quite 'common' for the technological innovations born in the defence, army or aeronautic industries and then transferred to mass and low-tech environments. It is assumed that future customers will necessarily be interested as they should be aware of the preparation of new regulations entailing the renewal of their quality control equipments. It is assumed that lobbying will trigger these changes. A 'cause–effect' analysis of lobbying and promoting the new technology has been achieved but without a proven impact on potential customers. The advanced acoustic technology is not advanced as an important parameter for the future as any other competitive technology could be used. The overall approach to technological opportunity is anchored in the technological diversification framework. Opportunity detection relies on individuals' alertness and open network of contacts.

The objective of the company is to commercialize a new portable device for the early detection of insects in silos of cereals. WEEN wishes to create a market through sensitization and conviction of key actors. They propose a series of actions to address the three identified groups of customers, each responding to different key success factors. Equipment manufacturers and distributors and quality control organizations are perceived as having a decisive role in the realization of the potential business. Cereals stockers are looking for productivity and quality and agroindustries are looking for quality and environmental respect. A major expected event which will trigger the business development of the new venture is the change of regulations at the European level as regards the accredited quality control methods. Sieves will have to be replaced by acoustic probes.

Within five years, the company should be one of the five major suppliers of this kind of equipment in Europe through both direct commercialization and licensing. In the long run, other agricultural products, such as tobacco, could be the target. A major strength of this project lies in its fit with current trends towards more quality and more environment-friendly activities but also in the difficulty of copying the combination of the two technologies, based on the integration of very different scientific knowledge and specific know-how. It has taken more than three years of collaboration with the French R&D centre to develop a suitable solution and to have it externally recognized by quality control organizations. The reputation of the expert in entomology was a determinant factor. Prototypes have proved effective when it comes to coping with future environmental drivers regarding the quality of cereals. Currently, this has been achieved with two potential customers. However, the new system is also coherent with potential customers' needs for more productivity and profitability. In fact, the industrial food chain is currently suffering a major paradox of using chemicals to reduce infestation and increase productivity while contributing to environmental pollution and enforcing laws. This field suffers from many diverging pressures from customers, competitors and legal actors. Hence, the new system proposed by WEEN seems to be an appropriate and acceptable solution to this difficult situation. The potential worldwide market is huge, following a slow growth rate but a rapid replacement of the old technology (sieves). A quantitative market study made by an external consultant specializing in microelectronics shows the high potential of this market worldwide. These results convinced the two scientists that it is worth launching a new business for the commercialization of this new family of products. The business plan has been set up to convince financial partners but also key distributors to support the creation and the development of this new business. Currently, market accessibility is still difficult as the distribution network is handled by a few major actors.

The items which have been gathered to constitute the potential opportunity include the elements in Table 1.5. WEEN's leaders are still willing to reinforce their knowledge about customers through direct collaborations to test and fine-tune their electronic probe. They are also active in lobbying for new European quality standards and in dialogue and bargaining with potential partners for distribution.

Table 1.5   Future market potential by WEEN

Dimensions of the opportunity	Items gathered
Potential future market	Trends and quantitative extrapolation of future markets at the global level
	Identification of market drivers and potential shift in drivers (communication with quality control organizations)
	Limitations on entering this potential market (distributors' negotiation power, cultural differences, existing standards for quality control devices, etc)
	Four different market segments identified and characterized
	Subjective creative approach of the added value perceived by customers
Path of actions (and feasibility)	Mastering of existing limitations on entering the market
	Optional paths according to the market segment receptivity
	Scenarios to capture the potential business value of the project
Expected outcomes	A new high-tech product combining technologies to provide unexpected performance and functionalities to customers
	Worldwide market through licensing and manufacturing for small market segments
	Launching of new ideas in the same or in other industries

The main anticipative approach handled by WEEN is a mix of type I and type II over a period of five years. They are telling another story of how to integrate high-tech products into low-tech industries through regulations drivers, thus causing a breach in continuity. Their main logic is one of actions directed at triggering events whose impact is mastered at least regarding the success of their new venture. They focus more on the evolution of drivers of change than on the change itself, which could lead us to think that the type I approach of anticipation is dominating. Hence, they are working with a specific network of dominant actors characterized by very strong ties and a high level of expertise as to the quality of cereals. The use of trends and quantitative market studies is a way to reinforce the accuracy of data on the importance of the potential market.

Learning from Successful Entrepreneurs

3.1   The concept of technology-based opportunity

Our study fully confirms the preliminary statements about the nature and content of innovation opportunity as a social construct (Gaglio, 1997). However, techno-entrepreneurs seem to insist on integrative knowledge to fully capture their potential opportunity. Beyond the marketing and R&D integration through specific interface mechanisms, other integration dimensions are to be emphasized. The integration of the technology-based opportunities into an industrial environment at both the potential market and the action path levels is to be underlined. The sense of the current climate is very important in giving plausibility to the opportunity. Many industries are characterized by a culture, past stories and cases that are well known by the actors playing the game. To be credible, techno-entrepreneurs have to show how they fit the acknowledged industrial model(s), even though they are aware that the development of their business will differ from their business plan. Little gaps may be tolerated if they are compensated by other assets, but techno-entrepreneurs seem to devote much attention to showing that they belong to the technological community they want to integrate thanks to common values and references.

The integration of market potential, path of actions and expected outcomes over a long period, going from a recent past to a long-term future, seems to be necessary. We can identify diverse approaches to this integration. It may be mechanically market-driven like AAT, influenced by actions led by dominant actors like WEEN, or co-developed and admitted by the community like LUM, where all actors agree upon the same technological roadmap. The uncertainty concerns the ability to handle the complexity and the dynamics of the way actions and outputs form chains to reach the target result without drifting too much because of environmental turbulence.

This type of integrative knowledge is techno-entrepreneurs' specific production coming from both subjective thinking and action learning to rationalize intuition. Typically, many authors in innovation assert that matching technology and market needs is a difficult issue requiring a careful interface management between R&D and marketing people. Our examples do not refer to this kind of problem as the R&D and marketing functions are handled by the same people, at least in the early stages of the opportunity recognition process. However, this matching issue is not solved by a 'two persons in one' strategy. It seems to be more a matter of critical learning done in strong association with all stakeholders. Beyond direct search through planned and controlled experimentation, our cases highlight that techno-entrepreneurs all implement various empirical approaches in a concurrent way. They all look for feedback, seeking both technology and market information and knowledge. An interesting point is that AAT, which has developed exploratory new applications out of scientific knowledge and under strong time pressure, has invested less in laboratory experimentation than LUM but is more active in the use of prototypes, in fast iterations and direct contacts. It appears as a compression strategy in which well-understood links in the system are squeezed together (Eisenhardt and Tabrizi, 1995). It is also worth noting that WEEN is somehow left out of this system of experimentation as the adoption will depend on regulations and lobbying.

The opportunity recognition process comprises both exploratory and exploitative knowledge (Levinthal and March, 1993). However, it sounds as if exploitative knowledge becomes more important as a way to demonstrate the ability to use available resources effectively. It also seems to be more difficult to handle for techno-entrepreneurs thus taking the risk to cease focusing on exploration for long-term business development. A similarity between our three cases is that they try to keep alive as many options as possible as long as possible and they always make sure that they have potential options to develop. For instance, a frequently perceived technological uncertainty is the tendency to deal substantially with engineering and production up scaling aspects of science and not with scientific knowledge production processes. Different uncertainty reduction processes are mentioned: application of existing models of reference, removing the problem to other actors of the industrial chain, learning through partnerships or progressive internal acquisition of knowledge.

As a consequence of the previous comments, we way see that information gathering is not linear, not guided only by systematic information search methods. These may be useful mainly to accumulate reassuring knowledge. The part of new knowledge generation through field experimentation, face-to-face confrontation seems to bring most added value into the concept creation. Daft and Weick (1984) argue that discovery may be achieved through enactment and interpretation as it cannot be obtained otherwise and, in highly novel settings, no base of cause and effect understanding exists.

A decisive skill seems to lie in the ability to select significant pieces of information from of huge flows of raw data. Information selection has hardly been evoked either by researchers or by practitioners (Blanco, 1998) even though it has been recognized as very important since Simon (1983). This information selection requires acquisition of both individual and collective awareness and know-how and integration of information perception and interpretation skills. To do this, a shared frame of reference is necessary. The three cases we present emphasize particularly this frame of reference, made of history, stories and values of their specific technological communities. This point should systematically be taken into account to enter and to be accepted by a high-tech group. As a synthesis, an emerging model of the opportunity recognition process allowing us to structure different types of heuristic rules is proposed in Figure 1.3.

3.2 Anticipative approaches by successful techno-entrepreneurs

We have deliberately chosen heterogeneous situations of opportunity recognition in order to explore potentially different approaches of anticipation and foresight: LUM is planning for a technological breakthrough on existing markets, WEEN is combining existing technologies to create a new market segment based on a new quality standard within an existing industry, AAT is improving an existing technology to enter new industries by bringing new products based on his technology into each of them.

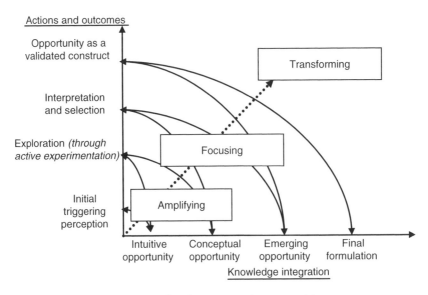

Figure 1.3   Structuring heuristic rules for opportunity recognition

Table 1.6 proposes a synthetic view of the use of anticipative approaches by the techno-entrepreneurs' cases we have presented. The table highlights how all techno-entrepreneurs may use all three identified anticipation approaches in parallel or in combination with for each one, however, a specific dominant style. They all use these methods without procedural awareness, except perhaps for statistical forecasts as they very often mention their limits. They necessarily implement cyclic interactive loops aimed at creating value in the short and medium term, as suggested by Tidd et al. (2001) mixing market-pull and technology-push approaches. The choice of appropriate anticipation methods seems to depend mainly upon the time horizon and prior knowledge of the team. However, these approaches are not implemented equivalently: some rely on aware approaches whereas others are implemented intuitively. It seems necessary to raise people's awareness about the philosophy and heuristic rules they implement intuitively so as to improve their efficiency and relevant use.

Beyond these acknowledged elements, a series of methods and approaches should be proposed to gather and interpret information and knowledge, to learn from the environment and entrepreneurial activities. It could emerge as a combination of existing procedural knowledge in anticipation coming from management, forecasting, sensemaking, cognitive sciences, information science and so on. Even though none of these approaches is sufficient and appropriate, 'intelligent' combinations may be useful to techno-entrepreneurs. Actually, the different cases we have presented highlight the complexity of this issue which does not call for deterministic reasoning.

Each anticipation approach's relevance, usefulness and usability for techno-entrepreneurs is still vague. For instance, direct contact may be used both to deepen and to validate an assumption and to explore potential applications and markets. Experimentation may relate both to planned operations to fine-tune existing know-how and to unplanned exposure to the environment to search for new ideas. Another point is the absence of explicit links

Table 1.6   Synthesis of anticipation approaches by successful techno-entrepreneurs

	Type I	Type II	Type III
AAT	Expected market growth through statistical forecasts for known applications in the same area	Stories about customers' pattern of innovation in the area and new European regulations Identification of multiple options for applications and markets	Current dissatisfaction of dominant actors Imagination regarding potential applications within various pre-identified markets Attention and careful listening to potential customers to detect early signs of change
WEEN	Expected total market growth	Scenario associated with a change in the European regulations and pattern of innovation adoption	
LUM	Long-term evolution of the electrical mass market	Scenarios telling how intermediary market segments will develop, based on change in market drivers	Experimentation with potential customers and signs of future change in their behaviour

between the early stages of the techno-entrepreneurial process and existing methods for anticipation such as prospective, technology and marketing intelligence methods and so on. Further, if these methods are of poor performance and use in such a context, building a flexible organization and developing models and tools to constantly reinterpret trajectories and achievements along them appears mandatory. What we observed through the successful stories we mentioned is mixed ways of doing. Entrepreneurs seem to be at the same time conscious and unconscious of building a future reality: more conscious for technology purpose (background and methods), then partly conscious for market (methods) and finally hardly aware as to future resources needs.

As a conclusion, we advocate the production and transfer of procedural knowledge to support techno-entrepreneurs while building their opportunity. It should rely on various anticipative approaches and consist of a mix of probability and plausibility elements. Storytelling as well as clockbuilding, forecasting as well as sensemaking should be used appropriately, with an emphasis on learning how to cope with weak signals as defined by Ansoff (1975).

Conclusion

Anticipation in entrepreneurship is handled very differently from anticipation in innovation. However, both contexts have a limited understanding of appropriate heuristics rules enabling the improvement of their anticipations. As a matter of fact, innovation people would tend to use very sophisticated business intelligence and environmental scanning tools to anticipate the future market of their potential innovation. They also systematically implement known patterns of innovation to enter a concrete action path with calculated outcomes according to past references. The problem is that, in this context, they are not able to handle disruptive innovations. Entrepreneurial people tend to disprove the usefulness and practicability of these sophisticated methods and to rely mainly on their intuition and prior knowledge. They would rationalize these approaches by using conventional methods provided that they reinforce their assumptions. In both cases, questioning past references and prior knowledge to optimize the creation of new venture remains superficial.

Under a high level of perceived uncertainty, it seems that most people are willing to gather as much data as possible to be as sure as possible that their vision will prove to be true. A major shift in the underlying paradigm is required. It consists of being aware of the value of applying appropriately bricks of procedural knowledge and of relying less on substantial rationality than on procedural rationality. Plausibility should be enhanced to balance accuracy and deterministic models. Sensemaking, intuition and sense of doubt should be recognized as the source of added value, provided that they are then examined through appropriate patterns of innovation. This means that more conventional managerial knowledge needs to be partly adjusted and combined with specific entrepreneurial contexts but also enriched with new concepts and new heuristics. This advocates combining scientific knowledge from more diverse fields of research into opportunity recognition in order to be able to design appropriate entrepreneurial decision systems.

Obviously, we are aware of the limits of this qualitative and exploratory research. One of its major weaknesses lies in the use of business plans whose aim is multiple, from communication to negotiation, evaluation and decision. However, the emerging conceptual model we propose can be a useful tool for researchers to refine the scientific knowledge in entrepreneurship and for practitioners to guide or to assess the opportunity recognition process. We are willing to go further into identifying heuristic rules dedicated to anticipation in techno-entrepreneurship by multiplying the cases through case-based learning methodology. Any practitioners or researchers willing to discuss, make suggestions or participate in this research work are welcome.

References

Ahuja, G., R.W. Coff and P.M. Lee (2005), 'Managerial foresight and attempted rent appropriation: insider trading on knowledge of imminent breakthroughs', *Strategic Management Journal*, **26**(9), 791–808.

Ansoff, I. (1975), 'Managing surprise by response to weak signals', *California Management Review*, **18**(2), 21–33.

Ardichvili, A., R.N. Cardozo and S. Ray (2003), 'A theory of entrepreneurial opportunity identification and development', *Journal of Business Venturing*, **18**(1), 105–23.

Baron, R.A. (2006), 'Opportunity recognition as pattern recognition: how entrepreneurs "connect the dots" to identify new business opportunities', *Academy of Management Perspectives*, **20**(1), 104–19.

Bettis, R.A. and C.K. Prahalad (1995), 'The dominant logic: retrospective and extension', *Strategic Management Journal*, **16**, 5–14.

Blanco, S. (1998), 'Gestion de l'information et intelligence stratégique: le cas de la sélection des signes d'alerte précoce de veille stratégique', PhD, CERAG, University of Grenoble.

Cohen, W.M. and D.A. Levinthal (1990), 'Absorptive capacity: a new perspective on learning and innovation', *Administrative Science Quarterly*, **35**, 128–52.

Collins, J. and M. Porras (1994), *Built to Last: Successful Habits of Visionary Companies*, New York: Harper Business.

Courtney, H. (2001), *20/20 Foresight: Crafting Strategy in an Uncertain World*, Worldwide Co. no place of publication, McKinsey & Company.

Daft, R.L. and K.E. Weick (1984), 'Toward a model of organizations as interpretation systems', *Academy of Management Review*, **9**(2), 284–95.

Davidsson, P. (2004), *Researching Entrepreneurship*, New York: Springer.

De Koning, A. (1999), 'Conceptualising opportunity formation as a socio-cognitive process', PhD dissertation, Fontainebleau, INSEAD.

Eisenhardt, K. and B. Tabrizi (1995), 'Accelerating adaptive processes: product innovation in the global computer industry', *Administrative Science Quarterly*, **40**, 84–110.

Gaglio, C.M. (1997), 'Opportunity identification: review, critique and suggested research direction', in J.A. Katz (ed.), *Advances in Entrepreneurship, Firm Emergence and Growth*, Volume 3, Greenwich, CT: JAI Press.

Hedberg, B. and S. Jonsson (1978), 'Designing semi-confusing IS for organizations in changing environments', *Accounting, Organizations and Society*, **3**(1), 47–64.

Hills, G.E. and R.C. Shrader (1998), 'Successful entrepreneurs' insight into opportunity recognition', *Frontiers of Entrepreneurship Research*, Wellesley, MA: Babson College, pp. 30–43.

Jolly, C. (1997), *Commercializing New Technologies: Getting from Mind to Market*, Boston, MA: Harvard Business School Press.

Kaish, S. and B. Gilad (1991), 'Characteristics of opportunities search of entrepreneurs: sources, interests, general alertness', *Journal of Business Venturing*, **6**(1), 45–61.

Klofsten, M. (1997), 'Management of the early development process in technology-based firms', *Technology, Innovation and Enterprise*, New York: Macmillan Press.

Levinthal, D.A. and J.G. March (1993), 'The myopia of learning', *Strategic Management Journal*, **14**, 95–112.

McMullen, J.S. and D.A. Shepherd (2006), 'Entrepreneurial action and the role of uncertainty in the theory of the entrepreneur', *Academy of Management Review*, **31**(1), 132–52.

Milliken, F.J. (1987), 'Three types of perceived uncertainty about the environment: state, effect and response uncertainty', *Academy of Management Review*, **12**(1), 133–43.

Mills, J.H. (2003), *Making Sense of Organizational Change*, London: Routledge.

O'Reilly, C.A. (1980), 'Individuals and information overload in organizations: is more necessarily better?', *Academy of Management Journal*, **23**(4), 684–96.

Schumpeter, J.A. (1934), *The Theory of Economic Development*, Cambridge, MA: Harvard University Press.

Shane, S. and S. Venkataraman (2000), 'The promise of entrepreneurship as a field of research', *Academy of Management Review*, **25**(1), 217–26.

Simon, H. (1983), 'Models of bounded rationality', Cambridge, MA: MIT Press.

Singh, R.P. (1999), 'Opportunity recognition through social network characteristics of entrepreneurs', *Frontiers of Entrepreneurship Research*, Wellesley, MA: Babson College, pp. 228–41.

Tidd, J., J. Bessant and K. Pavitt (2001), *Management Innovation: Integrating Technological, Market and Organizational Change*, Chichester: John Wiley & Sons Ltd.

Van der Ven, M. and I. Wakkee (2004), 'Understanding the entrepreneurial process', *ARPENT*, EFMD, **2**, 114–52.

Weick, K.E. (1995), *Sensemaking in Organizations*, New York: Sage Publications.

Wilensky, H.L. (1967), *Organizational Intelligence*, New York: Basic Books.

2   A model of technological entrepreneurship
Igor Prodan

Introduction

According to Schumpeter (1976), the function of entrepreneurs is to reform or revolutionize the pattern of production by exploiting an invention or, more generally, an untried technological possibility for producing a new commodity or producing an old one in a new way, by opening up a new source of supply of materials or a new outlet for products, by reorganizing an industry and so on. Since the end of the 1980s, the development of the knowledge-based economy, globalization and international competitive pressure has increased the importance of innovation in local economies (Camagni, 1995; Feldman, 1994; Malmberg, 1997; Porter, 1990; Ritsila, 1999; Storper, 1995) and also the importance of entrepreneurship, especially technological entrepreneurship, as one of the most important factors for regional development. The importance of technological entrepreneurship as a factor in the creation of both individual and regional wealth has recently generated considerable interest (Venkataraman, 2004).

The reason why some regions are more advanced than others lies in successful fostering of technological entrepreneurship of advanced regions. Schumpeter was the first (Schumpeter, 1976; Venkataraman, 2004) to clearly posit the centrality of the entrepreneur to economic progress. For Schumpeter, the entrepreneur is essential to the progress of capitalism because he creates change. And capitalism, according to Schumpeter, is distinguished by a striving for disruption, rather than stability, as innovations are introduced that reshape the existing structure of industry. Not only is 'the perennial gale of creative destruction' more typical than continuity in a capitalist economy, but disruption is also, ultimately, the source of the greatest social welfare as it ushers in the new and the better.

What is Technological Entrepreneurship?

There are several words used in scientific articles for technological entrepreneurship (technology entrepreneurship, technical entrepreneurship, techno-entrepreneurship, technopreneurship and so on) and several definitions of technological entrepreneurship, of which we chose three that are most important.

Dorf and Byers (2005) defined technological entrepreneurship as a style of business leadership that involves identifying high-potential, technology-intensive commercial opportunities, gathering resources such as talent and capital, and managing rapid growth and significant risk using principled decision-making skills. Technology ventures exploit breakthrough advances in science and engineering to develop better products and services for customers. The leaders of technology ventures demonstrate focus, passion and unrelenting will to succeed.

Shane and Venkataraman (2004) defined technological entrepreneurship as the processes by which entrepreneurs assemble organizational resources and technical systems, and the strategies used by entrepreneurial firms to pursue opportunities. Technological entrepreneurship (The Canadian Academy of Engineering, 1998) is the innovative application of scientific and technical knowledge by one or several persons who start and operate a business and assume financial risks to achieve their vision and goals. Technically, engineers are well-qualified in many respects for this activity, but often lack the necessary business skills and entrepreneurial mentality.

However, to really understand what technological entrepreneurship is and how we can stimulate regional development with technological entrepreneurship, we need to determine the key elements of technological entrepreneurship.

Key Elements of Technological Entrepreneurship

Technological entrepreneurship research occurs at many levels of analysis. We have identified seven levels of analyses or key elements of technological entrepreneurship that are linked to a new technology-based firm technological entrepreneur, universities, corporations, capital, market/customers, government and advisors. The research of technological entrepreneurship is thus necessarily interdisciplinary and multi-level.

Technological entrepreneur

The technological entrepreneur is an acknowledged key catalyst in the process of industrial formation and growth (Rothwell and Zegveld, 1982). There is usually more than one technological entrepreneur involved in the process of establishing a new technology-based firm.

Usually technological entrepreneurs have different knowledge, skills and other characteristics than non-technological entrepreneurs. They have sufficient technical knowledge but they lack business skills necessary for success. Because technological entrepreneurs usually lack the necessary knowledge of entrepreneurship, all technical universities should also include some entrepreneurial courses. They should know (Dorf and Byers, 2005) that entrepreneurship education is a wonderful way to teach universal leadership skills, which include being comfortable with constant change, contributing to an innovative team and always demonstrating passion in their effort. From a personality perspective technical entrepreneurs are found to be more extrovert, more intuitive and more thinking-oriented than their less entrepreneurial engineering and scientific colleagues (Roberts, 1989).

Motivational factors of the technological entrepreneur are the key drivers of success and are slightly different from non-technological entrepreneurs. Three major motives (Oakey, 2003) for beginning a new business are 'independence', 'wealth' and 'exploitation'. Most importantly, the desire for independence is divided into two sharply different, driving sub-motives: 'freedom' and 'control'. While the desire for freedom frequently derives from a need to escape the stifling bureaucracy of previous employment in large public or private sector bodies and pursue a personal (often research) agenda, the control motive is a more complex psychological driver.

The availability of resources enabled by entrepreneurial networks greatly enhances the survival and growth potential of new firms (Liaoa and Welsch, 2003) and, because of that, especially entrepreneurial social networks (friends, relatives and acquaintances) are very important. Walker, MacBride and Vachon (1977, p. 35) have defined a social network as

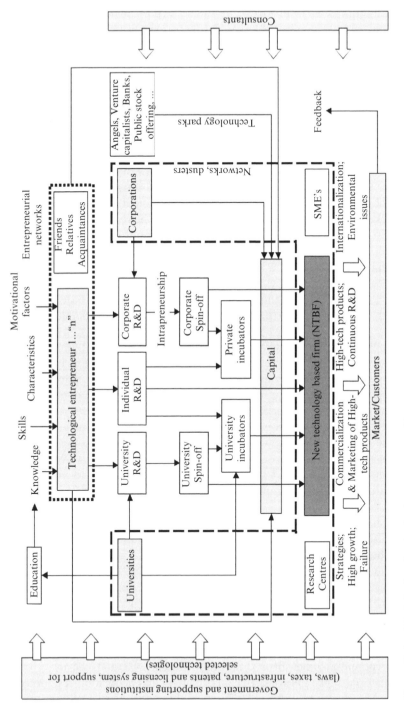

Figure 2.1   Model of technological entrepreneurship

the set of personal contacts through which an individual maintains his social identity and receives emotional support, material aid and services, information and new social contacts. There are some differences in networks of technological and non-technological entrepreneurs.

Major candidates for high-technology technical entrepreneurship are scientifically qualified staff that have 'spun off', either from public sector research establishments (including universities) or existing (usually large) industrial firms (Freeman, 1982; Harvey, 1990), but we should not forget those who started their new technology-based firm on their individual research and development, not within the universities or existing companies.

Universities

We have identified three important roles of universities linked to new technology based firms: an educational role, a role in establishing new high-tech companies with university-based research and development, university spin-offs and university incubators, and a role in cooperating with high-tech companies (clusters, technology parks and so on).

Universities and other higher education institutions are an important source of new scientific knowledge (Lofsten and Lindelof, 2005) – both technical and entrepreneurial. To ensure that technological entrepreneurs will have a higher probability of success in establishing a new technology-based firm, technical faculties have to cooperate with business faculties to train future technical entrepreneurs.

Nowhere is scientific discovery more salient to new venture creation than in research-oriented institutions of higher learning, the modern seedbeds for scientific breakthroughs and technological innovation (Markman et al., 2003). That is why university spin-offs and university incubators are extremely important. The term 'spin-off' means a new company that arises from a parent organization. Typically, an employee (or employees) leaves the parent organization, taking along a technology that serves as the entry ticket for the new company in a high-technology industry. Spin-offs are also known as 'start-ups' and 'spin-outs' (Steffensen et al., 2000). An important factor in the success of a spin-off company is the degree of support that it receives from its parent organization (ibid.), in the case of universities usually within university incubators. The creation of a university incubator is a popular policy aimed at promoting venture creation among their students and employees. It provides entrepreneurs with the expertise, networks and tools they need to make their ventures successful (Pena, 2002). Incubation is defined (NBIA, 2005) as a business support process that accelerates the successful development of start-up and fledgling companies by providing entrepreneurs with an array of target resources and services. These services are usually developed or orchestrated by incubator management and offered both in the incubator and through its network of contacts. An incubator's main goal is to produce successful firms that will leave the programme financially viable and freestanding. These incubator graduates have the potential to create jobs, revitalize neighbourhoods, commercialize new technologies and strengthen local and national economies.

The collaboration between universities, research centres, corporations, small and medium enterprises and new technology-based firms, as well as the interrelationship between them, is a fundamental tenet of success of new technology-based firms in the global market. For technological entrepreneurs particularly, clusters and technology parks are important.

Clusters

In terms of economy there are no new and old industries, just companies that are more or less successful in creating and mastering the development and usage of new technologies. Companies have to be able to compete in the markets of opportunities. The key factors of success lie in speed, adaptation, skill, knowledge and the organizational approaches. The new developmental concepts are based on the development of relationships with suppliers, customers and knowledge bearers, as well as other key figures of the local and global environment. Establishing a cluster could be viewed in the light of the old proverb that two heads are better than one.

Clusters include companies involved in similar or different business, knowledge bearers as well as other institutions and organizations ensuring the critical mass of knowledge, technologies, sources and funds needed for enhancing the competitiveness of individual companies and the group as a whole. The joint interests of the group pertain to suppliers, customers, specialized services, workforce and other resources.

The companies in a cluster have a common vision, but not necessarily all their business goals in common. Because each company focuses on its strongest activity and lets others deal with the rest, the companies cooperate on various common projects and compete with each other on others. The specialization of companies increases the demand for complementary and supplementary sources and also enhances the mutual trust along with the strength of the cluster.

Many examples around the world demonstrate that such cooperation is one of the key elements for ensuring the competitiveness of regions and countries because a cluster promotes the development of unique knowledge which is extremely difficult for the competition to match. It is precisely this kind of knowledge that ensures for companies, regions and countries certain advantages over their competition despite the growing globalization. Therefore it is no coincidence that clusters form an important element in the marketing structure of globally competitive economies.

A cluster has positive effects on innovation and competition, the gaining of experience and information, and growth and long-term development of business.

Technological parks

The main intention of technological parks is to ensure an interconnected environment, which accelerates interaction between resources, ideas, people and equipment. This occurs between companies and big research organizations, for instance the university (Prodan et al., 2004).

Technological parks, together with the university, the government, local authorities and the business environment, incubate small companies and offer them consulting, educational and administrative support and infrastructure. They also connect diverse knowledge as well as external and internal experts in science and business. In doing so, they manage to create a favourable environment for the development of entrepreneurial ideas. Moreover, the credibility of the parks helps ensure sources and, on the other hand, domestic and international business contacts. In this manner technological parks help companies on their road to independence or even internationalization, which is the goal of the majority of promising technological companies.

A technological park is a modern way of gaining new technological knowledge and consolidating the existing information at the local (microlocational), organizational and structural levels. It offers an all-round solution where technology centres operate side by side with established middle-sized and small companies.

The importance of parks at the world level is demonstrated by cases in which the government, districts, cities, major companies, universities, banks and so on contribute to their formation with non-refundable resources such as property, real estate and money. Technological parks are established on the basis of clearly expressed interests between economic firms, public research centres and other partners. They are most often a combination of research and business interests.

The goals of technological parks are (a) to establish technologically innovative companies which are guaranteed solid infrastructure and favourable working conditions due to the informational and consulting services, (b) to connect science with industrial usage and other fields, (c) to develop regional economies by retaining and incorporating skilled workers as well as to create appealing and creative jobs, and (d) to provide consulting services and establish new technologies.

The services offered by technological parks can vary. However, the most frequent ones are as follows.

Co-financing of business premises   Because of funding provided by the government, other institutions and companies, the amount of rent for the business premises and other resources is lower than the market price for the companies included in the technological park, at least for the first few years. The duration and amount of financial help depend on the policies of each technological park; however, the funding usually decreases with each year. In this manner the companies can gradually adapt to the market conditions.

Prestige   The companies included in an established technological park enjoy special renown which similar companies not included in the park do not. This is especially important when it comes to conducting business deals, raising extra funding (creditworthiness with financial institutions) and seeking help at university centres.

Possibility of informal contacts   Owing to the concentration of high-tech companies, a technological park offers ideal conditions for establishing informal contacts (common areas for socializing) and cooperation with research institutions.

General and administrative services   Companies within a park may use common administrative and secretarial services, courier service and photocopying. They may also rent the same conference and teleconference halls as well as telephones, fax machines, photocopiers and other similar equipment. A company can use all of the enumerated services or just some of them. The services of a technological park are normally less expensive than such services offered by other companies and are extremely professional. The manner of payment depends on the park's business policy.

Consulting services   Different kinds of training and consulting are organized by the management of the park, external experts and sometimes even companies in the park. Consulting usually consists of the initial help with forming a business plan, preparing documentation necessary for the granting of funds, advising on legal and financial matters, insurance, marketing, human resources and so on.

The companies in a technological park have access to various information bases, libraries and other documentation. Technological parks also organize national and international meetings for high-tech companies.

Entrepreneurial training   Most entrepreneurs do not possess an in-depth knowledge of finance, accounting, marketing, legislation and the rest, because they are focused primarily on the technological aspect of business. Training is therefore intended for companies in a technological park and its surroundings and can be co-financed by the government.

Funds   Companies operating within a technological park must provide funds for the equipment and the current expenses themselves. The experts employed by the technological park can provide help with raising the funds by obtaining guarantees, bank capital, subsidies and other types of help. As a rule technological parks do not invest their own funds into the companies.

Technological parks are an especially effective strategy for universities to diversify and at the same time retain their connection with the entrepreneurial world. The ways of expressing this connection are the following. Professors and researchers can expand their network of technological support. If they manage to attract high-tech companies into their technological park, they can use them to establish a broad enough network of research and solutions which successfully meet the needs of big companies. An additional advantage is the close link with the students, which is another important reason why a technological park should be associated with the university.

The university can use technological parks to establish its connections with companies as well as commercial and economic worlds and ensure for its employees the realization of their ideas, skills and research. Their ideas and solutions can be marketed with the formation of their own company or, as is more often the case, by establishing a partnership with another company. The latter often contributes to the development in a certain area.

Spatial proximity of the university and the companies means that the technological park uses the university's infrastructure. In the event that these two locations are displaced, it is impossible to establish such a close collaboration. Cooperation with the companies in the technology centre accelerates the development of academic curriculum and training adjusted to the entrepreneurial needs.

The university establishes competitive advantages over other universities, as it offers its students support in the realization of their entrepreneurial ideas and the transfer of their theoretical knowledge into practice.

Corporations

On one side corporations have a very important role in new business ventures and on the other side intrapreneurship 'is viewed as being beneficial for revitalization and performance of corporations' (Antoncic and Hisrich, 2001). Intrapreneurship is usually based on corporate research and development. It is an attempt to take the mindset and behaviours that external entrepreneurs use to create and build businesses, and bring these characteristics to bear inside an existing and usually large corporate setting. Start-up entrepreneurs are often credited with being able to recognize and capture opportunities that others have either not seen or not thought worth pursuing. Companies wishing to spur innovation and find new market opportunities are most often interested in trying to inculcate some of these entrepreneurial values into their culture by creating 'intrapreneurs' (Thornberry, 2003). Based on intrapreneurship, corporate spin-offs are established. Spin-offs are new business formations based on the business ideas developed within the parent firm being taken into an autonomous firm (Parhankangas and Arenius, 2003). Usually, if an establishment of a new firm is initiated by a corporation, the corporation is also an important source of capital.

Capital
The manner in which a business is financed depends on the type of company established by the entrepreneur, its creditworthiness, the entrepreneur's inclination towards risk taking and the various possibilities of access to the equity or the debtor funds and the conditions inherent therein (Ronstadt, 1988, p. 31).

A company obtains equity in various ways, depending on the stage of its development. When a company is established, it is usually the entrepreneurs and their families who invest in it. This type of equity usually encourages the entrepreneur–owner to do everything in his/her power for the company to operate successfully. In the next stages a company may obtain equity in a number of ways and from different sources, which depend on the one hand on the organizational structure of the company and on the other hand on the entrepreneurial capabilities (or incapabilities) of the company (Mramor, 1993, p. 251).

It is common practice in equity financing for the investor to obtain the ownership share of the company. The advantage of this kind of financing is that the entrepreneur is not liable for the funds obtained with the funds of the company since repaying the investor depends on the profit of the company. The down side of equity financing is that it leads to a loss in control over the company, as the entrepreneur gives not only the ownership share of the company to the investor, but also a proportionate right in controlling the company's management.

Technological entrepreneurs can acquire some of the required capital for establishing a new technology-based firm from friends, relatives or acquaintances, but that is not enough. Especially if they want to grow to a significant degree, they will need outside capital. Most important sources of outside capital for technological entrepreneurs are corporations (for their corporate spin-offs), venture capitalist, angels, public stocks, government grants and banks.

One of the most common ways of financing new technological companies is venture capital. A venture capitalist invests capital in certain companies on behalf of the investors. In return for the invested capital he receives ordinary shares, preference shares and fungible bonds. The returns from the company's growth are realized with the sale of the equity share. The institutional investors, banks, pension funds, insurance companies and the government can all form funds. At the same time there can be independent funds which are managed by professional teams of venture capitalists. Investors in a venture capital fund expect their investment to increase in the long term. The average life expectancy of a fund is approximately ten years. In that time the investors should get their stakes back along with the realized returns.

Good venture capitalists should (a) master different technologies, (b) be a successful manager, (c) assume responsibility for the company's returns, (d) assess the managerial and leadership qualities of the entrepreneurs and employees, (e) be persistent, (f) have a good sense of judgment, (g) know how to deal with the changes in technology and markets, and (h) have an expert knowledge of market conditions.

Besides equity financing, new technological companies can also apply for debt financing. However, this kind of financing is normally quite limited at first since the entrepreneurs of small companies usually do not have enough high-quality guarantees for the bank to grant them long-term loans, despite the fact that their projects are viewed positively.

In debt financing, the entrepreneur assumes the responsibility of paying off the principal and the corresponding interest. The advantage of debt financing is that the entrepreneur does not have to pay the whole sum at once, but postpones some payments for a future time. Also, the investor does not own a part of the company or have any control over it. The down side is that the entrepreneur must assume the responsibility of paying the debt off in the future – an obligation which does not hinge on the company's profits.

Market/customers

The main focus of all entrepreneurs should be the customer. Although technological entrepreneurs are often focused on technological challenges and product development, they should also focus on market feedback, on how to be successful in commercialization and marketing of high-tech products, the high growth strategies, the internationalization issues, the environmental issues and many other market-related issues.

Marketing of high-tech products

The last two decades of the twentieth century witnessed a marked growth in the use of marketing techniques in high-tech industries (Davidow, 1988; Davies and Brush, 1997; Davis et al., 2001; Easingwood and Koustelos, 2000; Grunenwald and Vernon, 1988; Lynn et al., 1999; Meldrum, 1995; Shanklin and Ryans, 1987; Smith et al., 1999; Traynor and Traynor, 1989; Traynor and Traynor, 1992; Traynor and Traynor, 1994; Traynor and Traynor, 1997; Wheeler and Shelley, 1987). While high-tech companies have historically relied on their unique technological advantage to remain competitive, the firms have found that it is becoming more and more difficult to maintain a competitive edge through technological advantage alone (Davidow, 1988; Davies and Brush, 1997; Davis et al., 2001; Smith et al., 1999; Traynor and Traynor, 1989; Traynor and Traynor, 1992; Traynor and Traynor, 1994; Traynor and Traynor, 1997; Wheeler and Shelley, 1987). It is clear that the marketing efforts of high-tech firms are as important as, if not more important than, the reliance on state-of-the-art technology (Traynor and Traynor, 2004).

Although all of the fundamental principles of marketing apply to the high-tech industry, there are industry and product-specific factors that affect the development and implementation of successful high-tech industry marketing strategies. These industry-specific factors include (Davies and Brush, 1997) the following.

The short life of high-tech products   Owing to the high rate of change in technological development, the proliferation of innovative products and the market demand for leading-edge capability, most products in the high-tech industry have an extremely short product life. This has several significant product development and marketing consequences and puts pressure on reducing time-to-market and ensuring that the product will be backward compatible. Short product life and the need to reach break-even within a compressed time frame has resulted in the need to sell in multiple markets, including international markets, almost simultaneously, and has resulted in the wide use of skimming strategies, rather than penetration strategies.

The interdependence of high-tech products   There is no other industry where what one company does technologically can require so many other companies to change their products and where both product developers and product purchasers are preoccupied by interconnect and interoperability concerns.

Tech-support   There is probably no more important factor in high-tech product marketing than tech-support.

Maintenance pricing   The pricing of maintenance agreements, service agreements and warranties in the high-tech industry is complex, but of extreme importance.

Strategic alliances   The high number of separate specialized companies, the high level of intra-industry interdependence and the high rate of industry expansion have resulted in the manic use of strategic alliances by the high-tech industry. Strategic alliances are used by high-tech companies to acquire technology, expand their areas of technical expertise, acquire operational expertise, increase the size of their market, acquire market access, increase their market share, increase their sales, increase their production capacity, acquire production skills and know-how, time-to-market, stretch their resources, acquire capital and so on.

Internationalization of new technology-based firms
Internationalization can be explained as the process of increasing involvement in international operations (Welch and Luostarinen, 1988, p. 36). The internationalization process of small and specialized high-technology firms is often different from that of more mature industries (Saarenketo et al., 2004). Traditional frameworks that explain firms' internationalization were already formulated two or three decades ago. At that time there were bigger barriers for entering foreign markets and internationalization was the luxury of the largest and strongest firms (Saarenketo et al., 2004). Because research and development of high-tech products is very costly and because high-tech products have a short life time, the internationalization of new technology-based firms is of extreme importance.

Government
The government must accelerate the formation of firms and stimulate the growth of small and medium-sized firms. Another goal should be to adopt certain measures to ensure a friendly business environment. The development of small and medium-sized firms can be boosted by (a) macroeconomic policy, specifically a stable economic environment; (b) legislation which lays down favourable conditions for small and medium-sized firms; (c) offering support aimed at solving problems of the small and medium-sized firms; and (d) promoting businesses and entrepreneurship and developing the entrepreneurial culture (Glas and Psenicny, 2000, p. 11).

The government must combine three aspects which are crucial if the support for the firms is to be successful: unity of strategy (policies), institutions (organizations) and the service programmes (Glas and Psenicny, 2000, pp. 12–13). In order to reach a favourable ratio between the cost for the support and its effectiveness, the government must clearly state the goals of its policies, identify appropriate programmes which will help it realize its goals in a certain time frame and appoint effective mechanisms (support organizations) for conducting these programmes.

It is advisable that the government organize types of support which provide (Glas and Psenicny, 2000, p. 40) the development of a business environment which stimulates entrepreneurship, simplification of procedures and tax cuts, development of new units, access to financial sources, information, consulting and guidance, help with technical and technological problems, links between small, medium-sized and big firms, and the development of distribution networks and support with internationalization of business.

The government may also offer support for firms at the national, regional and local levels by helping individual firms with favourable loans (subsidized interest rates, lesser guarantees, longer repayment periods), tax cuts, favourable amortization costs, non-refundable employment benefits and low costs for firms wishing to buy or rent business space and equipment, and also by developing business infrastructure: special financial institutions (funds), chambers, technology centres, incubators, business zones and the rest.

Advisors
Research on the problems of small firms has shown that there are typical gaps in the abilities of small firms, where it is reasonable to help with various types of consulting and training. These gaps are (Bolton, 1971) as follows.

Information gap   Entrepreneurs who have just recently established their own firm lack certain information necessary for the preparation of business plans and the making of sound business decisions. Advisors are therefore the people who offer entrepreneurs basic business information at the lowest level of services.

A gap in problem solving and technical capabilities   Individuals who are new at running their own business and are more used to the safety of the organizational environment of big firms where others make decisions, often never developed or tested their own analytical capabilities. They do not know how to recognize problems and solve them in a fast and efficient manner – advisors will help them in learning how to do just that.

Learning gap   Although many entrepreneurs start their business in the fields they are familiar with, it is often the case that they do not know all the aspects of such activities; their knowledge might be limited when it comes to other fields, the local market or just certain aspects of entrepreneurship. Consulting can therefore bridge the gap in knowledge and training of such individuals.

Also firms might have a gap in (available) resources, as entrepreneurs either have a limited amount of time to prepare and plan a new business or can not gain sufficient start-up resources because the firm is new and small. Such firms have a limited supply of resources, which can soon lead to a financial crisis in the case of early (unexpected) difficulties.

Therefore it is very important for the success of a technological entrepreneur to have advisors different from his social network (friends, relatives, acquaintances and so on) and different professional consultants. Advice from people in a technological entrepreneur social network are especially important in the process of establishing a new technology-based firm because of limited financial resources of new entrepreneurs. Professional advisors are of extreme importance when the new technology-based firm grows rapidly.

Conclusion

Since technological entrepreneurship is a relatively unexplored topic (Shane and Venkataraman, 2004) and is one of the most important factors of regional development, key elements of technological entrepreneurship should be determined to know how to foster technological entrepreneurship. In this chapter a model of technological entrepreneurship is presented. It includes seven key elements of technological entrepreneurship: technological entrepreneur, universities, corporations, capital, market/customers, government and advisors.

The model of technological entrepreneurship should aid researchers, form the basis for future research and serve as a guide for governments and regions willing to develop and stimulate technological entrepreneurship.

References

Antoncic, B. and R.D. Hisrich (2001), 'Intrapreneurship: construct refinement and cross-cultural validation', *Journal of Business Venturing*, **16**, 495–527.
Bolton, J. (1971), *Report of the Committee of Inquiry on Small Firms*, Cm 4811, London: HMSO.
Camagni, R.P. (1995), 'The concept of innovative milieu and its relevance for public policies in European lagging regions', *Papers in Regional Science*, **74**, 317–40.
Davidow, W.H. (1988), 'The ascendancy of high-tech marketing', *Electronic Business*, **14** (10), 130–32.
Davies, W. and K.E. Brush (1997), 'High-tech industry marketing: the elements of a sophisticated global strategy', *Industrial Marketing Management*, **26** (1), 1–14.
Davis, J., A. Fusfeld, E. Scriven and G. Tritle (2001), 'Determining a project's probability of success', *Research–Technology Management*, **44** (3), 51–62.
Dorf, R.C. and T.H. Byers (2005), *Technology Ventures: from Idea to Enterprise*, New York: McGraw-Hill.
Easingwood, C. and A. Koustelos (2000), 'Marketing high technology: preparation, targeting, positioning, execution', *Business Horizons*, **43** (3), 27–38.
Feldman, M.P. (1994), 'The university and high-technology start-ups: the case of Johns Hopkins University and Baltimore', *The Economic Development Quarterly*, **8**, 67–76.
Freeman, C. (1982), *The Economics of Innovation*, London: Frances Pinter.
Glas, M. and V. Psenicny (2000), *Podjetnistvo – izziv za 21. stoletje*, Ljubljana: Gea College.
Grunenwald, J.P. and T.T. Vernon (1988), 'Pricing decision making for high-technology products and services', *Journal of Business and Industrial Marketing*, **3** (1), 61–70.
Harvey, K.A. (1990), 'The impact of institution intellectual property on the propensity on individual UK universities to incubate NTBFs', in R.P. Oakey (ed.), *New Technology-based New Firms in the 1990s*, London: Paul Chapman Publishers.
Liaoa, J. and H. Welsch (2003), 'Social capital and entrepreneurial growth aspiration: a comparison of technology- and non-technology-based nascent entrepreneurs', *The Journal of High Technology Management Research*, **14**, 149–70.
Lofsten, H. and P. Lindelof (2005), 'R&D networks and product innovation patterns: academic and non-academic new technology-based firms on Science Parks', *Technovation*, **25** (9), 1025–37.
Lynn, G.S., S.P. Schnaars and R.B. Skov (1999), 'Survey of new product forecasting practices in industrial high technology and low technology businesses', *Industrial Marketing Management*, **28** (6), 565–72.
Malmberg, A. (1997), 'Industrial geography: location and learning', *Progress in Human Geography*, **21**, 573–82.
Markman, D.G., P.H. Phan, D.B. Balkin and P.T. Gianiodis (2003), 'Entrepreneurship and university-based technology transfer', *Journal of Business Venturing*, **20**, 241–63.
Meldrum, M.J. (1995), 'Marketing high-tech products: the emerging themes', *European Journal of Marketing*, **29** (10), 45–59.

Mramor, D. (1993), *Uvod v poslovne finance*, Ljubljana: Gospodarski vestnik.

NBIA (2005), 'What is business incubation?', retrieved 01/24/05 from World Wide Web: http://www.nbia.org/resource_center/what_is/index.php.

Oakey, R.P. (2003), 'Technical entrepreneurship in high technology small firms: some observations on the implications for management', *Technovation*, **23**, 679–88.

Parhankangas, A. and P. Arenius (2003), 'From a corporate venture to an independent company: a base for a taxonomy for corporate spin-off firms', *Research Policy*, **32**, 463–81.

Pena, I. (2002), 'Intellectual capital and business start-up success', *Journal of Intellectual Capital*, **3**, 180–98.

Porter, M.E. (1990), *The Competitive Advantage of Nations*, London: Macmillan.

Prodan, I., S. Dolinsek and J. Kopac (2004), 'Technology transfer and entrepreneurship in the traditional industrial environment', in A.Y. Hosni, M.T. Khalil and R. Smith (eds), *IAMOT 2004: 13th International Conference on Management of Technologies*, Washington: IAMOT.

Ritsila, J.J. (1999), 'Regional differences in environments for enterprises', *Entrepreneurship and Regional Development*, **11**, 187–202.

Roberts, B.E. (1989), 'The personality and motivations of technological entrepreneurs', *Journal of Engineering and Technology Management*, **6**, 5–23.

Ronstadt, R.C. (1988), *Entrepreneurial Finance: Talking Control of Your Financial Decision Making*, Dana Point, CA: Lord Publishing.

Rothwell, R. and W. Zegveld (1982), *Innovation in the Small and Medium Sized Firm*, London: Frances Pinter.

Saarenketo, S., K. Puumalainen, O. Kuivalainen and K. Kylaheiko (2004), 'Dynamic knowledge-related learning processes in internationalizing high-tech SMEs', *International Journal of Production Economics*, **89** (3), 363–78.

Schumpeter, J.A. (1976), *Capitalism, Socialism and Democracy*, New York: Harper and Row.

Shane, S. and S. Venkataraman (2004), 'Guest editors' introduction to the special issue on technology entrepreneurship', *Research Policy*, **32**, 181–4.

Shanklin, W.L. and J.K. Ryans (1987), *Essentials of Marketing High Technology*, Lexington: D.C. Heath and Company.

Smith, M.F., I. Sinha, R. Lancioni and H. Forman (1999), 'Role of market turbulence in shaping pricing strategy', *Industrial Marketing Management*, **28**, 637–50.

Steffensen, M., E.M. Rogers and K. Speakman (2000), 'Spin-offs from research centers at a research university', *Journal of Business Venturing*, **15**, 93–111.

Storper, M. (1995), 'The resurgence of regional economics ten years later: the region as a nexus of untraded interdependencies', *European Urban and Regional Studies*, **2**, 191–221.

The Canadian Academy of Engineering (1998), *Wealth through Technological Entrepreneurship*, Ottawa: The Canadian Academy of Engineering.

Thornberry, E.N. (2003), 'Corporate entrepreneurship: teaching managers to be entrepreneurs', *The Journal of Management Development*, **22**, 329–44.

Traynor, K. and S. Traynor (1989), 'Marketing approaches used by high-tech firms', *Industrial Marketing Management*, **18** (4), 281–7.

Traynor, K. and S. Traynor (1992), 'Educational backgrounds of high-tech salespeople', *Industrial Marketing Management*, **21** (2), 1–7.

Traynor, K. and S. Traynor (1994), 'Efficacy of strategic and promotional factors on the sales growth of high-tech firms', *IEEE Transactions on Engineering Management*, **41** (2), 126–34.

Traynor, K. and S. Traynor (1997), 'Degree of innovativeness and marketing approaches used by high-tech firms', *International Journal of Technology Management*, **14** (2/3/4), 238–47.

Venkataraman, S. (2004), 'Regional transformation through technological entrepreneurship', *Journal of Business Venturing*, **19**, 153–67.

Walker, K.N., A. MacBride and M.L.S. Vachon (1977), 'Social support networks and the crisis of bereavement', *Social Science and Medicine*, **35**, 35–41.

Welch, L.S. and R. Luostarinen (1988), 'Internationalization: evolution of a concept', *Journal of General Management*, **34** (2), 34–57.

Wheeler, D.R. and C.J. Shelley (1987), 'Toward more realistic forecasts for high-technology products', *Journal of Business and Industrial Marketing*, **2** (2), 55–64.

3 Exchange relationships in techno-entrepreneurship research: toward a multitheoretic, integrative view

Helena Yli-Renko

Introduction

New business creation and growth are not autonomous, isolated processes but collective processes that involve the establishment and sustaining of a network of relationships between the new organization and other parties in its environment. A firm needs to interact with the customers for and distributors of its outputs, and with the suppliers of inputs that the firm requires, such as funds, labour, material resources and knowledge. A young firm's relationships provide access to external resources, which compensate for internal resource constraints (Jarillo, 1988; Pfeffer and Salancik, 1977). Accumulated resources make it possible for firms to exploit the 'productive opportunities' (Penrose, 1959) in their environment, as well as to provide a buffer against 'environmental jolts' (Venkataraman and Van de Ven, 1998). Consequently, a young firm's external relationships have a significant and long-lasting impact on the behaviour, survival and success of the firms (Aldrich and Pfeffer, 1976; Birley, 1985; Larson, 1992; Venkataraman, 1989).

The influences of exchange relationships are particularly relevant for young, technology-based firms. Such firms usually operate in narrow market 'interstices' (Penrose, 1959) in highly volatile environments characterized by rapid changes in technologies and markets (Bruno and Tyebjee, 1982). Further, technology-based firms are highly knowledge-intensive, creating value through exploiting their distinctive technological knowledge and needing access to external sources of knowledge (Autio, Sapienza and Almeida, 2000). These are conditions that make it both increasingly important and increasingly difficult for young firms to establish and maintain exchange relationships successfully.

Recognizing the critical role of external relationships in new venture creation and performance, entrepreneurship scholars have increasingly focused their attention on issues such as nascent entrepreneurs' personal networks or social capital (for example, Aldrich and Zimmer, 1986; Birley, 1985; Davidsson and Honig, 2003; Dubini and Aldrich, 1991), the relationships between investors and entrepreneurs (for example, Sapienza and Gupta, 1994; Sapienza and Korsgaard, 1996; Shane and Cable, 2002; Steiner and Greenwood, 1995), the customer relationships of entrepreneurial firms (for example, Venkataraman et al., 1990; Yli-Renko et al., 2001a) and the use of strategic partners, R&D alliances and external resources by entrepreneurial firms (for example, Dollinger and Golden, 1992; McGee and Dowling, 1994; Shan, Walker and Kogut, 1994; Stuart et al., 1999). This research, mostly accumulated over the past 15 years, is highly fragmented; it has developed in a number of separate streams, characterized by varying theoretical frameworks, assumptions and terminology. Given that the research domain is at the intersection of two heterogeneous fields, interorganizational relationship/network research on the one hand,

and entrepreneurship on the other, the fragmentation and multiplicity of research on entrepreneurs' and entrepreneurial firms' external relationships are hardly surprising.

This fragmentation has resulted in inconsistencies in terminology, ambiguity in levels of analysis and a lack of cumulative theory building. Few attempts have been made to synthesize this body of research or to propose an integrative framework. A recent review article by Hoang and Antoncic (2003) summarized findings and indentified gaps in the 'network-based research in entrepreneurship', providing a useful categorization of this research into studies focusing on (1) content, (2) governance, and (3) structure of entrepreneurs' and entrepreneurial firms' networks as well as distinguishing between process- and outcome-oriented network research. However, they remained silent on the theoretical foundations and assumptions underlying this research, and because of their focus on networks, they largely omitted streams of research focusing on dyadic ties, such as the research on entrepreneur–investor relationships.

The current chapter presents an analytical framework for mapping the various streams of extant research on the external relationships of entrepreneurs and entrepreneurial firms, with a particular focus on technology-based entrepreneurship. The purpose of the framework is to create a holistic understanding of where this body of research currently is and how it can develop going forward.[1] Specifically, the chapter focuses on the theoretical foundations of the various research streams, seeking to explicate the differences in underlying assumptions, levels of analysis and the research questions addressed. Based on this review, I propose a multitheoretic, integrative perspective to understanding the external relationships of technology-based entrepreneurs and entrepreneurial firms. In this chapter the term 'entrepreneurial exchange relationship' is used to refer broadly to all external relationships of entrepreneurs or entrepreneurial firms. The term thus encompasses the full range of interpersonal and interorganizational relationships between entrepreneurs/entrepreneurial firms and other parties in their environment (customers, suppliers, investors, advisers, strategic alliance partners and the rest).

Research Streams on Entrepreneurial Exchange Relationships

The literature on entrepreneurial exchange relationships has developed in a number of separate streams, each of which focuses on a distinct domain in terms of research questions, draws on different theoretical frameworks and utilizes different levels of analysis. I have identified five distinct streams:

1. research focusing on the personal networks of the entrepreneur and on how these influence the formation and early development of entrepreneurial firms;
2. research focusing on how the use of alliances and external resources by entrepreneurial firms influences the firms' performance (in terms of, for example, innovativeness or growth);
3. research focusing on the formation, development and governance of entrepreneurial firms' exchange relationships;
4. research focusing on the relationships between entrepreneurs and investors (that is, venture capitalists, private investors or bankers);
5. research focusing on regional networks of entrepreneurial firms and how these networks foster innovation and growth.

The analytical framework for discussing these research streams consists of three elements: (1) level of analysis, (2) typical research questions and dependent variables, and (3) the theoretical approaches applied and the key assumptions about firms and exchange relationships in these theoretical approaches. By looking at each of the research streams through this lens, I will demonstrate that the streams are clearly distinct from each other, and will highlight the differences between the streams. I will also discuss the extent to which each stream has focused on or is applicable to techno-entrepreneurship. Further, the analysis will uncover potential for cross-stream integration that will lead to a more comprehensive, theoretically grounded view of entrepreneurial exchange relationships. Before reviewing the research streams, I will first introduce the three components of the analytical framework.

Level of analysis
Two dimensions can be used to distinguish the level of analysis: first, whether the research focuses on inter*personal* relationships or inter*organizational* relationships, and, second, whether relationships are conceptualized on a dyad, egocentric set or network level. Table 3.1 illustrates these different levels of analysis.

The distinction between the entrepreneur's personal relationships and the entrepreneurial firm's exchange relationships is often vague. This 'simultaneity of the entrepreneur's network and the emerging firm's initial network' (Hite and Hesterly, 2001) stems from the entrepreneur's role as resource coordinator and agent of the firm (Kirzner, 1973). Particularly at early stages in firm emergence, the entrepreneur relies on his or her personal social network, and thus the external ties of the new firm exist primarily on an interpersonal level. As the firm develops, these idiosyncratic personal ties become formalized into stable exchange relationships between organizations (Dubini and Aldrich, 1991; Larson and Starr, 1993).

The simplest way to analyse external relationships is to focus on a dyad between the entrepreneur/entrepreneurial firm and another actor in the environment. This type of

Table 3.1   Levels of analysis in research on entrepreneurial exchange relationships

	The entrepreneur's personal ties	The entrepreneurial firm's interorganizational ties
Dyadic relationship	One relationship between the entrepreneur and another person, e.g., entrepreneur–business angel, usually analysed from the entrepreneur's perspective	One relationship between the entrepreneurial firm and another organization, e.g., key customer, usually analysed from the entrepreneurial firm's perspective
Egocentric set of relationships	Fan-like structure mapping the entrepreneur's network of direct personal relationships	Fan-like structure mapping the entrepreneurial firm's network of direct relationships
Network	Network of direct and indirect ties between a group of people (including the entrepreneur)	Network of direct and indirect ties between a set of organizations (including the entrepreneurial firm)

research is usually carried out from the focal actor's perspective, but can also sometimes focus on comparing the two parties' perspectives regarding the relationship (Iacobucci and Zerrillo, 1996). The next level of analysis focuses on the egocentric, fan-like set of direct relationships of the entrepreneur or entrepreneurial firm, aggregating the network dyads into the larger network of the focal actor (Hite and Hesterly, 2001; Iacobucci and Zerrillo, 1996). The third level involves analysis of a network or group, focusing on the direct and indirect ties between a set of actors, all of whom may or may not be connected to each other. Considering the pragmatic difficulties involved in using a set of interconnected actors as the unit of analysis (as described by, for example, Iacobucci and Zerrillo, 1996), it is natural that most of the research on entrepreneurial exchange relationships has focused on dyads or egocentric sets of relationships, rather than true networks (Johannisson et al., 1994).

Research questions and dependent variables

Hoang and Antoncic (2003) distinguish between process-oriented and outcome-oriented network research; in the former, networks are considered the dependent variable, and research focuses on how entrepreneurial processes and influence network development over time; in the latter, networks are the independent variable, and the focus is on how networks affect the entrepreneurial process and lead to positive outcomes for the entrepreneurs or their firms. In the present chapter, I build on this distinction, and further differentiate between various outcome and process variables when discussing the five research streams.

Theoretical approaches and assumptions

Various theoretical approaches – most notably social network/social capital, resource dependence, agency, resource-based and knowledge-based theories – have been applied to the study of interpersonal and interorganizational relationships in the entrepreneurship literature. Each of the theories has different assumptions about the nature of firms and the conceptualization of exchange relationships (see Table 3.2); these differences will be discussed below as I review the five research streams.

1   Personal networks of the entrepreneur

First, there is a stream of research focusing on the personal networks of the entrepreneur and on how these influence the formation and early development of entrepreneurial firms. Birley (1985), Aldrich and Zimmer (1986) and Johannisson (1987) were among the first to draw attention to the social context of entrepreneurship, arguing that start-up is not a discrete, isolated event, but a socially embedded process influenced by the personal relationships of the entrepreneur, including friends, family, community and organizational ties. Since this initial realization, studies have looked at the way availability, choice and development of personal social networks can explain why some individuals start firms while others do not, arguing that a nascent entrepreneur's personal network is a source of information and other resources that enable the entrepreneur to recognize and exploit a new business opportunity (for example, Aldrich and Cliff, 2003; Davidsson and Honig, 2003; Johannisson, 1987; Ostgaard and Birley, 1994). Further, studies have focused on the way the entrepreneur's personal ties influence the emergent firm's strategy and performance (for example, Ostgaard and Birley, 1996; Zhao and Aram, 1995).

Table 3.2 Comparison of theoretical approaches in the study of exchange relationships

Approach	Conceptualization of the firm	Behavioural assumptions	Notion of external relationships	Main drivers for firms in managing relationships
Resource dependence perspective	Dependent on resource exchange with other actors in environment	Quest for autonomy	Structures of dependence and power	Minimizing dependence on others; controlling critical resources
Agency theory	Nexus of contracts	Opportunism, bounded rationality, risk avoidance	Principal–agent ties	Minimizing agency risks and costs
The resource-based view	Bundle of resources	Creativity, search, learning	A means to acquire or gain access to external resources	Building sustainable competitive advantage through new resource combinations
The knowledge-based view	Concentration of firm-specific knowledge	Capability to acquire, assimilate and diffuse knowledge	A means to acquire information and generate knowledge	Building the organizations' knowledge base, which is the basis for competitive advantage
Social capital theory	Social actor embedded in a network of social relationships	Deliberate construction of social relationships to achieve benefits	Consist of structural, behavioural and cognitive elements	Gaining access to resources

The level of analysis is typically the egocentric 'fan' of all relationships extending from the focal entrepreneur (or from each person in a team of entrepreneurs). Many studies have simply counted the number of contacts entrepreneurs have with other actors (for example, Birley, 1985; Hansen, 1995; Ostgaard and Birley, 1994); some have also focused on the heterogeneity and density, or the mix of weak and strong ties, in the entrepreneur's network (for example, Zhao and Aram, 1995). Research has identified a variety of benefits accruing to entrepreneurs from their personal networks; these benefits include access to physical, financial and organizational resources (for example, Birley, 1985; Hart et al., 1997), information and advice (for example, Johannisson, 1987), reputation and legitimacy benefits (for example, Starr and MacMillan, 1990) and emotional support (for example, Bruderl and Preisendorfer, 1998). These benefits, in turn, affect the emergence and performance of entrepreneurial firms. Typical dependent variables are gestation activities in the start-up process (such as writing a business plan, conducting customer tests and acquiring equipment or raw materials), the creation of a new venture and the sales or profitability of the new venture.

As its theoretical basis, the research on entrepreneurs' personal networks has largely relied on social capital theory[2] to explain why and how an entrepreneur's personal social relationships affect firm creation and performance. In this theoretical perspective, entrepreneurs and entrepreneurial firms are conceptualized as actors embedded in social networks of relationships, which influence behaviour, survival and success (Granovetter, 1985; Coleman, 1988). Actors are viewed as having the ability to extract benefits from their social structures, networks and memberships. The term 'social capital' is used to describe the relational resources that are embedded in these personal ties (Portes, 1998; Putnam, 1995). Social capital is clearly multidimensional, and has been suggested to consist of a structural dimension (existence of ties), a relational dimension (behavioural assets such as trust) and a cognitive dimension (shared understanding and goals) (Nahapiet and Ghoshal, 1998).

Drawing on its social capital theory foundations, the research on entrepreneurs' personal networks has created an in-depth understanding of the benefits accruing to entrepreneurs through social relationships. However, this research has remained silent on any costs, obligations or trade-offs involved for entrepreneurs in maintaining a personal network. Further, this stream of research has largely ignored the *process* of networking and the entrepreneurial *capabilities* required for successful networking.

Most of the research on entrepreneurs' personal networks has been carried out in non-technology settings. Thus, to date, there is very little knowledge on the importance and effects of personal networks for technology-based entrepreneurs in particular. It is likely that technology-based entrepreneurs will differ from other entrepreneurs in the types of personal networks they possess, in the way they utilize their networks and in the effects of these networks. Future research would clearly benefit from theory building and empirical studies exploring these issues.

2 Use of alliances and external resources by entrepreneurial firms
The second stream of research focuses on entrepreneurial firms' exchange relationships, and the research questions examine how the use of alliances and external resources by entrepreneurial firms influences the firms' performance. The level of analysis is the firm's set of exchange relationships (its egocentric network). Typical dependent variables in this research stream include innovativeness (number of new products or patents), sales growth (for example, Deeds and Hill, 1996; Dollinger and Golden, 1992; Jarillo, 1988, 1989; McGee and Dowling, 1994; Shan et al., 1994) and sometimes firm survival (for example, Venkataraman, Van de Ven, Buckeye and Hudson, 1990).

The rationales for the way external relationships influence firm performance are rooted in the resource-based and knowledge-based views of the firm. In the resource-based view, a firm is conceptualized as a collection of unique resources and relationships (Wernerfelt, 1984; Rumelt, 1984); firm growth is the process of using these resources to exploit the firm's 'productive opportunity' and increase the firm's resource base (Penrose, 1959). The essence of a firm's competitive advantage lies in the ways that existing resources are used and in the means to acquire or internally develop additional resources (Wernerfelt, 1984) – resources that are valuable, rare, imperfectly imitable and without a strategically equivalent substitute (Barney, 1991). Interorganizational alliances and collaboration are viewed as mechanisms to share and acquire resources, such as technological capabilities (Hagedoorn and Schakenraad, 1990; Eisenhardt and Schoonhoven, 1996). In the knowledge-based approach,[3] knowledge and competencies are viewed as the key resources of firms. Accordingly, the firm is conceptualized as a repository of knowledge (Nelson and

Winter, 1982; Spender, 1996). The organizational advantage of firms over market mechanisms arises from the capabilities of firms for creating and transferring knowledge (Kogut and Zander, 1992). The accumulation of knowledge through learning constitutes a driving resource for the development and growth of firms (Penrose, 1959; Spender and Grant, 1996), because learning opens new 'productive opportunities' (Penrose, 1959) for the firm, as well as enhancing the firm's ability to exploit these. Organizational learning takes place as information is exchanged between the firm and its environment; the firm learns as, through processing this new information, the range of its potential behaviours is changed (Huber, 1991; Steensma, 1996). Outside sources of knowledge are thus critical to organizational learning, the development of a firm's competencies and the innovation process (von Hippel, 1988). Interorganizational relationships, alliances and networks are important means to acquire this outside knowledge (Eisenhardt and Schoonhoven, 1996; Hagedoorn, 1993; Larsson et al., 1998; Steensma, 1996).

Parallel to the first research stream's focus on the benefits accruing to entrepreneurs through their personal networks, the second stream has focused on what resources entrepreneurial firms can acquire or mobilize through their interorganizational relationships; most research has focused on knowledge and other intangible resources such as reputation (Hoang and Antoncic, 2003). For example, Larson (1992) found that entrepreneurial firms benefit from customer and supplier relationships by acquiring information on new products, technologies and customer needs, and that the firms are able to develop their internal capabilities through the interaction with exchange partners. Similarly, Lipparini and Sobrero (1994) found that entrepreneurs' ability to generate new knowledge by combining firm-internal learning with learning in inter-firm ties was associated with industrial machinery firms' innovative capabilities. Stuart, Hoang and Hybels (1999) found that the signalling effect of prominent alliance partners allowed biotechnology firms to go public faster and with higher market capitalizations. Yli-Renko, Autio and Sapienza (2001a) showed that, through knowledge acquisition in their key customer relationships, young, technology-based firms were able to achieve higher levels of new product development and technological distinctiveness as well as lower sales costs. As the above examples indicate, much of the research on entrepreneurial firms' use of alliances and external resources has been carried out in technology-based industries, as knowledge- and resource-based theories are particularly applicable in such contexts (Yli-Renko, 1999).

Looking at this stream of research, it is clear that it has suffered from the often abstract and all-encompassing notions of resources and learning for which the resource-based and knowledge-based views have been criticized (Montgomery, 1995; Argote, 1999). Resource combination and learning processes are often considered as a 'black box'; research has instead focused on the tangible outcomes of resource combination or learning (Argote, 1999). Given the difficult-to-measure concepts, it is understandable that many studies have resorted to 'relationship counting', not considering the governance of or the exchange processes in the relationships. Further, in line with the resource- and knowledge-based views' 'penchant for the positive' (Montgomery, 1995), most studies assume that interorganizational relationships are beneficial in terms of knowledge generation and resource acquisition, while little attention has been paid to the costs of maintaining these relationships or the loss of proprietary knowledge that may take place. Some of these risks are likely to be particularly relevant in technology-based settings: the exchange of complex and often tacit technological knowledge is time-consuming and difficult, and losing proprietary technology may jeopardize the core competitive advantage of the firm.

3   Evolution of entrepreneurial firms' exchange relationships

In the first two research streams, the dependent variables were outcomes of the entrepreneurial process, that is, the various operationalizations of the emergence of a new firm or the performance of the young firm. The third research stream has a different perspective: it focuses on the formation, development and governance of entrepreneurial firms' exchange relationships. The dependent variables here are the relationships and networks themselves. The level of analysis is typically the dyadic interorganizational relationship; some studies have also focused on the entrepreneur's relationships or the firm's egocentric set of relationships.

Most of these studies have tended to be exploratory in nature, seeking to create a more in-depth understanding of entrepreneurial exchange relationships. Researchers have focused on understanding how the entrepreneur's personal ties are transformed into the firm's exchange relationships (for example, Dubini and Aldrich, 1991; Larson and Starr, 1993), the evolutionary patterns of the 'transaction set' of entrepreneurial firms (Venkataraman, 1989; Venkataraman and Van de Ven, 1998), as well as the nature and governance of exchange relationships (Larson, 1992; Uzzi, 1997). For example, Hite and Hesterly (2001) proposed that, as new firms move from emergence into the early growth stage, their networks evolve from cohesive, socially embedded personal networks to more sparse, intentionally managed exchange networks; Larson and Starr (1993) proposed a three-stage process through which an entrepreneur's one-dimensional exchanges are transformed into a stable set of multidimensional and multilayered relationships; Venkataraman and Van de Ven (1998) examined how 'environmental jolts' affect the maintaining or adding of customer and supplier relationships in the entrepreneurial firm's 'transaction set'. Larson (1992) focused on social governance mechanisms in entrepreneurial dyad relationships and proposed a process model of network formation, while Uzzi (1997) specified dimensions of entrepreneurial firms' embedded relationships and the mechanisms through which they influence economic action.

This research stream is primarily rooted in social exchange theory; it has also drawn on the social capital, resource-based and knowledge-based theories described above, and the resource dependence perspective. Social exchange theory emphasizes the social relationship between actors engaged in an interdependent series of transactions (Emerson, 1962; Levine and White, 1961). The key idea is that actors engage in transactions 'in honor of the social exchange relationship itself, that relationship being a series of reciprocating benefits extending into the experienced past and the anticipated future' (Emerson, 1981, p. 33). This approach differs significantly from neoclassical economic theory, which assumes that transactions are independent events and that actors are interchangeable. Building on the concepts of dependence and power in social exchange theory, the resource dependence perspective emerged, as Jacobs (1974) examined how organizations are controlled through exchange relationships with their environments. The resource dependence perspective posits that, because firms cannot generate all the resources they need internally, they depend on other organizations in the environment to acquire necessary resources, such as capital, materials, know-how and even reputation. The patterns of dependence produce interorganizational and intraorganizational power, which influences organizational behaviour (Aldrich and Pfeffer, 1976; Pfeffer and Salancik, 1978).

Building on this theoretical basis, this stream of research has created an important initial understanding of how entrepreneurial exchange relationships evolve and are governed, heavily emphasizing the social embeddedness of the actors in these relationships. The challenges for this research stream going forward are (1) to move beyond exploratory theory building to quantitative testing of the proposed frameworks, and (2) to complement the social exchange-based view of relationships with other perspectives, such as economic, resource-based and knowledge-based arguments. Further, little research has focused specifically on the evolution of technology-based firms' exchange relationships; there is clearly a need for theory building and empirical studies to better understand the idiosyncrasies of developing exchange relationships in technology-based settings.

4   Relationships between entrepreneurs and investors

A fourth distinct stream of research overlaps with the above three in terms of many of the research issues but it is clearly separate from them in that it focuses on the relationships between entrepreneurs and investors (venture capitalists, private investors or bankers) and draws primarily on agency theory. Much of this stream has been carried out in technology-based contexts, which is natural considering that venture capitalists often focus on technology-based firms, and that such firms are more likely to require external funding. Topics of interest within this stream include how contracts between entrepreneurs and investors are negotiated (for example, Kelly, 2000; Landstrom et al., 1998) and how the relationships are governed or maintained, for example, in terms of the level of investor involvement in managing the new ventures (for example, Sapienza, 1992; Sapienza and Korsgaard, 1996). This research seeks to uncover how the entrepreneur–investor relationships influence entrepreneurial firm performance. Dependent variables include perceived performance, perceived value-added by investors, Initial Public Offering (IPO) valuations, and survival of the entrepreneurial firms. The level of analysis is typically the dyadic relationship between an entrepreneurial firm and an investor/investment firm.

Agency theory has been the dominant framework in this research (for example, Barney et al., 1994; Fiet, 1995; Sahlman, 1990; Sapienza and Gupta, 1994). In agency theory, a firm is conceptualized as a nexus of contracts encompassing agency relationships with employees as well as with suppliers, customers, creditors and other external parties (Jensen and Meckling, 1976). The focus is on dyadic principal–agent ties between actors, who are assumed to be self-interested, rational and risk-averse. Following this logic, entrepreneurs are viewed as agents of investors, and the major activities of investors are aimed at minimizing the agency risk that arises from goal incongruence, information asymmetry and differences in risk preferences. This perspective is most suitable for explaining pre-investment, contract-writing and renegotiation phases, but its suitability for explaining post-investment monitoring, advising and value-adding activities in the entrepreneur–investor relationship has been argued to be limited (Manigart and Sapienza, 2000). Alternative theoretical approaches applied in this research stream include game theory (Cable and Shane, 1997), procedural justice theory (Sapienza and Korsgaard, 1996) and, most recently, the social embeddedness perspective (Shane and Cable, 2002).

The entrepreneur–investor research is particularly isolated from the other streams of research on entrepreneurial exchange relationships owing to the very different theoretical assumptions underlying this approach, namely the strict assumption of economic gain as the sole motivator of investors and entrepreneurs and the emphasis on minimizing agency risk (as opposed to the notion of maximizing value creation that underlies much of the other entrepreneurship research). In order to provide a more fine-grained and realistic view of entrepreneur–investor relationships, this research could build on the knowledge-based, social capital and relational contracting theories (Manigart and Sapienza, 2000).

5   *Research focusing on regional networks of entrepreneurial firms*

The fifth stream of research can be identified in regional studies which focus on how regional networks of firms (or 'industrial districts') foster innovation and growth. These studies often do not explicitly focus on *new* ventures, but rather on small and medium-sized firms. Nevertheless, because new firms often emerge and operate in these regional networks, the findings of these studies are highly relevant for understanding the role that networks play in entrepreneurial processes, on the one hand, and the role that entrepreneurial processes play in regional development, on the other. Much of this research stream has focused on technology-based regional clusters.

Researchers in this stream have examined topics such as the growth of firms through 'constellations' (Lorenzoni and Ornati, 1988; Shepherd, 1991), the regional environments which foster the growth of new, technology-based firms (Saxenian, 1990, 1991), the innovative role of small-firm networks (Lipparini and Sobrero, 1994), the structures and outcomes of participation in small-firm manufacturing networks (Human and Provan, 1997) and the dynamic complementarities between small and large firms in innovation (Acs and Audretsch, 1993; Rothwell, 1983; Rothwell and Dodgson, 1993). Often cited examples of industrial districts are Silicon Valley (Piore and Sabel, 1984; Saxenian, 1990, 1991), the Emilia-Romagna region in Italy (Lorenzoni and Oranti, 1988; Piore and Sable, 1984) and the Cambridge region in the UK (Keeble et al., 1999). The dependent variables in studies are usually the growth of the region/network (emergence of new firms and growth of existing firms), the evolving structure of the network, or the collective innovative outputs of firms in the network. The level of analysis is the network or region.

Theoretically, these studies draw on the Marshallian notion of industrial districts (Marshall, 1890; Krugman, 1991) and theoretical work on the network form of organization (for example, Imai et al., 1985; Håkansson, 1989). Marshall introduced the idea of concentration of specialized industries in particular localities, emphasizing the role of external economies of scale deriving from the division of tasks in an industry among many producers. Based on Marshall's work, the models of flexible specialization have explained how regional networks foster the exchange of ideas, information and goods, the accumulation of skills and innovative capability, and the development of cultural homogeneity allowing for cooperation and trust between firms (Brusco, 1982; Grabher, 1993; Piore and Sabel, 1984). Noting the cooperative, trust-based relationships between buyers, suppliers and, even among competitors, free flows of information and personnel in these networks, researchers proposed that networks are a distinct form of organization, between markets and hierarchies (for example, Jarillo, 1988; Thorelli, 1986). More recently, the research on industrial districts has also drawn on knowledge-based theory to develop a model of 'regional collective learning' (Camagni, 1991; Lorenz, 1996, 1997) describing the emergence of basic common knowledge and procedures

Table 3.3   Main streams of research on the external relationships of entrepreneurial firms

Research stream	Level of analysis	Dependent variables	Main theoretical approaches
Entrepreneurs' personal networks	Entrepreneur's egocentric set of interpersonal relationships	Benefits accruing to entrepreneurs through personal networks New venture formation; gestation activities New venture performance (e.g., survival, early growth)	Social capital theory, social network theory
Use of alliances and external resources by entrepreneurial firms	Entrepreneurial firm's egocentric set of interorganizational relationships	Benefits accruing to entrepreneurial firms through their external ties Firm performance (e.g., growth, innovativeness)	Resource-based view, knowledge-based view
Formation and evolution of entrepreneurial firms' exchange relationships	Interorganizational dyad or entrepreneurial firm's egocentric set of interorganizational relationships	Exchange relationships and networks of entrepreneurial firms	Social exchange theory, resource dependence perspective, resource-based and knowledge-based views
Relationships between entrepreneurs and investors	Dyadic relationship between entrepreneurial firm and investor/ investment firm	Firm performance (e.g., IPO valuation, survival) Perceived value-add by investor	Agency theory, procedural justice theory, game theory
Regional innovation networks (industrial districts)	Geographically concentrated network of firms	Growth or level of innovative activity of the network	Marshallian industrial districts, network theory

across a set of geographically proximate firms, facilitating cooperation, innovation and growth.

While this stream of research is distinct from the other four streams primarily owing to its regional focus and network level of analysis, the research topics such as leveraging external resources, information flows and trust in networks are very similar to those in the other streams. The regional network studies would greatly benefit from drawing more on the theory development that has been done in the other research streams on entrepreneurial exchange relationships, in particular those based on the social capital and knowledge-based theories.

The above discussion of the five streams of research on entrepreneurs' and entrepreneurial firms' external relationships is summarized in Table 3.3, illustrating the distinctions between the streams in terms of dependent variables, levels of analysis and theoretical perspectives. In the following, I will build on this review to propose a multi-theoretic, integrative perspective to research on entrepreneurial exchange relationships.

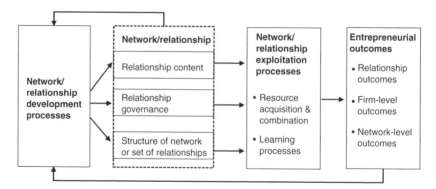

Figure 3.1   An integrative model of entrepreneurial exchange relationships

Toward a Multitheoretic, Integrative View

While research tends to be cumulative within each of the five streams, not many studies have attempted to draw insights from across streams. Each of the streams and each of the theoretical approaches sheds light on some aspects of entrepreneurial exchange relationships, with no one stream or approach providing a complete understanding of the phenomenon of interest. In the following, I argue that the perspectives provided are complementary, rather than conflicting, and should be combined to create a more holistic understanding of entrepreneurial exchange relationships. To provide a structure for this discussion, Figure 3.1 presents a general framework that conceptualizes entrepreneurial exchange relationships as follows. First, relationship/network development processes give rise to an entrepreneurial exchange relationship/network, characterized in terms of content, governance and structure. Then, through exploitation processes, the exchange relationships/networks result in entrepreneurial outcomes; these can be examined at the relationship, firm or network level. The feedback arrows in the framework indicate that the relationship/network characteristics and the entrepreneurial outcomes influence the continuing evolutionary processes of relationship/network development. This framework is applicable across the different streams of research and the different theoretical perspectives.

Content, governance and structure of relationships
Starting with the characteristics of the relationships/network, I follow Amit and Zott (2001) and Hoang and Antoncic (2003) in distinguishing between content, governance and structure. While each of these is discussed separately, it should be noted that the three components are not independent but, rather, closely interrelated.

Content refers to what is being exchanged and how much of it is being exchanged in a relationship. The traditional agency and transaction cost economics perspectives emphasize the economic transactions that constitute an interorganizational relationship, that is, the flow of money and goods. Similarly, the resource-dependence and resource-based views have focused on the resources to which the entrepreneur or entrepreneurial firm can gain access through external linkages, with the knowledge-based view focusing explicitly on the flows of information and know-how. The above perspectives create an 'undersocialized' understanding (Granovetter, 1985) of interorganizational relationships. Social capital theory brings balance into the picture with its emphasis on social elements of exchange relationships: the social interaction taking place in parallel to the economic transactions. Therefore, in order to create a holistic understanding of the content of entrepreneurial exchange relationships, a theoretical framework should include economic, knowledge-related and social exchange elements.

The second construct is governance, that is, the mechanisms that are used to coordinate and manage an exchange relationship. The traditional economic approaches and agency theory focus on contractual governance – how it can be used to manage problems of information asymmetry and goal incongruence – and the costs involved in maintaining the relationship and monitoring the other party's actions. In entrepreneurial settings, the applicability of this traditional approach is limited, because of the high level of uncertainty of future events and the limited resources of the entrepreneurial firm (limited resources do not allow for extensive monitoring activities or legal enforcement of contracts). Accordingly, the other theoretical approaches propose informal mechanisms for the governance of entrepreneurial exchange relationships: social capital theory focuses on social mechanisms such as trust, common goals or loss of reputation, whereas the social exchange theory and the resource dependence perspective focus on how power and dependence between actors dictate the behaviour of the exchange partners. Studies have focused on the use of a particular governance mechanism (such as trust, reciprocity and reputation [Larson, 1992] and contractual governance flexibility [Yli-Renko et al., 2001b]), with little effort to understand the complementarity, interaction or trade-offs between alternative mechanisms. Thus, in order to create a holistic understanding of the governance of entrepreneurial exchange relationships, a theoretical framework should include contractual, social and power/dependence-related governance mechanisms.

Aggregating the dyadic relationships of entrepreneurs and entrepreneurial firms to the network or set of relationships brings us to the third construct: structure, the pattern of relationships that comprise the ties between actors. A very different network structure will emerge, depending on which content elements are considered. Social network theory has focused on social structures in terms of network size, centrality of the actor and the diversity of an actor's links (mix of weak and strong ties). The resource dependence perspective emphasizes the patterns of dependence and power that arise from the actors' differential resource positions. The resource-based and agency perspectives focus on the flows of money and goods. Yet another picture will emerge from mapping the flows of information and know-how between actors, as proposed by the knowledge-based view. Therefore, to fully understand the structure of entrepreneurial exchange networks, a theoretical framework should include the patterns of direct and indirect flows of money and goods, power/dependence, knowledge and social interaction.

When studying the content, governance and structure of exchange relationships in technology-based contexts, it is particularly important to include and integrate different theories. Young, technology-based firms tend to be highly knowledge intensive; that is, the ventures' inputs, transformation processes and outputs depend on knowledge, rather than physical factors of production (Bud-Frierman, 1994). Young firms that compete in knowledge-intensive industries, such as biotechnology, software and electronics, are likely to have highly mobile resources (Sapienza et al., 2003) that are leveraged and developed in interorganizational relationships. Thus it is critical to integrate knowledge-based theory with the more traditional resource dependence and economic approaches when studying exchange relationships. Further, social capital has been shown to facilitate knowledge acquisition, combination and exploitation processes in exchange relationships (Nahapiet and Ghoshal, 1998; Yli-Renko et al., 2001a), indicating that social aspects of relationships may also be of particular relevance for technology-based firms.

Relationship development and exploitation processes
The extant research has provided a largely static, 'snap-shot' view of exchange relationships. In order to gain a more dynamic, in-depth understanding of entrepreneurial exchange relationships, scholars should examine two types of processes.

First, we need to understand the evolution of entrepreneurial exchange relationships, that is, the processes of establishing and maintaining these relationships and the factors that influence these processes. Most studies have, to date, focused on certain aspects of this development. Work rooted in social capital research has focused on the informal, social processes (Hite, 2001), while others, drawing on resource-based or social exchange theories, have examined the impact of environmental conditions on establishing relationships (Eisenhardt and Schoonhoven, 1996; Venkataraman and Van de Ven, 1998). Some exploratory, multitheoretic frameworks have been proposed, including both economic and social elements (Larson, 1992; Larson and Starr, 1993; Uzzi, 1997).

Second, we need to look inside the 'black box' of the processes involved in exploiting exchange relationships, in order to uncover how, when and to what extent entrepreneurs and entrepreneurial firms leverage their external relationships. To understand these exploitation processes, we could apply resource-based theory to understand interorganizational resource combination processes, and build on recent knowledge-based work that has focused on the way entrepreneurial firms acquire knowledge in their exchange relationships (for example, Lorenz, 1996; Soh, 2003; Yli-Renko et al., 2001a).

Understanding the dynamic processes and patterns associated with exchange relationships is particularly important in technology-based settings characterized by rapid changes in customer needs and competitive dynamics. Such changes may significantly alter the context and objectives of exchange relationships (Eisenhardt and Schoonhoven, 1996). Further, owing to the often rapid pace and complex nature of development in technology-based industries, these industries provide a particularly fruitful setting for longitudinal and qualitative studies of the evolutionary processes of entrepreneurial exchange relationships.

Outcomes of relationships
Following the conceptual framework in Figure 3.1, exchange relationships, through exploitation processes, result in entrepreneurial outcomes. As our review of the five research streams showed, the typical outcomes that have been studied are the creation, survival and performance of new ventures. I propose that a wider range of more fine-grained outcomes should be studied, incorporating (1) not only firm-level performance metrics, but also the immediate outcomes of relationships as well as network-level outcomes, and (2) outcomes derived from a variety of theoretical perspectives, including both positive and negative outcomes.

Much of the research has focused on outcomes for the firm as a whole. However, when the unit of analysis is one relationship or a subset of a firm's relationships, it can often be difficult to discern the incremental impact on overall firm performance; any impact will be entangled in the multitude of firm-internal, environmental or other interorganizational factors. Therefore, in addition to the firm-level outcomes, research should increasingly focus on the immediate outcomes of particular relationships. These may include, for example, the perceived success of the relationships, the economic outcomes of the relationships (generated revenues or profits) or the innovative outcomes of the relationship (such as number of new products developed). Similarly, when research is conducted at the network level, outcomes should naturally be measured at that level, as an aggregate of the firm-level outcomes in the network.

The different theoretical approaches have differing points of view on the outcomes of exchange relationships. Roughly categorizing, the resource dependence perspective and agency theory focus on the avoidance of the negatives in exchange relationships, while the resource-based, knowledge-based and social capital theories emphasize the creation of positives. The resource dependence perspective portrays firms as depending on their external relationships to acquire necessary resources, and assumes that this dependence is always non-beneficial. The focus is on negative outcomes, the mechanisms and dangers of dependence. Similarly, though recognizing the economic benefits of external relationships, agency theory heavily emphasizes risks and costs. The resource-based and knowledge-based views, on the other hand, seldom consider the potential negative outcomes involved in external relationships. For example, most studies assume that these relationships are beneficial in terms of knowledge generation, while little attention has been paid to the loss of proprietary knowledge that may take place as a result of opportunistic actions by the exchange partner. Similarly, social capital theory has been criticized for ignoring the costs and negative implications of social capital. In one of the few studies considering this possibility, Uzzi (1997) found that social embeddedness in inter-firm networks had positive effects until a threshold, after which embeddedness had a negative effect by making firms vulnerable to exogenous shocks or insulating them from information beyond their network.

I thus propose that, by including a variety of more fine-grained outcome measures derived from various theories, we can create a better understanding of entrepreneurial exchange relationships. Relationships will have an effect, not only on an entrepreneurial firm's economic performance (for example, growth, profitability), but also on other outcomes such as the firm's power position, reputation, social capital and knowledge stocks. For technology-based firms operating in highly uncertain and rapidly changing environments, the knowledge-related, reputational and social outcomes are likely to be of particular relevance (Yli-Renko, 1999).

Conclusions

This chapter has identified and analysed five distinct streams of research on entrepreneurial exchange relationships: research on (1) the personal networks of the entrepreneur, (2) the use of alliances and external resources by entrepreneurial firms, (3) the formation, development and governance of entrepreneurial firms' exchange relationships, (4) the relationships between entrepreneurs and investors, and (5) regional networks of entrepreneurial firms. Focusing on the theoretical foundations of the research streams, I have explicated the differences in the assumptions about the nature of firms and exchange relationships, levels of analysis and the research questions addressed. I have also discussed the extent to which each of the streams has considered issues specific to technology-based entrepreneurship. A number of conclusions can be drawn, based on the review.

The analysis demonstrated that the levels of analysis vary along two dimensions: inter*personal* vs. inter*organizational* relationships, and the dyad, egocentric set or network levels. This multiplicity contributes to the heterogeneity and ambiguity of the field. Greater conceptual precision in the use of terminology and the definition of the level of analysis is required to avoid confusion and to facilitate cross-stream leveraging of frameworks and findings. The framework presented in Table 3.1 provides a step in this direction.

In outlining the theoretical foundations of each research stream I have sought to make explicit the underlying assumptions and viewpoints that are often implied but not explicitly discussed in the research. I have argued that scholars should increasingly focus on theory building, and that there is significant potential to leverage theoretical frameworks across research streams; each of the approaches sheds light on some aspects of entrepreneurial exchange relationships and their outcomes, with no one approach providing a complete understanding of the phenomenon of interest. The perspectives are complementary, rather than conflicting, and they should be combined to create a more holistic understanding of entrepreneurial exchange relationships.

Accordingly, I have proposed an integrative, multitheoretic framework (Figure 3.1) that conceptualizes entrepreneurial exchange relationships in terms of (1) the development processes of relationships/networks, (2) the content, governance and structure of relationships/networks, (3) the exploitation processes of relationships/networks, and (4) the entrepreneurial outcomes of exchange relationships. I have suggested that a better understanding of these elements can be gained by combining insights from social capital, resource-based, knowledge-based, resource-dependence and economic theories.

Multitheoretic and cross-stream integration is particularly important in technology-based settings, which are characterized by high knowledge intensity, uncertainty, complexity and a rapid pace of development. While some of the research streams have often focused on technology-based settings (namely research streams 2, 4 and 5) there has been little emphasis on techno-entrepreneurship in the research on personal networks (research stream 1) or the evolution of exchange relationships (research stream 3). In techno-entrepreneurial contexts, researchers would benefit from increased application of knowledge-based theory in the study of entrepreneurs' personal networks, the relationships between investors and technology-based entrepreneurs, and regional technology clusters; social and economic approaches have largely dominated these streams of research. Research on the use of alliances and external resources by technology-based entrepreneurial firms would benefit from increased use of resource dependence and economic approaches in conjunction with the currently prevalent social and knowledge-based approaches.

This chapter has made several contributions to the entrepreneurship and interorganizational relationship research. First, by comparing and contrasting the separate streams of research on entrepreneurial exchange relationships, I have created a comprehensive understanding of the current state of this research that until now has remained fragmented in separate silos. Second, by explicating the theoretical bases, levels of analysis and research questions in each stream, I have identified opportunities for leveraging frameworks and findings across streams. Third, by proposing an integrative, multitheoretic framework, I have contributed towards the development of a 'relational theory of entrepreneurship'; such a theory will enable us to better understand the nature of and processes involved in entrepreneurial exchange relationships as well as the two-way relationship between this exchange and entrepreneurial outcomes. Finally, I have highlighted issues and research opportunities specific to techno-entrepreneurship, contributing to the development of this growing area of research.

Implications for future research
Rather than trying to maintain separation in traditional theoretical silos or to analyse rival hypotheses, future research should aim at finding ways to consolidate and combine elements from various approaches to form a more comprehensive understanding of entrepreneurial exchange relationships. To explore the development and content of exchange, research could focus on questions such as the following. As a relationship develops, how do the economic and social aspects of exchange hinder or facilitate each others' development? How does an entrepreneurial firm's resource position affect its willingness to take on agency risks and its ability to manage these risks? To create a better understanding of governance mechanisms, research questions could include the following. How can contractual and social governance mechanisms be used in parallel? In which situations are social vs. contractual mechanisms more important; does this depend on, for example, the resource or knowledge base of the exchange partner or the technology intensity of the setting?

For a more comprehensive view of the positive and negative outcomes of entrepreneurial exchange relationships, research could look at questions such as the following. In terms of the impact on firm performance, how do the negative effects (agency risks, dependence) compare in magnitude to the positive effects (acquired resources and knowledge)? How do the relationship outcomes of the different theoretical approaches interact? One such link, the intersection of social capital and knowledge-based theories, focuses on the way social capital facilitates the creation of intellectual capital (for example, Nahapiet and Ghoshal, 1998; Yli-Renko et al., 2001a). Other similar avenues should be pursued; for example, does resource dependence facilitate or hinder the building of social capital and knowledge? Further, which outcomes are most relevant in technology-based settings?

It will be a challenge to combine the various theoretical approaches into realistic models with high explanatory power, while maintaining conceptual precision and clarity. To achieve this, it is critical that we uncover the contextual and situational factors that determine the relevance of the different theoretical approaches. Looking at the different theoretical approaches – their differing assumptions, the wide range of issues studied, and the different settings in which they have been applied in entrepreneurship research – it is clear that not all approaches are going to be equally relevant in all situations. Therefore, the key question is: when is each approach helpful? The relevance of the theories will vary depending on key factors such as knowledge intensity, stage in the new venture life cycle or the type of exchange relationship. Knowledge-based and social capital theories may be more relevant in knowledge-intensive settings. Social capital-based models are likely to be most relevant at the pre-start-up and early stages of entrepreneurial firm development, whereas resource dependence and agency arguments are likely to increase in relevance as the firm develops and the relationships evolve from personal ties to interorganizational exchanges (Boyd, 1990; Hite and Hesterly, 2001). The applicability of the different theories is also likely to vary by type of exchange partner; that is, whether we are focusing on relationships with investors, customers, suppliers, advisors, competitors, strategic partners or other exchange parties. In buyer–supplier relationships, where exchanges are primarily structured around the economic transactions, the resource dependence and agency perspectives are likely to be more relevant than in informal situations. In the informal networks among competitors, strategic partners and support organizations in industrial districts, the social and knowledge-based aspects of exchange are likely to be in a central role.

Significant theory development and empirical testing is clearly required to uncover and develop the rationales for the contingencies involved in applying the different theories to the study of entrepreneurial exchange relationships in technology-based as well as other settings. As researchers increasingly tackle questions that span theoretical boundaries and leverage insights from previously separate research streams, a more complete understanding of entrepreneurial exchange relationships will be created.

Notes

1. This review is based on a survey of entrepreneurship, management and sociology journal articles matching the keywords 'entrepreneurial' or 'SME' and 'network', 'interorganizational relationship' or 'exchange relationship'. My search of the ABI/Inform article database uncovered 192 such articles, published between 1980 and 2003.
2. The term 'social capital' is used here as the 'umbrella concept' encompassing a range of theories and concepts such as social networks, social exchange, social embeddedness, informal organization, trust and relational contracts (Adler and Kwon, 2002).
3. The knowledge-based view of the firm evolved from the resource-based view, as knowledge and competencies were increasingly viewed as the key resources of firms. The knowledge-based view is often considered a part or an extension of the resource-based view. Alternatively, the resource-based view can be considered one of several knowledge-based approaches (Foss, 1996). There seems to be general agreement in the literature that Nelson and Winter's (1982) evolutionary theory, Hamel and Prahalad's (1990) work on core competencies and Teece, Pisano and Schuen's (1997) dynamic capabilities framework all represent different streams within the knowledge-based view.

References

Acs, Z. and D. Audretsch (1993), 'Innovation and firm size: the new learning', *International Journal of Technology Management*, Special Publication on Small Firms and Innovation, 23–35.
Adler, P.S. and S.-W. Kwon (2002), 'Social capital: prospects for a new concept', *Academy of Management Review*, **27**(1), 17–40.
Aldrich, H.E. and J.E. Cliff (2003), 'The pervasive effects of family on entrepreneurship: toward a family embeddedness perspective', *Journal of Business Venturing*, **18**(5), 573–97.
Aldrich, H.E. and J. Pfeffer (1976), 'Environments of organizations', in A. Inkeles, J. Coleman and N. Smelser (eds), *Annual Review of Sociology*, **2**, 79–105.
Aldrich, H.E. and C. Zimmer (1986), 'Entrepreneurship through social networks, in D. Sexton and R. Smilor (eds), *The Art and Science of Entrepreneurship*, New York: Ballinger, pp. 3–23.
Amit, R. and C. Zott (2001), 'Value creation in e-business', *Strategic Management Journal*, **22**, 493–520.
Argote, L. (1999), *Organizational Learning: Creating, Retaining and Transferring Knowledge*, Boston, Dordrecht, and London: Kluwer Academic Publishers.
Autio, E., H.J. Sapienza and J. Almeida (2000), 'Effects of age at entry, knowledge intensity and imitability on international growth', *Academy of Management Journal*, **43**(5), 909–24.
Barney, J. (1991), 'Firm resources and sustained competitive advantage', *Journal of Management*, **17**(1), 99–120.
Barney, J.B., L.W. Busenitz, J.O. Fiet and D.D. Moesel (1994), 'The relationship between venture capitalists and managers in new firms: determinants of contractual covenants', *Managerial Finance*, **20**(1), 19–31.
Boyd, B. (1990), 'Corporate linkages and organizational environment: a test of the resource dependence model', *Strategic Management Journal*, **11**, 419–30.
Birley, S. (1985), 'The role of networks in the entrepreneurial process', *Journal of Business Venturing*, **1**(1), 107–17.
Bruderl, J. and P. Preisendorfer (1998), 'Network support and the success of newly founded businesses', *Small Business Economics*, **10**, 213–25.

Bruno, A.V. and T.T. Tyebjee (1982), 'The entrepreneur's search for capital', *Journal of Business Venturing*, **1**, 61–74.

Brusco, S. (1982), 'The Emilian model: productive decentralisation and social integration', *Cambridge Journal of Economics*, **6**, 167–84.

Bud-Frierman, L. (ed.) (1994), *Information Acumen*, London: Routledge.

Cable, D.M. and S. Shane (1997), 'A prisoner's dilemma approach to entrepreneur – venture capitalist relationships', *Academy of Management Review*, **22**(1), 142–76.

Coleman, J. (1988), 'Social capital and the creation of human capital', *American Journal of Sociology*, **94**, S95–S120.

Camagni, R. (1991), 'Local "milieu", uncertainty and innovation networks: toward a dynamic theory of economic space', in R. Camagni (ed.), *Innovation Networks: Spatial Perspectives*, London: Belhaven, pp. 121–42.

Davidsson, P. and B. Honig (2003), 'The role of social and human capital among nascent entrepreneurs', *Journal of Business Venturing*, **18**, 301–31.

Deeds, D.L. and C.W.L. Hill (1996), 'Strategic alliances and the rate of new product development: an empirical study of entrepreneurial biotechnology firms', *Journal of Business Venturing*, **11**, 42–55.

Dollinger, M. and P. Golden (1992), 'Interorganizational and collective strategies in small firms: environmental effects and performance', *Journal of Management*, **18**, 695–715.

Dubini, P. and H. Aldrich (1991), 'Personal and extended networks are central to the entrepreneurial process', *Journal of Business Venturing*, **6**, 305–13.

Eisenhardt, K.M. and C. Schoonhoven (1996), 'Resource-based view of strategic alliance formation: strategic and social effects in entrepreneurial firms', *Organization Science*, **7**(2), 136–50.

Emerson, R.M. (1962), 'Power-dependence relations', *American Sociological Review*, **27**, 31–40.

Emerson, R.M. (1981), 'Social exchange theory', in M. Rosenberg and R. Turner (eds), *Social Psychology, Sociological Perspectives*, New Brunswick: Transaction Publishers.

Fiet, J.O. (1995), 'Reliance upon informants in the venture capital industry', *Journal of Business Venturing*, **10**(3), 195–214.

Foss, N.J. (1996), 'Knowledge-based approaches to the theory of the firm: some practical comments', *Organizational Science*, **7**(5), September–October, 470–76.

Grabher, G. (1993), 'Rediscovering the social in the economics of interfirm relations', in G. Grabher (ed.), *The Embedded Firm*, London and New York: Routledge, pp. 1–32.

Granovetter, M.S. (1985), 'Economic action and social structure: the problem of embeddedness', *American Journal of Sociology*, **91**(3), 481–510.

Hagedoorn, J. (1993), 'Understanding the rationale of strategic technology partnering: Interorganizational modes of cooperation and sectional differences', *Strategic Management Journal*, **14**, 371–85.

Hagedoorn, J. and J. Schakenraad (1990), 'Strategic partnering and technological cooperation', in B. Dankbaar, J. Groenewgwn and H. Schenk (eds), *Perspectives in Industrial Economics*, Dordrecht: Kluwer, pp. 171–94.

Håkansson, H. (1989), *Corporate Technological Behavior, Co-operation and Networks*, London and New York: Routledge.

Hamel, G. and C.K. Prahalad (1990), 'The core competence of the corporation', *Harvard Business Review*, **68**(3), May–June, 79–93.

Hansen, E.L. (1995), 'Entrepreneurial networks and new organization growth', *Entrepreneurship: Theory and Practice*, **19**(4), 7–19.

Hart, M.M., P.G. Greene and C.G. Brush (1997), 'Leveraging resources: building an organization on an entrepreneurial resource base', *Babson – Kauffman Entrepreneurship Research Conference*.

Hite, J.M. (2001), 'Evolutionary processes and paths of embedded network ties in emerging entrepreneurial firms', *Academy of Management Proceedings*.

Hite, J.M. and W.S. Hesterly (2001), 'The evolution of firm networks: from emergence to early growth of the firm', *Strategic Management Journal*, **22**, 275–86.

Hoang, H. and B. Antoncic (2003), 'Network-based research in entrepreneurship: a critical review', *Journal of Business Venturing*, **18**, 165–87.

Huber, G.P. (1991), 'Organizational learning: the contributing processes and the literature', *Organization Science*, **2**(1), 88–115.

Human, S.E. and K.G. Provan (1997), 'An emergent theory of structure and outcomes in small-firm strategic manufacturing networks', *Academy of Management Journal*, **40**(2), 368–403.

Iacobucci, D. and P.C. Zerrillo (1996), 'Multiple levels of relational marketing phanomena', in D. Iacobucci (ed.), *Networks in Marketing*, Thousand Oaks, CA: Sage Publications.

Imai, K., I. Nonaka and H. Takeuchi (1985), 'Managing the new product development process: how Japanese companies learn and unlearn', in R.H. Hayes and C. Lorenz (eds), *The Uneasy Alliances*, Cambridge, MA: Harvard Business School Press.

Jacobs, J. (1965), *The Death and Life of Great American Cities*, New York: Penguin Books.

Jacobs, D. (1974), 'Dependency and vulnerability: an exchange approach to the control of organizations', *Administrative Science Quarterly*, **19**, 45–59.

Jarillo, J.-C. (1989), 'Entrepreneurship and growth: the strategic use of external resources', *Journal of Business Venturing*, **4**, 133–47.

Jarillo, J. (1988), 'On strategic networks', *Strategic Management Journal*, **7**(1), 37–51.

Jensen, M.C. and W.H. Meckling (1976), 'Theory of the firm: managerial behavior, agency costs and ownership structure', *Journal of Financial Economics*, **3**, 305–60.

Johannisson, B., K.N. Alexanderson and K. Senneseth (1994), 'Beyond anarchy and organization: entrepreneurs in contextual networks', *Entrepreneurship and Regional Development*, **6**, 329–56.

Johannisson, B. (1987), 'Anarchists and organizers: entrepreneurs in a network perspective', *International Studies of Management and Organization*, **17**, 49–63.

Keeble, D., C. Lawson, B. Moore and F. Wilkinson (1999), 'Collective learning processes, networking and "institutional thickness" in the Cambridge Region', *Regional Studies*, **33**(4), 319–32.

Kelly, P. (2000), 'Private investors and entrepreneurs: how context shapes their relationship', unpublished PhD dissertation, London Business School, London, UK.

Kirzner, I.M. (1973), *Competition and Entrepreneurship*, Chicago, IL: University of Chicago Press.

Kogut, B. and U. Zander (1992), 'Knowledge of the firm, combinative capabilities, and the replication of technology', *Organization Science*, **3**(3), 383–97.

Krugman, P.R. (1991), *Geography and Trad*, Leuven: Leuven University Press.

Landstrom, H., S. Manigart, C. Mason and H.J. Sapienza (1998), 'Contracts between entrepreneurs and investors: terms and negotiation processes', in P. Reynolds, W. Bygrave, N. Carter, S. Manigart, C. Mason, D. Meyer and K. Shaver (eds), *Frontiers of Entrepreneurship Research*, Boston, MA: Babson College.

Larson, A. (1992), 'Network dyads in entrepreneurial settings: a study of the governance of exchange relationships', *Administrative Science Quarterly*, **37**(March), 76–104.

Larson, A. and J. Starr (1993), 'A network model of organization formation', *Entrepreneurship Theory and Practice*, **17**(Winter), 5–15.

Larsson, R., L. Bengtsson, K. Henriksson and J. Sparks (1998), 'The interorganizational learning dilemma: collective knowledge development in strategic alliances', *Organization Science*, **9**(3), 285–305.

Levine, S. and P.E. White (1961), 'Exchange as a conceptual framework for the study of interorganizational relationships', *Administrative Science Quarterly*, **5**, 583–601.

Lipparini, A. and M. Sobrero (1994), 'The glue and the pieces: entrepreneurship and innovation in small-firm networks', *Journal of Business Venturing*, **9**, 125–40.

Lorenz, E. (1996), 'Collective learning processes and the regional labour market', research note, European Network on Networks, Collective Learning and RTD in regionally-Clustered High Technology SMEs.

Lorenzoni, G. and O. Ornati (1988), 'Constellations of firms and new ventures', *Journal of Business Venturing*, **3**, 41–57.

Manigart, S. and H.J. Sapienza (2000), 'Venture capital and growth', in D. Sexton and H. Landstrom (eds), *Handbook of International Entrepreneurship*, Oxford, UK: Blackwell.

Marshall, A. (1890), *Principles of Economics*, London: MacMillan Press.

McGee, J.E. and M.J. Dowling (1994), 'Using R&D cooperative agreements to leverage managerial experience: a study of technology-intensive new ventures', *Journal of Business Venturing*, **9**, 33–48.

Montgomery, C.A. (1995). 'Of diamonds and rust: a new look at resources', in C.A. Montgomery (ed.), *Resource-Based and Evolutionary Theories of the Firm*, Norwell, MA: Kluwer Academic Publishers, pp. 251–68.

Nahapiet, J. and S. Ghoshal (1998), 'Social capital, intellectual capital and the organizational advantage', *Academy of Management Review*, **23**(2), 242–66.

Nelson, R. and S. Winter (1982), *An Evolutionary Theory of Economic Change*, Cambridge: Belknap.

Ostgaard, T.A. and S. Birley (1994), 'Personal networks and firm competitive strategy – a strategic or coincidental match?', *Journal of Business Venturing*, **9**, 281–305.

Penrose, E. (1959), *The Theory of the Growth of the Firm*, Oxford: Blackwell.

Pfeffer, J. and G.R. Salancik (1978), *The External Control of Organizations: A Resource Dependence Perspective*, New York: Harper & Row.

Piore, M.J. and C.F. Sabel (1984), *The Second Industrial Divide: Possibilities for Prosperity*, New York: Basic Books.

Portes, A. (1998), 'Social capital: its origins and applications in modern sociology', *Annual Review of Sociology*, **24**, 1–24.

Putnam, R.D. (1995), 'Bowling alone: America's declining social capital', *Journal of Democracy*, **6**(1), 65–78.

Rothwell, R. (1983), 'Innovation and firm size: the case of dynamic complementarity', *Journal of General Management*, **8**(6), 5–25.

Rothwell, R. and M. Dodgson (1993), 'Technology-based SMEs: their role in industrial and economic change', *International Journal of Technology Management*, Special Publication on Small Firms and Innovation, 8–22.

Rumelt, R.P. (1984), 'Toward a strategic theory of the firm', in R.B. Lamb (ed.), *Competitive Strategic Management*, Englewood Cliffs, NJ: Prentice-Hall.

Sahlman, W.A. (1990), 'The structure and governance of venture-capital organizations', *Journal of Financial Economics*, **27**, 473–521.

Sapienza, H.J. (1992), 'When do venture capitalists add value?', *Journal of Business Venturing*, **7**(1), 9–28.

Sapienza, H.J., E. Autio and S. Zahra (2003), 'Effects of internationalization on young firms' prospects for survival and growth', paper presented at the *Academy of Management Meeting*, Seattle, WA.

Sapienza, H.J. and A.K. Gupta (1994), 'Impact of agency risks and task uncertainty on venture capitalist – CEO interaction', *Academy of Management Journal*, **37**(6), 1618–32.

Sapienza, H.J. and M.A. Korsgaard (1996), 'Procedural justice in entrepreneur-investor relations', *Academy of Management Journal*, **39**(3), 544–74.

Sawyerr, O.O. and J.E. McGee (1999), 'The impact of personal network characteristics on perceived strategic uncertainty: an examination of new high technology manufacturing firms', Babson College – Kauffman Foundation Entrepreneurship Research Conference.

Saxenian, A. (1990), 'Regional networks and the resurgence of Silicon Valley', *California Management Review*, **33**(1), 89–112.

Saxenian, A. (1991), 'The origins and dynamics of production networks in Silicon Valley', *Research Policy*, **20**, 423–37.

Shan, W., G. Walker and B. Kogut (1994), 'Interfirm cooperation and startup innovation in the biotechnology industry', *Strategic Management Journal*, **15**, 387–94.

Shane, S. and D. Cable (2002), 'Network ties, reputation, and the financing of new ventures', *Management Science*, **48**(3), 364–82.

Shepherd, J. (1991), 'Entrepreneurial growth through constellations', *Journal of Business Venturing*, **6**, 363–73.

Soh, P.-H. (2003), 'The role of networking alliances in information acquisition and its implications for new product performance', *Journal of Business Venturing*, **18**(6), 727–40.

Spender, J.-C. (1996), 'Making knowledge the basis of a dynamic theory of the firm', *Strategic Management Journal*, **17**, 45–62.

Spender, J.-C. and R.M. Grant (1996), 'Knowledge and the firm: overview', *Strategic Management Journal*, **17**, 5–9.

Starr, J.A. and I.C. MacMillan (1990), 'Resource cooptation via social contracting: resource acquisition strategies for new ventures', *Strategic Management Journal*, **11**, 79–93.

Steensma, H.K. (1996), Acquiring technological competencies through inter-organizational collaboration: an organizational learning perspective, *Journal of Engineering and Technology Management*, **12**, 267–86.

Steiner, L. and R. Greenwood (1995), 'Venture capital relationships in the deal structuring and post-investment stages of new firm creation', *Journal of Management Studies*, **32**(3), 337–57.

Stuart, T.E., H. Hoang and R.C. Hybels (1999), 'Interorganizational endorsements and the performance of entrepreneurial ventures', *Administrative Science Quarterly*, **44**(2), 315–49.

Uzzi, B. (1997), 'Social structure and competition in interfirm networks: the paradox of embeddedness', *Administrative Science Quarterly*, **42**(March), 35–67.

Teece, D.J., G. Pisano and A. Schuen (1997), 'Dynamic capabilities and strategic management', *Strategic Management Journal*, **18**(7), 509–33.

Thorelli, H.B. (1986), 'Networks: between markets and hierarchies', *Strategic Management Journal*, **7**(1), 37–52.

Venkataraman, S. (1989), 'Problems of small venture start-up, survival, and growth: a transaction set approach', PhD dissertation, University of Minnesota.

Venkataraman, S. and A.H. Van de Ven (1998), 'Hostile environmental jolts, transaction set, and new business', *Journal of Business Venturing*, **13**, 231–55.

Venkataraman, S., A.H. Van de Ven, J. Buckeye and R. Hudson (1990), 'Starting up in a turbulent environment: a process model of failure among firms with high customer dependence', *Journal of Business Venturing*, **5**, 277–95.

von Hippel, E. (1988), *The Sources of Innovation*, New York: Oxford University Press.

Wernerfelt, B. (1984), 'A resource-based view of the firm', *Strategic Management Journal*, **5**, 171–80.

Yli-Renko, H. (1999), *Dependence, Social Capital, and Learning in Key Customer Relationships: Effects on the Performance of Technology-based New Firms*, Doctoral Dissertation, Espoo, Finland: Acta Polytechnica Scandinavica, Industrial Management and Business Administration Series.

Yli-Renko, H., E. Autio and H.J. Sapienza (2001a), 'Social capital, knowledge acquisition, and knowledge exploitation in young technology-based firms', *Strategic Management Journal*, **22**, 587–613.

Yli-Renko, H., H.J. Sapienza and M. Hay (2001b), 'The role of contractual governance flexibility in realizing the outcomes of key customer relationships', *Journal of Business Venturing*, **16**, 529–55.

Zhao, L. and J.D. Aram (1995), 'Networking and growth of young technology-intensive ventures in China', *Journal of Business Venturing*, **10**, 349–70.

PART 2

PROCESSES

4 S&T commercialization strategies and practices
Dianne I. Isabelle[1]

Reviewed in this section are various S&T commercialization strategies and supporting mechanisms, primarily within the North American context. The goal is to explore such strategies, their evolution and trends. International practices and insights are cursorily covered.

North American Strategies and Practices of Laboratories and Universities

Governments worldwide are seeking ways to generate economic impact from the R&D carried out by their universities and laboratories. There is an effervescence of 'new and improved' commercialization strategies involving government laboratories, universities, intermediary organizations and the private sector, aiming at bridging the commercialization chasm. The numerous conferences, recent international comparative studies, benchmarking and the like attest to this priority. Although universities have traditionally seen their roles to be in research and teaching, they are now taking on a third role in terms of the commercialization of research findings, becoming even more important contributors to regional and national economies.

Creation of new technology-based firms (NTBFs)

> Wherever you see a successful business, someone once made a courageous decision. (Peter Drucker)

New technology-based firms can be spin-outs from public research, large firms or created ex nihilo. They account for between 1 per cent and 3 per cent of all firms. Although the use of NTBFs to commercialize technology is not new, Canadian institutions, as in the US, generally give priority to licensing their technologies (Association of University Technology Managers, 2002). A line of reasoning further emphasized by DC Technologies Ltd. (2004) is that it is preferable to try and license Intellectual Property (IP) into existing SMEs rather than taking the high-risk route of starting up a new company. Consequently, Vohora, Wright et al. (2004) believe that university spin-out is an underdeveloped, yet potentially important option to create wealth from the commercialization of research.

The focus in this section is on NTBFs created with the purpose of further developing and commercializing university or government lab technologies. Perhaps not surprisingly, there does not appear to be a commonly adopted definition of public research spinoffs; the Association of University Technology Managers (AUTM) in the US defines a spin-off as a 'start-up company that is dependent upon licensing the institution's technology for initiation' (a spin-out firm is generally defined as a firm created by a graduate who has some links to the university but no university-linked IP). Adding to this challenge, some terminologies are used interchangeably in the literature. Various taxonomies have been developed, each with its own perspective. For instance, Hindle and Yencken (2003) has reported a taxonomy of public research spin-off ventures from recent studies in Australia (Thorburn, 2000; Upstill and Symington, 2002). These studies suggest three main classes of new ventures derived from public research agencies, classified primarily by the relationships back to the host or parent organization. *Direct research spinoffs* are new ventures created to commercialize IP arising out of the research institution. The staff may be seconded or transferred from the research institution to the new firm. *Technology transfer companies* are companies set up to exploit commercially the university's tacit knowledge and know-how, where no formerly protected IP and/or exclusive licensing is involved. Usually such companies are in the area of process rather than product innovation. These companies are considered as consultancy and R&D contracting in taxonomy below. Their activities are an extension of the research activities that are core competencies of academic researchers. *Start-ups or indirect spin-off companies* are companies set up by former or present university staff/students, with no formal IP licensing or similar relationships to the university.

Hindle and Yencken (2003) add a further class, *spin-ins* (to existing companies), defined as new ventures derived from the licensing or other agreed exploitation of new knowledge generated by public research agencies, whether or not separate incorporated entities are set up. They may also operate as discrete ventures within the existing company.

Several other studies (Stankiewicz, 1994; Bhidé, 2000; Upstill and Symington, 2002) have also developed such taxonomies. Of interest, Stankiewicz (1994) has suggested a taxonomy based on the NTBFs' main modes of activity: first, consultancy and R&D contracting; second, product-oriented mode (advanced development, production and marketing of the product); third, Technology asset-oriented mode (development of technologies subsequently commercialized through spinning out new firms, licensing, JVs or other types of alliance). Many of the spin-off firms operate solely or predominantly in one of these modes, or move along these modes over time.

Roberts and Malone (1996) developed five structural models for spinning off NTBFs from universities, government laboratories and other R&D organizations, taking into account key roles (technologist, entrepreneur, licensing office, venture investor) and a spin-off stages approach: invention, disclosure, evaluation, protection, new venture creation, product development, incubation, business development and sales/Initial Public Offering (IPO). The five process models describe the sequence of interactions between the parties and the objectives of these interactions: technology push/business pull, inter-party processes at each spin-off stage. Using a results, policy, environment perspective, the authors then mapped eight R&D organizations in the US (MIT, Stanford, Argonne National Laboratory, University of Connecticut, Boston University, Harvard University) and the UK (British Technology Group, King's College London Enterprises Ltd). The authors found a wide variety of internal and external environments relative to spin-offs, as well as different policies and results. Some of the organizations in their study have drawn back from the promotion of company spin-offs either because of lack of success, long-term pay-offs, or the need to alter the internal environment, that have contributed to financial issues with licensing, and have chosen instead to concentrate on traditional licensing. Organizations successful at achieving a high spin-off rate, such as Boston University, Harvard, MIT and Stanford, benefit from an existing entrepreneurial and venture capital-rich environment even though they do so at the expense of traditional licensing. Another aspect of their study deals with the impact of the technology focus of the R&D organization; as expected, if the focus is towards large specialized projects that are somewhat removed from the needs of commercial markets, then the amount of technology that can be transferred is more limited and consequently so is the number of spin-offs.

Lehrer and Asakawa (2004) coined the term 'science entrepreneurships', the simultaneous dedication of scientists to academic science and to commercial profit, pointing out that this phenomenon has a well-established history in the US but is relatively new in other countries such as Germany and Japan, where stronger compartmentalization between academia and industry has been the norm. The biotechnology sector is a sector with blurred boundaries between basic and applied research with feedback loops among among basic and applied research, development and commercialization, with biotech scientists often engaged in multiple stages simultaneously. Not surprisingly in this context, biotechnology scientists tend to be science entrepreneurs, as evidenced by the high number of university spin-offs in biotechnology.

In the past, strong emphasis was placed on forming NTBFs such as spin-offs, in part to overcome the lack of receptor capacity. There now appears to be recognition that these small NTBFs are struggling to reach the scale and scope needed for sustained and profitable growth in the global economy. Consequently, several of these NTBFs have been taken over by multinational corporations that shift development and production to another country, hence decreasing jobs, growth and economic benefits to the home country. NTBFs in biotechnology – and in particular biopharmaceuticals – are a case in point in Canada. The current literature emphasizes that a successful process of commercialization should be a process of building future companies that can compete successfully rather than simply pushing the creation of high numbers of NTBFs: quality prefered to quantity.

There is also a growing awareness that different sectors face different commercialization challenges, hence a need for sector strategies. Taking the example of biotechnology again, it is well known that successful commercialization is an expensive, high-risk and long-term process. This is currently a challenge in Canada, as roughly half of publicly traded biotechnology companies have less than one year's cash available, compared to the US, with 15 per cent, and Europe, with 20 per cent, and lack the necessary infrastructure to test and develop new products.[2]

Several studies have been conducted on best commercialization strategies for new technology-based firms in a variety of technology sectors. One of them, Kwak (2002), surveyed 118 start-ups that had successfully commercialized a new technology, looking at the external environment to determine whether competition or cooperation (through licensing, strategic alliance or being acquired) is the preferred road. It was found that strength of IP along with importance of complementary assets helped determine whether cooperation or competition was the preferred route to commercialization. For instance, cooperation would be the preferred route for a start-up possessing strong IP and needing to gain access to complementary assets critical for success, such as in the pharmaceutical industry. In this analysis, start-ups are considered to be in the strongest competitive position when IP rights are strong and complementary assets relatively unimportant, a situation Palm Inc (Palm Pilot products) found themselves in.

Concerning the commercialization strategies for disruptive technologies, several researchers (Christensen, Walsh, Schumpeter; see Garner and Termouth, 2004) are advocating that disruptive technologies are best commercialized by spinning off a new start-up NTBF, a finding substantiated by the OECD (2003) study of sources of economic growth.

Established firms have sustainable competitive advantages with many satisfied customers that provide satisfactory profits, hence the difficulty for such organizations to pursue a technology which is highly risky, potentially competitive to their own products and difficult to market since applications are in unfamiliar industries. Moreover, small firms can presumably focus on one technology and have relatively low operating costs and are not encumbered by sunk costs of older technology capital. For similar reasons, Bower and Christensen (1995) advocate that such spin-offs not be integrated into the mainstream organization. Surveying 72 micro-electro-mechanical systems (MEMS) manufacturing firms, Walsh, Kirchhoff et al. (2002) confirmed that established firms rarely commercialize disruptive technologies while new firms select primarily disruptive technologies, using market-pull strategies more often than technology-push strategies. A significant finding from their small survey is that time to market is much shorter for new firms than for established firms – roughly one-fourth that for established firms.

Nerkar and Shane (2003) explored in greater detail the impact of industry environment, specifically industry concentration, on the survival of start-ups exploiting patented academic knowledge. They found empirical evidence that a strategy to exploit competence-destroying radical technology as a way for new firms to compete only works in fragmented industries. In concentrated industries, this does not provide an advantage as concentrated industry environments hinder efforts of the new firm to build the manufacturing and marketing assets necessary to compete. The authors also provided insight into the argument that new technology firms will perform better if they have broad scope patents (Merges and Nelson, 1990, cited in Nerkar and Shane, 2003), but again, contingent upon founding the company in fragmented industries.

Entrepreneurship is another commercialization mechanism for publicly sponsored technology. Radosevich (1995b), for instance, has explored two kinds of entrepreneurs: the inventor-entrepreneurs, who are or were laboratory employees and who actively seek to commercialize their own inventions, and surrogate entrepreneurs who are not the inventors but who acquire rights to the federally-sponsored technology to launch a new venture. He concentrated on New Mexico, considered a state with a plethora of raw S&T, with three research-oriented universities, test facilities and over 20 000 scientists and engineers working at three large federal laboratories and their contractors, but with low receptor capacity. He reports that risk capital and technical entrepreneurs (both inventor-entrepreneurs and surrogate entrepreneurs) are below critical mass to stimulate and support a substantial flow of new ventures, a conclusion also reached by Roberts and Malone (1996). The primary advantage of the inventor-entrepreneur model is the knowledge of the technology carried by the inventor into the new firm, although it may still be insufficient unless considerable technical assistance is available from the technology source, a situation experienced at the National Research Council of Canada (NRC) with their spin-offs (called 'new ventures'), even with a number of key individuals leaving to form a new venture. Conversely, the primary advantage of the surrogate entrepreneur model is the previous entrepreneurial experience and accumulated business knowledge, while an important disadvantage is less commitment to, and knowledge of, the technology. Table 4.1 below summarizes Radosevich's views on advantages of large and small firms as a technology transfer recipient and commercialization agent.

Canadian spin-offs are produced at a much higher rate per research dollar than in the US, a fact demonstrated repeatedly via analysis of surveys performed by the Association

Table 4.1 Advantages of large and small firms in technology commercialization

Large firms	Small firms
Market power	Ability to move rapidly, both in technology development and in commercialization activities
Adequate internal technical capacity	Strong commitment to the technology, especially if the inventor becomes involved in the enterprise
Established linkages to customers, distributors, suppliers, regulators, potential strategic alliances, etc	More efficient job and wealth creators
Access to capital markets (especially for asset-based financing)	
Potential synergy with the current production operations	
Better protection of proprietary technology positions	Less bureaucratic, more innovative
Professional management for later-stage growth	Entrepreneurial management for early-stage growth
Ability to absorb large fixed transactions cost – time and money	Lower cost of development and operations

Source: Radosevich (1995).

of University Technology Managers (AUTM), among others. Clayman and Holbrook (2002) claim that, in 2000, Canadian universities created 2.5 times more spin-offs per dollar spent on research than US universities, likely owing to the recognized lack of receptor capacity in Canada. Major areas for spin-offs overall are biotech and ICT (also substantiated by Stankiewicz, 1994). ICT clusters can be considered 'textbook cases' of clusters in Canada: the 1960s saw the splitting up of Western Electric by US consent decree and resulted in Bell Northern Research (originally Northern Electric, in Montreal, Quebec) which later drove the ICT cluster in Ottawa, Ontario, developed through the wartime (WW II) activities of the National Research Council and the Defence Research Telecommunications Establishment. Bell established its Canadian research facilities in Ottawa, primarily because of the proximity of government laboratories. When spun off by Bell for regulatory reasons, Northern Electric (today Nortel) invested further in its Ottawa laboratories. The subsequent role of the public sector has been complex, since it has involved not only support for basic research in universities and, upon occasion, direct procurements, but also regulatory activities and their consequences.

According to Statistics Canada, there were 648 university spin-offs in 2001, compared with 454 in 1999, a significant 43 per cent increase. Various sources report that between 70 and 80 per cent of these spin-offs are still in business five years after start-up. However, other sources such as the Advisory Council on Science and Technology (ACST), paint a bleaker survival picture. In any event, most would agree that academic spin-offs do contribute to the competitiveness of Canada. For instance, Cooper (2004) notes that, in 2002, academic spin-offs accounted for C$5.9 billion in annual sales and 25 000 jobs. Interestingly, there are examples in Canada where university spin-offs have fostered development of clusters, such as the Waterloo ICT cluster (Clayman and Holbrook, 2002). On a global note, Stankiewicz (1994) finds that, although academic spin-offs' ability to survive is on the whole impressive, their growth rates have been disappointingly low. However, he acknowledges the inherent difficulties in assessing their success, given the abundance of definitions and policies.

Spatial Concentration

Spatial concentration includes such strategies as regional innovation systems, clusters, incubators, research/science/technology parks, innovation centres, industrial estates and centres of excellence.

The terms 'small business incubator', 'enterprise centre', 'business technology centre', 'technology business incubator' and 'innovation centre' are often used interchangeably, creating challenges in distinguishing between incubators that support new firms in general and the more specialized incubators that deal with technology-related problems associated with the start-up of technology-oriented new firms. For instance, the terminology innovation centre is often used for incubators close to, or on, a university campus. Incubators may also be located on an S&T park (Phillimore and Joseph, 2003).

A technology business incubator is generally defined as converted or purpose-built industrial buildings that offer accommodation and a supportive, growth-oriented environment for newly formed companies having technology development as a core component of their business plan. The range of services offered by such parks is broader than those offered by small business incubators. Incubators tend to focus on new enterprise development while S&T parks (interchangeably called 'research park', 'science park' and 'technology park') aim to establish concentrations of firms or industries in a particular area. Today, it is estimated that there are 1000 business incubators in North America (around 120 in Canada) and over 3500 worldwide. In 2001, NRC launched its own incubator strategy, called 'Industry Partnership Facilities' (IPFs). It currently has a national network of 12 such IPFs across the country, each with a focus on a different technology sector based on the specialization of its host institute, and is considered a very unusual model, both in Canada and globally.[3]

Incubating new technology-based firms in federal labs can be done under an entrepreneurship activated by an external entity, referred to earlier as '*surrogate entrepreneur*', while another mechanism could be a spin-off from the lab by one or more employees, typically the inventor of the technology as inventor–entrepreneur, alternatively called 'intrapreneur', the latter being more traditional. University research laboratories are becoming more responsive to the long-term needs of industry. Although the phenomenon of incubating new firms is quite common in high-profile universities in the US, Canadian universities are starting to take the new-firm spin-out route in addition to creating new sources of funding through licensing of IP, and business venturing with industry. University spin-off may occur with a professor or a technical staff person finding an opportunity to develop and exploit a market niche, or the university itself may initiate a new firm with a technology developed within the university. Kumar and Kumar (1997) studied best practices of incubating new technology-based firms, by interviewing representatives of various technology-based incubators of government R&D laboratories, universities and large technology corporations. For the purpose of their study, they define a technology incubator as 'a facility that aids the early-stage growth of technology-based companies by providing shared facilities such as space and office services, and business consulting assistance'. Their study describes the following six dimensions of an incubator that have a direct impact on its success: facilities and location, shared services, tenant entry and exit criteria, mentoring and networking, funding and support, and incubator governance. The best practices identified in the study relate to these dimensions:

1. The incubator has a minimum of 30 000 ft^2. with room to expand in order to be able to generate enough income to become self-sustainable.
2. There are at least ten in-residence members for generating enough networking activity and sustaining the variety of shared services and support operations.
3. The incubator is located either near a university or near a research laboratory so that tenants have easy access to technical facilities, scientists and engineers, state-of-the-art equipment/testing facilities, students, faculty members, research labs and libraries.
4. In both cases 'image' is an added bonus.
5. The incubator is situated in a high tech, top-quality building, preferably with the telecommunications infrastructure to connect companies with each other and the outside world electronically.
6. A selection committee is set up to pre-screen the clients.
7. An advisory committee consisting of five or six experts from different business areas assisting in developing a business plan, in obtaining funding, and for marketing and legal issues.
8. The incubator is creating opportunities for its tenants to network.
9. The incubator has the funding and support from private, public or government organizations.
10. The incubator's manager is a highly motivated visionary individual whose goal is to see the tenants' firms succeed.

Boards of directors are generally responsible for policy development, leaving day-to-day operations to the incubator manager, and keeping bureaucracy to a minimum. Phillimore and Joseph (2003) define an S&T park (Research or Science Parks) as a property-based initiative that has a high-quality, low-density physical environment, is located within a reasonable distance of a university or research institute, and emphasizes activities which encourage the formation and growth of a range of research, new technology or knowledge-based enterprises. Appold (2004) emphasizes the policy intervention purpose of research parks that is to promote a particular type of industrial activity, R&D, in locations where it would otherwise not take place. There are now more than 400 science parks spread throughout the world, while, 50 years ago, there were only two: Stanford Research Park in California and the Research Triangle Park in North Carolina. The number of parks continues to grow. The first parks appeared in the USA, with the UK and France following suit in the 1960s and 1970s. Australia and Canada experienced their first main science park growth from the mid-1980s, with Continental Europe getting on board in the 1990s. China and other countries in the Asia-Pacific have now become the major growth area for science parks.

Several objectives are listed for science parks: economic development, local benefits, transfer of technology, reindustrialization, regional development and creation of synergies. Emphasis on one or a few of these objectives depends on the specific needs of a country or region. For instance, in Australia, the first motivation was for industrial development, while in other countries such as Japan and Korea, decentralization of economic and technological activities was an important goal. In all countries, however, knowledge transfer from universities and government research institutions to the commercial sector has been the primary goal of science park development.

In his analysis of university–private sector technology interactions, Shane (2002) found that S&T parks have a larger influence on university–industries interaction for entrepreneurial firms than for large firms. Appold (2004) tested the ability of research parks to affect the growth in the number of local laboratories, looking at Singapore data from 1960 to 1985, but found no such correlation. His analysis indicates that research parks do not appear to be effective local development tools. He concludes that the ability to shape the geography of innovation through local policy efforts appears to be limited. On the other hand, Shane (2002) found that companies actively participating in an incubator typically have a lower failure rate than other new businesses. Although science parks have been in existence now for over 50 years, there is no clear indication that S&T parks actually meet their objectives. However, their numbers are increasing, hence a need to learn from existing S&T parks and formulate a way forward based on past successes and best practices, as proposed by Phillimore and Joseph (2003):

1. Enlist more proactive and supportive science park management.
2. Use the existing and expanding international science park network as a source of value-added for park tenants.
3. Encourage science parks to integrate more closely to the wider community.
4. Create new science parks with a more specific focus, such as particular technologies or environmental objectives.
5. Move beyond a linear view of innovation towards a network view.

Science and engineering advance largely at centres of excellence – physical locations where research and advanced training are carried out, often in collaboration with other centres, institutions and individuals. The Canadian Networks of Centres of Excellence (NCE) are 'unique partnerships among universities, industry, government and not-for-profit organizations aimed at turning Canadian research and entrepreneurial talent into economic and social benefits for all Canadians'.[4] It has been operating for 15 years and in 1997 the government established the NCE as a permanent programme with a budget of $77.4 m. per year. There are currently 21 Centres of Excellence within the NCE. The NCE is supported by three Canadian federal granting agencies and Industry Canada. In 2002–2003, the NCEs supported 1613 researchers in 68 Canadian universities. The networks partnered with 184 provincial and federal government departments, 44 hospitals and 232 other organizations, thus accelerating the use of research results by organizations that can employ them to benefit Canadians. The networks also built partnerships with 756 Canadian and foreign companies.[5] The InterAcademy Council (2004) considers such centres crucial to innovation and are advocating creation of such centres to grow S&T capacities of developing nations, along with the creation of virtual networks of excellence to extend throughout the developing world.

Despite the digital capabilities of our 'virtual' world, it appears that many of the fundamentals of human and economic geography hold, hence the accrued interest in 'clusters' or 'regional systems of innovation' (Traversy, 2004). Ideas-driven growth and cluster theory focus on the economic impact of geography (spillovers tend to be localized), while the national innovation systems literature focuses more on the political implications of geography; for instance, the impact of policies and institutions is circumscribed by national borders (Stern et al., 2000). Overall, the innovation literature stresses the diversity in national and regional approaches to innovation in terms of national structures, policies and institutions. Research has shown that firms are much more likely to interact with sources of public R&D that are relatively close by, the median distance being 75 to 100 miles. Although firms using public R&D prefer proximity, they also find advantages in being near other firms in their industry, a diverse environment and business services, most likely found in larger cities. Therefore it was concluded that, while public R&D in any location can stimulate industrial innovation, its impact tends to diminish in smaller areas. Looking at knowledge spillovers, Jaffe et al. (1993), cited in Agrawal (2002), investigated the degree to which such spillovers are geographically localized by examining citations of patents and found that indeed the citations are significantly localized. He also found that patents occur in those states where public and private knowledge-generating inputs are the greatest, even after controlling for industrial R&D. Many scholars argue that tacit knowledge is 'sticky' and remains geographically localized.

Interest in cluster development has exploded recently across North America, Europe and newly industrialized countries, in part because of fascination with the success of Silicon Valley and, in part through the efforts of other regions to emulate the Silicon Valley model (Wolfe and Gertler, 2004). Perhaps the most commonly cited definition of a cluster is that advanced by Michael Porter (1998) as 'a geographically proximate group of interconnected companies and associated institutions in a particular field, linked by commonalities and complementarities'. However, a clear and common understanding of what a cluster is has yet to emerge as far as the Conference Board of Canada is concerned. In any case, a central element in most definitions is the idea of geographic proximity of an agglomeration of firms. Porter's work on clusters, his renowned Diamond model, find that innovation and productivity growth at the cluster level are driven by the interaction of the four determinants identified in Figure 4.1.

Innovation tends to be facilitated by the presence of a cluster; firms within a cluster are often able to perceive more clearly and rapidly new buyer needs than can isolated competitors. Importantly, such firms can often commercialize innovations more rapidly and efficiently. Here again, though, caution is required in comparing and emulating clusters: for instance, in Italy, different geographic regions enjoy remarkably different circumstances in both their innovative capacity and realized level of innovation, hence the importance of investigating innovative capacity at the regional level (Porter and Stern, 1999). This last point is echoed by Wolfe and Gertler (2004) in their comparative study of cluster development, warning against a 'cookie cutter' approach to clusters.

Clusters have generally been perceived in one of two ways. First, they may be seen as the product of *traditional agglomeration economies*, dating back to the work of economist Alfred Marshall (1890). Firms co-located in the cluster benefit from the easier access to, and reduced costs of, certain collective resources (infrastructure, local labour market and

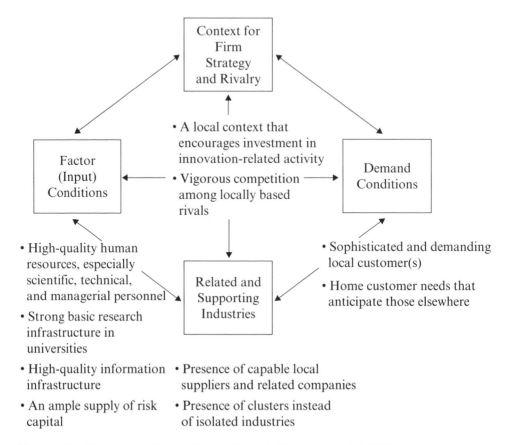

Figure 4.1   Cluster-specific conditions (Porter's Diamond model, 1990)

so on). Second, clusters may have a role involving *knowledge and learning processes*, often on the basis of local flows of spatially sticky tacit knowledge, at both local and global levels ('economics of place').

In Canada, the Innovation Systems Research Network (ISRN) was established in 1998 to support interaction among researchers and their partners. A cluster initiative was launched in 2001 to investigate the process of Canadian cluster development in knowledge-intensive and traditional sectors, in metro and non-metro regions (Wolfe and Gertler, 2003). The following summarizes initial findings from this broad comparative study of cluster development across a wide range of industrial sectors and virtually all regions of the Canadian economy. In this study, sources of competitive advantage in *regional economies* were found to be as follows:

1. Distance: strong geographic spillovers between public research centres and industrial R&D. (In the US, Reamer et al., 2003, found that size and location matter: public R&D is even more geographically concentrated than patenting.)
2. Knowledge and practices transferred between firms: technological spillovers, not always codified or explicit (tacit dimension) transferred through networks. (In the US,

Reamer et al., found that personal interaction and geographic proximity tend to be more important in the early stages of a technology life cycle.)

3. Networking, based on trust: shared intelligence of a group of firms, grounded in a regional economy.
4. Social capital: shared norms and trust facilitate cooperation among firms and sectors.

Interestingly, Wolfe and Gertler (2004) note that, given the openness and strong export orientation of much of the Canadian economy, many of the firms interviewed in their case studies indicate that their markets and competitors are overwhelmingly outside the region and the country, especially for firms in the ICT, biotechnology and aerospace sectors. In their view, this suggests that at least two corners of Porter's diamond (sophisticated and demanding local customers and strong rivalry between local competitors) are not consistently present in the Canadian context. This points to a potential area of future cluster research, concentrating on the dynamics of Canadian clusters in the ICT, biotechnology and aerospace sectors, all sectors of crucial importance for Canada.

While Porter does not suggest that the presence of a large public-sector research institution is a necessary condition for the existence of the cluster, research by ISRN is leading to the conclusion that, at least in Canada, a large public sector investment in relevant science and technology is a prerequisite for the creation and sustainability of viable high-tech industrial clusters. They point to organizations such as NRC Labs in telecom, health-based biotechnology and agricultural biotechnology as examples. Analysis of the rationale behind this apparent prerequisite for Canadian clusters could help determine gaps needing to be addressed. For instance, it may be that lower private R&D investments in Canada compared to other countries such as the US create the need for sustained public sector investment.

The researchers found the emergence of two models of clusters:

Regionally embedded: anchored (for instance, Montreal biotech, Ottawa telecom/photonics). Global knowledge flow is important but a local knowledge/science base is a major contributor. Local universities/research institutes are an important part of this base. One or a few lead, anchor firms or institutions.

'Entrepot': (for example, Montreal aerospace, Saskatoon agri-biotech). Much of the knowledge base is acquired through market transactions and global sources. Local institutions and firms exploit this knowledge effectively and combine it with local assets and capabilities for success.

The ISRN lists the following competitive advantage of clusters: (a) superior access to specialized inputs, including availability of specialized and experienced personnel, reduces transaction costs; (b) diverse specialization focuses on core competences and increases flexibility, improving capacity to innovate through access to knowledge; (c) the process of firm formation through start-ups and spin-offs is stimulated.

The ISRN also believes the critical factors for cluster emergence are the following:

1. Strong, diverse and 'tech-savvy' talent pool.
2. Presence of established pillar companies with global reach.

3. Strong knowledge infrastructure (research university, government labs, etc.).
4. Specialized support services.
5. Risk-tolerant venture capital and angel investors.
6. Entrepreneurial culture that nourishes innovation.
7. Sustained development strategies by civic entrepreneurs and local governments.

These findings are echoed in international studies. For instance, the Department of Trade and Industry (DTI, UK[6]), through a global literature search, found that the following five top critical success factors in cluster development were mentioned in over 50 per cent of the number of articles mentioning success criteria: networking partnership, innovative technology, human capital, physical infrastructure and presence of large firms.

In its experience to date, building 13 technology clusters, NRC has determined the following key set of required building blocs:

1. A critical mass of R&D, conducted within firms and in collaboration with other firms and research organizations.
2. Attraction and development of a highly skilled workforce.
3. A knowledgable and accessible source of financing.
4. A supportive policy environment at all levels of government, conducive to innovative growth.
5. Business support programmes, services and tools to effect S&T knowledge, business management and technology transfer.
6. Incubators and mentors to nurture new enterprises.
7. A growing company base made up of thriving start-ups and SMEs as well as established companies that can act as role models.
8. Effective public and private networks to share resources, information and expertise, and create cluster synergy.

The Australian Institute for Commercialisation (2003a) concurs that clusters are crucial, but notes that only Silicon Valley has it all: a third of all the venture capital raised around the world goes on nurturing innovations in Silicon Valley, which is a web of local services (from chip designers and specialized software writers to patent lawyers, high-tech marketers, head hunters, and PR experts, not to mention super-smart venture capitalists) that make innovation in Silicon Valley so easy.

As more publicly funded R&D institutions and universities reach out to the community-at-large to promote cluster development, the incubators associated with these institutions are gaining a new role. Incubators are proving to be effective focal points through which cluster proponents can launch business and scientific networks, coordinate the development and interplay of the innovation infrastructure and attract new resources to the selected region.[7]

The Conference Board of Canada (2004) conducted a study on clusters to attempt to determine whether they do contribute to regional economic growth, by surveying executives at 171 firms belonging to ICT or biotechnology clusters across Canada and augmented by 11 case studies of clusters around the world. The answer is a qualified 'yes'; as clusters evolve through a number of life cycle stages (early stage, growth, maturity, renewal or decline stage), they can make important contributions to both regional *economic* growth and regional *knowledge* growth. Furthermore, the authors found that the dynamic interplay between clusters and innovation suggests that firms belonging to a cluster yield greater economic results, albeit one-third of respondents 'strongly disagree' that belonging to a cluster provides them with competitive advantages related to introduction and speed of introduction of new products, services or processes, ability to keep up with competitors, their profitability or their productivity. Concerns are raised as well: opportunities arise with clusters, but so do risks. The three major risks reported by the Conference Board of Canada (2004) are as follows.

1. Failure to keep knowledge flowing: if the 'local buzz' (knowledge that flows between firms and institutions in the region) dwindles, a cluster risks dissolving. Conversely, if it drowns out the knowledge from '*global pipelines*' (knowledge that flows into the region from other parts of the world), a cluster risks becoming insular and impermeable to new ideas.
2. Increased volatility: three cycles affect a cluster: the economy, the technology platform and its own maturity. These cycles can align to produce tremendous success or devastating results.
3. Becoming the modern mining town: regions relying too heavily on a single cluster risk negative impact should that cluster decline. Clusters can also be susceptible to boom–bust cycles that can leave a region reeling.

In September 2004, Ottawa hosted the Competitive Institute's Annual International Cluster Conference, a not-for-profit alliance of cluster practitioners. Insights include the following. First, clusters are recognized as an important instrument for promoting industrial development, innovation, competitiveness and growth. Although primarily driven by the efforts made by private companies and individuals, clusters are influenced by various actors, including governments and other public institutions at national and regional levels.

Second, there is a continuing debate related to identifying key drivers for clusters: the conclusion seems to be that place does matter in the way a cluster takes shape but that it is the people who are critical to its formation and success. Overall, key drivers appear to be 'smallness', place and linkages.

Third is the importance of industry competitiveness within a cluster: past conferences have focused on the need for collaboration.

Fourth, untraded interdependencies involve tacit and codified knowledge that requires face-to-face interaction. Trust is inherent in the interactions and, while it has economic value, it has no price (cannot be sold in the marketplace), but clusters cannot succeed without it. Trust is the social capital of the cluster.

Finally, public policies have one specified purpose but also unintended consequences. The serendipitous character of clusters underlines their randomness; investigation will usually uncover a set of preconditions or actions that led to the creation of the cluster in that locale.

Government-created clusters have a poor record, and success is often by inadvertence.

Cluster blind spots: failing to see where the disruptive technologies are coming from. Knowledge management and generation of knowledge are getting increasingly weak in large corporations as a result of outsourcing research to universities or small firms, pointing to the need for a new economic geography – open innovation.

The level of education is not an element of competitiveness but the size of the pool of high-tech workers is very significant. However no one knows what is the impact on clusters of mobility of educated workers.

Fostering the innovation process in clusters is difficult (proximity does not equate to interaction).

There is a need to shift from sector-specific to convergent technology cluster thinking.

There is danger in political cluster selection: political allegiance shifts and selection often mean forgetting about the unselected.

There is still no resolution about the entity that drives clusters (government, universities, industry). However, all need to cooperate.

The cluster phenomenon is relatively recent in Canada and a number of initiatives are under way to seek to understand what clusters are, how they form and what impact they have (Institute for Competitiveness & Prosperity, ISRN). Canada has set a goal of developing at least ten internationally recognized technology clusters by 2010. As Canadian clusters evolved, in-depth case studies would enhance understanding of critical Canadian success factors within clusters and within the Canadian environment. Of interest would be a greater understanding of history and factors enabling successful creation of clusters, impacts of collaboration versus competition, mechanisms to foster greater interactions, and impacts of government, universities and federal laboratories.

Public–Private Partnerships

A variety of public–private partnerships exist to facilitate commercialization of S&T from federal government labs and universities such as R&D consortia, exchange programmes, licensing, R&D contracts and demonstration projects, along with a myriad of activities aimed at creating awareness. Nevertheless, it is estimated that only a small percentage of federal technology innovations are researched by or transferred to the private sector for development and commercialization (Lombana et al., 2000). An appealing metaphor is offered by Dorf (1988):

> The effective commercialization of new technologies is less of a relay race where players hand off a baton to the next buyer than it is a basketball game where players pass the ball back and forth as they advance towards the goal. Clearly a team effort is required for most new technology development. Unfortunately, working with a federal laboratory or a university is difficult for an industrial firm since they are not on the same team.

The direct involvement of universities in technology commercialization is commonly accepted (Stankiewicz, 1994; Roberts and Malone, 1996; Mansfield, 1991; Lowe, 1993; Lee and Gaertner, 1994). Statistics gathered by Canadian federal funding groups[8] also support the contention that universities are attempting to commercialize research outputs (Industry Canada, 2003). Academic institutions are seriously pursuing and developing commercialization activities and the setting up of licensing/technology transfer offices is on the rise, with some university technology transfer offices now being significant profit centres. The Canada Foundation for Innovation (2003) found that, when commercialization activity per $1 million of research support at Canadian universities is compared to that in the US, the Canadian performance is quite impressive: Canadian universities created 2.5 times more spin-off companies per dollar spent on research than US universities, disclosed as many inventions as their US counterparts per dollar spent and were as successful as US universities in licensing their inventions; however, they only generated half the licence revenues of US universities.

Canadian universities have developed a strong partnership with industry, in fact the highest among the G7 countries (Advisory Council on Science and Technology, 1999). For instance, the Industrial Research Assistance Program (IRAP) of NRC is an important player in nurturing young companies and fostering university–industry partnerships from the industry side. Canadian universities have set a clear objective to triple commercialization outputs by 2010. Nonetheless, Lee and Gaertner (1994) warn that technology commercialization is not a main mission of the research university (which is teaching and basic research) and therefore any shift of resources from this basic mission to others may undercut the very strength on which the national system of innovation depends, let alone the societal objectives. On that very point, the Advisory Council on Science and Technology (1999) noted that, in the vast majority of research universities in the US, the revenues from commercializing research constitute a small addition to university budget, generally well below 1 per cent. It would therefore not be realistic to expect much more in Canada. In contrast, the underlying practical orientation in much of the government laboratory system suggests a significant role in public technology transfer. For instance, NRC has a legislated public purpose to produce industrially useful results.

According to Lowe (1993), 'the issue of which route to follow for academic commercialization depends crucially on an understanding of the alternative routes to *appropriability*, that is the way in which a university can maximize the value of its research to either the organization or the individual inventors. Discussions of appropriability usually consider the *exogenous* factors, that is the technological and market opportunity, and *endogenous* factors, or complementary assets and protection afforded to the innovation'. Mansfield (1991) surveyed 76 major American firms in seven manufacturing industries in an attempt to identify and measure the links between academic research and industrial innovation. His findings suggest that about one-tenth of the new products and processes commercialized during 1975–85 in information processing, electrical equipment, chemicals, instruments, drugs, metals and oil could not have been developed (without substantial delay) without academic research. The average time lag between the conclusion of the relevant academic research and the first commercial introduction of the innovations based on this research was about seven years (and tended to be a little longer for large firms). Mansfield concludes that these results provide convincing evidence that, particularly in industries like drugs, instruments and information processing, the contribution of academic research to industrial innovation has been considerable.

In conclusion, public/private partnerships need to balance the desire for knowledge diffusion with legitimate rewards for appropriation.

Other types
Government as first users/demonstrators is an often cited mechanism to enhance commercialization of public or private R&D. Another mechanism is a more extensive use of Technology Road Maps to bring government laboratories, universities and the private sector together to focus resources on technologies that have a strong commercialization

potential. Broker partnerships encourage the establishment of support mechanisms to facilitate better collaboration between researchers and companies in particular sectors. Examples are 'fourth pillar' organizations such as Precarn, a Canadian member-owned industrial consortium that funds, coordinates and promotes collaborative pre-competitive research in the area of intelligent systems conducted by industry, university and government researchers; and existing industry associations or newly created private/public partnerships such as Fuel Cells Canada and Genome Canada.

(Gibson and Stiles, 1998) talk of the linking of talent, technology, capital and business know-how through global networked entrepreneurship, given that the emphasis is shifting from fostering regionally based technology-intensive wealth and job creation toward international collaboration. While they support the importance of a regional focus, they also emphasize the fostering and leveraging of global linkages through regionally based research universities, large and small companies, local government and support groups, a concept they dub worldwide technopoleis. A related concept, innovation boot camps, aims at taking seasoned executives out of established corporations, locating them in an entrepreneurial environment and teaming them nationally and globally. An example is 3M corporation's Innovation Boot Camp that focuses on technology innovation and commercialization in an attempt to avoid key individuals losing their entrepreneurial and creative instincts over time.

Highlights of Selected International Practices

The practice of technology transfer and commercialization in Canada has a history, direction and evolution that is significantly different from that in the US, which developed a number of key, well-established programmes at a very early date. By contrast, although Canadian universities made significant commercial discoveries, no formal technology transfer programme existed in Canada until the early 1980s, which unfortunately led to a 'potpourri' of IP policies evolving across Canada. In addition, up to 1991, IP developed by research contracts sponsored by the federal government was retained by the Crown.

The Canadian Patents and Development Limited (CPDL) was formed in 1947 by NRC initially to exploit NRC developed technologies and eventually that of other Crown technologies. The CPDL was dissolved in 1990, which then led to a confusing array of IP policies. Subsequently, the Interdepartmental Working Group on IP, led by NRCan, was formed in 1990. The Working Group was then formalized in 1996 as the Federal Partners In Technology Transfer (FPTT), led and financed by NRC, to share best practices and seek training opportunities (Association of University Technology Managers, 2002).

By contrast, the US has developed since the 1980s aggressive policies with respect to transferring technology among themselves and to various industry segments. Legislation includes the Stevenson–Wydler Technology Innovation Act (1980), making transfer of federal technologies to industry, states and regions a national policy; the Bayh–Dole Act (1980) which allows universities, not-for-profit research institutes and small businesses doing research under government contract to keep the technologies they have developed and apply for patents in their own names and also authorizes the granting of exclusive and partially exclusive licences (previously all IP was owned by the US government and all licences were non-exclusive); the Cooperative Research Act (1984), permitting industry to form consortia; the Federal Technology Transfer Act (1986), amendment to the Stevenson–Wydler legislation, making technology transfer a responsibility of all federal lab scientists; and the National Competitiveness Technology Transfer Act (1989), amendment to the Stevenson–Wydler Act, to establish technology transfer as a federal laboratory mission and to permit Cooperative R&D Agreements (CRADAs) for government-owned, contractor-operated laboratories (Greenberg, 1995).

The passing of such Acts in the US had huge impacts:[9] industry funds invested in university R&D have increased by 160 per cent since 1980; the number of patents from universities has increased by 500 per cent since 1980; and the Bayh–Dole Act created the unequalled US biotechnology industry (which is clustered around the major universities).

Most recent data suggest that every dollar invested in research at a leading US university still produces around 50 per cent more in licence income than a dollar invested in research at a leading Canadian university (Martin, 2003). Although it is likely that different national systems require differing patent legislation solutions, several believe that Canada needs a Bayh–Dole equivalent to truly capitalize on knowledge generated in its universities. This presents an attractive avenue of research into IP strategy gaps in Canada, such as critical factors required to emulate a Bayh–Dole Act, taking history and cultural factors into consideration to develop a national and forward-looking IP policy aligned with international IP policies.

US CRADAs are contractual arrangements between a federal laboratory and a participating firm that enables the laboratories to conduct joint R&D projects with private firms. Rights to IP are negotiated between the laboratory and participant firm. CRADAs may involve multiple firms or consortia. The CRADA's assignment to a private party of the IPR to technologies developed in federal laboratories is intended to provide incentives to commercialize the technologies. The Federal Technology Transfer Act was subsequently amended in 1989 to allow contractor-operated federal laboratories to participate in CRADAs (Ham and Mowery, 1997).

The Bayh–Dole Act gave rise to a significant surge in university activity during the 1980s and 1990s with substantial flow-on effects to other parts of the world. Shane (2002) notes that, since the introduction of the Act, universities have experienced tremendous growth in the number of companies forming around academic inventions, particularly in biotechnology and software. Positive impacts also include significant increases in contract research sponsored by industry, patenting and technology licensing, with an increasing portion of this interaction taking place with younger and smaller firms. The Jaffe and Lerner (2001) empirical and case study analyses suggest that the policy reforms of the 1980s had a dramatic and positive effect on technology commercialization, findings that challenge the general picture of bleak failure.

A similar change in UK government policy towards universities has also resulted in a positive effect on the transfer of technology and commercialization from British universities: the UK government, via the Department of Trade and Industry (DTI), proposes a 'third mission' for universities: excellence in the support of industry, alongside their research and teaching responsibilities. Universities in Australia may soon follow the US and the UK.[10]

The DTI considers that the UK has a strong science, engineering and technology base but that the record of knowledge transfer and exploitation by business has generally been weak, with some notable exceptions such as pharmaceuticals, telecommunications and aerospace. Several initiatives have been undertaken in recent years to work with industry, knowledge transfer, coordination and streamlining of activities. The UK has undertaken a review of its university–business links (Lambert, 2003); findings revealed that a key challenge is to raise the overall level of demand by business for research from all sources. The UK's position in the OECD has been dropping in recent decades, adversely affecting the overall productivity of its economy. In 1981, the UK's total spending on R&D as a proportion of its GDP surpassed that of any other member of the G7, apart from Germany, but by 1999, it was lagging behind Germany, the US, France and Japan, and only just keeping pace with Canada. The Lambert report's proposed recommendations include making the Higher Education Innovation Fund a permanent third stream of funding (alongside teaching and research) to enhance the capacity in the university sector for knowledge transfer and collaboration with business; enhancing the role of English Regional Development Agencies (RDAs) in strengthening university–business links; and working with universities and business to develop a set of model research–collaboration contracts and an IP protocol to cut bureaucracy and prevent disputes between partners.

The Australian government's interest in the commercialization of public sector research and the growth of technology-based companies gradually built up over the period 1983–98 so that, by 1998, there was a significantly better set of policies and funding in place. However, Australia's commercialization policies still had not reached world best practice standards, and its performance in commercializing publicly funded research is considered well behind international best practice (Australian Institute for Commercialisation, 2003b). Thorburn (2000) interviewed 75 people from 48 Australian spin-offs and found that new firms have been successful carriers of technology from the public to the private sector and enjoy the very high survival rate after five years of 88 per cent overall. The author believes that the tacit knowledge of the founders is likely a success factor, together with the ability to maintain informal ties with the research sector. The author acknowledges, however, that the picture is incomplete owing to a lack of data from Australian universities and other research agencies.

Declining public funding of tertiary education in New Zealand has encouraged universities to grow research-funding links with business and industry, and to commercialize technology and other IP arising from staff and student research, via university–industry liaison offices (Raine and Beukman, 2002).

In Europe, several governments now aim for 'the commercial exploitation of science' instead of the old aim of 'increased innovation capacity'. In the US, clusters and academic spin-offs have been part of the American academic landscape for decades and have been popularized by the development of the legendary 'Silicon Valley' and 'Route 128 Boston' around prestigious universities, such as Stanford and MIT. According to Ndonzuau et al. (2002), the phenomenon of academic spin-offs is still in its infancy in Europe, however. A growing number of clusters around the globe, from Scotland to Bangalore and from Singapore to Israel, claim direct lineage from the original model in northern California (Wolfe and Gertler, 2004).

Recent studies suggest that, for every dollar of public subsidy provided to North American incubators, clients and graduates of member incubators generate over $30 in local tax revenue alone.[11] From the Arctic Circle to South Africa, universities, governments and corporations are using incubators to accomplish a range of wealth creation and social goals. In China, East Germany and the Ukraine, for example, incubators have been used to facilitate the transition to a market economy. In Israel, incubators have played a key role in helping to integrate immigrants from Russia and the ex-Soviet bloc into the mainstream economy.[12] There are approximately 1100 technology-based incubators in Asia, the majority being located in China, Korea and Taiwan. These incubators tend to be larger than those in the US and the EU. They are linked to universities and technology parks and are regrouped under the Association of Asian Business Incubators.

The Dutch recently launched an Innovation Platform to strengthen innovation as the future driver of economic growth. Specific policy suggestions include tax incentives for private sector R&D in SMEs, and stimulation of more collaborative R&D. In Korea, the 2001 Science and Technology Framework Law places emphasis on the coordination of national science and technology and R&D policies and investments. The Korean government has also initiated new programmes to promote technology transfer, diffusion and commercialization of new technologies.

Analysis from Porter and Stern (1999) suggests that a number of historically less advanced countries such as Taiwan, Singapore and South Korea are developing innovative capacities that have or will soon approach the levels of at least the middle tier of the OECD countries. Beyond the Pacific Rim, both Israel and, to a lesser extent, Ireland seem to have established the underlying infrastructure together with several clusters consistent with strong national innovative capacity. The authors predict that Taiwan, Israel, Singapore, South Korea and Ireland are rapidly moving from fast followers to true innovators.

Notes

1. PhD. student at the Eric Sprott School of Business, Carleton University, Ottawa, Canada, Diane A. Isabelle, P.Eng., MBA, is a researcher, innovation management, at the National Research Council of Canada.
2. David Crane, Re$earch Money, 16 July 2004.
3. Speech from former president of the National Research Council, Dr A Carty, to the 2003 Incubators and New Venture Conference, Montreal.
4. www.nce.gc.ca.
5. NCE Annual report (2002–2003).
6. Department of Trade and Industry, UK, *A Practical Guide to Cluster Development* (www.dti.gov.uk/clusters).
7. Ibid., p. 2.
8. NSERC, CFI, NCE, Precarn, Genome Canada Inc., NRC, NRC-IRAP, Canadian Space Agency, SRED, TPC.
9. National Technology Transfer Centre (www.nttc.edu) 2004.
10. AIC, 'This week in Commercialisation', 13 August 2004.
11. Country Update, National Business Incubation Association (2004).
12. Ibid., p. 2.

References

Advisory Council on Science and Technology (1999), 'Issues with respect to commercializing Canadian university research', *Project Number 98848, Final Report*, 37 pages.
Agrawal, A. (2002), 'Innovation, growth theory, and the role of knowledge spillovers', *Innovation Analysis Bulletin, Statistics Canada*, **4**(3).
Appold, S.J. (2004), 'Research parks and the location of industrial research laboratories: an analysis of the effectiveness of a policy intervention', *Research Policy*, **33**, 225–43.
Association of University Technology Managers (2002), 'Canadian universities' and research institutions' technology transfer practices: how Canada differs from the U.S.A.', *AUTM Manual*, **XIV**(Chapter 1), 1–18.
Australian Institute for Commercialisation (2003a), 'Critical factors in successful R&D – an international comparison', discussion paper for the Australian Institute for Commercialisation, Erskinomics Consulting Pty Limited, 1–62.

Australian Institute for Commercialisation (2003b), 'The economic impact of the commercialisation of publicly funded R&D in Australia', *The Allen Consulting Group Pty Ltd*, 72 pages.

Bhidé, A.V. (2000), *The Origin and Evolution of New Businesses*, Oxford: Oxford University Press.

Bower, J.L. and C.M. Christensen (1995), 'Disruptive technologies: catching the wave', *Harvard Business Review*, 43–53.

Canada Foundation for Innovation (2003), 'Summary of institutional activities on the commercialization of research', *Second Annual Report*, 68 pages.

Clayman, B.P. and J.A. Holbrook (2002), 'The survival of university spin-offs and their relevance to regional development', *Centre for Policy Research on S&T*, 12 pages.

Conference Board of Canada (2004), 'Clusters of opportunity, clusters of risk', *The Canada Project*, 21 pages.

Cooper, D.G. (2004), 'The socio-economic impact of a government assistance program on the growth of university spin-off firms in Canada', *National Research Council*.

DC Technologies Ltd. (2004), 'An innovation and commercialization model for a network of ICT centres in Ontario', *Final Report*.

Dorf, R.C. (1988), 'Models for technology transfer from universities and research laboratories', *Technology Management Publication*, 302–12.

Garner, C. and P. Termouth (2004), 'Spin outs and start ups – new companies to commercialise intellectual property from university research', *Management of Intellectual Property in Health Research and Development MIHR*, 1–5.

Gibson, D.V. and C. Stiles (1998), 'Global networked entrepreneurship: linking the world's technopoleis for shared prosperity at home and abroad', *IEEE Proceedings, 31st Annual Hawaii International Conference on System Sciences*, 291–8.

Greenberg, J.S. (1995), 'Technology transfer and commercialization', *Aerospace America*, **February**, 39–43.

Ham, R.M. and D.C. Mowery (1997), 'Technology transfer and collaboration between industry and national laboratories', *International Journal of Industrial Engineering*, **4**(4), 244–53.

Hindle, K. and J. Yencken (2003), 'Public research commercialisation, entrepreneurship and new technology-based firms: an integrated model', *Technovation*, **24**(10), 793.

Industry Canada (2003), 'Strengthening industry relationships with research organizations and access to R&D funds'.

InterAcademy Council (2004), 'Inventing a better future: a strategy for building worldwide capacities in S&T', 143 pages.

Jaffe, A.B. and J. Lerner (2001), 'Reinventing public R&D: patent policy and the commercialisation of national laboratory technologies', *Rand Journal of Economics*, **32**(1), 167–98.

Kumar, U. and V. Kumar (1997), 'Incubating technology: best practices', *Federal Partners in Technology Transfer FPTT*, 1–75.

Kwak, M. (2002), 'What's the best commercialization strategy for startups?', *MIT Sloan Management Review* **43**(3), Spring.

Lambert, R. (2003), 'Lambert review of business–university collaboration', 148 pages.

Lee, Y. and R. Gaertner (1994), 'Technology transfer from university to industry: a large-scale experiment with technology development and commercialization', *Policy Studies Journal*, **22**(2), 384–99.

Lehrer, M. and K. Asakawa (2004), 'Pushing scientists into the marketplace promoting science entrepreneurship', *California Management Review*, **46**(3), 55–76.

Lombana, C.A., A.D. Romig et al. (2000), 'Accelerating technology transfer from federal laboratories to the private sector by increasing industrial R&D collaborations – a new business model', *IEEE*, 380–85.

Lowe, J. (1993), 'Commercialisation of university research: a policy perspective', *Technology Analysis and Strategic Management*, **5**(1), 27–37.

Mansfield, E. (1991), 'Academic Research and Industrial Innovation', *Research Policy*, **20**, 1–12.

Martin, P. (2003), 'Building the 21st century economy', speech to the Montreal Board of Trade.

Ndonzuau, F.N., F. Pirnay and B. Surlemont (2002), 'A stage-model of academic spin-off creation', *Technovation*, **22**(5), 281–9.

Nerkar, A. and S. Shane (2003), 'When do startups that exploit patented academic knowledge survive?', *International Journal of Industrial Organization*, **21**, 1391–1410.

OECD (2003), *The Sources of Economic Growth in OECD Countries*, Paris: OECD.

Phillimore, J. and R. Joseph (2003), 'Science parks, a triumph of hype over experience?', in L.V. Shavina, *The International Handbook of Innovation*, Oxford: Elsevier, pp. 750–8.

Porter, M.E. (1998), 'Clusters and the new economics of competition', *Harvard Business Review*, **76**(6), 77–91.

Porter, M.E. and S. Stern (1999), 'The new challenge to America's prosperity: findings from the innovation index', Council on Competitiveness.

Radosevich, R. (1995b), 'A test of the surrogate-entrepreneurship model of public-technology commercialization', *Proceedings of the 28th Annual Hawaii International Conference on System Sciences*, 681–8.

Raine, J.K. and C.P. Beukman (2002), 'University technology commercialisation offices – a New Zealand perspective', *International Journal of Technology Management*, **24**(5/6), 627–47.

Reamer, A., L. Icerman and J. Youtie (2003), 'Technology transfer and commercialization: their role in economic development', U.S. Department of Commerce, 141.

Roberts, E.B. and D.E. Malone (1996), 'Policies and structures for spinning off new companies from research and development organizations', *R&D Management*, **26**(1), 17–48.

Shane, S. (2002), 'Executive forum: university technology transfer to entrepreneurial companies', *Journal of Business Venturing*, **17**, 537–52.

Stankiewicz, R. (1994), 'Spin-off companies from universities', *Science and Public Policy*, **21**(2), 99–107.

Stern, S., M.E. Porter and J.L. Furman (2000), 'The determinants of national innovative capacity', *NBER Working Paper Series* (7876), 1–56.

Thorburn, L. (2000), 'Knowledge management, research spinoffs and commercialization of R&D in Australia', *Asia Pacific Journal of Management*, **17**, 257–75.

Traversy, V. (2004), 'Commercial innovation: a policy stocktaking', *The Innovation Journal: The Public Sector Innovation Journal*, **9**(2), 1–24.

Upstill, G. and D. Symington (2002), 'Technology transfer and the creation of companies: the CSIRO experience', *R&D Management*, **32**(3), 233–40.

Vohora, A., M. Wright and A. Lockett (2004), 'Critical junctures in the development of university high-tech spinout companies', *Research Policy*, **33**(1), 147–75.

Walsh, S., B.A. Kirchhoff and S. Newbert (2002), 'Differentiating market strategies for disruptive technologies', *IEEE Transactions on Engineering Management*, **49**(4), 341–51.

Wolfe, D.A. and M.S. Gertler (2003), 'Policies for cluster creation: lessons from the ISRN research initiative', Innovation Systems Research Network, University of Toronto, 19 pages.

Wolfe, D.A. and M.S. Gertler (2004), 'Clusters from the inside and out: local dynamics and global linkages', *Urban Studies*, **41**(5/6), 1055–77.

5 From the exploration of new possibilities to the exploitation of recently developed competencies: evidence from five ventures developing new-to-the-world technologies

Annaleena Parhankangas and David L. Hawk

Introduction

Entrepreneurship in general and technology-based entrepreneurship in particular is a process of experimentation and learning (Woo et al., 1994). Entrepreneurs start their venturing process by exploring a newly 'theorized' opportunity in a highly uncertain situation. After a certain period of exploration, entrepreneurs will try to gain profits from the experimented opportunities (Choi and Shepherd, 2004). Using the terminology of the organizational learning literature, successful entrepreneurs are able to proceed from the exploration of new possibilities to the exploitation of recently acquired competencies.

The postulate of a trade-off between exploration and exploitation processes is one of the most enduring ideas in organizational theory (see, for instance, Adler et al., 1999). The contradictory nature of exploration and exploitation activities (Abernathy, 1978; Adler et al., 1999; March, 1991) has led several scholars to question whether it is possible for organizations to pursue both types of activities simultaneously. Some scholars have suggested that organizations engage in multiple forms of learning by adopting features from both organic and mechanistic structures (Hedberg et al., 1976; Brown and Eisenhardt, 1997). A contrasting view suggests that corporations should completely separate (Christensen, 1998) or buffer experimenting units from exploiting ones (March and Simon, 1958, p. 198). Some studies argue that ambidextrous or dual organizational forms are the key to managing exploration and exploitation activities simultaneously (Bradach, 1997; Tushman and O'Reilly, 1997). While a great deal of attention has been paid to organizational structures conducive to either exploration or exploitation processes, the students of organizations have largely ignored the question of how organizations shift from the exploration of new possibilities to the exploitation of recently developed competencies (Choi and Shepherd, 2004). This is a question which, in our view, ultimately determines the success of exploration activities. Furthermore, most studies provide a snapshot view of organizations exploring the potentials of new technologies. This sets the stage for neglecting the fact that technological diversification can often become a decades-long process.

We set out to partly fill this gap in existing knowledge by following the development of five new-to-the-world technologies as they emerged over nearly three decades. The developers of these new technologies faced many challenges along the way to successful commercialization of the technology. First, they often had a limited understanding of the technical and commercial aspects of their invention. Second, novel technologies offered a wide array of application directions of which developers were not initially aware. Third, formalizing agreements with the first customer and then scaling up the production process proved to be a very significant challenge for the development team. We are seeking to answer the following questions: how did the managers choose amongst the array of technological possibilities and then how did they select from amongst the numerous means to apply the technology? In addition, our goal was to identify the factors that promoted the shift from exploration of new possibilities to the exploitation of recently developed competencies. Most importantly, we are interested in how the modes of governance changed along this process.

All the technologies studied in the work described herein were new both to the parent organizations and to the world providing the context of the organizations. Common to these technologies was the trait that they appeared as 'solutions looking for problems', triggered by recent advances in science and technology. During their life cycle, these technologies became embedded in various networks and ownership structures. The changes in the governance structure tended to help an organization avoid the tendency of becoming too closely tied to traditional attitudes and forms, some of which were seen clearly to impede the further development and application of a technology. Moving from one set of connections to another was found to exert a major impact on improving the speed and the direction of technology development and adoption. These changes in the context aided the organizations in embarking on new exploration paths as well as cashing in on their earlier exploration processes. Most interestingly, shifts in governance structures, as well as in technology development and commercialization, were seen to come from happenstance, luck, chance associations and social connections. This gives us reason to believe that coincidence, luck and personal networks are better pathways to explaining the milestone events in technology development than are pre-ordained strategy and reason. Finally, we found that, in the case of new-to-the-world technologies, the parent firm's benefits accruing from technology development are more likely to materialize in the form of revenues from technology-based transactions that take place outside the firm than from internal strategic benefits of building a new business area.

Exploration and Exploitation in Organizational Learning

The organizational learning literature makes a distinction between the exploration of new possibilities and the exploitation of old certainties (March, 1991; Levinthal and March, 1993; Schumpeter, 1968; Holland, 1975; Kuran, 1988). Organizations engaged in exploration consciously move away from current organizational routines and knowledge bases. Exploration includes things captured by terms such as search, variation, risk taking, experimentation, play, flexibility, discovery and innovation. Exploration activities involve second-order learning, resulting from the realization that certain experiences cannot be interpreted within the current belief system (Watzlawick et al., 1974; Hedberg et al., 1976; Argyris and Schon, 1978).

The exploitation processes refer to those activities and investments committed to gaining returns from a new product or service through the building of efficient business systems for full-scale operations (March, 1991; Choi and Shepherd, 2004). Exploitation includes things such as refinement, production, efficiency, selection, implementation and execution. In other words, exploitation involves first-order learning, gaining a competence in a well-defined activity, routine or technology.

Organizations that engage in exploration to the exclusion of exploitation are likely to find that they suffer the costs of experimentation without gaining many of its benefits. Compared to returns from exploitation, returns from exploration are systematically less certain, more remote in time, and organizationally more distant from the locus of action and adaptation. Conversely, systems that engage in exploitation to the exclusion of exploration are likely to find themselves unable to change or, stated differently, in a competency trap (March, 1991). Thus a critical challenge facing organizations is the dilemma of maintaining the capability for both exploitation and exploration. According to the organizational theory literature (March and Simon, 1958; Cyert and March, 1963), the balance between these two enables the organization both to function efficiently and to remain flexible over time. Various theoretical perspectives have addressed this paradox, including ecological theories (Hannan and Freeman, 1977, 1987), contingency theories (Lawrence and Lorsch, 1967; Galbraith, 1973) and bureaucratic theories (Perrow, 1986).

The contradictory nature of exploration and exploitation activities (Abernathy, 1978; Adler et al., 1999; March, 1991) has led several scholars to question whether and how it is possible for organizations to pursue both types of activities simultaneously. It has been suggested that exploitation requires a bureaucratic form of organization with high levels of standardization, formalization, specialization and hierarchy, whereas exploration activities are associated with organic structures, fluid processes, informality and absence of hierarchy (Burns and Stalker, 1961). In previous literature, there are multiple points of view on the way organizations may strike a balance between exploration and exploitation activities. Some scholars suggest that organizations engage in multiple forms of learning by adopting features from both organic and mechanistic (organizational) structures (Hedberg et al., 1976; Brown and Eisenhardt, 1997). A contrasting view suggests that corporations should completely separate (Christensen, 1998) or buffer experimenting units from exploiting ones (March and Simon, 1958, p. 198).

While a great deal of attention has been paid to the organizational structures conducive or detrimental to these two forms of learning (Bradach, 1997; Tushman and O'Reilly, 1997; Benner and Tushman, 2003), less is known on the way organizations are able to transfer successfully from the exploration of new possibilities to the exploitation of recently developed competencies. Scholars of entrepreneurship appear to have been somewhat more active in this realm. Even though most of the work has focused on the discovery and recognition of opportunities to bring into existence new products (Busenitz and Barney, 1997; Shane, 2000; Shaver and Scott, 1991), there are studies addressing the question of right timing of exploiting opportunities (Schoonhoven et al., 1990) and the important public support measures facilitating exploitation (Chrisman and McMullan, 2000; Manning et al., 1989; Rice, 2002). In addition, some scholars have focused on the market and resource-based factors encouraging entrepreneurs to start the exploitation of recently recognized opportunities (Alvarez and Busenitz, 2001; Choi and Shepherd, 2004).

Our goal is to add to the existing knowledge by analysing how corporations are able to shift from the exploration of new possibilities to the exploitation of the recently recognized and developed competencies. We set out to address this question by taking a somewhat novel approach by following how fundamental discoveries in science and technology spawn subsequent research, discovery and commercialization in five technology-based ventures initiated by large corporations seeking to broaden their technological base.

Method

Others have called for the need of qualitative, longitudinal analysis of technology diversification and interorganizational relationships (Parkhe, 1993; Smith et al., 1995). Our
study adopts this approach and follows a multiple case study research design by Yin
(1984). We chose to analyse five technology-based ventures from large Finnish and
Swedish corporations. These examples were selected on the basis of two considerations:
they represent new-to-the-world technologies defying the frontiers of scientific knowledge, and they have been in operation for a sufficient period of time, so that the interactions between the two forms of learning and governance structures could be expected
to have surfaced. These technology-based ventures differed in terms of their orientation
to exploration vs. exploitation, organizational design, parent firm characteristics and
country. We believe that this research setting provides many possibilities for comparison, which enables richer theory development (Glaser and Strauss, 1967; Eisenhardt,
1989).

We collected both interview and archival data. We interviewed the venture managers,
corporate managers of the parent firm, and alliance partners to cover the entire lifetime
of the technology-based venture from its inception to the time of the study. The initial
data collection focused on developing an overall understanding of the milestones and outcomes of technology development in each of these ventures. In later interviews, we asked
more specific questions to refine and elaborate themes that emerged from the earlier interviews, and to check factual data. Data collection was stopped at the point of theoretical
saturation (Strauss, 1987).

The interviews were conducted individually with each participant. In addition, we conducted some group interviews with various combinations of participants. The interviews
were semi-structured and ranged from 45 to 180 minutes. The interviews were carried out
between October 2001 and May 2002. All the interviews were taped and transcribed. The
interviewees read and commented on the interview transcriptions for accuracy. Archival
data were employed to complement the interview data as a means to triangulate the validity of our findings (Eisenhardt, 1989). Archival data include minutes of the board meetings, Internet sites, organization charts and internal newsletters, as well as technical and
market reports.

In analysing our data, we first applied a narrative strategy involving the construction
of a detailed story of the raw data (Langley, 1999). The narrative strategy was followed
by a visual mapping strategy, which offers a means of data reduction and synthesis. Using
our comparison of five technology-based ventures, we sought regularities in the exploration and exploitation processes, their contexts, governance and outcomes, serving as a
basis of proposed hypotheses to be tested in the future studies.

**Research Setting: Five Technology-based Ventures developing New-to-the-World
Technologies**

In the following, we will briefly describe the evolution of five technology-based ventures
initiated by large Finnish and Swedish corporations as they proceeded toward the market
place.

Conductive polymers

In the early 1980s, a large chemical corporation (CHEMCO)[1] decided to diversify into the battery business, in an effort to pursue and enhance its international competitiveness. It was then believed that it would be technically possible to replace the heavy lead batteries with much lighter plastic batteries for use, for instance, in electric cars. In order to develop plastic batteries, an improved knowledge of conductive polymers was called for. Conductive polymers were discovered only a couple of years earlier by Alan Heeger, Alan MacDiarmid and Hideki Shirakawa of the University of Pennsylvania. To gain access to this new-to-the-world knowledge, CHEMCO ended up recruiting a young PhD who had been working with Alan MacDiarmid in Philadelphia at the time of the discovery.

Applying the conductive polymer technology to plastic batteries proved to be a disappointment from the operational point of view. It seemed that plastic batteries could never replace the lead, nickel and cadmium batteries because of quality problems. This realization marked the end of the battery research at CHEMCO. However, the knowledge related to conductive polymers did not go to waste. In those days, the parent firm CHEMCO was a leading international plastic producer, and decided to explore the possibilities of blending conductive polymers with commercial mainstream plastics. It was believed that these polymer blends could be used in computers and emergency room equipment to protect this equipment from becoming electrically charged. The venture team started experimenting with various polymers and allied itself with several Nordic firms and research institutions. In the mid-1980s, this phase was ended by another disappointment. It seemed that making a polymer chain conductive would also render it more rigid, and thus difficult to mould for various product applications. However, during this phase, the venture team was able to build up production facilities, while all the competitors were still operating on a laboratory scale.

The venture team presented their results at a research conference in New Mexico. Following the conference presentation, two leading scientists of the University of California expressed their willingness to collaborate with the venture team. They had developed a dissolvable polyaniline derivative without sacrificing its conductive properties. CHEMCO, in its turn, had the production facilities matching the needs of the University of California. As a result, CHEMCO decided to establish a joint venture with these two American scientists, dedicated to the development of conductive polymers and their applications.

The subsequent years marked a very intensive period in the development of the technology, resulting in a pre-commercial product line of insolvable polyaniline and polymer-LEDs. The number of people working for this project grew rapidly in the late 1980s. However, in the mid-1990s, the strategic importance of the venture for the parent corporation decreased as CHEMCO decided to divest all its plastic-related businesses. In 1998, a spin-off company was formed to continue the development of conductive polyaniline applications. Today, the spin-off company is active in selling additives for basic polymers and developing applications related to anti-corrosive paints, and conductive surface applications.

Immobolization technology

In the late 1970s, a large Nordic life science corporation, FOODCO, was exploring new business areas to exploit recent developments in biotechnology. Their strategy was to move further into the biotech industry. At the same time, quite unexpectedly, FOODCO got an opportunity to acquire a manufacturing plant suitable for fermentation purposes. At that time FOODCO also entered into an alliance with a large US corporation, where FOODCO provided the production facilities and the partner technological competences related to the production of industrial enzymes. As a by-product of this alliance, FOODCO adopted many technologies from its partner, among them so-called 'immobilization technology', potentially applicable for enzyme immobilization, ion exchange, chromatography and protein separation.

A project team was set up to explore potential product applications of the technology. By accident, the project manager found out about a parallel research project going on at the National Technical Research Centre. The mission of this project was to apply immobilization technology in beer fermentation. FOODCO participated in this project, which resulted in an alliance between a large brewery and FOODCO. Besides beer fermentation, the venture team got gradually involved in the development of various other product applications, such as soft drinks, non-alcoholic beers and extremely pure lactic acid, just to mention a few. All these applications were developed in alliances with other firms or research institutes. Only the applications related to beer fermentation generated a continuous revenue stream. However, this revenue stream was not enough to pursue the development of other applications of the immobilization technology. The fact that the project team was not able to come up with product applications for the core businesses of FOODCO made the technology less valuable in the eyes of the corporate management. Struggling with financial distress, the parent firm decided to sell the rights to the technology to an international engineering company in 1997.

Atomic layer epitaxy (ALE) technology

The foundation of the atomic layer technology was laid in the early 1970s, when Dr Technology Champion was developing sensors at the National Research Centre. A friend recruited him to a large pharmaceutical company, PHARMCO, where he was expected to apply his knowledge to the manufacture of high-quality flat panels for medical devices. The first prototype was introduced in 1978, and the product was launched on the market in the mid-1980s. However, technology development proved to be too time and resource consuming for PHARMCO. Thus, the corporate management decided to sell all the rights related to technology to ELECTRO, a large Nordic corporation specializing in the manufacture of consumer electronics. ELECTRO planned to apply the technology in the manufacture of TV displays. However, after only a couple of years, ELECTRO decided to divest some of its business divisions, among them the business developing the ALE technology. As a result, this business unit became part of a US corporation.

In 1987, a large energy corporation, ENERCO, recruited Dr Technology Champion and 20 of his co-workers to apply their technological knowledge in various emerging business areas of the corporation, such as the manufacture of solar panels and catalysts. The project team received international recognition for its scientific achievements. By the late 1990s, the venture team came up with a prototype for solar panels. However, commercial production of the solar panels did not prove to be a commercially feasible solution. ALE technology was also applied to the manufacture of catalysts. The most important application of the technology was the ALE reactor developed for the manufacture of flat panels and thin layer membranes for the needs of the electronics industry. Except for catalysts, all the applications of the technology lay outside the core areas of ENERCO. That is why the corporate management ended up selling the business unit to a global semiconductor company in 1998.

Speciality resins
In the 1960s, FOODCO was a pioneer of chromatographic separation in various industrial applications. The successful implementation of chromatographic separation requires hardware, software and speciality resins. In the 1970s, speciality resins were not available on the market. As a result, FOODCO decided to start the in-house production of resins for chromatographic separation purposes. The in-house production of resins first came under the R&D unit. Later on it was transferred to an engineering unit specializing in separation technologies. After some years of experimentation, the venture team was able to produce speciality resins on a commercially viable scale.

In 1990, FOODCO decided to terminate the production of speciality resins, now widely available on the market. The personnel expressed their willingness to continue the development of the technology in an independent firm. As a result, six people from FOODCO transferred to a newly formed spin-off company. The very first challenge faced by the SPIN-OFF COMPANY involved decreasing the dependence on its first and only customer, FOODCO, by broadening the clientèle and developing new applications of the technology. By the year 2001, the SPIN-OFF COMPANY had diversified successfully into two new product areas, including resins and special polymers.

Miniaturization technology
The roots of the miniaturization technology at BIOCO date back to the late 1980s, when the corporation was taking its first steps toward a better understanding of biosensor development. In 1990, a new ambitious CEO decided to establish an exploratory research group searching for new areas of interest, although the corporation as a whole was under financial distress and laying off personnel in more established areas. Most of the people forming the newly founded exploratory research group had engaged in the corporation's earlier efforts in biosensor development in a subsidiary spun off from BIOCO. By 1996, a number of patent applications had been filed. However, the research group anticipated that launching the product on the market would still take at least five more years. In those days, BIOCO had a tendency to discontinue projects that would not generate short-term revenue. For some reason, this project was not discontinued, but it almost starved to death under the meagre financial support from the parent.

In 1997, BIOCO merged with a large global pharmaceutical corporation. The new owner had a much bolder attitude toward risk taking and exploratory research. As a result, the project was revitalized. Another stroke of luck came in the form of a new vice president in R&D. He saw great potential in the technology and soon became a dedicated venture champion for the whole research group. However, the other business units were unwilling to invest in a technology that they considered too risky and too unrelated to their current operations. As a result, the venture was spun off in 2000, with a considerable venture capital backing. By 2002, the newly founded spin-off firm had specialized in proteomics and launched its first product on the market.

Governance of Exploration and Exploitation Processes: Organizational Structures, Networking and Ownership

Prior research has suggested that organizations may shift between exploration and exploitation by adapting mainly their *internal* organization structures (Hedberg et al., 1976; Brown and Eisenhardt, 1997; Christensen, 1998; Bradach, 1997; Tushman and O'Reilly, 1997). The data from this research indicate a somewhat different view. It looks like our sample corporations' tendency to engage in *interorganizational* relationships varied according to whether they were involved in searching or developing new products, concepts or processes (exploration activities) or whether they sought to exploit previously developed products, concepts or processes (exploitation activities). It seems to us that major technological breakthroughs were achieved in close collaboration with other organizations, with relatively little concern for the allocation of ownership rights. Later, as opportunities for commercial exploitation of the technology emerged, the organizations tended to rush to secure their access to continuous revenue streams through hierarchical control and shying away from previous collaborative arrangements.

> *Proposition 1: Exploration and exploitation activities differ from each other in terms of their networking orientation.*
> *Proposition 1a: Exploration activities are more often associated with inter-firm collaboration than the exploitation activities.*
> *Proposition 1b: Exploitation activities are more often controlled through hierarchical governance than exploration activities.*

Table 5.1 summarizes this study's empirical evidence related to the governance structures used during the evolution of our five technology-based ventures. Figure 5.1 presents event chronologies associated with the technology-based ventures. The form of the boxes indicates whether the event described represents a decision (sharp-cornered rectangles), an activity undertaken by the firm (round-cornered rectangles) or an activity outside the control of the firm (ovals). The arrows leading from one box to another indicate the interrelatedness of these events. Exploitation activities have a dotted background. In our study, we used the following procedure to distinguish exploration activities from their exploitation: exploration refers to those activities experimenting with the potentials of technological and scientific phenomena, potentially leading to the introduction of a new product, process or service. Exploration activities include basic research and early product development prior to the introduction of the first prototype or product concept. Exploitation processes aim at generating a revenue stream from the product concepts developed during the exploration phase, thus encompassing activities such as refinement and fine-tuning of the product, the development and scaling-up of the manufacturing facilities, and establishing presence in the market place.

While analysing the evolution of the conductive polymer technology, it became obvious that there were five distinct partnership governance structures that came into use over time: (1) an alliance between CHEMCO, the National Technical Research Centre and a domestic lead battery manufacturer; (2) a Nordic research consortium between CHEMCO, the National Technical Research Centre, Nordic universities and research institutions; (3) a joint venture between CHEMCO and two scientists of the University of California; (4) AMERICAN COMPANY continuing the development of polymer-LEDs after the

Table 5.1 Comparison of the technology-based ventures

	Conductive Polymer Technology (1982–2002)	Immobilization Technology (1980–2002)	Atomic Layer Epitaxy Technology (1980–2002)
Original goal	A plastic battery for electric car	To explore recent developments in biotech	Medical device monitors
Role of coincidence, luck and non-planned (chance) events	'Our conference presentation caught the interest of two leading US scientists. Quite unexpectedly, they suggested collaboration to us.'	'Quite unexpectedly, we got an opportunity to acquire production facilities not far from here. They were suitable for fermentation purposes and that is how it all began.'	'Our conference presentation led to 4000 product inquiries. We should have saved that presentation for a moment when our product was ready.'
	'The decision to terminate the plastic battery research project coincided with a change in the corporate strategy. The new interest of CHEMCO lay in the applications where conductive polymers were blended with main stream plastics.'	'As a by-product of our alliance with this US corporation, we learned the immobilization technology.'	'Quite unexpectedly, ELECTRO decided to divest its consumer electronic divisions. As a result, our project was terminated.'
	'The severe economic recession of the early 1990s made it necessary for CHEMCO to divest its plastic-related businesses, thus leaving a venture without a home in the restructured parent corporation.'	'Quite by chance, I heard about a research project going on at the National Research Center pursuing similar interests.'	
	'The application for the paper industry occurred to me just because of my prior job in that industry.'	'In the search for potential applications for the technology, we engaged in a thorough and systematic search of existing literature. However, all the applications that actually worked and were implemented were found by chance. Many times companies aim at modelling processes and using well-structured management methods. However, our experience shows that often intuition can lead to exactly the same results.'	
		'Many of these things just happened. It seemed to me that there was no systematic management of technology in this organization, at least you couldn't see it at the lower levels.'	

92

Milestones in technology development	Plastic Battery → dead end Experimentation with polytiofene derivatives Scaling up the production facilities Conductive polyaniline→ a commercial product Polymer LEDs→ a commercial product Additives → a commercial product Anticorrosive paints→ under development Conductive textiles→ under development Conductive surface application→ under development	Beer fermentation-→ a new product line at BREWERY Fermentation of soft drinks→ patents Fermentation of non-alcoholic beers→ new production lines at NON-ALCOHOLIC BREWERY → design and sales bioreactors to other breweries Control of the PH level of beer → patent, in use at NON-ALCOHOLIC BREWERY Production of extremely pure lactic acid→ development delayed at FOODCO Manufacture of food ingredients→ development delayed at FOODCO Manufacture of ciders and long drinks→ under development under a global research consortium	Medical device application→ discontinued TV monitor application→ alive and well Catalyst application→ under development at the parent Solar panel application→ alive and well with the new parent ALE reactor application→ alive and well with the new parent
Governance structures and technologies developed within them	Alliance between CHEMCO, National Technical Research Center, and lead battery Manufacturer → development of plastic battery A Nordic research consortium → experimentation with polytiofene derivatives and scaling up the production A joint venture between CHEMCO and University of California → conductive polymers and polymer LEDs AMERICAN COMPANY: Commercialization of polymer LEDs Spin-off firm from CHEMCO in alliance with the paper manufacturer, textile company and paint producer→ additives, anticorrosive paints, conductive textiles, conductive surface applications	Joint venture between FOODCO and a US corporation→ basics of immobilization technology A project under R&D centre→ experimentation with polytiofenes RIFB consortium→ beer fermentation Alliances with BREWERY, SOFTDRINK, and NON-ALCOHOLIC BREWERY → fermentation of beers and soft drinks, a business unit under ENGINEERING COMPANY→ design of fermentation systems	R&D lab of PHARMCO→ a flat panel display for medical devices A business unit under ELECTRCO→ TV monitor applications A subsidiary of a US corporation→ a world leader in TV monitor-related technologies A subsidiary of ENERCO→ catalyst, ALE reactor and solar panel applications A subsidiary of a global semiconductor firm→ ALE Reactor and solar panel applications

Table 5.1 (continued)

	Conductive Polymer Technology (1982–2002)	Immobilization Technology (1980–2002)	Atomic Layer Epitaxy Technology (1980–2002)
Outcome	A spin-off company selling conductive polymers. High-tech applications acquired by a global chemical corporation	Beer fermentation applications sold to an ENGINEERING COMPANY. The rights to other applications are retained by the parent	Most promising applications sold to a global semiconductor corporation. Catalyst applications retained by the parent

	Speciality Resins (1970–2002)	Miniaturization Technologies (1986–2002)
Original goal	In-house production of special resins for the use of parent corporation's chromatographic separation processes	Building a new business area around the potentials of miniaturization and microfluidics technologies
Role of coincidence, luck and non-planned (chance) events	'We found our second major product group thanks to the fact that big manufacturers lost their interest in this business. As a result, customers came to us and asked if we could do it.' 'The decision to spin us out had to do with general refocusing tendencies of the parent. This decision was further confirmed by the fact that resins for chromatographic separations started to become available on the market. As a result, in-house production was not a necessity anymore.'	'The corporation didn't really know what all this [microfluidics] was going to be about . . . it was very much like early stage research without knowing the directions.' 'Later on when I started thinking about the possibilities of CDs, I remembered the name of the company I got to know in Liechtenstein some years ago. That is how it all started. It would have never happened if I hadn't gone to Liechtenstein back then.' 'We met a researcher at a conference and noticed that we are doing similar kinds of things. The positive feedback we got from him gave us enough courage to start the whole process.' 'Attendance at a seminar brought us into contact with TELCO and that is how our collaboration started.' 'The merger of the parent and GLOBAL BIOTECH CORPORATION created a new situation where some projects put on the shelf prior to the merger were revitalized. This is because GLOBAL BIOTECH CORPORATION had a more positive attitude

	Case 1	Case 2
		toward risky technology development projects than BIOCO had.' 'The new VP in R&D was able to detect the huge potential of the technology. That is why the project was revitalized.' 'At that time, the drug screening and drug development were hungry for very high throughput devices. The existence of chemical libraries, for instance, made it necessary to have a high throughput analysing technology. This was not the case before.'
Milestones in technology development	Resins for chromatographic separations→ a commercial product Powered resin mixtures for water treatment and nuclear applications→ a commercial product Special polymers for clothing, furniture and paint industries→ a commercial product	a patent portfolio a proof of principle the first product application in the proteomics area: a sample preparation disc for use with mass spectrometers→ development ongoing
Governance structures and technologies developed within them	Research Centre of FOODCO and Engineering Department of FOODCO: early development of resins Manufacturing facilities of FOODCO: manufacture of resins for chromatographic separations SPIN-OFF FIRM in collaboration with a TECHNOLOGY SUPPORT ORGANIZATION, FOODCO, LOCAL UNIVERSITY and PAPERMAKER: manufacture of resins for chromatographic separations development and manufacture of powered resin mixtures development and manufacture of special polymers	subsidiary of BIOCO 1986–90: basic understanding of the microfluidics area and the CD applications was built Exploratory research group within BIOCO: 1990–95 in collaboration with many universities and TELCO: patents and patent applications 'On the shelf' (1995–97) Revitalization of the project at BIOCO (1997–2000): patents, patent applications and a proof of principle Spin-off in collaboration with DISC MAKER: product development in the proteomics area
Outcome	A successful spin-off firm developing and exploiting numerous applications of the technology Chromatographic separation resins developed by the venture contributed to the technology and product development at the parent corporation	A spin-off company launching the first product on the market

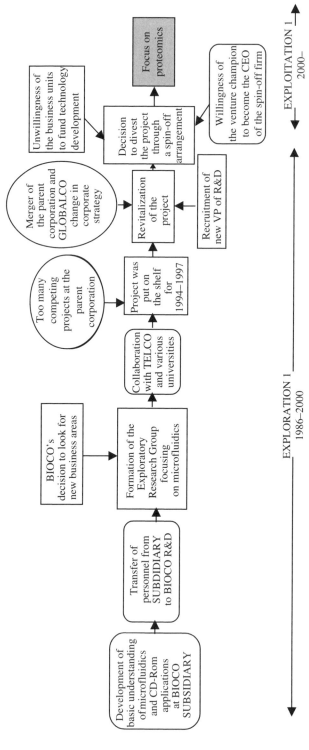

(a) Miniaturization technology

(b) *Atomic layer epitaxy technology*

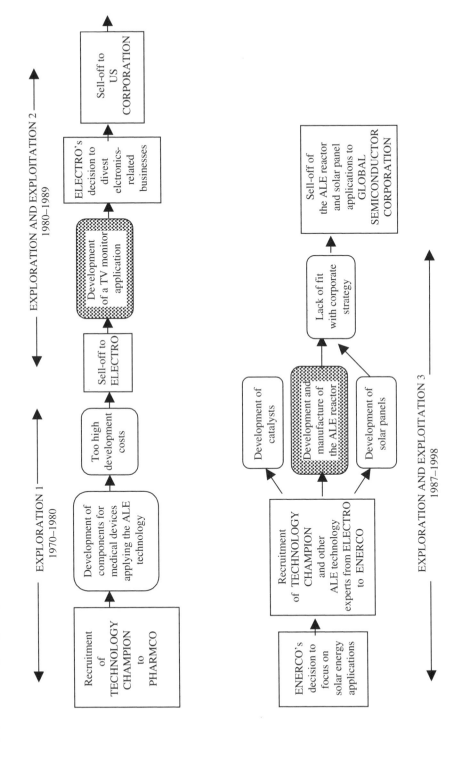

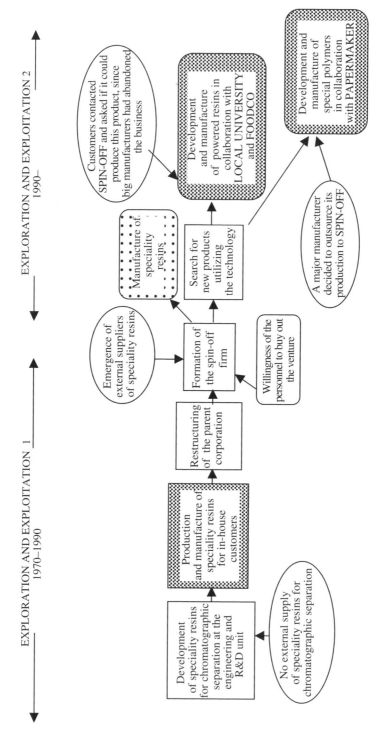

(c) *Speciality resins*

EXPLORATION AND EXPLOITATION 1
1970–1990

EXPLORATION AND EXPLOITATION 2
1990–

Development
of speciality resins
for chromatographic
separation at the
engineering and
R&D unit

No external supply
of speciality resins for
chromatographic separation

Production
and manufacture of
speciality resins
for in-house
customers

Restructuring
of the parent
corporation

Formation of
the spin-off
firm

Emergence of
external suppliers
of speciality resins

Willingness of the
personnel to buy out
the venture

Manufacture of
speciality
resins

Search for
new products
utilizing
the technology

Development
and manufacture
of powered resins in
collaboration with
LOCAL UNIVERSITY
and FOODCO

Customers contacted
SPIN-OFF and asked if it could
produce this product, since
big manufacturers had abandoned
the business

A major manufacturer
decided to outsource its
production to SPIN-OFF

Development and
manufacture of
special polymers
in collaboration
with PAPERMAKER

(d) Immobilization technology

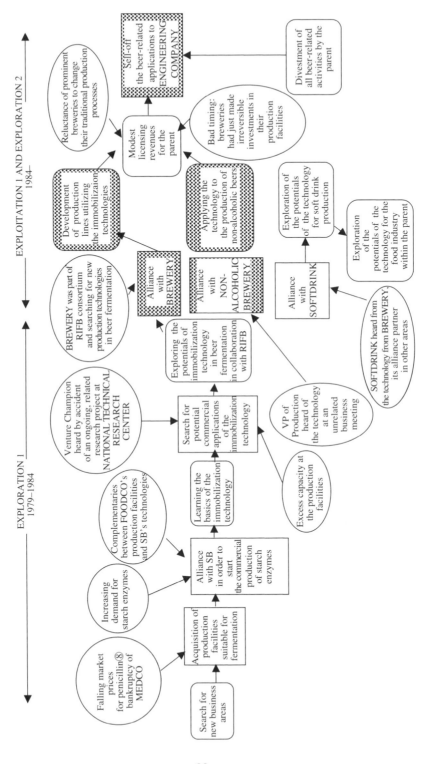

(e) Conductive polymers

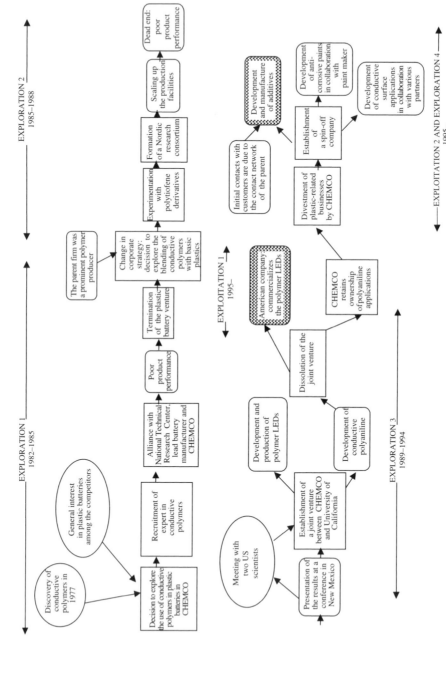

Figure 5.1 Five technology-based ventures

dissolution of a joint venture; and (5) a spin-off firm from CHEMCO in alliance with a domestic paper producer, a paint manufacturer and a textile manufacturer. The first three organizational arrangements were dedicated to exploring the potentials of conductive polymers in plastic batteries, and evaluating the suitability of polytiofene and polyaniline derivatives for industrial applications. Most notably, all these exploration activities were conducted in collaboration with external organizations. The exploitation activities (the commercialization of polymer-LEDs and polyaniline applications) were conducted in independent small firms with little or no collaboration with others.

While developing speciality resins for in-house chromatographic separation, FOODCO moved very fast from the exploration to full-scale exploitation. Some years later, FOODCO decided to transfer the technology development to an independent spin-off firm, as the strategic importance of speciality resins for its own operations decreased. The spin-off firm focused on cashing in on the competencies developed within the former parent and exploring new applications of the technology in collaboration with other partners, as shown in Figure 5.1. The evolution of the venture focusing on the miniaturization technology follows a similar pattern. The exploration of the potentials of micro-fluidics took place within BIOCO in collaboration with various research institutes and other corporations. The commercialization of these activities was conducted in a spin-off firm with minimal reliance on external collaboration partners. The same pattern was repeated with the immobilization technology, where the shift from exploration to exploitation also marked the end of the collaboration with numerous alliance partners. The example of the atomic layer epitaxy technology tells a slightly different story. Here, all the exploration and exploitation activities were carried out within a single organization with no external partners. However, all these exploration processes were triggered by knowledge transfer from external entities, as the venture champion moved from one organization to another.

Why do organizations tend to rely on interorganizational relationships when exploring the potentials of new technologies? Why does it seem that exploitation is best governed within a single firm? Previous literature views innovations as new combinations of existing materials and forces (Schumpeter, 1968; User, 1971, p. 50; Kogut and Zander, 1992). In a similar vein, Cohen and Levinthal (1990) suggest that knowledge diversity contributes to learning by enabling individuals to make new associations between apparently unrelated knowledge items, potentially triggering the discovery of new technological possibilities. While knowledge diversity may facilitate the recognition of new opportunities, it may also have an adverse effect on the successful implementation of projects pursuing these opportunities (Wilson, 1966). Exploitation activities, such as manufacturing, marketing and fine-tuning of existing products, services or processes, call for efficiency in carefully chosen areas. Such efficiency requires high levels of common knowledge among the development team, 'whether in the form of language, shared meaning, or mutual recognition of knowledge domains' (Grant, 1996, p. 117). It appears likely that such knowledge commonality is best achieved through hierarchical forms of governance within a single organization. In a similar vein, Levinthal and March (1993) highlight the importance of departmentalization as the most basic way of segregating experience and simplifying the learning environment. Thus organizations seek to transform confusing, interactive environments into less confusing and less interactive ones by decomposing domains and treating sub-domains as autonomous in their quest for efficiency and exploitation.

An alternative and perhaps more cynical explanation for the perceived shift from relatively informal network relationships to hierarchical governance highlights the eagerness of venture managers to secure steady revenue streams as the venture proceeds toward the market. Contracts and ownership may appear as less relevant when the developers of new technology are only flirting with new ideas and possibilities, but may gain in importance as opportunities for profit generation come into sight.

The Necessity of Breaking Loose from the Current Organizational and Social Setting

The social embeddedness literature highlights how social structure assists economic performance.[2] Prior research has demonstrated the concept's usefulness in illustrating how actors use network contacts to secure resources and critical information, to manage organizations (Granovetter, 1973; Uzzi, 1996) or to recognize economic opportunities (Young, 2002; Jack and Anderson, 2002). In addition, network partners may signal the importance of technology development to the third parties and spur innovativeness of an organization (see, for instance, Lee et al., 2001; Cohen and Levinthal, 1990; Hagedoorn, 1993; Teece, 1987; Goes and Park, 1997). However, it has been found that these positive effects rise up to a threshold, after which overembeddedness may derail performance by making firms vulnerable to exogenous shocks or insulating them from information that exists beyond their networks (Uzzi, 1997). Even though there are some longitudinal studies on the evolution of alliances and networks (see, for instance, Ariño and de la Torre, 1998; Larsson et al., 1998; Kumar and Nti, 1998), the time span covered is too short to help one understand the context of important new-to-the-world technologies.

Our data suggest that shifting from exploration to exploitation or embarking on new exploration paths is positively associated with the changes in network relationships and ownership. Teaming up with an external organization may help developers of novel technologies recognize opportunities they would not have been able to detect on their own. In addition, our data suggest that technologies may become transferred from one organization to another because of an inability of the original owner to further develop or commercialize the technology. Using our data, we suggest the following.

> *Proposition 2: Changes in exploration and exploitation activities are positively associated with changes in network relationships and ownership.*
> *Proposition 2a: A shift from exploration to exploitation in technology development is positively associated with changes in network relationships and ownership.*
> *Proposition 2b: New exploration activities are triggered by changes in network relationships and ownership.*

We saw some evidence of established organizations being seen to seek solutions in the neighbourhood of their existing solutions while relying on past historical experience for a guiding rationale (see, for instance, Ahuja and Lampert, 2001) and thus unable to realize the full potential of the technology being developed. In the words of the Vice President in R&D of BIOCO: 'If you are working for a sugar mill, it is hard for you to see how your technology could be applied in a paper mill.'

Besides deficiencies in opportunity recognition, parent firms often lacked resources required for the development of novel technologies. For instance, it would not have been possible for FOODCO to pursue beverage-related applications without allying themselves with leading domestic and international breweries. In a similar vein, establishing a spin-off firm may serve as a means of separating a technology-based venture from a parent corporation not interested in or capable of its further development. For instance, BIOCO was not willing to fund the commercialization of miniaturization technology, which was then transferred to an independent firm.

In some instances, abandoning old contacts and connecting to new ones was seen as a necessity to provide a great boost to a technology-based venture successfully approaching a market. The clearest manifestation of this emerged from an interview with the technology director at CHEMCO, where he stated that his professional contacts were too technical in nature to facilitate the commercialization of the conductive polymer technology and, therefore, it was necessary to bring new people into the picture. In a similar vein, the CEO of the spin-off company found it necessary to break free from the old networks of CHEMCO in order to take a new product application to the market. Finally, the CEO of SPIN-OFF from BIOCO stated, 'When talking to customers, I make clear to them that we are not a BIOCO company . . . Having a strategic industrial partner can really be a burden to a company like us, unless it is really an active shareholder that somehow contributes to the success of the company. Otherwise a lot of customers will avoid you because of your parent corporation.'

The necessity of breaking loose from the old organizational setting may also be explained by the parent corporation's structural and social complexity, creating resistance to fundamental change (Tushman and Romanelli, 1985, p. 191). Therefore, the advocates of novel technologies may find it easier to pursue their ambitions beyond the boundaries of the parent corporation, starting with a clean slate.

Role of Coincidence, Luck, Chance Events and Strategic Planning

Although there are studies recognizing that the actions of the organizations are to some degree shaped by the occurrence of the unexpected or otherwise random events (Barney, 1986; Hannan and Freeman, 1987; Woo et al., 1994), the mainstream of management literature seems implicitly to presume a high degree of focused rationality on the part of the corporate managers deciding on the direction and mode of a diversification move. By 'rationality', we refer to an assumption that the actions of the organizations are intentional, reflective of a strategic mission of the organization (or the individual manager), as well as carried out through formal and careful planning. There is an apparent overemphasis on rationality and an avoidance of issues connected to luck, chance or serendipity in technology development (Woo et al., 1994).

We suggest that such a perspective fails to describe the realities of technology-based venturing and severely limits our understanding of the phenomenon being studied. Contrary to previous literature, our discussions with venture managers increasingly led us to believe that coincidence, luck and chance events (non-planned activities) played a very major role in shaping the development paths of these novel technologies, as illustrated by Table 5.1. Therefore, we suggest the following.

Proposition 3: Shifting from exploration to exploitation activities and embarking on new exploration paths are triggered by forces of coincidence, luck and opportunities stemming more from personal networks than from deliberate corporate strategy and related rationalizations.

First, we set out to explore the role of rational planning in the evolution of these five technologies. In the case of conductive polymers, the parent corporation had a clear mission for technology development activities, namely the development of a plastic battery. In those days, there was a strong belief that plastic batteries could compete against traditional ones in terms of quality. The decision to diversify into the plastic battery business seemed very rational given the state of knowledge at the time of the decision. However, years of development work proved this initial optimism to be wrong, where it seemed that the development team's efforts were defying the laws of nature. As a result, the venture team decided to back off and apply their accumulated knowledge in closely related areas.

In the immobilization technology example, the parent firm was looking for new business areas utilizing biotechnology. At the beginning of this exploration, the parent corporation did not restrict its search to any specific applications. By chance, the parent corporation acquired a fermentation plant. The possession of the plant made it possible for FOODCO to enter into an alliance with a corporation with complementary knowledge on enzyme manufacture. As a by-product of this alliance the parent firm was able to adopt the immobilization technology and started looking for commercial applications. To us, this story is a good illustration of the serendipitous nature of technology development.

The development of the ALE technology was triggered by the parent firm's desire to explore new business areas with the help of new-to-the-world technologies. However, the novel technology did not result in commercially viable products. As a result, the parent firm decided to divest the technology through a sell-off arrangement. This started a chain of transactions where the technology was transferred from one organization to another, resulting in numerous product applications during its decades-long history in various organizations.

The unavailability of speciality resins for chromatographic separation served as a trigger for FOODCO to start in-house production. This well-defined objective was achieved. However, this achievement soon lost its significance owing to changes in corporate strategy and the emergence of external suppliers of speciality resins. As a result, the development and manufacture of speciality resins were transferred to a spin-off company also exploring other applications of the technology.

In the case of the miniaturization technology, the parent corporation was exploring the potentials of nanotechnology and microfluidics. In the words of vice president of R&D at BIOCO, 'The corporation didn't really know what all this [microfluidics] was going to be about . . . it was very much like early stage research without knowing the directions.'

After decades of exploration and a spin-off arrangement, the venture team decided to focus on the proteomics area, partly following the recommendations of their new investors.

In four out of five examples, the parent firms were searching for new business areas by exploring new-to-the-world technologies. In only two of our examples, the parent firm had an unambiguous goal of technology development. Ironically, this goal either was never realized or it lost its significance soon after its realization. In the three other examples, the parent firm had only a vague idea of what it was after. The potential product applications were identified after a series of ownership changes. Many of the applications were nothing like the corporate management imagined at the beginning. In addition, most of these applications ended up being exploited by other firms than the parent corporation. How can we explain the relatively insignificant role of strategic planning in our technology-based ventures?[3] First, perhaps due to market and technology uncertainties, managers found the role of formal planning of less relative importance during the process. In the words of the technology manager at FOODCO, 'Many of these things just happened. It seems to me that there was no systematic management of technology in this organization, at least you couldn't see it at the lower levels.'

This applies to the identification of new applications for the technology in particular:

> In search of potential applications for this technology, we engaged in a thorough and systematic analysis of existing literature and existing customer base. However, all the applications that actually worked and were implemented were found by chance. Companies often aim at modelling processes and using well-structured management methods. However, our experience shows that intuition can often lead to exactly the same results.

This intuition was mainly based on the venture team's networks of contacts, relying on the personal history or chance events. For instance, the CEO of a spin-off firm from CHEMCO states that the identification of a market opportunity in the paper industry was purely due to his previous employment at a leading Finnish paper manufacturer. This is in line with prior network literature stating that opportunity recognition relies heavily on individuals' existing business and personal contacts (Gulati, 1995; Wong and Ellis, 2002; Mitsuhashi, 2002). Reliance on personal contacts and close business associates may become extremely important in situations where no objective data exist to be collected since the technology being developed has no counterpart in the past. This is typically the case with a new-to-the-world technology (Woo et al., 1994).

In some instances, the impetus for technology development stemmed simply from being in the right place at the right time. In the words of a venture manager at FOODCO, 'By chance, I heard about a research project going on at the National Research Centre pursuing similar interests.' In a similar vein, participation in a research conference led to an establishment of joint venture focusing on certain applications of conductive polymers: 'Our conference presentation in New Mexico caught the interest of two leading US scientists. Quite unexpectedly, they wanted to collaborate with us.'

For the technology-based venture developing speciality resins, an unexpected call from the future customer led to a discovery of a whole new product application and market: 'We found our second major product group due to the fact that big manufacturers lost their interest in this business. As a result, customers came to us and asked if we could do it.'

Also unpredictable and somewhat random changes in corporate strategy added to uncertainty in the development of novel technologies. Unexpected changes in corporate strategy were seen to open up new applications for the technology, as was witnessed with the development of conductive polymers. Alternatively, sudden changes in corporate strategy were seen to lead to a tightening of philosophy and later closing of some important windows of opportunities, as we perceived with the ALE technology and conductive polymers. Also the parent corporation's merger with a competitor may represent a chance event increasing the strategic importance of the technology within the parent corporation, as demonstrated by our venture developing the miniaturization technology.

Profiting from Innovation through the Mastery of Technology-based Transactions

Exploration activities, if successful, result in opening up new opportunities for a company to prosper in the form of new products, services or processes. According to conventional wisdom, successful exploration activities lead directly to their exploitation. The fruits of the exploitation activities, in their turn, contribute to the bottom line of a company. Following this logic, our sample corporations do not appear particularly successful. The outcomes of these five technology development projects are summarized at the end of Table 5.1. It is striking that, besides the revenues resulting from divestments, the parent firms appeared to benefit very little from decades of intensive investment in the development of the novel technologies. CHEMCO retained no rights related to the conductive polymer technology. FOODCO decided to keep those applications of immobilization technology in-house that had links to its core businesses, yet, eventually, the development activities were put on the shelf to wait for better times. ENERCO divested most of the applications of the ALE technology, although it did retain its catalyst applications. After the formation of SPIN-OFF COMPANY, BIOCO cut all its ties to the miniaturization technology.

Does this mean that most of these projects failed in the strategic sense? None of them fulfilled the corporate mission, supported its strategic formulation or created any new major business areas for the parent. Nevertheless, all become an important basis for the creation of numerous product applications and new firms. Paradoxically, it seemed, in all instances, that corporations other than the parent were best able to unleash the potential of these technologies. We do not believe that our results could be explained away by biased sample selection, or by bad management practices on the part of our sample corporations. More likely, we suspect that the challenges associated with the development of new-to-the-word technologies require different approaches and mindsets from what we have got used to when operating in more stable and traditional environments. Therefore, we suspect that the success in exploration activities is positively associated with the corporation's ability to form and sustain new network relationships. In addition, we expect that the degree to which the parent firm will be able to cash in on its investments in novel technologies is heavily dependent on its ability to conduct technology-based transactions (licensing, sell-offs, spin-offs) within these networks.

Proposition 4: When developing new-to-the-world technologies, the ability to form and sustain network relationships is positively associated with success in the introduction of new applications of a technology.

Proposition 5: With new-to-the-world technologies, the parent firm's benefits accruing from technology development are more likely to materialize in the form of revenues from technology-based transactions that take place outside the firm, than from internal strategic benefits of building a new business area.

Previous literature has discussed 'the division of labour' in innovative activities, suggesting that small, entrepreneurial firms are strong at creating new product concepts, whereas large, established corporations dominate in their commercialization (see, for example, Rothwell, 1983). Our evidence does not directly support this statement. Rather, it seems to us that moving from one network of contacts to another, per se, helped creating new products, regardless of whether these new networks consisted of small firms, large corporations or universities. By changing their social and organizational context, the developers were able to tap into new combinations of resources. It has been argued elsewhere that new technology-based ventures undergo several ownership changes and thereby become embedded in multiple networks during their lifetime (Lindholm, 1994; Parhankangas,

1999). The results from this study emphasize the boundary-spanning nature of innovation activities and take this line of reasoning even further. We argue that gaining a competency in technology-based transactions and networking is essential for any technology manager under the conditions of extreme ambiguity with limited knowledge of the outcomes of his or her actions. As the uncertainty around the new technology decreases, venture managers may find themselves either unwilling or incapable to make a commitment in the further development of the technology. Thus the ability to let go of an invention and to identify an optimal recipient for its further development may better serve the interests of the parent corporation and the technology-based venture than stubbornly continuing technology development in-house. In the words of the Vice President in R&D of BIOCO,

> If the project had stayed at BIOCO, my guess is that it would have been closed down. There was just not enough support on the part of the headquarters or business units. The patents would have been just sitting there, whether the project would ever have been revitalized, it is hard to say. By then, however, the key people might have left. I mean they are experts in microfluidics, and they came to work for BIOCO, because this was the only company in Europe in this area. Most of these guys are entrepreneurial spirits, young scientists wanting to conquer the world. If you close their project, they'll move on.

The results of our study seem to be in line with Levinthal and March (1993), stating that the fruits of successful exploration are public goods and that they tend to diffuse over populations of organizations. However, our evidence does not fully support their statement according to which the risks and the costs of exploration are private goods, and they tend to be borne by organizations carrying out such initiatives. Judging by the historical data from these five ventures, networking with private and public organizations as well as well-managed ownership changes help organizations share the costs and risks of technology development as well as cashing in on their initial investments.

Conclusions and Discussion

In this chapter we followed the development of five new-to-the-world technologies as they emerged over several decades in a complex, paradoxical, systemic, even messy, real-life context. Our aim was to explore how these ventures shifted from the exploration of new possibilities to the exploitation of recently recognized and acquired competencies, a transition that is the ultimate measure of success for any technology development process.

Our findings not only suggest that exploration and exploitation activities differ in terms of their networking orientation, but also highlight the importance of moving from one social network to another in order to be able to embark on a new exploration path or start the exploitation of previously acquired competencies. In addition, our results give a reason to believe that corporations other than the parent were best able to unleash the potential of these technologies. These results extend and complement the work on organizational structures conducive or detrimental to exploration and exploitation processes. While the focus of previous literature has primarily been on the organization of innovative activities within a single firm, our study clearly indicates developing radically new technologies is a process for subsequent changes in ownership and network membership.

Although our chapter is firmly anchored in the literature of organizational learning, our results have interesting implications for the corporate diversification literature. Our findings tend to refute the assumed rational nature of corporate management, diversification and development (see, for instance, Ramanujam and Varadarajan, 1989; Silverman and Castaldi, 1992). In our study, more of the direction of successful technology-based diversification was found to be dependent on coincidence and luck, rather than strategic (rational) intentions. Stated differently, the success in pursuing certain applications of a novel technology accrues more from being 'in the right place at the right time' than from predicting the right places and times. Personal, informal contacts were seen to play a significant role in helping venture managers 'get lucky' and connect into new constellations of resources, including first customers. In addition, our study contributes to the vast literature on inter-firm networks and alliances. Even though there are some longitudinal studies on the evolution of alliances and networks (see, for instance, Ariño and de la Torre, 1998; Larsson et al., 1998; Kumar and Nti, 1998), the time span covered is too short to help one understand the context of important new-to-the-world technologies. In a similar vein, most studies limit their analysis to the evolution of a single alliance or a network. The special contribution of our study is to analyse the evolution of changes in governance forms over the long term, all viewed in parallel with the technological change process.

It is important to note, however, that our results are based on a longitudinal analysis of radically new technologies developed by large Northern European corporations. Finland and Sweden are known to be the most networked countries in the innovation activities in the European Union (European Commission, 2001). Therefore future studies are called for to confirm the robustness of our findings in different cultural and industrial settings.

Notes

1. For confidentiality reasons, we do not use the real names of the companies or persons in this report.
2. Embeddedness may be defined as the nature, depth and extent of an individual's ties into the environment (Jack and Anderson, 2002).
3. We are fully aware that the more recent approaches to corporate strategy have broken free from the strict rationalism of the early planning school represented by Ansoff (1965). However, even the more incremental or evolutionary schools of strategy tend to treat the behaviour of managers as attempts to adapt to the environment or learn from it. We argue that these perspectives, too, tend to ignore the non-rational nature of behaviour and the concept of coincidence and luck.

References

Abernathy, William J. (1978), *The Productivity Dilemma: Roadblock to Innovation in the Automobile Industry*, Baltimore, MA: Johns Hopkins University Press.
Adler, P.S., B. Goldoftas and D. Levine (1999), 'Flexibility versus efficiency? A case study of model changeovers in the Toyota production system', *Organization Science*, **10**, 43–68.
Ahuja, G. and C.M. Lampert (2001), 'Entrepreneurship in the large corporation: a longitudinal study of how established firms create breakthrough inventions', *Strategic Management Journal*, **22**, 521–43.
Alvarez, S.A. and L.W. Busenitz (2001), 'The entrepreneurship of resource-based theory', *Journal of Management*, **27**, 755–75.
Ansoff, Igor (1965), *Corporate Strategy*, New York: McGraw-Hill.
Argyris, Chris and David A. Schon (1978), *Organizational Learning*, Reading, MA: Addison-Wesley.
Ariño, A. and J. de la Torre (1998), 'Learning from failure: towards an evolutionary model of collaborative ventures', *Organization Science*, **9**(3), 306–25.
Barney, J. (1986), 'Strategic factor markets: expectations, luck and business strategy', *Management Science*, 1231–41.
Benner, M.J. and M.L. Tushman (2003), 'Exploitation, exploration, and process management: the productivity dilemma revisited', *Academy of Management Review*, **28**(2), 238–56.

Bradach, J. (1997), 'Using the plural form of managing restaurant chains', *Administrative Science Quarterly*, **42**, 276–303.

Brown, S.L. and K.M. Eisenhardt (1997), 'The art of continuous change: linking complexity theory and time-paced evolution in relentlessly shifting organizations', *Administrative Science Quarterly*, **47**, 1–34.

Burns, Tom and G.M. Stalker (1961), *The Management of Innovation*, London: Tavistock.

Busenitz, L. and J.B. Barney (1997), 'Differences between entrepreneurs and managers in large organizations: biases and heuristics in strategic decision-making', *Journal of Business Venturing*, **12**, 9–30.

Choi, Y.-R. and D.A. Shepherd (2004), 'Entrepreneurs' decision to exploit opportunities', *Journal of Management*, **30**(3), 377–95.

Chrisman, J.J. and W.E. McMullan (2000), 'A preliminary assessment of outsider assistance as a knowledge resource: the longer-term impact of new venture counselling', *Entrepreneurship Theory and Practice*, **24**(3), 37–53.

Christensen, Clayton M. (1998), *The Innovator's Dilemma: when New Technologies Cause Great Firms to Fail*, Boston: Harvard Business School Press.

Cohen, M. and D. Levinthal (1990), 'Absorptive capacity: a perspective on learning and innovation', *Administrative Science Quarterly*, **35**, 128–52.

Cyert, Richard M. and James G. March (1963), *A Behavioral Theory of the Firm*, Englewood Cliffs, NJ: Prentice-Hall.

Eisenhardt, K.M. (1989), 'Building theories from case study research', *Academy of Management Review*, **14**, 532–50.

European Commission (2001), *Towards a European Research Area: Key Figures 2001*, special edition.

Galbraith, Jay R. (1973), *Designing Complex Organizations*, Reading, MA: Addison-Wesley.

Glaser, Barney G. and Anselm L. Strauss (1967), *The Discovery of Grounded Theory: Strategies for Qualitative Research*, Chicago, IL: Aldine.

Goes, J.B. and S.H. Park (1997), 'Interorganizational links and innovation: the case of hospital services', *Academy of Management Journal*, **40**(3), 673–96.

Granovetter, Mark (1973), 'The strength of weak ties', *American Journal of Sociology*, **78**, 1360–80.

Grant, R. (1996), 'Toward a knowledge-based theory of the firm', *Strategic Management Journal*, Winter Special Issue, 109–22.

Gulati, R. (1995), 'Social structure and alliance formation patterns: a longitudinal analysis', *Administrative Science Quarterly*, **40**, 619–52.

Hannan, M.T. and J. Freeman (1977), 'The population ecology of organizations', *American Journal of Sociology*, **82**, 929–64.

Hedberg, B., P.C. Nystrom and W.H. Starbuck (1976), 'Camping on seesaws: prescriptions for a self-designing organization', *Administrative Science Quarterly*, **21**, 41–65.

Holland, John H. (1975), *Adaptation in Natural and Artificial Systems*, Ann Arbor, MI: University of Michigan Press.

Jack, S.L. and A.R. Anderson (2002), 'The effects of embeddedness on the entrepreneurial process', *Journal of Business Venturing*, **17**, 467–87.

Kogut, B. and U. Zander (1992), 'Knowledge of the firm, combinative capabilities, and the replication of technology', *Organization Science*, **3**(3), 383–97.

Kumar, R. and K.O. Nti (1998), 'Differential learning and interaction in alliance dynamics: a process and outcome discrepancy model', *Organization Science*, **9**(3), 356–67.

Kuran, T. (1988), 'The tenacious past: theories of personal and collective conservatism', *Journal of Economic Behavior*, **10**, 143–71.

Langley, A. (1999), 'Strategies for theorizing from process data', *Academy of Management Review*, **24**(4), 691–710.

Larsson, R., L. Bengtsson, K. Henriksson and J. Sparks (1998), 'The interorganizational learning dilemma: collective knowledge development in strategic alliances', *Organization Science*, **9**(3), 285–305.

Lawrence, P.R. and J.W. Lorsch (1967), 'Managing differentiation and integration', Graduate School of Business Administration, Harvard University.

Lee, C., K. Lee and J.M. Pennings (2001), 'Internal capabilities, external networks, and performance: a study of technology-based ventures', *Strategic Management Journal*, **22**, 615–40.

Levinthal, D.A. and J.G. March (1993), 'The myopia of learning', *Strategic Management Journal*, **14** (Winter Special Issue), 95–112.

Lindholm, Åsa (1994), 'The economics of technology-related ownership changes. A study of innovativeness and growth through acquisitions and spin-offs', doctoral dissertation, Chalmers University of Technology, Department of Industrial Management and Economics, Gothenburg, Sweden.

Manning, K., S. Birley and D. Norburn (1989), 'Developing a new venture's strategy', *Entrepreneurship Theory and Practice*, **14**(1), 67–76.

March, J.G. (1991), 'Exploration and exploitation in organizational learning', *Organization Science*, **2**(1), 71–87.

March, James G. and Herbert A. Simon (1958), *Organizations*, New York: John Wiley.

Parhankangas, Annaleena (1999), 'Disintegration of technological competencies: an empirical study of divestments through spin-off arrangements', doctoral dissertation, Acta Polytechnica Scandinavica, Series 99 (Finnish Academy of Technology, Espoo).

Parkhe, A. (1993), ' "Messy" research, methodological predispositions and theory development in international joint ventures', *Academy of Management Review*, **18**, 227–68.

Perrow, Charles (1986), *Complex Organizations: A Critical Essay*, Glenview, IL: Scott, Foresman and Company.

Ramanujam, V. and P. Varadarajan (1989), 'Research on corporate diversification: a synthesis', *Strategic Management Journal*, **10**, 523–51.

Rice, M. (2002), 'Co-production of business assistance in business incubators: an exploratory study', *Journal of Business Venturing*, **17**, 163–87.

Rothwell, R. (1983), 'Innovation and firm size: a case for dynamic complementarity; or, is small really so beautiful?', *Journal of General Management*, **8**(3), 5–25.

Schoonhoven, C.B., K.M. Eisenhardt and K. Lyman (1990), 'Speeding products to market: waiting time to first product introduction in new firms', *Administrative Science Quarterly*, **35**, 177–207.

Schumpeter, Joseph (1968), *The Theory of Economic Development*, Cambridge, MA: Harvard University Press (first published 1911).

Shane, S. (2000), 'Prior knowledge and the discovery of entrepreneurial opportunities', *Organization Science*, **11**, 448–69.

Shaver, K.G. and L.R. Scott (1991), 'Person, process, and choice: the psychology of new venture creation', *Entrepreneurship Theory and Practice*, **16**(2), 23–42.

Silverman, M. and R.M. Castaldi (1992), 'Antecedents and propensity for diversification: a focus on small banks', *Journal of Small Business Management*, **April**, 42–52.

Smith, K.G., S.J. Carrol and S.J. Ashford (1995), 'Intra- and inter-organizational cooperation: toward a research agenda', *Academy of Management Journal*, **19**(1), 7–23.

Strauss, Anselm L. (1987), *Qualitative Analysis for Social Scientists*, New York: Cambridge University Press.

Tushman, Michael L. and Charles O'Reilly (1997), *Winning through Innovation*, Boston, MA: Harvard Business School Press.

Tushman, Michael L. and Elaine Romanelli (1985), 'Organizational evolution: a metamorphosis model of convergence and reorientation', in L.L. Cummings and Barry M. Staw (eds), *Research in Organizational Behavior*, vol. 7, Greenwich, CT: JAI Press, pp. 171–222.

User, A. (1971), 'Technological change and capital formation', in Nathan Rosenberg (ed.), *Economics of Technological Change*, Harmondsworth: Penguin Books.

Uzzi, B. (1996), 'The sources and consequences of embeddedness for the economic performance of organizations', *American Sociological Review*, **61**, 674–98.

Uzzi, B. (1997), 'Social structure and competition in interfirm networks: the paradox of embeddedness', *Administrative Science Quarterly*, **42**, 35–67.

Watzlawick, Paul, John Weakland and Richard Fisch (1974), *Change: Principles of Problem Formulation and Problem Resolution*, New York: W.W. Norton and Company.

Wilson, John G. (1966), 'Innovation in organization: notes toward a theory', in John D. Thompson (ed.), *Approaches to Organizational Design*, Pittsburgh, PA: University of Pittsburgh Press, pp. 193–218.

Wong, P.L-K. and P. Ellis (2002), 'Social ties and partner identification in Sino-Hong Kong international joint ventures', *Journal of International Business Studies*, **33**(2), 267–89.

Woo, C.Y., U. Daellenbach and C. Nicholls-Nixon (1994), 'Theory building in the presence of "randomness": the case of venture creation and performance', *Journal of Management*, **31**(4), 507–24.

Yin, Robert K. (1984), *Case Study Research: Design and Methods*, Newbury Park, CA: Sage.

Young, N. (2002), 'Social embeddedness and entrepreneurial opportunity: the case of African Americans', working paper, University of St. Thomas, Graduate School of Business.

6 Fostering entrepreneurial firms: recognizing and adapting radical innovation through corporate venture capital investments

Behrend Freese, Thomas Keil and Thorsten Teichert

Introduction

Technological change is often an incremental, cumulative process punctuated by short revolutionary periods in the form of discontinuities (Tushman and Anderson, 1986). Some of these discontinuities are major technological and market shifts that are so significant that no change in scale, efficiency or design can keep existing technologies and business models competitive (Anderson and Tushman, 1990; Tushman and Anderson, 1986), thus rending the competitive advantages of incumbents obsolete and challenging them to develop new competencies to retain their market lead. Such radical innovations frequently arise from outside an incumbent's industry (Tushman and Anderson, 1986) or are initiated by start-ups created to capitalize on rival technological paradigms (Shane, 2001).

Faced with radical innovation, incumbents often do not recognize and adapt to the changes taking place on the fringes of their industries (Henderson, 1993; Henderson and Clark, 1990). These problems arise from incumbents' inability to recognize emerging technologies in a timely fashion and to develop (or acquire) the skills necessary to create and exploit these technologies. To improve their ability to recognize and adopt technological change incumbents have reverted to a variety of mechanisms ranging from internal R&D activities, corporate venturing, joining alliances and technology development consortia, to acquiring other companies that control rival technologies. More recently, some incumbents have also made use of corporate venture capital (CVC) investments to monitor radical technological change in and outside their industries (Keil, 2002). CVC investments refer to established companies' participation in the private equity market by providing start-ups with funding in return for equity positions (Gompers and Lerner, 1998). For example, Intel, Dell, Siemens and Nokia have developed formal CVC programmes in which they provide funding and related services to start-ups in return for an equity stake. These investments show the growing recognition that start-ups are often the vanguard of technological change and incumbents should study these firms to track promising and often rival technologies across multiple fields (for example, Winters and Murfin, 1988). Despite the increased popularity of CVC investments as a mechanism for recognizing and adopting radical innovations, we lack a solid conceptual understanding of ways CVC programmes can help to address the challenges of radical innovation.

In this chapter, we aim at addressing this gap in the literature by analysing how the demands from three key stakeholders of a CVC unit (the corporate parent, the start-up it invests in, and other actors in the private equity market) create challenges in three areas. We show how CVCs need to reconcile these stakeholder demands in the areas of (1) balancing financial versus strategic objectives, (2) managing knowledge transfer and value added, and (3) balancing autonomy with operational integration. In particular, we argue that CVC units need to focus on financial returns within a strategic mandate and that learning in CVC investments takes place in a triangular relationship between the start-up, the CVC unit and mainstream business units of the corporation. This triangular configuration allows CVC units to act as a knowledge broker, bridging the social networks of start-ups and venture capitalists on the one hand and the incumbent on the other hand. To act effectively as a knowledge broker, the CVC unit has to maintain a relatively high level of autonomy. We show how this configuration allows incumbents to overcome some of the challenges that they face when confronted with radical innovations. Our theoretical perspective further allows us to explain some of the inherent challenges of the CVC model and in particular of recognizing and adopting radical innovations through CVC investments.

Our chapter is structured as follows. In the next section we briefly introduce CVC programmes as a response to the challenges of radical innovation. Then we investigate the perspectives of the three main stakeholders and their demands from CVC units. Next we discuss how these stakeholder demands are reconciled in three areas. On the basis of this analysis, we identify and discuss challenges for the CVC model. We conclude with implications for theory and practice.

Incumbents and Radical Innovation

Incumbents' failure to recognize and exploit radical innovation
Faced with radical innovation, incumbents often do not recognize and adapt to the changes taking place on the fringes of their industries (Henderson, 1993; Henderson and Clark, 1990). These problems arise from incumbents' inability to recognize emerging technologies in a timely fashion and to develop (or to acquire) the skills necessary to create and exploit these technologies. Radical innovation is often based on a different set-up of engineering and scientific principles and requires incumbents to process different kinds of information (Henderson and Clark, 1990). Existing competencies of the firm act as information filters that effectively blind the incumbent to information that does not fit into existing mental models and knowledge schemata (Bettis and Prahalad, 1995; Levinthal and March, 1993). When radical innovation calls dominant mental models held in the firm into question (Bettis and Prahalad, 1995; Levinthal and March, 1993), the firm might even actively suppress any such information (Leonard-Barton, 1995).

Even when incumbents recognize radical innovations they frequently fail to adopt and exploit them. Research on radical innovation has shown that, in the light of radical innovations, incumbents often prefer to invest in incremental innovation to enhance current assets and gain a larger market share rather than adopt radical innovations which could cause current technological assets and competencies to become partially obsolete (Utterback, 1994). Incumbents' failure to invest in developing radically new technology is often driven by a focus on existing customers (Christensen and Bower, 1996). When radical innovation addresses emerging markets instead of the needs of existing customers, incumbents rationally focus on serving existing customers and improving existing capabilities instead of focusing on the new technology. Even when incumbents invest in exploiting radical innovations their efforts fail to reach the level of new entrants. Henderson (1993) points out that frequently the research productivity of established firms pursuing radical innovation is significantly lower than that of entrants and therefore start-ups create or capitalize on emerging radical technologies (Shane, 2001) while incumbents fail to keep pace with these developments.

Mechanisms to address radical innovation

The academic literature has discussed a broad variety of mechanisms that incumbents can use to improve their ability to recognize, adopt and exploit radical innovation. One group of authors stresses internal organizational structures and processes that allow the corporation to separate radical innovation projects from incremental research and development. Under such headings as 'innovation hub' (Leifer et al., 2001), 'corporate venturing divisions' (Chesbrough, 2000) or 'ambidextrous organizations' (Tushman and O'Reilly, 1997) several authors have argued for dedicated organizational units within the organization to support radical innovation in the corporation.

A second set of authors stresses the use of interorganizational relationships to complement internal innovative activities. Incumbents use these relationships to gain access to external sources of radical innovations. Alliances (for example, Dussauge, Garrette and Mitchell, 2000), joint ventures (for example, Shenkar and Li, 1999), and acquisitions (for example, Roberts and Berry, 1985) are important approaches that incumbents frequently use to acquire knowledge and resources from these sources.

During the late 1990s, corporations increasingly started to use CVC investments (Chesbrough, 2002) as a mechanism to monitor technological and market development and to gain an early window on emerging technologies (Chesbrough, 2002; Rind, 1981; Siegel, Siegel and MacMillan, 1988). CVC investments are in most corporations conducted by a separately managed unit (Block and MacMillan, 1993). CVC investments are typically syndicated with venture capital firms (Birkinshaw, van Basten Batenburg and Murray, 2002); that is, several firms jointly invest and thereby share financial risks, pre- and post-investment monitoring and financial returns (Bygrave, 1988; Podolny, 2001). Aside from the financial relationship with the start-up, investments typically provide the corporation with strong access to the start-up. Through proprietary relationships the incumbent can connect to start-ups that are likely to develop and introduce radical innovations. Start-ups offer learning opportunities to incumbents and expose them to new technological paradigms and evolving capabilities that could be applied in adopting and exploiting radical innovation.

While research repeatedly argues for the potential advantages of CVC investments as a mechanism to support early access to emerging radical innovations (for example, Chesbrough, 2002; Keil, 2002; McNally, 1997), we have only limited research helping us to understand how a CVC unit should be structured to support the recognition and adoption of radical innovation. We propose that analysing CVC activities through the lens of three important stakeholders allows us to better understand the necessary trade-offs that CVC units face and to explain some of the challenges CVC units have faced in practice.

Stakeholders in CVC Investments

In its operations, a CVC unit has to manage relationships with start-ups, the corporate parent and other participants in the private equity market. Each of these stakeholders is important for the success of the CVC unit but each creates slightly different demands that the CVC unit has to balance in its activities.

Corporate parent relationship

The first stakeholder relationship the CVC unit has to manage is with its parent corporation. Most corporations enter CVC investments with both strategic and financial objectives but strategic objectives often prevail (Chesbrough, 2002; Siegel et al., 1988; Sykes, 1990). Strategic objectives can cover a wide range, including learning about new markets and technologies, creating demand for existing products or scouting for acquisition targets, but learning about new technologies has been reported as a prominent objective in many previous studies (Block and MacMillan, 1993; Chesbrough, 2002; Keil, 2002; Maula, 2001; Siegel et al., 1988).

A corporate venture capital unit is connected to the parent company through multiple links. Financial funding commitment of the parent company results in a strong governance connection and duty of financial reporting for the corporate venture capital unit. At the same time the corporate venture capital unit gains access to executives and the attention of the parent company's top management. This is an important relationship to raise attention to emerging technologies and associated radical innovation.

In addition to links with top management, the corporate venture capitalist needs active support from the different business units and R&D function of the parents' corporation. Major business units and the R&D function are able to transfer resources like expert knowledge and support due diligence processes to assess venture technologies as well as to inform the corporate venture unit about current and planned developments within the organization. At the same time, linkages of corporate venture capitalists to research and development and business units are important for infusing information about emerging radical innovation and facilitating knowledge transfer to these units.

While these linkages to different parts of the corporate parent are important for the operations of the corporate venture capital unit, they expose the CVC unit to potentially conflicting objectives of different business units. For instance, operating units often have relatively short time horizons, might not be able to recognize the importance of emerging radical technologies, or might even try actively to suppress competing technologies. Furthermore, operating units or the corporate parent might have little interest in developing a fragile new venture and might try to internalize technologies from start-ups the venture capital unit invests in and so exhausts knowledge of (outlearn) the venture.

Start-up relationship

The second stakeholder group the CVC unit faces are start-ups it invests in. In the private equity market, new ventures seek growth capital as well as value added services (Maula and Murray, 2002). Traditional venture capitalists provide start-ups with services such as providing the entrepreneur team with a sounding board, helping the firm obtain further sources of equity financing, interfacing with the investor group, monitoring financial and operating performance, and helping their portfolio firms to attract alternative sources of debt financing (MacMillan, Kulow and Khoylian, 1989). To be attractive to start-ups, CVC units might provide complementary sources of value added that traditional venture capitalists lack (Maula, 2001; McNally, 1997). Start-ups frequently seek resources such as access to distribution channels, technological support and managerial expertise from a corporate investor (Maula and Murray, 2002). Large corporations often have deep technological know-how that neither the start-up nor the traditional venture capitalists possess. Since start-ups frequently suffer from lack of legitimacy in product markets, corporate investors can provide important endorsement in these markets, thus lending their credibility to the young firm (Stuart, Hoang and Hybels, 1999).

While CVC units can be value added investors for start-ups, the start-up might perceive potential threats in the relationship with the CVC unit. Start-ups could perceive the risk that the corporation might strive to maximize, not the economic value of their portfolio firms, but that of their parent company: for instance, to minimize the costs of later acquiring firms from its portfolio (Maula, 2001). The firm might further perceive the risk that the corporation would use the investment as a stepping stone to develop internal activities if the emerging business area which is the target of the start-up becomes commercially important (Keil, 2002; Maula and Murray, 2002; McGrath, 1997). In this regard, the start-up firm might perceive the risk of being outlearned in a too close relationship (Hamel, 1991). These potential threats might prohibit a CVC investment or a close relationship between the CVC unit and a start-up.

VC relationship
Beyond the aforementioned two stakeholders, CVC units face the demands of other actors in the private equity market. In most investments, venture capitalists coinvest with other venture investors to share some of the financial risk. Coinvesting also helps to share the burden of due diligence and monitoring. In venture investments, VCs are forced to make decisions based on limited information provided by the start-up. This can create adverse selection problems of 'hidden information' and moral hazard problems of 'hidden action' that can only be overcome by significant efforts in pre-investment due diligence and post-investment monitoring (Amit, Brander and Zott, 1998). In syndicated investments, venture capitalists can avoid some of these costs by relying on the efforts of their syndicate partners.

Investment syndicates are typically formed by a lead investor who invites other potential investors. Syndicated investments account for over 50 per cent of all venture capital funds invested in entrepreneurial companies in the United States (Wright and Lockett, 2003). Since investment syndication require a substantial amount of trust among the syndicate partners, over time, VCs have formed tightly coupled networks (Bygrave, 1988). These networks are often clustered by geographic and industry boundaries, as US venture capital research shows (Sorenson and Stuart, 2001). More importantly, these venture capital networks are highly exclusive and positioning is critical for the financial performance of venture capitalists providing them with information, resource and status benefits. As a result attractive deals are often shared only among an exclusive group of centrally positioned venture capitalists. Lack of such a central position might translate into access to inferior deal flow, for instance, hampering the CVCs' ability to recognize technological discontinuities (Maula, Keil and Zahra, 2003). This might constitute a major problem to CVC units, as they regularly entered the venture capital industry during the late 1990s (Maula, 2001) and therefore often lack the investment track record and central position of traditional venture capitalists.

To coinvest with successful corporate venture capitalists a CVC unit has to fulfil the financial return requirements of these venture capitalists and provide additional value added to become an attractive syndicate partner. In particular, the CVC has to confirm with the expectations of other venture capitalists in respect of their requested high rates of return on the investment as well as with their limited time horizon of five to seven years.

Within this time period, the coinvesting partners seek to exit the investment through either an initial public offering or a trade sale to a corporation.

Reconciling stakeholder demands

Building on the three stakeholder relationships discussed above, it becomes clear that corporate venturing investments constitute a complex political system that serves to integrate differing objectives. Stakeholders follow their own objectives and compare benefits and costs of their voluntary participation with those of alternative engagements. Since all stakeholders are needed for ensuring long-term success, the CVC must adjust its set of objectives by integrating stakeholders' different objectives. This requires balancing immediate against long-term effects and considering economic, technological and socio-organizational effects for the participating partners of the joint undertaking (Brockhoff and Teichert, 1995).

According to the above, three areas emerge in which stakeholder objectives and demands either complement each other or create conflicts for the corporation. First, the CVC unit needs to balance and reconcile strategic and financial demands imposed upon the programme by the corporate parent and the private equity market. Second, it needs to manage the relationships with the start-up and the corporate parent to ensure balanced knowledge transfer to the corporate parent and creation of value added for the start-up. Third, the CVC unit needs to balance parent firm demands for operational integration with demands for operational autonomy by the start-up. CVC units need to address these dimensions to utilize successfully corporate venture capital investment to recognize and adopt radical innovations.

Strategic versus Financial Objectives in CVC Programmes

CVC units face the challenge of balancing strategic and financial goals. Traditional venture capitalists are solely focused on financial returns as their investment criterion and judge syndication opportunities with corporate investors accordingly. In contrast, the corporate parent is driven by a combination of strategic and financial goals and thus it might trade off financial return against perceived strategic returns. For instance, from 1968 to 1976, GE was using a CVC investment fund (GEVENCO) to experiment with diversification opportunities. During that time its operating mandate was to put GE into new businesses, not to make a profit. Similarly, INTEL has used a hurdle rate for its strategic investments, but does not select investment opportunities strictly according to a return on investment criterion.

Compromising return on investment for strategic criteria can make a CVC unit an unattractive syndication partner for traditional venture capitalists. This might lead to inferior deal flow that ultimately might as well compromise the desired strategic benefits. For instance, GEVENCO failed to reach both financial and strategic targets and was reorganized as a profit-oriented unit in 1976. It became a financial success only by becoming more independent from the strategic agenda of the corporate parent (Hardymon, De Nino and Salter, 1983).

While a too dominating strategic objective might compromise the quality of the deal flow, a too weak strategic agenda might compromise the survival of the CVC unit. The value of venture capital portfolios typically follows a J-curve (Gompers and Lerner, 1999) that is, investments are made during the early stage of a portfolio while returns are only realized several years later when exits occur. This leads to negative cash flows during the early period of the fund. Without strategic benefits to show from early on, CVC units might be discontinued before they have the opportunity to create financial value (Gompers and Lerner, 1998), in particular during an economic downturn, as experienced after 2000. To the contrary, the corporate investor might become unattractive for start-ups without sufficient relatedness to the operations of the corporate parent, as the venture can only be provided with limited added value.

Financial and strategic objectives might also conflict at the exit stage of investments. When venture capitalists aim to exit the investment through an initial public offering or a trade sale, their only goal is to maximize the price achieved for the venture. In contrast, corporate venture capital units might keep an option to acquire the portfolio company if it proves to be strategically valuable from a technological or market perspective (Kann, 2000; Keil, 2002). In such a situation, the CVC unit faces a conflict of interest between its objective to maximize its own financial return and its corporate parent's objective to minimize the cost of acquiring the start-up. To avoid such conflict of interest situations, trade sales to the corporate parent are extremely rare (Maula, 2001).

Corporations and their CVC units strike this balance by using two forms of investment policies (Keil, 2002). One model is to tie investments of the CVC unit to sponsorship by an operational unit, for instance through co-funding the investment or through entering into a commercial relationship with the start-up. Accordingly, Siemens Corporation's Mustang Fund has made investments contingent upon a commercial relationship with Siemens' telecommunications business unit. Similarly, Novell aligns Novell Ventures' investments with corporate strategy by requiring its venture group to collaborate with an equity review team of senior employees from various functional areas. With crucial input from the business units, this team determines whether promising start-up companies can create both strategic and financial value (van der Oord et al., 2000). Having to gain approval and sponsorship from business units forces the CVC unit to focus on strategic benefits for the business unit. However, this strong form of operational binding might hamper recognition of radical innovations since the same innovation filters that prohibit a business unit recognizing and adopting the technology directly might hamper the gaining of support for a CVC investment. Therefore, a less restrictive set of investment policies has been adopted by some CVC units, such as Nokia Venture Partners. In this model, the CVC unit focuses solely on financial investment criteria. Strategic benefits are ensured by defining an investment focus that supports the strategic agenda of the corporation. Earlier findings show that corporate venture capital programmes bound to the portfolio companies' financial success support both parties' interests (Siegel et al., 1988; Block and MacMillan, 1993). Financial investment goals and investments in the financially most promising companies give a window to the best venture companies with promising products and reduce conflicts of interest (Maula, 2001). This model seems to provide the required flexibility for the recognition of radical innovations since the CVC unit can step outside of the capabilities and mental frameworks that guide business unit decision making.

Technology transfer and value added
The CVC unit needs to manage the relationship with the corporate parent and the start-up to ensure simultaneously that the corporate parent receives strategic benefits through knowledge transfer and that the start-up receives value added from the corporation (see

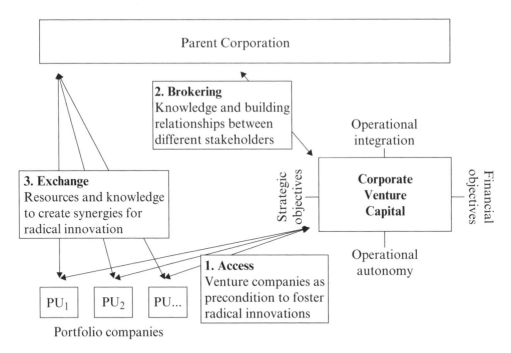

*Figure 6.1   Triangulation between CVC unit, portfolio companies and parent
corporation*

Figure 6.1). Corporate venture capital activities take place in a triangular relationship
between the start-up companies, the corporate venture capital unit and the business units
of the parent corporation in which the CVC unit plays the role of a broker between the
start-up and the parent corporation (Hargadon, 2002). This triangulation is an important
precondition to support access to both actors, to build trustworthy relationships and to
facilitate the exchange between the corporation and the start-up.

To facilitate the knowledge transfer and value creation processes, the CVC needs to gain
rich access to the start-up and the corporate parent. Corporate venture capitalists as
active investors usually take a board seat in portfolio firms, thoroughly monitor the
company's development and build tight relationships to the business leader. Board meetings are not a place to learn exclusively about the company, but rather to meet as well
board members of different organizations and positions. The CVC unit is equally dependent upon trusted relationships to the parent corporation. Access to corporate resources
or information often requires strong social networks in the corporation and informal
support from business units.

To ensure knowledge transfer but also creation of value added for the corporation
requires strong interaction between the three actors. The degree to which incumbents learn
about new opportunities and exchange knowledge is a function of the extent of their participation in relationships (Levinthal and March, 1993). CVC units might employ a wide
variety of mechanisms to ensure interaction. These mechanisms range from participation
on the board of the start-up, developing joint projects between start-ups and business
units, establishing knowledge transfer and integration committees, holding face-to-face

meetings with top management, and participating in venture fairs (for example, Dushnitsky and Lenox, 2002; Keil, 2002). For instance, Motorola improves information transfer between the corporation and its portfolio of venture investment companies by using a knowledge transfer team that is charged with developing relationships between each start-up company and the parent corporation. Supervised by an investment professional, each team comprises a technical expert and a product manager from one of the corporation's related business units (van der Oord et al., 2000).

Despite the need for strong interaction, the CVC unit also needs to insulate the start-up from the corporate parent and vice versa. When start-ups possess valuable knowledge, they face the threat of being outlearned by the corporation (Hamel, 1991). To protect its investment but also to protect the corporation from legal action, the CVC unit needs to manage interactions so that knowledge does not spill over inavertedly. For instance, in its investment in Berkeley Networks, Intel Corp. limited its interactions with the venture to avoid its engineers' copying the architecture that Berkeley Networks was developing (Lane and Chesbrough, 2000). Managing such an insulation of the start-ups from threats of being outlearned is important to avoid a negative reputation in the private equity market. Failure to do so can hamper a firm's ability to gain access to innovative start-ups. For instance, Microsoft has over the years suffered from such a negative reputation. For instance, in one of its investments it co-developed a computer networking product in cooperation with Citrix. After the development proved successful, Microsoft notified Citrix that it might develop a competing product (Petreley, 1997). The loss of reputation that Microsoft has suffered has forced the company to take a more careful approach in the private equity market, as Mr Maffei, chief financial officer of Microsoft, points out: 'Our investment strategy of the last few years is an explicit acknowledgement that Microsoft has no great lock on innovative ideas' (Red Herring, 1998).

Overall, the CVC unit's role as a broker between the start-up and the corporate parent resembles the role of a knowledge broker as introduced by Hargadon and Sutton (Hargadon, 2002; Hargadon and Sutton, 1997). Radical innovation often requires the combination of new knowledge with past knowledge to solve existing problems. This process usually takes place in individuals and groups by bridging multiple knowledge sources and moving ideas from where they are known to where they are not known (Hargadon, 2002). To foster radical innovation, corporate venture needs (1) to access distinct sources of knowledge and resources in different social networks, (2) to recognize valuable knowledge and resources, (3) to learn the knowledge and (4) to transfer the knowledge to business units where it is most valuable (Hargadon, 2002). This process can create a potential for synergies that can be exploited in a cooperative interorganizational relationship between the two firms and therefore the parent corporation can benefit from alliances with entrepreneurial firms. In this process the CVC unit can draw from several sources. Brokered knowledge can derive from the relationships with portfolio companies, from business plan screening, due diligence in venture companies, collaboration with independent venture capital, and monitoring the entrepreneurial developments through venture capital networks and venture capital associations (Maula, 2001; Kann, 2000; Sykes, 1990; Winters and Murfin, 1988).

Managing conflicting corporate agendas and autonomy
From an organizational perspective the corporate venture capital unit needs to balance autonomy with organizational integration. Traditional venture capital funds are organized

around managing partners that have large investment decision authority (Gompers and Lerner, 1999). Decision making in private equity markets is therefore often rapid and informal (Chesbrough, 2000). In comparison, decision making in most large corporations can be characterized as more hierarchical, slower and more formal (for example, Chesbrough, 2000). In addition, corporate decision making is often characterized as a political process in which different business unit agendas compete for resources (Henderson and Leleux, 2002). To be effective investors in the private equity market, CVC units would need to maintain a high degree of autonomy. Some corporate venture capital units have established such autonomy, for instance, by setting themselves up as limited partnerships with the corporation acting as the sole limited partner. Nokia Venture Partners, for instance, have gone so far as inviting other corporations and financial institutions as additional limited partners. Given the financial interests and right of multiple limited partners, the corporate parent has less opportunity to influence the decision making of the CVC unit to discontinue its operations, allowing the CVC unit to position itself in the private equity market as relatively independent. In line with this argument, previous studies have found that a higher level of corporate venture autonomy is associated with more successful corporate venture capital activity (Siegel et al., 1988) and with greater financial returns (Block and MacMillan, 1993; Kann, 2000).

While a high degree of autonomy allows the CVC unit to make rapid decisions, it limits its ability to participate in corporate decision-making processes. To be effective in influencing conflicting agendas of business units requires tighter integration into the corporation (Keil, 2002). Tighter operational integration might allow the CVC unit, for instance, to avoid direct competition with business unit activities and might help to manage the competition for financial resources. On the contrary, loosening the operational integration might also sever the linkages with business units that are necessary to realize strategic returns, for instance, through the access to resources of the parent corporation. Less linked corporate venture capital units are more dependent upon strong personal social connections to the parent company to keep business units collaborative. Too high autonomy might also sever linkages with top management that are necessary. Without these linkages support might become arbitrary and short-term, hampering the CVC unit's ability to put innovative ideas into action. Without strong support through the top management to overcome internal obstacles within the corporate parent, as with for instance the refusal of external technologies (or knowledge) by business units, CVC will not be able to develop its whole potential strategic contribution. Thus strong executive support is a precondition to overcoming internal resistance in infusing external knowledge and gaining attention for radical innovation.

The degree of necessary operational integration is likely to depend on the type of investments sought by the CVC unit (Burgelman, 1984). Dushnitsky and Lenox (2002) argue that most corporate venture capital investments do not compete with internal corporate R&D, but rather complement internal R&D. For such complementary ventures, operational integration of the CVC unit should be beneficial since it facilitates the operational cooperation between the venture and the parent corporation. In addition, strategic agendas of business units become more transparent with tighter integration, thus the CVC unit more easily understands which investment opportunities have the potential to complement the corporation.

If the CVC unit is focusing on identifying radical innovations in the vicinity of the incumbent's industry, tight operational integration might be disadvantageous for at least three reasons. First, radical innovations are likely not to fit with existing technologies or business models. Too tight integration might bias the CVC unit towards the technologies and business models currently held in the corporation. Thus the CVC unit might fail to recognize these innovations. Second, adopting and exploiting radical innovations requires that the firm can at least invest in technologies that have the potential to cannibalize the existing resource base of the corporation. Being tightly integrated with business units might give these business units the means actively to suppress competing technologies. Finally, tight integration and resulting conflicts of interest might hamper investments in ventures pursuing radical innovation with the potential to cannibalize existing technologies held by the corporation. Previous research has argued that, in the case of competing technologies, entrepreneurs prefer independent venture capitalists (Hellmann, 2002) not to conjure up direct competition with the corporations business units. The more independent a CVC unit is perceived to be, the smaller this risk might be perceived in the market.

Analysing weaknesses of the CVC model and radical innovation

Our arguments regarding the challenges of reconciling stakeholder demands allow us to reinterpret previous findings regarding the weaknesses and to further analyse the suitability of CVC as a mechanism to address radical innovation in an incumbent's industry.

Explaining earlier findings

Several studies have questioned the financial viability of the CVC model. Some studies have suggested that returns on investments in start-ups frequently fail to meet corporate expectations (Henderson and Leleux, 2002). Others have found that returns of CVC funds do not match those of independent venture funds (Gompers and Lerner, 1998). Our discussion suggests that many of these disappointing results stem from a failure to balance strategic and financial objectives. In line with this argument, empirical research has shown that competing objectives are among the most prominent causes of failure of CVC units (Sykes, 1990). CVC programmes with a well-defined strategic focus appear to be as stable as traditional independent venture organizations and seem to achieve financial success (Gompers and Lerner, 1998; Gompers and Lerner, 1999).

A second frequent criticism stresses the cyclicality of corporate engagements in corporate venture capital. While corporate venture capital investments exploded during the second half of the 1990s, a large number of corporations have discontinued their CVC programmes during the years following the bursting of the Internet bubble (Henderson and Leleux, 2002). Our analysis suggests that the design and objective setting has in many CVC units failed to incorporate the demands and dynamics of stakeholders such as the private equity market and start-ups that have fundamentally different time horizons than large corporations (Kanter, 1985).

Some CVC programmes have also faced acceptance difficulties among entrepreneurs and venture capitalists (Hardymon et al., 1983). While there are clear benefits from a relationship with the corporate venture capitalists for start-ups (Maula, 2001), some CVC funds have failed to address potential concerns of venture capitalists regarding conflicts of interest, or of start-ups regarding risks of being outlearned. Balancing these concerns is an important factor that could make a CVC unit more effective in the private equity market and ultimately for the corporation.

CVC and radical innovation

Our analysis helps us to better understand how CVC units can be used to enhance an incumbent's ability to recognize and adopt radical innovation. First of all, the positioning as a knowledge broker between start-ups pursuing radical innovation and the corporate parent suggests that the CVC model is suitable for addressing some of the information filtering problems of incumbents. The literature of innovation has shown that specialized personnel such as technological gatekeepers, specialized organizational arrangements such as transfer groups (Katz and Allen, 1988) and mediating groups such as knowledge brokers (Hargadon, 2002) can have a significant effect on the transfer of information and innovation between organizations. By setting up an independent CVC unit, the corporation can create a unit that is less bound by existing technologies, capabilities and business models. To be an effective monitor of markets and technologies, the CVC unit should possess relatively large autonomy. Furthermore, investment policies should not link investments too closely to the short-term needs of business units. The more the CVC unit is designed to operate according to the demands of the private equity market, the more likely it will be able to access high-quality deals helping it to identify potentially threatening technologies. This calls for focusing on financial returns as an investment criterion. To ensure strategic relevance of deals made by the CVC unit, the investment focus in such a set-up has to be clearly defined and frequently updated according to the changing strategic priorities of the corporation. The challenge of such a market monitoring set-up is that the CVC unit might fail to create strategic value for the corporation, since autonomy might lead to isolation of the CVC unit. Thus strong social networks to the parent corporation are necessary in order to be able to infuse knowledge into key processes of the corporate parent.

Discussion and Conclusions

In this chapter we have discussed corporate venture capital investments as an instrument to recognize and adopt radical innovation. We have argued that, for successful CVC activities, the demands of corporate parents, start-ups and the private equity market need to be reconciled. CVC units need to balance strategic and financial objectives, need to exploit their knowledge broker position to facilitate knowledge transfer to the corporate parent and create value added for the start-up, and need to balance autonomy with operational integration. Our arguments suggest that, by addressing these areas, corporations can create CVC units that can enhance their ability to address radical innovation.

Implications for theory

Our arguments inform two main bodies of literature. Literature on radical innovation has been dominated by studies that have focused on mechanisms internal to the corporation. While these studies have been valuable in improving our understanding of the barriers to radical innovation and have helped to increase incumbents' ability to renew themselves, their inward focus is a serious limitation. Even if incumbents increase their ability to create radical innovation, a large fraction of innovations originate outside of the boundaries of the incumbent, making it necessary to monitor and tap these sources of potential disruptions. The increasing complexity of the innovation process (Brusoni, Prencipe and Pavitt, 2001; Ritter and Gemünden, 2003) is likely to further amplify this trend.

Therefore incumbents need effective processes to recognize potentially threatening innovations in their environment and to adopt these. While previous research on interorganizational relationships has analysed some of these mechanisms, we still lack a solid understanding of the alternative mechanisms and their strength and weaknesses. We suggest that CVC is such a mechanism that incumbents can employ as a strategic radar for the recognition of innovation. Our arguments regarding the knowledge broker structure of CVC investments suggest that CVC is different from alliances and acquisitions in important dimensions that might make it particularly useful to monitor the emergence of radical innovation. Therefore research should further explore this mechanism and its unique properties.

Our arguments also inform literature on corporate venture capital investing. Recent research has begun to explore the linkages between CVC investments and different stakeholders. Recent studies have started to link CVC investments with the performance of initial public offerings of start-ups (Gompers and Lerner, 1998; Stuart et al., 1999). Others have shown antecedents and consequences of syndication with traditional venture capitalists (Maula et al., 2003) and performance impacts of CVC investments (Dushnitsky and Lenox, 2002). However, these studies lack an integrating framework. Utilizing our stakeholder approach allows us to reconcile the findings of this research. Future research should build on this framework, for instance, by moving beyond the focus on secondary data-driven research that has dominated during past years towards explicitly measuring choices of corporate venture capitalists in the areas that we have laid out. Such primary research would have the potential to test some of our arguments and so add more depth to our understanding of the way managers address the paradoxes of corporate venture capital investment.

Implications for managerial practice
Our arguments suggest that CVC can be a valuable tool to improve the corporation's ability to recognize radical innovation. However, to use this tool effectively, managers have to look beyond the boundaries and viewpoints of their own organization. By making CVC investments the corporation enters the private equity market and needs to at least partly play to the rules of this market. Similarly, to become an attractive partner to start-up firms, the corporation has to be concerned with the start-up's value added. These two perspectives are typically not found within the realm of large corporations. This suggests that CVC units should be at least partly staffed by personnel that possess experience from these two stakeholder groups.

When setting up CVC units, managers have consciously to manage the balance of different stakeholder demands. In many instances, this might require the management of paradoxes. For instance, strategic learning requires close interaction between start-ups and the corporate parent. However, at the same time, the CVC unit has to ensure autonomy and needs to keep a distance from operating units to maintain its ability to invest in potentially threatening technologies. To create value added for the start-up, the business area and the technologies of the start-up and the corporate parent have to be closely related. However, this relatedness poses a threat to the independence of the start-up and increases the risk of the corporation outlearning its technology. To manage these paradoxes it is important to make the positions of all stakeholders explicit to be able to make conscious trade-offs and to communicate the positioning of the CVC unit.

References

Amit, R., J. Brander and C. Zott (1998), 'Why do venture capital firms exist? Theory and Canadian evidence', *Journal of Business Venturing*, **13** (6), 441–66.

Anderson, P. and M.L. Tushman (1990), 'Technological discontinuities and dominant designs: a cyclical model of technological change', *Administrative Science Quarterly*, **35** (4), 604–34.

Bettis, R.A. and C.K. Prahalad (1995), 'The dominant logic: retrospective and extension', *Strategic Management Journal*, **16** (1), 5–14.

Birkinshaw, J., R. Van Basten Batenburg and G. Murray (2002), *Corporate Venturing: The State of the Art and the Prospects for the Future*, London: London Business School.

Block, Z. and I.C. MacMillan (1993), *Corporate Venturing: Creating New Business within the Firm*, Boston, Mass: Harvard Business School Publishing Corporation.

Brockhoff, K. and T. Teichert (1995), 'Cooperative R&D and partners' measures of success', *International Journal of Technology Management*, **10** (1), 111–23.

Brusoni, S., A. Prencipe and K. Pavitt (2001), 'Knowledge specialization, organizational coupling, and the boundaries of the firm: why do firms know more than they make?', *Administrative Science Quarterly*, **46** (4), 597–621.

Burgelman, R.A. (1984), 'Designs for corporate entrepreneurship in established firms', *California Management Review*, **26** (3), 128–67.

Bygrave, W.D. (1988), 'The structure of the investment networks of venture capital firms', *Journal of Business Venturing*, **3**, 137–57.

Chesbrough, H.W. (2000), 'Designing corporate ventures in the shadow of private venture capital', *California Management Review*, **42** (3), 31–49.

Chesbrough, H.W. (2002), 'Making sense of corporate venture capital', Harvard Business Review, **80** (3), 90–99.

Christensen, C.M. and J.L. Bower (1996), 'Customer power, strategic investment, and the failure of leading firms', *Strategic Management Journal*, **17** (3), 197–219.

Dushnitsky, G. and M.J. Lenox (2002), 'Corporate venture capital and incumbent firm innovation rates', paper presented at the Academy of Management Meetings, Denver, Colorado.

Dussauge, P., B. Garrette and W. Mitchell (2000), 'Learning from competing partners: outcomes and durations of scale and link alliances in Europe, North America and Asia', *Strategic Management Journal*, **21**, 99–126.

Gompers, P. and J. Lerner (1998), 'The determinants of corporate venture capital successes: organizational structure, incentives, and complementarities', working paper 6725, National Bureau of Economic Research, Cambridge, Mass.

Gompers, P. and J. Lerner (1999), *The Venture Capital Cycle*, Cambridge, Mass: The MIT Press.

Hamel, G. (1991), 'Competition for competence and interpartner learning within international strategic alliances', *Strategic Management Journal*, **12**, 83–103.

Hardymon, G.F., M.J. DeNino and M.S. Salter (1983), 'When corporate venture capital doesn't work', *Harvard Business Review*, **61**, 114–20.

Hargadon, A.B. (2002), 'Brokering knowledge: linking learning and innovation', *Research in Organizational Behavior*, **24**, 41–85.

Hargadon, A. and R.I. Sutton (1997), 'Technology brokering and innovation in a product development firm', *Administrative Science Quarterly*, **42**, 716–49.

Hellmann, T. (2002), 'A theory of strategic venture investing', *Journal of Financial Economics*, **64**, 285–314.

Henderson, J. and B. Leleux (2002), 'Corporate venture capital: effecting resource combinations and transfers', *Babson Entrepreneurial Review* (May), 31–46.

Henderson, R. (1993), 'Underinvestment and incompetence as reponses to radical innovation: evidence from the photolithographic alignment equipment industry', *RAND Journal of Economics*, **24** (2), 248–70.

Henderson, R.M. and K.B. Clark (1990), 'Architectural innovation: the reconfiguration of existing product technologies and the failure of established firms', *Administrative Science Quarterly*, **35** (1), 9–30.

Kann, A. (2000), 'Strategic venture capital investing by corporations: a framework for structuring and valuing corporate venture capital programs', unpublished dissertation, Department of Management Science and Engineering, Stanford University.

Kanter, R.M. (1985), 'Supporting innovation and venture development in established companies', *Journal of Business Venturing*, **1**, 47–60.

Katz, R. and T.J. Allen (1988), 'Organizational issues in the introduction of new technologies', in R. Katz (ed.), *Managing Professionals in Innovative Organizations: A Collection of Readings*, Florida: Ballinger.

Keil, T. (2002), *External Corporate Venturing: Strategic Renewal in Rapidly Changing Industries*, Westport, Conn: Quorum Books.

Lane, D. and H.W. Chesbrough (2000), 'Intel capital: the Berkeley networks investments', Cambridge, Mass: Harvard Business School Press.

Leifer, R., C.M. McDermott, G.C. O'Connor, L.S. Peters, M.P. Rice and R.W. Veryzer (2001), *Radical Innovation: How Mature Companies Can Outsmart Upstarts*, Cambridge, Mass: Harvard Business School Press.

Leonard-Barton, D. (1995), *Wellsprings of Knowledge: Building and Sustaining the Source of Innovation*, Boston, Mass: Harvard Business School Press.

Levinthal, D.A. and J.G. March (1993), 'The myopia of learning', *Strategic Management Journal*, **14** (8), 95–112.

MacMillan, I.C., D.M. Kulow and R. Khoylian (1989), 'Venture capitalists' involvement in their investments – extent and performance', *Journal of Business Venturing*, **4** (1), 27–47.

Maula, M. (2001), 'Corporate venture capital and the value-added for technology-based new firms', unpublished dissertation, Helsinki University of Technology, Espoo.

Maula, M. and G. Murray (2002), 'Corporate venture capital and the creation of U.S. public companies: the impact of sources of venture capital on the performance of portfolio companies', in M.A. Hitt, R. Amit, C. Lucier and R.D. Nixon (eds), *Creating Value: Winners in the New Business Environment*, Oxford: Blackwell Publishers, pp. 164–87.

Maula, M., T. Keil and S.A. Zahra (2003), 'Corporate venture capital and recognition of technological discontinuities', paper presented at the Academy of Management Meetings, Seattle, 2–7 August.

McGrath, R.G. (1997), 'A real options logic for initiating technology positioning investments', *Academy of Management Review*, **22** (4), 974–96.

McNally, K. (1997), *Corporate Venture Capital: Bridging the Gap in the Small Business Sector*, London: Routledge.

Petreley, N. (1997), 'Is Microsoft building a partnership or giving Citrix a stay of execution?', *InfoWorld*, 05/19/97, **19** (20), 134.

Podolny, J.M. (2001), 'Networks as pipes and prisms of the market', *American Journal of Sociology*, **107** (1), 33–60.

Red Herring (1998), 'The new startup', Red Herring (http://www.redherring.com) accessed June 2004.

Rind, K.W. (1981), 'The role of venture capital in corporate development', *Strategic Management Journal*, **2** (2), 169–80.

Ritter, T. and H.G. Gemünden (2003), 'Network competence: its impact on innovation success and its antecedents', *Journal of Business Research*, **56** (9), 745–55.

Roberts, E.B. and C.A. Berry (1985), 'Entering new business: selecting strategies for success', *Sloan Management Review*, **26** (3), 3–17.

Shane, S. (2001), 'Technology regimes and new firm formation', *Management Science*, **47** (9), 1173–90.

Shenkar, O. and J. Li (1999), 'Knowledge search in international cooperative ventures', *Organizational Science*, **10** (2), 134–214.

Siegel, R., E. Siegel and I.C. MacMillan (1988), 'Corporate venture capitalists: autonomy, obstacles and performance', *Journal of Business Venturing*, **3** (3), 233–47.

Sorenson, O. and T.E. Stuart (2001), 'Syndication networks and the spatial distribution of venture capital investments', *American Journal of Sociology*, **106** (6), 1546–88.

Stuart, T.E., H. Hoang and R.C. Hybels (1999), 'Interorganizational endorsements and the performance of entrepreneurial ventures', *Administrative Science Quarterly*, **44** (2), 315–49.

Sykes, H.B. (1990), 'Corporate venture capital: strategies for success', *Journal of Business Venturing*, **5** (1), 37–47.

Tushman, M.L. and P.A. Anderson (1986), 'Technological discontinuities and organizational environments', *Administrative Science Quarterly*, **31**, 439–65.

Tushman, M.L. and C.A. O'Reilly (1997), *Winning Through Innovation: A Practical Guide to Leading Organization Change and Renewal*, Boston, Mass: Harvard Business School Publishing Corporation.

Utterback, J.M. (1994), *Mastering the Dynamics of Innovation: how Companies can Seize Opportunities in the Face of Technological Change*, Boston, Mass: Harvard Business School Press.

Van der Oord, F., N. Rosenberg, G. Morton, A. Landis, S. Winslow and T. Monahan (2000), 'Corporate venture capital managing for strategic and financial returns', *Working Council for Chief Financial Officers* (http://www.cfo.executiveboard.com).

Winters, T.E. and D.L. Murfin (1988), 'Venture capital investing for corporate development objectives', *Journal of Business Venturing*, **3** (3), 207–23.

Wright, M. and A. Lockett (2003), 'The structure and management of alliances: syndication in the venture capital industry', *Journal of Management Studies*, **40** (8), 2073–2102.

7 Mentoring of Malaysian high-tech entrepreneurs in their pre-seeding phase

Khairul Akmaliah Adham and Mohd Fuaad Said

Introduction

Entrepreneurial firms that generate technological innovations not only bring economic returns to their investors, but also play an important role in helping to develop the general economy of their society (Tether, 2000). Nevertheless, because they are involved in either unproven technology or new markets, have limited human resources and money, and face other challenges associated with forming and growing a new venture, these enterprises often need a number of support infrastructures to help move their products and services rapidly to market. By helping to provide such infrastructures, their investors are more likely to derive a return on their investments, and society will sooner be able to benefit from these new contributions to the economy.

In reviewing the literature, two most important support factors for new ventures appeared to be mentors and business incubators (Leonard and Swap, 2000; Peters, Rice and Sundararajan, 2004). Mentors, in the context of this study, are individuals with pertinent expertise, who help entrepreneurs to create a sound foundation for their companies. Business incubators are facilities in settings equipped with certain specific components deemed necessary to support a fledgling venture. Support components ranged from bare office spaces with basic utilities, to extensive services helping with such things as connecting entrepreneurs with key collaborators (Hansen, Chesbrough, Nohria and Sull, 2000).

In Malaysia, the high-tech industry is among the few in which new ventures have received structured support from the government. Since the mid-1990s, government has vigorously sought to create an environment conducive to nurturing the development of high technology. The aim is to attract well-known established high-tech companies to the country, as well as to lay a base that directly encourages new enterprises. Government-sponsored support facilities have been concentrated in one particular geographical area south of Kuala Lumpur, known as the Multimedia Super Corridor (MSC) (Ramasamy, Chakrabarty and Cheah, 2004).

The MSC was designed to encompass a cluster of high-technology companies, along with supporting agencies and businesses (Porter, 1998). Several business incubators have been built there. Research facilities and large pools of skilled workers from the universities and research institutes are located nearby, and financial support mechanisms and other start-up essentials have been developed specifically for MSC residence companies (Ramasamy et al., 2004). The Malaysian government also provides support to some high-technology companies that are located outside the MSC region. The support comes in the form of grant programmes, among other things. One such programme is managed by the government-established Malaysia Venture Capital Management Berhad (MAVCAP), a venture capital company. MAVCAP's Cradle Investment Programme (CIP) offers eligible entrepreneurs funding during their 'pre-seeding' phase, regardless of their business location. CIP pre-seeding grants are usually combined with mentoring systems, to ensure that these nascent entrepreneurs receive both the needed funding and expert guidance, both of which are of utmost importance at the earliest stages of venture development.

Although Malaysia now appears to have in place most, if not all, of the infrastructures and support mechanisms needed to nurture new high-tech ventures, their operations have not been well documented. This leaves open the question of how such support programmes help development of new ventures in the country. Therefore the general purpose of this study was to collect information that might help answer that question, by first focusing on only one important support mechanism for high-tech ventures, *the mentoring of entrepreneurs*. After reviewing the research literature on the subject, we arrived at our first main research question: *What types of assistance are being provided by mentors to their entrepreneur mentees?* In a preliminary investigation conducted in December 2004, it was found that both the MSC Central Incubator, and MAVCAP's Cradle Investment Programme (CIP) offered structured mentoring programmes. (There may be other mentoring programmes as well; our investigation was not exhaustive.) MAVCAP was given responsibility for managing allocated funds from the Malaysian Ministry of Finance for high-technology development, and it had created CIP to help in managing the funds specifically for financing entrepreneurs during their 'pre-seeding phase', which is the earliest stage within the start-up phase of a new venture. It is the time during which entrepreneurs more fully develop their initial ideas. In this phase, entrepreneurs are usually preoccupied with determining the technical and business feasibility of their product concepts (Kazanjian, 1988; Hamm, 2002) and assistance with the financial aspects is especially welcomed. The CIP financing is referred to by MAVCAP as an 'entrepreneur idea developmental fund', and CIP is responsible first for assessing the viability of an entrepreneur's project before financial backing from the pre-seeding developmental fund will be granted. CIP makes recommendations to the Ministry of Finance, which gives final approval and disburses the funds. CIP then has the responsibility to help all its grant recipients successfully complete the pre-seeding phase.

This CIP funding during the earliest stages of a venture enables entrepreneurs to achieve a certain credibility and to increase their chances of obtaining further funding from the larger financial community for development of an actual product and a business structure for bringing it to market. By the end of this pre-seeding phase, entrepreneurs are expected to have developed their idea fully, in the form of a business model or plan and/or a prototype that serves as a 'proof of concept'. To help entrepreneurs achieve these objectives, the CIP added a structured mentoring system to the funding part of the programme. CIP now requires its grant recipients to have a mentor, believing that it is a support element vital for the entrepreneur's success (see the CIP web site at www.cradle.com.my and the MAVCAP web site at www.mavcap.com).

This study described and analysed the mentoring programme at CIP, providing an in-depth examination of the roles carried out by four mentors in the programme. The study's analysis focused on (1) identifying the types of assistance provided by the mentors (including a way of categorizing the predominant mentoring role(s) taken by each mentor); (2) examining the methods each mentor employed in delivering advice and opinions to their entrepreneurs (including a way of categorizing mentoring styles); (3) determining any significant patterns of similarities and differences in roles and styles among the four mentors; and (4) examining whether, and how, mentor and entrepreneur backgrounds appeared to influence the mentoring process.

Literature Review: Mentoring and New High-tech Ventures

Background: mentoring in organizational settings

Traditionally, mentoring has been viewed as a process whereby an individual who has seniority in rank in a particular job position or role (and/or experience and skill in a given field) provides assistance, knowledge and advice to a person with less status/rank, skill and experience. Over time, the mentor helps steadily to build up the junior person's career. The relationship may provide benefits to the mentor as well. The mentor may derive a sense of fulfilment in seeing a subordinate's career progress, and the mentor's position within the organization may thereby be strengthened, because the subordinate's progress is thought to reflect the mentor's ability to recognize new talent. (See Higgins and Kram, 2001; and Hill and Kamprath, 1998), for a comprehensive review of literature on this subject.)

A contemporary expansion of the mentoring concept involves an individual learning from a constellation of mentors (Higgins and Kram, 2001; Hill and Kamprath, 1998). It has been observed that a one-to-one mentoring relationship puts more responsibility on the mentor to help the learner advance his or her career, while the use of multiple mentors shifts more pressure onto the learner to become a 'perfect' protégé. To advance their careers, protégés are expected continually to seek opportunities to learn, and to gain access to needed resources directly from their network of mentors, as well as indirectly from the networks of each mentor. These authors point out that this newer style of mentoring has come about partly because of the huge information explosion that characterizes our times. In the fast-developing business environment, they see that success increasingly depends on the rapid exchange of information, and anything that helps information to flow smoothly is of value. Many sources of information and knowledge must be continually used in order to keep up, they say, and thus it is an advantage to acquire an array of different mentors for different purposes.

Regardless, the central evolving idea in developing mentoring relationships, whether with a single mentor or several, is that the assistance provided by mentors has come to be seen as developmental in nature, contributing directly to both the career growth and the psychosocial functioning of the entrepreneurs (Hill and Kamprath, 1998).

It may be argued that supportive mentoring relationships for entrepreneurs building their own companies are just as vital as to individuals building a career. In fact, entrepreneurs involved in start-up and growth of a new venture face an environment that is more complex, entangled with more responsibilities and complicated problems, and – most of the time – requiring more rapid decision making than the environment faced by most individuals trying to climb the corporate ladder (Bhide, 1996). Therefore, entrepreneurs need mentoring relationships even more than individuals in organizations need them. However, in mentoring for entrepreneurs, the focus shifts from developing careers to developing fledgling ventures into robust companies.

Mentoring within the contexts of new high-tech ventures

Entrepreneurs who are in high-tech businesses face even greater challenges than most other entrepreneurs, because they are continually involved in new technology, and often must operate in an unfamiliar market as well. To do well requires a high level of both technical ability and conceptual decision-making ability. Therefore, high-tech entrepreneurs especially need mentors who not only can help them obtain pertinent information and resources, but also can teach them how to make sound decisions to support the development of their ventures (see Champion and Carr, 2000). Because of these factors, we concluded that research focusing specifically on mentoring within the contexts of high-tech ventures, and also assistance needed by entrepreneurs during different phases of venture development, would add significantly to our understanding of mentoring for entrepreneurs in general.

An exemplary mentoring culture exists in the high-tech environment of the 'Silicon Valley' near San Francisco, in northern California, which is considered to be the foremost technology business cluster in the world (Leonard and Swap, 2000). The cluster comprises technology-based businesses, along with leading universities, financial support groups and a highly-skilled workforce, all located in close proximity. Communications among the various components are facilitated by a networking culture, which is embedded in the community (Rosenberg, 2002, pp. 1–37). Altogether, the very important 'eco-system' of Silicon Valley has been called 'mentor capitalism' – a situation in which experienced people are willing to 'mentor', or 'coach' younger or less-experienced members of the community, to improve their chances of success (Leonard and Swap, 2000; BusinessWorld, 2003).

In general, mentoring within the contexts of new ventures is offered by both venture capitalists and mentor capitalists. However, *venture capitalists*, who are usually representatives of established venture capital firms, mainly focus on providing financial support to entrepreneurs, and their business advice to the entrepreneurs is given mostly out of a desire to protect their financial investments (Gorman and Sahlman, 1987; Sapienza, Manigart and Vermeir, 1996). *Mentor capitalists*, on the other hand, are individuals who pour knowledge capital into the entrepreneurs' business, and may also provide small amounts of money as well (Leonard and Swap, 2000). Their intention is more toward grooming new entrepreneurs to build robust companies that will benefit the society at large. Their personal motivation derives mainly from a desire to 'give back' to the business community that has served them well in the past, but many are older experts who are also motivated by their intrinsic need to 'stay in the game'. Thus they are more willing to be personally and emotionally involved in their mentoring roles as they work to ensure the success of the new ventures (Leonard and Swap, 2000).

Mentors who provide only advice, mostly on product- and business-related matters, can be further divided into two types: *formal* and *informal* mentors. The *formal* ones work within a structured system, with assignments that are clearly defined at the beginning of the mentor–learner relationships. The mentoring programme is usually hosted by government-sponsored agencies that are involved in supporting entrepreneurial development in general. On the other hand, *informal* mentors are those who come from within the entrepreneur's own circle of friends and family. They may have known the entrepreneurs previously, or may be introduced to the entrepreneurs, either by chance or by arrangement, by those who are within that close circle. The roles of these informal mentors are not well defined, and their relationships with the learners are the most personal and wide-ranging of all the mentoring types (see Bisk, 2002). Leonard and Swap (2000) provided extensive discussion on the assistance provided by mentors to their would-be entrepreneurs in Silicon Valley. They categorized the roles taken by the mentors in their study into seven groups, based on the kinds of assistance mentors extended to their learners: sculptor, psychologist, diplomat, kingmaker, talent magnet, process engineer and rainmaker. A mentor taking the role of a sculptor helps in establishing the strategic course of action for the venture, takes part in finalizing the prototypes to be introduced to venture capitalists and is involved in managing initial market reaction to the product when it is introduced. Alternatively, when a mentor mediates any disagreements arising from different personalities and backgrounds of expertise among members of the entrepreneurial team, and sometimes acts as an intermediary between the entrepreneurs and important external parties, he or she is acting as a diplomat. A mentor acting in a psychologist role calms down worried entrepreneurs in times of uncertainty, provides moral support and keeps them focused on the venture. Acting as a kingmaker, a mentor helps turn inexperienced entrepreneurs into highly competent general managers, by coaching them on the most vital aspects of running a business. As a talent magnet, a mentor helps in hiring suitable employees for the ventures. When in the role of a process engineer, the mentor advises on setting up the venture's reporting and decision-making structure. Lastly, as a rainmaker, the mentor helps by contributing seed money of his/her own, or coming from his network of 'angels', and assists in opening the door to venture capitalists, especially if the entrepreneurial venture requires a large amount of funding. All these different roles highlight the different general types of assistance that entrepreneurs usually require in turning their fledgling ventures into successful companies. Through playing these roles, mentors help inexperienced entrepreneurs in developing their ventures. Mentors, therefore, can be considered part of the entrepreneur's developmental network. Formal mentoring involves a structured form, while the informal kind is mostly unstructured (Bisk, 2002; Higgins and Kram, 2001; Hill and Kamprath, 1998).

Leonard and Swap (2000) further classified the styles and techniques that mentors use in advising entrepreneurs, as follows:

1. *Learning by doing*: showing, by 'hands-on' coaching, how things are done;
2. *Socratic learning*: asking tough questions to encourage logical thinking;
3. *Stories with a moral*: offering timely anecdotes from the mentor's own past experiences, to show what worked in similar business situations;
4. *Rules of thumb*: offering general guidelines about how to handle certain types of business situations;
5. *Specific directives*: directly instructing the entrepreneurs about what is required in a given situation;
6. *Learning by observing*: pointing out methods that have been used successfully by others.

Regardless of the roles mentors play, or the styles and techniques they use, or whether they operate within a structured programme or a more informal relationship, mentoring makes important contributions to the development of new ventures. However, previous studies have indicated that the type of assistance needed at any given time is usually determined by the venture's stage of development at that time. For example, development of the basic business concept can usually be managed by the entrepreneurial team, with little or no help from outsiders (Bricklin, 2001; Hamm, 2002), but, as their ventures progress into the development stages, expert help is needed from a variety of individuals (Bricklin,

2001; Hamermesh, Heskett and Roberts, 2005; Kazanjian, 1988; Hamm, 2002). This indicates a need to examine the research literature on the different phases of new venture development, to see how it relates to the mentoring of entrepreneurs. Information on the needs entrepreneurs have at each stage of venture development gives direction to decisions about what kinds of assistance mentors should offer at each stage (Sullivan, 2000).

Specific capabilities needed in each phase of new venture development

A composite of findings from several researchers who have studied the development of new ventures (Hamermesh et al., 2005; Greiner, 1998; Kazanjian, 1988; Kroeger, 1974; Timmons, 1994, pp. 207–33), indicates that they typically go through four main stages: start-up (a pre-seeding phase, followed by a stage of fully developing the actual product), commercialization, growth and stability. However, these venture development stages are not necessarily well-defined, separate and strictly sequential. There may be considerable overlapping of needed resources and functions to be performed across stages, and sometimes there may be a temporary backtracking to an earlier stage as well (Sullivan, 2000).

Continuing to draw from the above-cited writers, it appears that moving a new venture all the way from start-up to the stabilized stage depends on the entrepreneurial team's capability of recognizing and addressing the needs specific to each stage, using abilities and skills developed from within the team, plus seeking help from outside experts as needed. In the *start-up* stage, when entrepreneurs are striving to develop their ideas into product prototypes, an extremely disciplined focus on the tasks at hand is critical, and there is a need especially for seed funding and technological capabilities. In the *further development* and *commercialization* phases, entrepreneurs are involved with the actual product development and its eventual launching. This requires refining the prototypes to meet directly the needs of the market, and either developing production capability in-house or selecting the right party to outsource manufacturing. In the *growth* stage, new ventures need to address tasks related to organizational development, including those of managing production and setting up investment and reporting structures. More funding is also required at this stage to support increases in product development, production and marketing. To survive this stage, new ventures require competent general management – again, either with managers developed from within the organization or those hired from outside. By the time the *stability* stage is reached, the number of products and stakeholders typically has multiplied, and the new venture requires even more capable general managerial hands to put in place the most appropriate and sustainable management structures. At the same time, the management team must strive to avoid pitfalls that may lead to a stage of decline. Therefore, to be effective, support mechanisms such as mentoring should match the kinds of assistance needed by entrepreneurs at each specific phase of venture development.

Building on literature findings to design this study

While studies of entrepreneurship have highlighted that there are variations in the kinds of assistance needed by entrepreneurs in different stages of their venture development, we found no study that explicitly described the pre-seeding phase. Therefore, in this study, we set out to examine the mentor assistance needed, and that which was actually provided in the four cases studied, specifically in the pre-seeding phase, the critical stage in which the basic idea of the product, system or service is developed.

All learners included in this study were recipients of an RM50000 (approximately US$13000) CIP pre-seeding grant, along with the services of the mentoring programme. Recipients were expected to develop their ideas into a business model or plan, and/or to build a prototype, that would serve as 'proof of concept', by the end of their six-month pre-seeding phase. Success in this phase meant that their technological product prototypes, and/or proofs of concepts, would be developed sufficiently for them to be ready to move on to the next stage, which would focus on fully developing the product or concept and making it ready for the commercial market. (At the end of that pre-seeding period, the entrepreneur is required to submit an executive summary about their business concept to a depository, called the CIP Idea Bank. The CIP then takes the concepts that are judged to have been successfully proved, and markets them to the venture capital communities, seeking further funding for development. The concepts are also offered to large corporations that may wish to make use of or acquire the new technology embodied in the concepts. The details of the CIP support facilities and its mentoring programme are summarized in Table 7.1.)

Understanding that the mentoring assistance required by the entrepreneurs during this phase necessarily had to focus on the designated end goal, we wanted to find out exactly how both mentors and their protégés described the mentoring process: the types of assistance provided, the manner and methods by which assistance was given patterns of differences and similarities, and any key factors that appeared to influence the whole process. Our investigation took place after the pre-seeding phase was completed for these learners.

Research Methodology

This study began with the identification of Malaysian support facilities and structures for entrepreneurs that included mentoring programmes. Information about them was gathered from published materials, web sites of relevant agencies and companies, and interviews with certain staff members from those agencies and companies.

At least two agencies were identified as having mentoring programmes, the Cradle Investment Program (CIP) and the Multimedia Super Corridor's Central Incubator (MCI), located in Cyberjaya. The two were visited and their managers were interviewed, to gather information about their respective mentoring systems. Published materials about these agencies were also obtained to supplement the interview data.

It was decided that the primary data collection would be from in-depth interviews with mentors and their respective protégés with the purpose of gaining further insights about the mentoring process, focusing on the research questions stated earlier. All interviews were conducted in January and February of 2005.

Mentors under the CIP were invited to participate in the study (not those from MCI) because CIP had been operating its mentoring programme since 2003, and 18 entrepreneurs had completed their mentoring 'contract', whereas MCI had just started its more structured mentoring programme in late 2004, and it was believed that there would not be sufficient data from MCI to support the analysis required by this study, which was aimed at getting a good picture of the mentoring roles and techniques, and of other factors that might influence the mentoring process.

Four of the CIP mentors agreed to be interviewed. Each mentor's personal background was different from the others, and each of their learners was involved in a different kind of

Table 7.1   Services offered and mentoring programme at the Cradle Investment Program (CIP)

Services Offered and Mentoring Programme	Details
Type of provider	A grant distribution programme that provides pre-seed funding to entrepreneurs in the technology sector and other fields of high growth potential
No. of entrepreneurs helped by the programme so far	Number of grant recipients = 150
Types of Services Offered	
Funding	Provide pre-seeding grant (once grant recipients submit completed concepts to CIP Idea Bank, they can apply for MAVCAP venture capital funding)
Office space	Does not provide office space for grant recipients, but allows those who require labs to use such facilities located in MSC Central Incubator (MCI)
Support for concept/ product development	Helps set up labs through partnering with well-known computer businesses, to assist grant recipients in developing prototypes Assists entrepreneurs who utilize labs to access technical mentoring of companies who sponsor lab development
Opportunity for commercialization	By end of pre-seeding period, requires grant recipients to submit executive summaries of their project to the CIP Idea Bank Submits concepts to venture capital communities to obtain further funding for entrepreneurs Offers the concepts to large corporations so that they can acquire new technology in exchange for funding of the entrepreneurs
Other support services	Organizes classes for CIP grant recipients, for example, on writing a business plan Arranges get-togethers between grant recipients and successful entrepreneurs for networking purposes Helps entrepreneurs in writing executive summaries on their concepts for marketing purposes
Structured mentoring programme	Helps assign a mentor to each grant recipient and requires the mentor to report learner's progress to CIP, via an online system
Characteristics of Mentoring Programme	
No. of registered mentors	160 (community includes members of industry and academia, researchers and scientists)
Methods in selecting potential mentors	Determines learner's requirements, approaches potential mentors, does presentations and persuades them to join the programme Invites experts to register via CIP web site. Requests their services when their CV matches the needs of a grant recipient Introduces the mentor to the matched learner
Requirements for mentors	Must have more that eight years of work experience Must be willing to commit at least two hours a week to meeting assigned entrepreneur Must report weekly progress of entrepreneur, via online reporting system
Reason for instituting the structured mentoring programme	To protect government investments To help entrepreneurs commercialize products
Remuneration for mentors	Disburses RM5000 (approximately US$1300) to mentor from the RM50 000 (approximately US13 000) granted to each entrepreneurial team

technology application, with each also representing a different industry (see Appendices 1 and 2). The four mentors were interviewed using an interview protocol that contained three sections: (1) their personal and business background; (2) their roles (what they do); and (3) their mentoring techniques (how they do it). For the second section, the descriptions of possible roles played by mentors were taken from those that were developed by Leonard and Swap (2000). In this section, variations in mentor roles that occurred as stages of the venture's idea development unfolded were also explored. Possible continued association with their respective learners, after their 'contract' was over was also examined. For the third section, the classification of mentoring techniques developed by Leonard and Swap (2000) was utilized. In this section, possible variations in mentoring techniques that may have occurred as stages of idea development unfolded were also examined.

These mentor interviews were then followed up by interviewing their respective learners. This dyadic interview procedure was performed to add depth to the data collection and to compare perceptions from both sides of the mentor–learner relationship (Fombrun, 1982). CIP required that each of its grant recipients be an entrepreneurial team of at least two members. In this study, in three of the four cases, only the lead entrepreneur was interviewed; in case 4 both members of the entrepreneurial team were interviewed. The interview protocol for learners had five sections: (1) the entrepreneur's background, (2) the specific nature of their business venture, (3) the mentoring process in general, (4) the roles taken by their mentor, and (5) the mentoring techniques used by their mentor. Questions for the first two sections were adapted from Timmons (1994, pp. 35–7). Questions for the last two sections mirrored questions for sections (2) and (3) in the protocol used for mentors. Interviewees were promised confidentiality of identity, and therefore pseudonyms were used in all reporting of the results.

Findings and Discussion

CIP's structured mentoring programme

The CIP's mentoring system involved a large community of experts registered as mentors under the programme. This made it possible for the CIP to meet the needs of the high number of CIP grant recipients, including both technical and business mentoring help during their critical pre-seeding developmental phase – the time when such help is usually most needed. At the CIP, the prerequisites for mentor 'recruitment' were quite relaxed, and outside volunteers were accepted as mentors. The aim of CIP is to maintain a large pool of mentors with varied expertise, to enable ready access to important knowledge networks. This approach gives them maximum flexibility to help meet the needs of a large and ever-changing, but predictably diverse, community of entrepreneurs (for further information about CIP, see www.cradle.com.my).

Types of mentoring assistance and roles taken, mentoring styles, patterns and influences observed and other significant findings

Details of the findings from the interviews of the four mentors are organized in a chart format in Appendix 1, and details of the learner interviews are displayed in Appendix 2. The following discussion concerns our observations, analysis and interpretations of those findings. The types of mentoring assistance provided were categorized according to the breakdown of types presented by Leonard and Swap (2000) and some elaboration was provided by the researchers in the appendixes. In all four cases, the mentors helped the entrepreneurial teams to develop their business models or plans and/or to build proto-types to serve as 'proofs of concept', by providing advice regarding the technical and business feasibility of the product. In addition, all four mentors contributed significantly in managing the development process, mostly by acting as project managers. They pushed learners to be focused on the tasks at hand, which were to complete the tasks necessary to develop proofs of concepts within the stipulated six-month period. This suggests that *sculpturing* was the dominant role played by the mentors.

Moreover, three of four mentors (mentors 1, 3 and 4) provided access to needed resources for their learners, acting in a version of the *diplomatic* role. For example, mentor 1 assembled a team of experts from his own research institute to support his learner in the technical aspects of developing his product. Mentor 4's *diplomatic* help mainly consisted of introducing his learners to potential customers from among his company's existing clients. Mentors 1 and 3 also helped introduce their learners to venture capitalists or angels that they knew personally, although the introductions did not result in sealed deals. Thus these mentors not only provided direct advice, but also helped the learners to become a part of their own social and professional networks, giving the learners access to information, facilities and other needed resources. Only one mentor (mentor 1) assisted in the actual formation process of a company. He helped refine the learner's business plan, plan equity sharing among learners' team members, and give extra credibility to the learn-ers' product in the presence of investors. Mentor 2 was not involved in the formation of his learner's company because the learner already had business investment 'angels' who helped them with company formation issues. In the case of mentor 3, the actual product development was not pursued by his learner, and therefore no company formation process was carried out. Mentor 4 was not involved in his learner's company formation because the venture's product concepts required further development. The plan was to complete its development and then join an existing company. Therefore, contacts with their learners after the pre-seeding phase were mainly social for mentors 3 and 4. Mentor 2 agreed to continue mentoring his mentee during the second module of product concept development.

Some other kinds of mentoring assistance that had been discussed in the research lit-erature appeared not to apply to the mentors interviewed in this study, mainly because of the way the pre-seeding funding programme was structured. The CIP funding and men-toring were designed only to help entrepreneurs develop their product concepts within the six-month stipulated time period. Therefore, the focus taken by the participants in the programme was expected to be narrow and short-term. The short time period and limited funding were a barrier to the hiring of any extra hands for the project, so mentors did not have a reason or opportunity to be *talent magnets*. In certain cases, this may have com-promised the robustness of the ventures, because having more team members can con-tribute a greater range of needed expertise; see Champion and Carr (2000).

In regard to being *rainmakers*, mentors 1 and 3 did help introduce learners to financing communities, but as long as they were CIP mentors they were not themselves allowed to make personal investments in learners' projects. Similarly, the mentors had little oppor-tunity to perform the role of *process engineers* as long as the organization structure of the ventures had yet to take form. Furthermore, because the mentors were only assigned to be involved during the six-month pre-seeding phase, and in doing that they had to focus on the tasks at hand, opportunities for them to be involved in grooming the entrepreneurs to become CEOs – playing the role of *king makers* – were very limited.

In reference to mentoring style, among all four cases the *Socratic* style was most prevalent. This way of delivering advice and opinions was sometimes complemented by learning by doing, stories with a moral, rules of thumb and specific directives. These styles were appropriate for addressing the nature of entrepreneurial teams' tasks during the pre-seeding phase.

Information obtained from the mentors on their styles and types of assistance was verified by information provided later by the entrepreneurs. Findings from learner interviews were congruent with the descriptions recounted by their respective mentors, with no significant discrepancies. In addition, the entrepreneurs' data highlighted the important role of MAVCAP's CIP contributions in the survivability of their ventures. The contributions can be divided into several categories. First, without the CIP grants many budding entrepreneurs would be without any financial sources during their pre-seeding phase. Second, it seems clear that for many of the grant recipients their business idea would be unlikely to survive the pre-seeding phase without a mentor's helping hand. Third, the CIP provided a structured commercialization programme that included a mechanism for matching new business knowledge, ideas and products with the commercial demand for them, through interested third parties. Fourth, the CIP provided an additional funding channel for its grant recipients through its connection with MAVCAP, its parent venture capital company. Fifth, it provided its entrepreneurs with networking opportunities within the CIP community. For example, because the CIP is a government-backed programme, entrepreneur 3 could utilize his CIP-grant recipient status to gain access to potential markets controlled by other government-linked companies.

Despite its demonstrated success, the CIP programme had its limitations. The limited amount of funds (RM50 000 or approximately US$13 000) granted, along with the short development time (six months) enforced by MAVCAP for the entrepreneurs' pre-seeding phase, may be considered as two such limitations. By having such limited funding and time, and being impelled to focus only on product development, the entrepreneurs were hampered in developing their business as a whole. This limitation was best demonstrated by case 3, in which the concept was technologically successful, but several business issues were neglected because of the time and financial constraints. Because of this neglect, the entrepreneurial team failed fully to consider ways to gain market acceptance of their product, and the sad result was termination of its development before becoming an actual business, even after successful completion of its proof-of-concept pre-seeding phase. This feature of the CIP (separating the product development phase from the business development phase) is a different approach from that in several cases reported by Vinod Khosla in Champion and Carr's 2000 article. In those cases, entrepreneurs deliberated about how to uncover the full potential of their product concepts, but there was concurrent development of their products and businesses during the same time frame. The success of this approach was possible apparently because the venture capital company partnering with the entrepreneurs allocated larger amounts of funding and allowed longer periods for development.

Another limitation found was the cumbersome process involved in obtaining the pre-seeding funds. All four of the interviewed entrepreneurs highlighted the difficulties they encountered in going through the funding process. This compounded their financial woes, as they had had no initial funding to finance their proof of concepts, and had not been able to get any funding elsewhere. Entrepreneur 2 explained the inefficient way CIP disburses its grants. He related that, after managing to secure a pre-seeding grant from CIP, there were times when they did not receive the money on time, even though his team had fulfilled all the conditions for funding disbursements. This created many financial difficulties for the entrepreneur, who had been counting on the money to pay his programmers' salaries.

Moreover, obtaining post-seeding funds was also an exhausting process. After completing their concept development under the CIP programme, the entrepreneurs faced hurdles in getting more funding to develop and launch their actual products. For example, entrepreneur 2 struggled to obtain additional funding for actual product development after completing his prototype. When submitting a proposal (with customer endorsements) to get more funding from a government-backed venture capital company, the entrepreneur was required to make a sale first, before any funds would be approved. But a sales contract could only be obtained from a potential customer by selling a fully developed product, which necessitated the development of a prototype into a fully marketable product, requiring additional financial investment. Unfortunately, at this stage of product development, the financial backing for this entrepreneur nearly dried up, putting him in a 'Catch-22' situation. In the case of entrepreneur 4, the financing community considered his venture's product as still embryonic, and insisted that they further develop it before they could apply for more funding. Only one entrepreneur (entrepreneur 1) had managed to gain further funding, and then only after experiencing numerous difficulties.

Another area of concern was the lack of support from the local community business environment for those entrepreneurs who developed novel concepts. Although entrepreneur 3's team had operated within the Klang Valley, a neighbouring area of MSC, the team did not gain substantial benefits from locating within close proximity of the MSC cluster. The team faced difficulties in getting their prototype's required components from local vendors, and they eventually had to order them from China. This shows either weak linkages between technology component suppliers and their buyers, or perhaps simply the absence of such supplying groups in the local setting. Thus it appears that some of the envisioned benefits of being in or near the MSC business cluster have yet to be realized for new high-tech ventures. A truly effective cluster would be expected to facilitate more rapid prototype development, in comparison to an 'unclustered' environment (Porter, 1998). If an entrepreneur faces problems in developing his venture's prototypes, it seems there may also be a high probability that he will face difficulties in the development of the actual product.

There are also several other findings worth noting. First, entrepreneur interviews revealed that they acquired a broad range of sources for important help, in addition to their assigned CIP mentors. The entrepreneurs disclosed that they also had a number of informal mentors who assisted them in solving problems, in areas where they lacked certain skills and knowledge. These informal mentors were drawn from both previously existing relationships and newly formed ones. Entrepreneur 1 sought help from new relationships, formed through introductions by his assigned mentor, to help him solve product-related problems. In addition he strengthened some relationships with people he knew from his previous job, to help him in his company formation process. Entrepreneur 2 would contact his friends at his previous workplace to help solve technical issues related to his products. Entrepreneur 3 contacted his previous partners for technical assistance, and he also capitalized on his networking within the CIP community and its related government connections, for market-related problems. Entrepreneur 4 utilized the networks of his mentors as a platform from which to meet potential buyers, and those contacts proved critical to defining their product concepts. Thus, in addition to formal mentoring provided under the CIP, the entrepreneurs extended their networks of experts by drawing on numerous other sources, greatly extending their own social and professional networks.

Another finding showed correlations between the mentors' and entrepreneurs' backgrounds (for example: age, educational background, work experience and current position) and the types of mentoring provided for the entrepreneurs. When age was considered, it appeared not to be significant in affecting the mentoring process, but a gap in age between a mentor and an entrepreneur did have an influence on the mentor–learner relationship. For example, there was a tendency for mentors to serve as psychologists when the age gap was larger (entrepreneurs 1 and 3), while for mentor–learner pairs closer in age, their relationship was more often focused simply on completing tasks.

Regardless of their educational background, work experience or current position, all mentors seemed willing to assist their entrepreneurs in whatever way possible to complete the pre-seeding phase successfully. All were willing to support the needs of their learners directly and, if that was not possible, they would help broker the needed assistance. However, most of the assistance was offered only on request by the learners. That is, if help was asked for, mentors tried their best to assist. Mentors were most assertive in giving their advice and opinions when the requested assistance was within their areas of expertise, and also when they believed their learner lacked knowledge or skill in those areas. In relation to this, mentoring styles employed by mentors were shaped by their perceptions of learners' ability to complete the tasks, and perceptions of their needs to be educated in the specialized knowledge possessed by the mentor. When the mentors could not meet learners' requests directly, they tried to acquire help from third parties. The extent of sourcing for outside help was determined by the existing nodes of the mentors' networks, which in turn tended to be determined by the mentor's educational background, work experience and current position. A mentor's willingness to help was mainly triggered by a mixture of (1) their empathy toward entrepreneurs in general (based on a combination of mentor work experience and current position, as all four mentors had been entrepreneurs themselves and two were currently running their own business); (2) the 'chemistry' between the mentor and the assigned learner (which seemed to result either from the learner's enthusiasm, which attracted mentor interest, or from a closeness of the learner's venture concepts to the mentor's own area of interest and expertise – a combination of mentor work experience and current position); and (3) above all, the mentor's satisfaction from seeing a learner experience success. Entrepreneurs, on the other hand, regardless of their background, were doing everything possible to push through the pre-seeding phase to fulfil their own intrinsic needs, meet the business objectives of their developing ventures, and fulfil their contractual obligations to the CIP.

On the part of the entrepreneurs, their previous experience (working in or starting up a business) helped strengthen their chances of survivability in the pre-seeding phase. Entrepreneur 3, for example, had been involved in many partnership projects previously, and can be referred to as a 'serial entrepreneur'. Entrepreneur 4 also had started up his own business previously. Both of them came into the CIP with a number of advantages from their prior entrepreneurial experience. Thus it seems logical that such previous entrepreneurial business experience helps mentees to push their new ventures successfully through the pre-seeding phase.

An interesting finding of this study is that mentoring also helped provide these new high-tech ventures with a protected environment in which to develop their product concepts. The mentees' ventures were being virtually incubated by the advice and other support services provided by the mentors, without having to relocate to a designated physical location. This suggests correlations between the concept of mentoring and the general concept of incubating new ventures. Mentoring can be designed into a given incubating project as a support programme (Peters et al., 2004), but it can also be established as an integral part of a total environment designed to incubate new ventures.

Possible Implications for Entrepreneurs, Mentors and Entrepreneurial Support Programme Sponsors, Policy Makers, Developers and Managers

This study has found that entrepreneurs linked with groups of people rather than relying only on the single assigned CIP mentor. Therefore, it seems highly desirable that entrepreneurs establish their networks of advisers, through structured mentoring programmes and/or on their own. It is also important that sponsors and managers of support programmes for entrepreneurs help facilitate their development of needed relationships. Existing and potential mentors can play a key role in such development of important networks.

This study also identifies some problems faced by entrepreneurs in the pre-seeding phase, including difficulties in (1) getting funding to prove their concepts, (2) obtaining access to expert advice concerning the technical and business feasibility of product concepts, (3) sourcing components for prototype development, (4) the process of forming a new company, and (5) getting funds for actual product development and commercialization. Awareness of such problems is important to all relevant parties – entrepreneurs, mentors, entrepreneur programme sponsors and policy makers – but particularly to new entrepreneurs, because they must be aware of what help is currently available, be willing to receive help and be able to gain access to and benefit from the help that is available. In fact, the extent of entrepreneurs' readiness and willingness is a significant determinant of success, both their own success and the success (in terms of effectiveness) of the support facilities designed for them (Rice, 2002). The identification of these problems may also serve as a guide for programme sponsors and managers in designing more effective programmes to support new venture development in Malaysia (and perhaps elsewhere) and as a guide also for existing and would-be mentors advising new entrepreneurs.

From the entrepreneurs' descriptions of their struggle in forming a new company, it is seen as desirable that, before setting up a venture, a new entrepreneur equip himself or herself with considerable knowledge about how to 'grow' a company. This is especially critical for entrepreneurs who had not previously had the experience of starting up their own businesses, as well as for those whose mentors do not have much experience in this process because they are experts mainly in some area related to developing of the product. These inexperienced entrepreneurs are advised to enrol in business development classes and to seek help from experts in gaining basic knowledge about forming a new business. In relation to this, entrepreneur support programme sponsors, developers and managers could help by organizing classes and introducing entrepreneurs to relevant experts.

The beneficial components of the CIP model highlighted in this study could be adapted to other support programmes. The most beneficial components appear to include (1) the roles and styles undertaken by CIP mentors; (2) CIP's method of matching mentor and entrepreneur; and (3) CIP's function as an important networking platform for entrepreneurs. However, there are several weaknesses in currently existing programmes supporting new venture development, that especially need to be addressed. Since most of these are related to financial support for entrepreneurs, solutions must lie in the hands of policy makers. CIP and other entrepreneur support developers and managers should seriously consider the problems entrepreneurs have in obtaining sufficient funding, during both the pre-seeding and actual product development/commercialization stages. This issue is particularly critical because the study found that getting funding is a precondition to creation of the venture itself. Solving the funding problems should help accelerate the venture creation and development process, which is essential if the number of successful new ventures in Malaysia is going to increase significantly.

Policy makers should also look into the way the MSC cluster is being developed and managed. Since the cluster was designed to nurture the development of new enterprises, it should be monitored closely to see if it is being effective overall. If locating new ventures within or near the MSC cluster is not being seen as an advantage, as reported by one of the entrepreneurs in our study, an in-depth analysis should be conducted to find out why. This should be of interest to policy makers especially because of the large amount of public money already invested in the MSC project and the additional sums committed to development of similar clusters in Malaysia for the future. The results of this analysis may help policy makers plan a course of action to improve the effectiveness of the MSC cluster as well as others in Malaysia.

Conclusions and Suggestions for Future Research

This study has described and analysed the work of four mentors as they assisted four entrepreneurial teams in a structured mentoring programme under the Cradle Investment Programme (CIP) in Malaysia, a government-backed programme that focuses on assisting high-tech entrepreneurs during the pre-seeding phase of their start-up ventures. It was found that, in this pre-seeding phase, the assistance that the four entrepreneurial teams requested most was related to developing their technological capabilities, managing the overall idea development project, and obtaining funding. Work on the formation of a business structure was not required during this phase, but did occur in some cases. In getting through their pre-seeding phase, the entrepreneurs availed themselves of the CIP's financial and technical help, facilities, some general business advice, and project management assistance. In addition to the assigned CIP mentors, the four entrepreneurial teams received help from a constellation of other experts as well. They found some of these other experts on their own, and connected with others through the CIP mentors and their social and professional networks. The actual amount of support and time requested and acquired by these four entrepreneurial teams seemed to depend on the nature of their products, their reasons for starting up the venture, and their previous experience with the product, as well as their experience with the workplace environment in which it would be used, and with general business management. As valuable as the mentoring was seen to be, money was a precondition for starting up the new ventures in all four cases. Mentoring alone, without the financial support, seemed very unlikely to have resulted in a techno-logically successful concept or prototype in these four cases.

Because the findings have implications for policies regarding future development of new high-tech ventures, further studies may be needed to confirm the benefits to be derived from allocating additional funding to the current MAVCAP programme, in order to introduce additional programmes, or to expand the CIP. Also the question arises as to whether potential entrepreneurs are as aware as they might be of the help that could be available from participation in this type of programme. Research to determine the general level of awareness would be helpful, therefore, to decide how much effort should be expended to raise awareness, especially among groups likely to give rise to high-tech entre-preneurs: the business community, universities and research institutes, and so on.

The information provided by this study regarding some of the critical needs of entre-preneurs during their pre-seeding phase, as well as the kinds of assistance they received from mentors, may indeed help policy makers and others find new ways to meet those needs. Nevertheless, as this is a descriptive study of a very small sample, care must be taken when thinking about how the findings might apply to cases not included in this study. Further research is needed that will include a larger population sample of mentors and entrepreneurs, in order to develop firmer conclusions and a deeper understanding of how mentoring affects the latter's performance in all phases of venture development.

In addition, future studies should also examine cases in which entrepreneurs were unsuccessful, to see what might have gone wrong, or what might have been lacking, in the mentoring relationships and other forms of assistance provided. If ineffective mentoring is found to be a factor, it would be of interest to identify the possible reasons: whether they might lie in the advice given, in the styles of mentoring, in a mismatch of mentor and learner (for example, in age, background, personality and so on) or in some other factors.

Further analysis of the styles of mentoring might allow conclusions to be drawn con-cerning the impact of that factor on the learners' success. (In the four instances examined by this study, all mentors took a 'Socratic learning' approach, and this seemed agreeable to the temperaments of their learners. However, the question arises as to whether, if the style had been different, or changed during the time covered (for example to a predomi-nantly 'specific directive' type), how might that have affected the four entrepreneurial teams and their respective ventures?) Future studies should also explore the possible exis-tence of other relationships which may have a negative impact on entrepreneurs – persons or groups within the entrepreneurs' formal or informal networks who in some way appear to exert a negative influence on their personal development and/or on their business venture. Such findings might help entrepreneurs to be aware of kinds of relationships to avoid, and entrepreneurial support programmes could include such awareness training in their assistance offerings, as well as finding ways to be more effective in helping the entre-preneurs to find suitably positive relationships.

Since this present study only includes mentors and learners under the CIP mentoring programme, some future studies should focus on those under the MSC Central Incubator (MCI) and other mentoring systems. Studying MCI in particular would give researchers additional insight into support programmes for new venture development, because MCI is an incubator, as well as being a host for mentoring programmes for its tenants. The results of such a study would contribute to our understanding of a wider variety of support structures, and of how they are utilized in combination with mentoring.

Researchers should also identify other organizations that are using mentoring systems, and study them to find elements that might be adapted for effective use by programmes supporting new venture development. As additional knowledge about mentoring is gathered, mentoring systems can be continually refined to be even more effective than at present, and the use of mentoring to nurture development of new enterprise in Malaysia may become more widespread, not only in the high-tech industry but in other industries as well.

References

Bhide, A. (1996), 'The questions every entrepreneur must answer', *Harvard Business Review*, **74**(6), 120–30.
Bisk, L. (2002), 'Formal entrepreneurial mentoring: the efficacy of third party managed programs', *Career Development International*, **7**(5), 262–70.
Bricklin, D. (2001), 'Natural-born entrepreneur', *Harvard Business Review*, **79**(8), 53–8.
BusinessWorld (2003), 'In tough times, it takes more than money to make a business operation', Manila, Financial Times Information Limited, 21 March.
Champion, D. and N.G. Carr (2000), 'Starting up in high gear: an interview with venture capitalist Vinod Khosla', *Harvard Business Review*, **78**(4), 92–100.
Fombrun, C.J. (1982), 'Strategies for network research in organizations', *The Academy of Management Review*, **7**(2), 280–91.
Gorman, M. and W.A. Sahlman (1987), *What Do Venture Capitalists Do?*, HBS no. 9-288-015, Boston: Harvard Business School Publishing.
Greiner, L.E. (1998), 'Evolution and revolution as organizations grow', *Harvard Business Review*, **76**(3), 55–63.
Hamermesh, R.G., J.L. Heskett and M.J. Roberts (2005), *A Note on Managing the Growing Venture*, HBS no. 9-805-092, Boston: Harvard Business School Publishing.
Hamm, J. (2002), 'Why entrepreneurs don't scale', *Harvard Business Review*, **80**(12), 110–15.
Hansen, M.T., H.W. Chesbrough, N. Nohria and D.N. Sull (2000), 'Networked incubators: hothouses of the New Economy', *Harvard Business Review*, **78**(5), 74–83.
Higgins, M.C. and K.E. Kram (2001), 'Reconceptualizing mentoring at work: a developmental network perspective', *The Academy of Management Review*, **26**(2), 264–88.
Hill, L. and N. Kamprath (1998), *Beyond the Myth of the Perfect Mentor: Building a Network of Developmental Relationships*, HBS no. 9-491-096, Boston: Harvard Business School Publishing.
Kazanjian, R.K. (1988), 'Relation of dominant problems to stages of growth in technology-based new ventures', *Academy of Management Journal*, **31**(2), 257–79.
Kroeger, C.V. (1974), 'Managerial development in the small firm', *California Management Review*, **17**(1), 41–7.
Leonard, D. and W. Swap (2000), 'Gurus in the garage', *Harvard Business Review*, **78**(6), 5–12.
Peters, L., M. Rice and M. Sundararajan (2004), 'The role of incubators in the entrepreneurial process', *Journal of Technology Transfer*, **29**(1), 83–91.
Porter, M.E. (1998), 'Clusters and the new economics of competition', *Harvard Business Review*, **76**(6), 77–90.
Ramasamy, B., A. Chakrabarty and M. Cheah (2004), 'Malaysia's leap into the future: an evaluation of the Multimedia Super Corridor', *Technovation*, **24**(11), 871–83.
Rice, M.P. (2002), 'Co-production of business assistance in business incubators: an exploratory study', *Journal of Business Venturing*, **17**(2), 163–87.
Rosenberg, David (2002), *Cloning Silicon Valley: The Next Generation High-Tech Hotspots*, London: Reuters.
Sapienza, H.J., S. Manigart and W. Vermeir (1996), 'Venture capitalist governance and value added in four countries', *Journal of Business Venturing*, **11**(6), 439–69.
Sullivan, R. (2000), 'Entrepreneurial learning and mentoring', *International Journal of Entrepreneurial Behavior & Research*, **6**(3), 160–75.
Tether, B.S. (2000), 'Small firms, innovation and employment creation in Britain and Europe: a question of expectations . . . ', *Technovation*, **20**(2), 109–13.
Timmons, Jeffry, A. (1994), *New Venture Creation: Entrepreneurship for the 21st Century*, 4th edn, Massachusetts: Irwin.

Appendix 1   Mentors – Personal Background, Mentoring Roles and Techniques

Factors Studied	Mentor 1	Mentor 2	Mentor 3	Mentor 4
Personal background				
Educational background	Has a PhD in animal husbandry	Trained in aeronautical engineering	Trained in maths and computer science	Trained in architecture and has an MBA
Work experience	Has been a senior researcher at his current research institute for more than 20 years	Has work experience in aviation industry for more than 36 years; after retiring, became CEO of an IT company for one year	Last job was as a managing director of marketing research company	Previously ran own business, then joined the multinational company as an executive. Has been in the current managing director position for 1 year
Current position	Senior scientist	Retiree from government service	Free-lance consultant	Managing director of a reputable multinational advertising company
		Currently running his own company	Independent director of a public-listed company	North American citizen, has worked in Malaysia for 3 years
Age	50+	60	50	Late 30s
Previous experience in running a business	Had past experience in running a family business (Believed that experience starting up his own business has helped a lot in mentoring)	Was hired as CEO of a company right after retirement After one year with the company, left to start own business Believed that starting up own business caused him to emphasize and explain to learner the importance of meeting customer needs	Currently, running own sole-proprietor business	Had experience in running own business 'I think being an entrepreneur previously made me a little bit more sympathetic, and I also know what it's like when you are unsure about the future. And you don't know whether your project is going to be successful or not. And it requires all

Factors Studied	Mentor 1	Mentor 2	Mentor 3	Mentor 4
				dedications. It helps me to become very committed as a mentor because I have been through that before, so I could at least understand their point of view'
Mentoring, general				
The process of becoming a CIP mentor	Had job specs that required the transferring of technology to industry. Had a good reputation in the industry, and was introduced to CIP via word of mouth. Was selected by one grant recipient who required assistance in technical matters related to his expertise	Was introduced to CIP mentoring programme via a personal friend who works for MAVCAP. Was asked to mentor CIP grant recipient whose business is in the aviation industry	Registered in CIP web site himself because of his intrinsic need to 'give back' to the society, then got invited by CIP, when there was a match. 'The main thing is . . . with all my experience, I just want to share back after working for so many years. Because I was a managing director, I know about management, HR, systems, technology, people, finance issues, almost all aspects of a business. So, I can guide them'	Was introduced to CIP mentoring programme via a personal friend who works for MAVCAP. 'I happened to know the person who is managing MAVCAP at that time. She told me about CIP and she actually recommended me as a mentor. She knows about me and my background. So she makes the connection between those learners and me, and then we manage the process to apply, and I fill out the form online in CIP web site'

Reasons for agreeing to becoming a mentor for this particular person	Motivated by seeing new company develop. Has personal interest in learner's product. Is impressed by learner's obsession with the product and commitment to its success	Passionate about the development of aviation industry in the country. Has stated that he had 'a very strong wish to provide assistance in developing the aviation industry and helping individuals to succeed in it'. Has some 'spare time' for such work	Agreed to become mentor because of his interest in the media industry. 'When CIP asked me at that time, we know that the learner was involved in something related to the media only. I don't even know who they are. But I knew they were in media-related industry, so I agreed'	Agreed to be a mentor because the business plan of learners was interesting. Was interested in the business model proposed by the learner. 'I didn't know the entrepreneurs at that time, but I saw their business plan on the web site, and I think it was quite interesting. And I saw it has a big potential, actually. The business plan to me is very exciting and interesting'
Previous mentoring experience in the CIP programme	None. (First time in any structured entrepreneur mentoring system; previously advised mainly as a consultant, not through formal mentoring)	None. (First time in structured entrepreneur mentoring system. Had mentored his subordinates during his tenure in government service)	None (First time in structured entrepreneur mentoring system)	None (First time in structured entrepreneur mentoring system)
Previous or concurrent formal mentoring experience outside of the CIP programme	None previously. However, is currently involved in mentoring 'juniors' in the research institute where he is currently employed	Had worked as mentor during his tenure in government service	Was mentor to his subordinates in previous workplace	Had participated in structured mentoring programme at the workplace when he was a junior executive
Ultimate goal of mentoring	To ensure that the learner makes progress, and that his/her ideas can become viable commercially	To see the learner's product and company develop their potential	'It is more on seeing the success of the learners. Sometimes you guide them, and they recognize your	'It was satisfying to know that I was helping. It was just personally rewarding. It also helps me to know a

Appendix 1 (continued)

Factors Studied	Mentor 1	Mentor 2	Mentor 3	Mentor 4
			contribution from there. They'll feel like you guide them in the right direction. Sometimes they call you . . . they respect you. Even after the project is finished for so long, we still talk'	new type of business. . . . and the industry. Because since then, the knowledge (that I have gathered) has been useful in dealing with my own clients. It was good to meet them, to make new contacts' 'The ultimate goal, I think it was just the experience and the exposure. So, learning about a new area in business and the experience of helping some entrepreneurs, and getting going. And opening up some opportunities to them'

What have you done as a mentor?

Factors Studied	Mentor 1	Mentor 2	Mentor 3	Mentor 4
Roles taken	Played the role of *sculptor*, provided help with the technical aspects of the project 'He has problems; luckily I was in that field, so I have been able to help him' Helped support learner in building the company (for example, preparing business	Has helped mainly with product-related issues Has acted most like a *sculptor*, but also played a bit of a *psychologist* role, when learner was discouraged over problems related to delay in receiving disbursements from CIP Also has worked as a	Has helped most with project management, acted mainly as *sculptor* 'Because I was previously a managing director, I can guide in almost everything From technical, finance, all aspects of it. So if they have a specific problem, I'll help them. I don't actually do	More of a *sculptor*, also played the *psychologist* role Did recommend learners to relevant external parties Had accompanied learners when they made presentation to clients There was no company formation as actual product development was not yet

	plan to be submitted to financing communities, and accompanying learner in meeting venture capitalists)	project manager, making sure learner's work progress is on schedule Did not help learner form a company. Learner sought help from his 'angel' to form the company	for them. Of course as a mentor I wouldn't do for them. The team I mentored was young . . .30 plus only . . . but they are not business people. They are technology people. And sometimes they enjoy playing with the technology equipment, software . . . just enjoy doing it. And a lot of time they forget the original objective. This is the problem' There was no company formation because actual product development was not yet carried out	carried out; financing community considered concepts as embryonic, thus more development work is required
Frequency of meetings with learner	Initially, 3–4 hours a week in person, met learner during weekends at site, then mainly on the phone as needed	Face-to-face contact for about 1 to 1½ hours a week Spends a few hours more to study, prepare, etc. Average 3–4 hours a week total on the venture	Every week, on average 2 hours a week 'It varies. Sometimes from 2 hours, we can go to 4 or 5 hours. Not so much on the specific product or business, sometimes we just go for teh tarik[1] and then just talk. End up sometimes for 4 hours. At least 2 hours, usually 3 or 4 hours a week'	Every week, on average 2 hours a week Also took some time to introduce learners to his network. 'After the meetings, sometimes I will follow up on my side to get some information, or to approach my clients, and introduce the entrepreneurs to these clients. Its basically doing more on networking. So besides meeting with them, I did some networking for them'

Factors Studied	Mentor 1	Mentor 2	Mentor 3	Mentor 4
Availability of mentor's social and professional networks to the learner	Has provided learner with access to technical support (machines and people) either at his research institute or at others, and has acted as liaison for all communications Has referred learner to financial community	No access provided	Helped introduce learner to venture capitalists that he knew personally	'Yes, I helped introduce them to potential partners, who mostly are my clients'
Personal financial investment in the venture	Has so far made no investment, but learner had expressed interest in making him a partner	Has made no investment	Has made no investment	Has made no investment. Learner had invited him to invest in venture, but he decided that it was too risky
Progressions of mentoring roles and styles according to venture development	Yes, from role of technical adviser to more of a personal relationship. First, as technical adviser, then, mentor acts as *psychologist* and *diplomat* 'Probably I'm older than him, he looks up to me and I am willing to share my time with him. I think that is very crucial. You know if he calls me in the middle of the night, I still entertain him'	No. Have remained as 'technical adviser' 'The ideas have been developed much earlier, even before I got involved with mentoring . . . For them, it is just to develop their ideas into a deliverable product. That is the part where I come in and help them, to make sure they deliver the product the right way. This group is clear on exactly what they want'	From mere mentoring to a more 'trusting' relationship. 'At first, we get together, we're not so comfortable yet. The relationship then gets better. In my case . . . I think it clicked . . . we feel comfortable'	'. . . as time progressed, I became more like a partner. I'm still a mentor but, I'm a bit closer to them, and a bit closer to the project. So I felt like a little bit of participating. Even though I was not investing. But I felt like participating. Which is good . . . towards the end. Its more than a mentor. So I would recommend this mentorship to other people. I think it's a very good programme'

Anticipation of future relationship with learner	Has maintained working relationship with learner, even though the 'mentoring contract' is over, and is willing to help learner, without pay, to form a company	'So, when we meet, we look at what we are supposed to do, what is the status . . . And then, of course, they will demonstrate on the PC what they have done so far.' Was rehired to be involved in the second phase of learner's project Has agreed to be involved in second project phase of the venture	Still keep in touch with learners socially	Still keep in touch with learner 'After the project was finished, we still met. Future relationship . . . because one of the partners started looking at other types of related businesses; sometimes he will ask me for some advice or recommend his idea to my clients. So there was some continuance'

How did you do it?

Mentoring techniques	Hybrid style – 'Learning by doing' for technical aspects, and 'Socratic style' for other issues	Hybrid style – a combination of 'Socratic style' and 'stories with a moral', as it seemed appropriate	More of a 'Socratic style'	More of 'Socratic style', giving general guidelines and instructions ('rules of thumb') and sometimes use 'specific directives' 'I gave them some general guidelines on how to make the business plans. They were thinking about how to market the product. . . .'

149

Appendix 1 (continued)

Factors Studied	Mentor 1	Mentor 2	Mentor 3	Mentor 4
				about how expensive it would be . . . I gave guidelines about what price they could charge for their product. So it is more like business guidelines' 'I also gave some specific directions . . . not very often, occasionally when they needed them. For example, they're trying to calculate the potential revenue. I suggested a certain approach to help them do the calculations, because I don't think they had any experience on this before'

Appendix 2   Learners – Personal Background, Venture Information and Perception of Mentor Roles and Techniques

Factors Studied	Mentee 1	Mentee 2	Mentee 3	Mentee 4[2]
About the entrepreneur/learner				
Educational background	Trained as journalist	Trained as a mechanical engineer	Trained as an electronic engineer	Mentee 4a was trained as an electrical engineer. Mentee 4b was trained as a musician
Working experience	Has 10 years' work experience in journalism	Has 25 years' work experience in the aviation industry	Had mixed work experience – of being self-employed and of working for others	Mentee 4a initially worked in an industry related to his tertiary training and then he started up his first business. In 1998, he set up an Internet-based content provider company. Mentee 4b was involved in music-related marketing before becoming general manager of a musical artists consortium, which is his current job
Current position	Full-time entrepreneur	Full-time entrepreneur	Currently hired as a consultant by a large client that needed him to put the product concepts to use	Mentee 4a is a CEO of a small-sized company. Mentee 4b is a general manager of a music consortium, which protects artist rights
Age	Early 30s	Late 40s	Mid-30s	Both are in their late 30s
Previous experience in starting venture?	No, but had experimented with several ideas. The current project emerged as most promising	No, the current business is the first venture	Yes, had experience in starting up 2 business ventures and had also worked in a start-up company	Since 1996, Mentee 4a had been involved in setting up four companies. Mentee 4b was a full-time employee up to now

Appendix 2 (continued)

Factors Studied	Mentee 1	Mentee 2	Mentee 3	Mentee 4[2]
Influence by entrepreneurial parents/close relatives in starting the venture?	No	There are siblings in business ('They are all in a "struggling" stage'), but he is not influenced by them	No. But low-income family background influenced him to become an entrepreneur. 'No one in my family was involved in business. I have been working since I was in secondary school. In college, I had to support myself because my family was poor'	Mentee 4a's decision to start up his own company in 1996 was not directly influenced by his businessman father; but he imitated his father's way of managing business Mentee 4b did not come from an entrepreneurial family
Influence of education/work experience in starting the venture?	Yes. Work experience as a journalist and continuous experimentation with new ideas are helpful in getting necessary connections to gain understanding about building up a company and getting funds	Yes. Current industry is similar to previous work experience Work experience provides opportunity to tap 'friends' for product-related knowledge	Family background, i.e. being poor, was main influence	Past bad experience as struggling musicians was one major motivation for starting product development. They wanted to help protect intellectual property of artists
About the venture				
How product or concept development was started	The idea for the project emerged while experimenting with his previous project When experimenting with this previous project, saw a huge potential market for this particular protein-based product Talked to friends at	Started to do groundwork while still working, then was introduced to student programmer Then, together with programmer, started tinkering with the idea, and he came to realize that he would need to	'I was always involved in new projects; I was lucky that I saw the advertisement for the CIP grant in a Chinese newspaper. "Very interesting", I said. "Why not just give a try?" So, I logged onto the CIP web site, applied for the grant,	Many variables triggered the concept development: (1) learner 4a involvement in Internet industry; (2) participation of both in music industry; (3) their empathy toward other musicians as they have been struggling artists themselves

	The concept was envisioned as one way to safeguard artists' intellectual property. It is a community-building concept for artists on a technology-based platform so that they could protect their intellectual property	'There are very few entrepreneurs who have a music background. So, we have the capability to develop the content ourselves and we also know how to make the technology work. Thus, we have the advantage compared to other operators who need to rely on others for content'
	and then I was called for the interview'	'I would say it was a combination of having a concept in mind, and getting the funding. It is a natural course of action for me because I am always looking for new projects'
Motivations for starting new venture/developing product or concept	work full-time on it, if he were to be successful. So he decided to become a full-time entrepreneur	Realized the growth potential for the industry and noticed the high level of technology content in the industry. Believed that the current software in the market could not meet users' requirements; there is an open niche market for new products. 'I truly believe that after 25 years in the aviation industry, I need to share my knowledge with somebody, with the local people. Why not do it now? If I waited until my retirement age, probably I will not be as productive'. 'I see this as creating an opportunity for the next generation, there is a niche market for the
	MAVCAP, was informed of CIP grant, decided to apply and was approved pre-seeding fund	Saw huge potential for protein-based product because believed that there is a shortage of protein and the product would certainly address this shortage. Believe that Malaysia's weather is conducive for developing agro-based/resource-based industry because its climate is best to breed certain animal species for producing protein as food

Appendix 2 (continued)

Factors Studied	Mentee 1	Mentee 2	Mentee 3	Mentee 4[2]
Composition of entrepreneurial team	Was lead entrepreneur for two-person venture, but the other was silent partner; so venture was essentially like a single-founder project	Is a lead entrepreneur for 3 team members Has background in aviation industry, the other two are IT experts locals to enter this aviation industry'	Is the lead entrepreneur of a two-person venture Partner was a freelance programmer	It was a two-person venture; both interviewed team members had known each other for 20 years
Funding sources and current status of venture development	At the beginning from personal savings, friends and families, eventually get pre-seed funding from CIP Currently in the process of forming a company and already receiving venture capital funding Has fully developed the idea, is in the process of developing the business, and in the course of registering it as a company	Initially from personal savings, but from September 2003 received pre-seed funding from CIP Currently in the process of getting more funding for actual development Has successfully developed the first module of prototype, in the process of developing the second module of prototype Has formed a company with a partner	Received pre-seeding funding from CIP in 2003 RM50 000 was enough to develop prototype because the components were sourced out from China; the money was not enough if components were sourced in Malaysia Has successfully developed a prototype Actual product development was not yet carried out, as product requires acceptance by the consortium that has control over the target market for the product	Received pre-seeding funding in September 2003 RM50 000 is enough to develop the product concepts Financing community considered concepts as embryonic; therefore, more development work is required. Planned to house the concept in learner 4a's existing business for further development
Business goals	'I want to turn the product of this project into the next primary commodity industry in Malaysia' 'I want to get rich, so that I can go fishing every day!'	To see that product is accepted by industry	'I liked to be involved in new projects; I would like to see that the concepts that we have developed generate money, but I am always working on new projects'	'To see that our concept is able to generate profit and that the company gets a listing in MESDAQ (Malaysian Exchange of Securities Dealing & Automated Quotation)'

Problems encountered	Initially, mainly technical issues related to developing the product. Then, problems related to building the company, such as seeking money from venture capitalists and company structuring	Most prevalent problem is getting funding. Faced problems in obtaining pre-seed funds when began operations – aviation industry viewed 'unfavourably' by local fund managers. Funding was not obtained until 2003. There are already established players in the market. Also faced funding problems in actual product development	Most prevalent problem was getting software/hardware houses to help develop prototype components. All required high volume ordering and expensive investments. Eventually resorted to source development to China, and managed to get prototype developed within stipulated budget and time	Most problematic was getting further funding because financing community considered product concepts as embryonic (MESDAQ is a market for listing of high-growth and technology-based companies) To be able to contribute toward protecting artists' intellectual property in the country
Mentoring, general Previous structured mentoring accessibility	None (First time in structured entrepreneurial mentoring system)	None (First time in structured entrepreneurial mentoring system)	None (First time in structured entrepreneurial mentoring system)	None (First time in structured entrepreneurial mentoring system)
Assignment of mentor to learner	'I found that the thing I lacked most at that time, was the technical skill – and	The mentor was assigned by CIP 'He was the only mentor	'I know that I need to know the industry well, so I told CIP that I want	The mentor was assigned by CIP The learners were first

155

Factors Studied	Mentee 1	Mentee 2	Mentee 3	Mentee 4[2]
	knowledge of science and agriculture. I am a journalist, a "jack of all trades' . . . But I did not know enough about those things' I asked my personal friend whether he knew anybody who is in the agricultural industry and all that related stuff. He suggested this mentor' So we met, and I found that I liked him very much	listed who had experience in the industry we are in'	someone from the advertising industry. This is because they already know the "in's and out's" of the business; you can make a product with interesting features, but it will all be useless if it doesn't meet what the industry needs'	assigned a mentor from a large telecommunication company, but he was replaced by this managing director of a multinational advertising company 'We feel more grateful with our mentor because advertising is one major element for our project. We want advertising expertise'
Availability of other mentors (*informal*) while developing products/concepts	Had depended a lot on informal mentors for non-product-related issues: Had about 10 informal mentors who mainly give advice on business structuring-related issues, such as how to set the valuation, what kinds of share structures to issue, etc	Quite a number of informal mentors, who are 'old' friends, and who help especially to solve technical matters Seek advice from informal mentors for product-related issues only	Has a number of informal mentors who advise him on technical matters	Through mentors' professional networks, learners were introduced to potential clients which allow learners to gain valuable knowledge about industry and product pricing and inputs to their product concepts
Learner's opinion of CIP mentoring programme	Very good, 'if not for mentor, I would not be in this business'	'Very good' Benefited from regular CIP get-togethers, where CIP invites successful entrepreneurs Benefited from classes	'Without the mentor's help, the project would be delayed. Without him, we would have missed out on the actual value of the CIP funding. The actual value	'I think the mentorship programme actually works very well for us because we need to have somebody with advertising and media background to

156

What mentors do
Roles of mentor

Technical adviser and teacher
Consultant and coach – purveyor of knowledge/expertise
'Mentor was very instrumental in helping me to acquire the technical understanding regarding how to achieve optimal performance for my product, to the point that

Product designer and manager
'Sculptor'
'and a little bit of a psychologist (when it comes to money matters only)'
Mentor assists more on issues related to product development, thus helping to ensure product meets project

'Sculptor'
'His major contribution is giving us the information on the TV advertising industries. As such he directly contributed to the development of our product'
Mentor also helped in finding investors because of his knowledge of the industry – 'diplomatic role'

'Sculptor'
Mentor's biggest contribution was to attract advertiser, which is a major revenue generator for learner's project, besides subscription fees
'Mentor gave valuable input on Malaysian advertising industry . . . . how it works and what are the trends that are

organized by CIP, such as those on business plans
Benefited from CIP help to write executive summaries for submission to the venture capital community

to me is to make use of the money and the *connection* behind it'

give us some very good advice in terms of generating revenues from advertising, to enable us to develop our revenue projections, which is of utmost importance to affirm the viability of our business. For example, what are the potential trends that advertisers are looking at?'
'Without mentor input, our revenue projections would not be convincing to the venture capital community. As such, the possibilities that our concepts would be commercialized would be very low'

Factors Studied	Mentee 1	Mentee 2	Mentee 3	Mentee 4[2]
	now I can independently figure out such problems. He gave me an understanding of the industry, the business, the market price, and what sources of protein are available now.' Mentor also helped with company formation	datelines and industry requirements	'He knows the industry, so he knows the industry players, and he knows who the rich industry players are.' Mentor was also project manager 'Mentor asked a lot of questions; the usual question is 'Have you completed ___?' Because we have milestones that we need to achieve. When work is not completed, then we share the problems'	happening.' Mentor introduced learners to his big clients. 'He brought us to present to potential mobile advertising client. Directly talking to potential clients is so valuable to us, we can directly see how clients react to this advertising concept'
Frequency of meetings with learner	Initially, three to four hours a week, then mainly on the phone 'I call him almost every day. I called him at midnight, when I could not sleep, something is disturbing me, and when I wanted to meet the potential partners, potential investors, I will ask him to come along'	3–4 hours a week, on average	'We met at least once a week. In terms of how many hours per meeting, that is interesting. Officially it was supposed to be 2 hours, but usually every time we spend more than 2 hours. We will use 1–2 hours to talk about the project, but after that we talked about anything'	Every week, on average 2 hours a week
Access to mentor's social and professional networks and other resources	Mentor provides access to his social and professional networks. 'He refers me to investors, when he met certain people, he will tell	No access yet, but the learner will probably ask for access when the time is appropriate	Mentor introduced learner to venture capitalists within the industry	Mentor provided mentees with access to his clients He also gave access to useful expensive literature and statistical data

	them the idea, he will call me and say this person is interested, can you call him and talk about it. So far, he has referred about 4–5 people' Access to resources and people in the research institute Access to other relevant government agencies	None	Mentor used his current position as a managing director to solicit primary data from his company's sister unit for the learners
Did mentor make personal financial investment in the business	None, but mentee had expressed interest in making him partner	None	None, but mentees have plans to invite mentor as a business partner
Progression of mentoring roles and styles according to venture development	First, served only as technical adviser, then as 'real' mentor. Over time, the relationship becomes more informal. When the 'contract' is over, the types of assistance provided by mentor are more focused on helping learner source out for funding and forming the company	Has remained mainly as a 'product' adviser throughout Rehired mentor for second phase of project, to capitalize on specific mentor's expertise Thought that mentor was able to help much more in second phase of the project	'He was sceptical during the initial part. The funny thing is that the mentor and the learner did not have the chance to meet before official appointment. But eventually, our relation with the mentor is like friends – we are very close; that is why we keep contacting each other. Even when the project is completed, we still get in touch'
Anticipation of future relationship with mentor	Wants to make the mentor a business partner	Still in the process of 'thinking about it'	'We didn't know him before, then we found out that he is about the same age as we are after the mentoring program was over. We joked with him, saying that we are not sure if you're old enough to become a mentor . . . so, mentor-mentee becomes more like a friendship' Wants to make the mentor a business partner

Appendix 2 (continued)

Factors Studied	Mentee 1	Mentee 2	Mentee 3	Mentee 4[2]
How mentors do it				
Mentoring techniques	Hybrid style, a combination of learning by doing and Socratic style	Hybrid style: a combination of Socratic style and stories with a moral, as appropriate	'Socratic style'	'Socratic style' 'Most of the time, we initiated the discussion, but rather than asking him what to do, we would show him, then say, "This is what we came up with; what do you think?" It is more that we ask the question, and he answers. We need his feedback because of his experience in the advertising industry. He will share with us some of the current practices in the advertising industry – the mentality and the way they practise the business'

Notes:
1. Having *teh tarik* in Malaysian culture usually refers to going in the company of friends to an inexpensive open air restaurant which serves tea with condensed milk, as a way of taking a break. Malaysian style.
2. CIP required that each of its grant recipients be an entrepreneurial team of at least two members. In three of the four cases, only the lead entrepreneur was interviewed; in case 4, both members of the team were interviewed.

PART 3

INCUBATORS AND TECHNOLOGY TRANSFERS

8 University technology transfer through university business incubators and how they help start-ups
Christian Lendner

Introduction

Universities play a major role as a source of technology, leading-edge research and for potential entrepreneurs, formerly academics, research staff, doctoral candidates or students. This know-how, human capital and network access are critical resources to entrepreneurial companies in general. Research commercialization and technology transfer is a main task of the universities, also teaching, research and executive education. The even more challenging task of universities is to transfer the intellectual property out of the university to industry or, better, to use it for the creation of new companies (start-ups). An incubator assists start-ups in setting up their business and starting operations. The specific requirements of knowledge based start-up firms differ according to their industry focus and technology level. Technology-based companies tend to emphasize R&D investments and a firm with a new 'high-tech' product wants to achieve proof of concept or to build a prototype. Incubators assist such firms in the pre-seed and seed phase. Universities can facilitate the transfer of critical resources to the business through the process of research commercialization. University business incubators (UBIs) can be distinguished from other public or private incubators, private business parks, corporate incubators and 'virtual' incubator organizations without a physical structure. The priority of public or private science parks is to rent space to young companies. They seldom offer further advice or support to the companies. In comparison, private business incubators lack a relationship with university with its complementary assets and services. Corporate incubators are only oriented towards the technological or business focus of the related company.

History of Incubators

The first incubators supporting start-up companies were set up in the USA. The oldest incubator in the world is Student Agencies Inc from Ithaca, New York, which began supporting student entrepreneurial initiatives as early as 1942. The first business incubator was the Batavia Industrial Center, founded in 1959 in Batavia, New York, USA. By 1980, there were already 12 incubators in the USA, and by 1984 the number had risen to 63 (Allen, 1985, p. 42). In 2000, the number of incubators in the USA was estimated by different sources to be between 800 and 1000 (McKinnon and Hayhow, 1998, p. 4). There have been a variety of studies conducted in the USA on the influence of incubator organizations on company development. These studies show that the success rate is higher for start-ups in incubators, with 87 per cent of all companies started in an incubator surviving the first five years successfully (Molnar et al., 1997, p. 17). Without an incubator, over half of the start-ups disappear during the first five years (Smilor and Gill, 1986, p. 13). As early as 1992, over 50 US universities or colleges had their own university incubators (Mian, 1994, p. 516). According to a survey by the NBIA (National Business Incubation Association, 2002, p. 1), in 1998 approximately 19 per cent of all US incubators were run by universities or colleges.

University-based incubators do often have the objective of technology transfer and research commercialization from universities, entrepreneurship education and providing opportunities for external research. Further objectives of incubators in general could be regional economic development and entrepreneurial teaching.

Theoretical Background and Previous Research

There is a lack of academic research on business incubation focusing on university-based incubators. In particular, there are almost no recommendations, best practices and guidelines coming out of the research for practising technology transfer from university by a UBI. There have as yet been no exclusive UBI surveys conducted globally involving a large, comprehensive sample size (Steffensen et al., 1999, pp. 93–111). The focus has been primarily on a direct technology transfer from universities (Shane, 2002, p. 540) typically using cases. A young business foundation usually has a single definite resource (Arbaugh and Camp, 2000, p. 313),[1] such as a technologically unique selling point. However, new foundations especially are characterized by the paradigms liability of newness and resource poverty. Regarding the university business incubator's resources and additionally applying the resource-based view, which is about the achievement of sustainable competitive advantage,[2] it is furthermore considered that this view is focused on competing businesses. The securing of survival and additionally the encouragement of growth of the incubatees is the primary competitive advantage of a university business incubator. Thus it is not the matter of competitive advantages in a narrower sense, meaning the realization of an above-average rate of return and the acquisition of market shares, but a matter of competitive advantages in a wider, rudimentary sense, meaning the securing of survival and the enablement of growth in the business's early phases. In particular, according to the paradigms of liability, of newness and of resource poverty, new foundations lack crucial know-how gained from experience during the early growth stages. This foundation specific treasury of experience can only be provided by the employees (and also, in a wider sense, by the network partners) of the university business incubator.

The UBI provides a formal mechanism for embedding start-up companies more quickly in entrepreneurial networks and thereby can help such companies to develop their own set of relationships (Schmude, 2002, p. 256) more quickly. Such relationships increase the probability of survival (Hisrich and Smilor, 1988, pp. 28ff; Uzzi 1996, p. 674). A UBI represents a node in the developing network for a start-up company that includes partners for research, financing, consulting and regulatory matters. The most important success factors to be considered for many technology-based firms in UBIs are recruitment of qualified employees and the acquisition of further intellectual property. Universities often represent an important source of additional personnel and know-how for the start-up firms, in particular in the area of R&D. Professors at universities often serve as research consultants or a scientific advisory board. The university partners may consist of other universities or colleges, research institutions or other higher educational institutions.

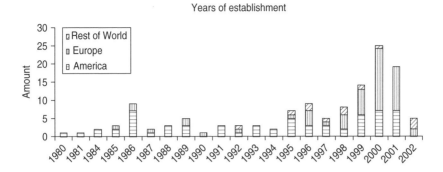

Figure 8.1   Year of establishment of the UBI (Lendner, 2004a, p. 114)

Methodology and Results

A database of 310 UBIs worldwide was created by the author, 46 per cent of which are located in America (90 per cent of these in the US), 42 per cent in Europe (49 per cent of them in Great Britain), 10 per cent in Asia, and 2 per cent in Australia. We believe that this database includes almost all existing UBIs worldwide. To ensure that the answers had a high validity, questionnaires were sent only to UBI managers. The final sample consists of 130 UBIs (44 per cent response rate) (Lendner, 2004a, p. 106). Regarding the age of university business incubators the data show that there are two focal points in the years of establishment: 1986 and 2000, as shown in Figure 8.1. The second focal point is quite obviously due to the new economy hype.

The success of a UBI can be measured by the success of the start-ups in the incubator and then transferred to their UBI. Success measures are the growth rate in employees and sale, the survival rate and the rate of gaining external finance.

Organizational Structure and Importance of the Related University

To maintain a legal or organizational relationship with a university was a formal criterion for being included in this study as a UBI. Some 51 per cent of the UBIs are located on the campus of the related university and 22 per cent of the respondents stated that they were located near the university campus. Only 27 per cent are located far away from campus at an average distance of 8.6 km (Lendner, 2004a, p. 121). Of the related universities, 36 have a research focus, 35 have a teaching focus and 30 have a teaching and research focus (n=101). This has no influence on the success of the start-ups in the UBI. More than three-quarters of the UBIs use university facilities (n=104), in most cases laboratory space and facilities but also IT network, library, conference rooms and catering were used. The technology focus of the UBI has a significant impact on the finance rate and growth rate of employees. The entrance and exit criteria of a UBI can also serve as a rating criterion for the incubatee (Lendner and Lichtinger, 2004, p. 353). The potential to grow and the innovativeness of the business as an entrance criterion for start-ups shows a high influence on all of the success rates (Table 8.1).

Table 8.1   Influence on entrance criteria of university business incubators

		Criterion for acceptance, potential to grow	Criterion for acceptance, innovativeness of the business
Survival rate	correlation	0.219*	0.188
	significance (2-sided)	0.038	0.078
	N	90	89
Finance rate	correlation	0.213	0.051
	significance (2-sided)	0.061	0.658
	N	78	77
Sales growth rate	correlation	0.219	0.213
	significance (2-sided)	0.073	0.084
	N	68	67

Note: * Significance level at 0.05 (2-sided).

Table 8.2   Professional services offered by a UBI

Professional services provided (yes/no)	All (%)
Business plan/development and strategy planning	88
Assistance with starting business operations	86
Assistance with raising external financing	83
Entrepreneurship education	76
Market research, marketing and sales assistance	72
Research and development	63
Accounting, tax and legal assistance	63
Human resource consulting	55
Human resources and organization	42
Providing seed financing	41

Source: Lendner (2003, p. 112).

Providing physical and/or non-material services for start-ups is one of the important characteristics for a UBI. The types of services which are critical for start-ups in the seed phase or early stages were collected. The frequency of provision of professional services is shown in Table 8.2.

Expertise of the UBI Employees

Apart from providing network contacts the related university can provide critical resources. For example, the university can serve as a committee member on the board of directors, in the advisory board or the investment committee of the university business incubator. In addition, the university can contribute to the finance of the university business incubator by providing equity, grants, subsidies, loans and donations. The related university can also contribute to create its own cash flow for the university business incubator. In particular, because the financing by 'intelligent capital' is expected to be a

Table 8.3   University involvement in the funding of UBIs

Funding from university through MW	Employee growth of incubatees						
	Yes		No		Avg.		
	MW	n	MW	n	MW	n	Significance
Equity	94.78	32	92.48	95	93.06	127	0.876
Grants/subsidies	108.93	28	88.58	99	93.06	127	0.187
Donations	79.43	7	93.86	120	93.06	127	0.607
Own cash flow	76.81	26	97.25	101	93.06	127	0.197

Source: Lendner (2004b, p. 331).

Table 8.4   Strength and influence of academic network

		Strength of relationship between incubator and other universities	Strength of relationship between incubator and research institutions	Average network strength in all academic network
100% minus survival rate	correlation	0.225*	0.006	0.109
	significance (2-sided)	0.032	0.956	0.305
	N	91	91	91
Sales growth rate	correlation	0.195	0.362**	0.266*
	significance (2-sided)	0.111	0.003	0.028
	N	68	67	68

Note: * Significance level at 0.05 (2-sided), ** significance level at 0.01 (2-sided).

crucial resource for young companies, the involvement of a university in the finance of its business incubator may contribute to the success of the companies which can be expressed in the employee growth rate. The results shown in Table 8.3 underline this expectation. UBIs who receive grants or subsidies from the related university do have a higher employee growth rate of their incubatees (108.93) than UBIs who do not receive grants (88.58).

Network of the UBI

The network of the university business incubator consists of a certain number of network partners (nodes) and the strength of the relationship with these partners (weak or strong ties): see Table 8.4. For technology transfer and research commercialization, there is a strong network of the UBI with other academic network partners necessary to secure the successful support of the young firms. This academic network may consist of other universities or research institutions. The correlation of the sales growth rate to all academic network partners on average is 0.3, with a significance rate of 0.025.

Implications and Conclusions

There is a very efficient means of technology transfer and research commercialization through young start-up companies, using university business incubators. This study of UBIs has brought useful insights on the factors that influence the successful technology transfer of universities to young and small firms. These results may also be of practical relevance for institutions planning to establish, or that are already running, a UBI. Network ties to other academic institutions may be the key to the success of the firms in the incubator and therefore to the UBI itself. Young firms that have a choice should look for the incubator with the strongest set of such academic relationships.

Young firms thinking about joining a UBI should also consider the number and kind of professional services which a UBI offers. Both directly and via its network, the UBI also provides its firms with critical resources, such as seed financing and human capital. The growth of firms in a UBI will also be positively influenced by the level of entrance criteria of the UBI. There is a valuable impact from the related university to the start-ups via the UBI. Representatives of the university can serve as a member of the advisory board of the UBI.

Notes

1. Arbaugh and Camp (2000, p. 313) speak of 'available resources', 'controlled resources' and 'required resources' in the entrepreneurial process.
2. As in the transaction costs approach.

References

Allen, D.N. (1985), 'An entrepreneurial marriage: business incubators and startups', in J.A. Hornaday, E.B. Shils, J.A. Timmons and K.H. Vesper (eds), *Frontiers of Entrepreneurship Research*, Wellesley, MA: Babson College.

Arbaugh, J.B. and S.M. Camp (2000), 'Managing growth transitions: theoretical perspectives and research directions', in D.L. Sexton and H. Landström (eds), *The Blackwell Handbook of Entrepreneurship*, Malden, MA: Blackwell Publishers Ltd.

Hisrich, R.D. and R.W. Smilor (1988), 'The university and business incubation: technology transfer through entrepreneurial development', *Technology Transfer*, **13**(1), 14–19.

Lendner, C. (2003), 'The organizational structure and university business incubators: an international study', in H. Klandt and A.Z. Bakar (eds), *IntEnt 2002 Internationalizing Entrepreneurship Education and Training – Proceedings of the IntEnt-Conference Johore Bahru, Malaysia, 8–10 July 2002*, Lohmar, Germany: Josef Eul.

Lendner, C. (2004a), *Organisationsmodell und Erfolgsfaktoren von Hochschulinkubatoren*, Lohmar, Germany: Josef Eul.

Lendner, C. (2004b), 'University involvements in university business incubators and their impact on the start-ups', *3rd International GET UP-Workshop Conference Proceedings: International Cooperation of Universities and its Impact on University Based Start-Ups*, Jena, Germany: University of Applied Sciences Jena, pp. 313–32.

Lendner, C. and H. Lichtinger (2004), 'Existenzgründerrating und Aufnahmekriterien in Hochschulinkubatoren', in A. Achleitner and O. Everling (eds), *Existenzgründerrating*, Wiesbaden, Germany: Gabler.

McKinnon, S. and S. Hayhow (1998), *The State of the Business Incubation Industry*, Athens, OH: National Business Incubation Association.

Mian, S.A. (1994), 'US university-sponsored technology incubators: an overview of management, policies and performance', *Technovation*, **14**(8), 515–28.

Molnar, L.A., D. Adkins, Y. Batts, D. Grimes, H. Sherman and L. Tomatzky (1997), *Business Incubation Works*, Athens, OH: National Business Incubation Association.

National Business Incubation Association (2002), 'Executive summary of NBIA's 1998 state of the business incubation industry findings' (online source: http://www.nbia.org/info/facts.html).

Schmude, J. (2002), 'Standortwahl und Netzwerke von Unternehmensgründern', in M. Dowling and H.-J. Drumm (eds), *Gründungsmanagement – Vom erfolgreichen Unternehmensstart zu dauerhaftem Wachstum*, Berlin: Springer.

Shane, S. (2002), 'Executive forum: university technology transfer to entrepreneurial companies', *Journal of Business Venturing*, **17**, 537–52.

Smilor, R.W. and M.D. Gill (1986), *The New Business Incubator – Linking Talent, Technology, Capital and Know-how*, Lanham, MD: Lexington University Press.

Steffensen, M., E.M. Rogers and K. Speakman (1999), 'Spin-offs from research centers at research universities', *Journal of Business Venturing*, **5**, 93–111.

Uzzi, B. (1996), 'The sources and consequences of embeddedness for the economic performance of organizations: the network effect', *American Sociological Review*, **61**, 674–98.

9 Determinants and consequences of university spin-off activity: a conceptual framework
Rory O'Shea

Introduction

The rapid rate of technological change, shorter product life cycles and more intense global competition has radically transformed the current competitive position of many regional economies. With the drive to generate knowledge-based employment opportunities, policy makers are now placing a greater emphasis on the role of universities in the commercialization of scientific and technological knowledge produced within research laboratories. This increased emphasis on technology transfer from universities to industry and the need to develop more 'rapid' linkages between science, technology and utilization (Allen, 1977, 1997) has led to the emergence of a number of entrepreneurial initiatives within academic institutions.

The term 'entrepreneurial university' was coined by Etzkowitz (1998) to describe instances in which universities have proved themselves critical to regional economic development. Although some authors refer to European universities (Chiesa and Piccaluga, 2000; Jones-Evans et al., 1999), the case of MIT is the reference example (Etzkowitz, 2002; Roberts, 1991). By encouraging faculty members to pursue private ventures outside the research lab, the Bank of Boston (1997) calculated that MIT start-up companies generated $240 billion worth of sales per year and provided an additional 1.1 million new jobs for the US economy. Another known example cited in the literature relates to the University of Texas at Austin in promoting the emergence of the city of Austin, Texas, as a technopolis. UT-Austin contributed to local economic development by launching and running one of the most successful business incubators in the US, the Austin Technology Incubator (Gibson and Smilor, 1991).

Explaining spin-off behaviour and why some universities are better at it has become an important research objective within the domain of entrepreneurship research. Referred to broadly as 'academic entrepreneurship', this domain has received increased attention from scholars in recent years.[1] The objective of this chapter is to review the academic entrepreneurship literature systematically, to synthesize this research and to provide directions for future research. Extant research has sought to identify the determinants and the consequences of university spin-off activity. We argue that the existing literature can be divided into six distinct research streams: (1) studies that focus on the individual and the personality of the individual as the key determinant of whether spin-off activity occurs; (2) organizational configuration studies that seek to explain spin-off activity in terms of the resources of the university; (3) socio-cultural development studies that explain spin-off activity in terms of culture and the rewards within the university; (4) studies that explain spin-offs in terms of external environmental influences; (5) studies that measure the performance of spin-offs; and (6) studies that seek to measure the economic impact of spin-off activity. While these research domains are clearly not orthogonal, we employ them as classifications of convenience to facilitate a discussion on the literature and the development of a conceptual framework that explains the determinants, constituents and consequences of university spin-off activity.

This chapter is organized in the following manner. First, we provide an overview of the evolving role of the university in economic development. Second, we outline six distinct research streams that we have identified in the 'academic entrepreneurship' literature. Third, we identify the limitations of existing research and we suggest new avenues for future research. Fourth, building on our review of the literature, we present a theoretical framework of the determinants, constituents and consequences of spin-off activity.

Role of the University in Economic Development

The primary mission of the traditional university is to engage in research and disseminate knowledge across both academic and student communities. The importance of this function of the university is well documented in the literature (Bok, 2003; Geiger, 1993; Newman, 1996). Universities can also play a key role in technology transfer activities by providing research and development (R&D) activities, by assisting in patenting innovations and by providing students with the skills that allow them to become highly qualified personnel (Roberts and Malone, 1996; Smilor et al., 1990). According to Segal (1986), not only do universities provide a source of technical expertise for faculty members, but their students also acquire a wealth of codified and tacit knowledge through learning and living at the university. Rogers (1986) supports this view and contends that universities influence the innovation process through a number of mechanisms, such as scientific publications that expand the technological opportunity set of firms; training of engineers and natural scientists; training of PhDs with its essential provision of background knowledge, skills and personal networks; and participation in common informal networks, joint R&D projects, research funding and contract research with an associated sharing of explicit and tacit knowledge. In essence, such universities place a strong emphasis on training, tacit knowledge and indirect benefits rather than codified information (or products) as being the main output of academic research into industry (Bok, 2003; Mansfield and Lee, 1996).

However, recent research suggests that traditional universities could play a greater role in regional and national economic development. A number of factors explain why universities are increasingly important to economic development: the growing role of knowledge in the development of national economies and employment; technical advances in information and communication technologies; and the increasing importance of regional high-technology clusters. These factors are explained in greater detail below.

The contribution of knowledge to economic development
There is a growing recognition among policy makers of the need to place more emphasis on knowledge creation and knowledge exploitation, and specifically on technology-based entrepreneurship, which converts new scientific discoveries into new opportunities (Chiesa and Piccaluga, 2000). Economic development is increasingly linked to a nation's ability to acquire and apply technical and socio-economic knowledge and the process of globalization is accelerating this trend. A recent World Economic Forum global competitiveness report states that 'without technological progress, countries may achieve a higher

standard of living through a higher rate of capital accumulation, but they will not be able to enjoy continuously high economic growth' (2003). Thus comparative advantages come less from abundant natural resources or cheap labour and more from technical innovations and the competitive use of knowledge. Economic growth can be seen as much as a process of knowledge accumulation as of capital accumulation.

Economies looking to meet the aim of developing a comparative advantage based on the enhancement and exploitation of the national knowledge base must look to foster university-based entrepreneurship as a central component of their strategy to develop a knowledge-based society (OECD, 1998). This is particularly so because of the rapid acceleration in the rhythm of creation and dissemination of knowledge, which means that the life span of technologies and products gets progressively shorter and that obsolescence comes more quickly. The ability to develop technologically sophisticated and knowledge-led regions has already provided Greater Boston and Silicon Valley regions with wealth creation and quality of life improvements (Kenney, 2000; Roberts, 1991). As a result, governments increasingly recognize the need to support the process of technological change with the aim of spawning high-growth, knowledge-intensive companies from university research.[2]

The information and communications technologies revolution
Advances in information and communication technologies have revolutionized the way people work, the way organizations are structured and the way businesses compete. For example, rapid developments in information and communication technologies have eased the difficulty of communicating and enabled the development of widespread ventures and global supply chains. This has resulted in what is popularly referred to as the knowledge-based, interdependent, global village. Competition is much less likely to be localized and may now come from any corner of the world. To compete in such an environment, economies have to accelerate the generation of new knowledge, which in turn requires a continuous process of learning. Universities have historically been the centre for the accumulation, creation and dissemination of new knowledge and must now use this knowledge to enhance the competitive advantage of their regions.

The role of regional high-technology clusters
In many national economies, policy makers argue that universities need to place increased emphasis on transferring and commercializing knowledge, as opposed to solely generating and disseminating knowledge within the academic community itself, in order to stimulate regional technological clusters. Universities and high-technology clusters are important to the attraction of inward foreign-direct investment because human capital and R&D capability play a key role in determining where high value-added R&D projects from multinational corporations are located (Etzkowitz, 2000). Economies that possess a sophisticated technology infrastructure and that are populated by start-ups are better positioned to attract knowledge-seeking investment from multinational corporations. For example, traditional pharmaceutical companies such as Novartis and Wyeth located their R&D facilities around successful universities such as Harvard and MIT and spin-offs such as Alnylam and Genzyme in Cambridge (US) to acquire critical expertise in biotechnology. The clustering effect resulting from the interchange of knowledge among such corporations and universities resulted in high-quality employment and increased wealth for the greater Boston region.

Review of Academic Entrepreneurship Literature

The study of university spin-offs within the 'entrepreneurial university' framework came to the fore with Roberts' seminal study on entrepreneurial activity in MIT (1991). Many subsequent studies of spin-off activity have followed Roberts' early work by investigating the factors that stimulate the creation of spin-off companies from universities. Indicative of this research, and of the general prescriptive findings that characterize this literature, is a cross-national study of five highly successful European universities that identified elements common among successful entrepreneurial institutions (Clark, 1998):

1. Strong top-down leadership and policies that support and encourage the process of academic entrepreneurship and which merge entrepreneurial orientation objectives with the traditional academic values of the university.
2. Strong ties between the university and industry in research projects of mutual gain and 'robust' structures, policies and procedures to enable such activity (for example, industrial liaison offices and flexible contracting procedures).
3. A diversified funding base such as industry and private benefactors, though much of university funding is still derived from government sources.
4. A strong academic base, what the authors referred to as 'a steeple of excellence approach', whereby the universities recruited the top candidates in those fields where it has built its 'steeple'. Tenure and academic promotions are granted solely on academic achievement and not thanks to individual entrepreneurial endeavours.
5. An entrepreneurial culture that embraces change and sustains the fundamental values of the institution.

Such findings are underpinned by a body of research that has explored individual determinants of spin-off activity. Our review of the literature suggests six primary research groups or domains. The first four focus on the determinants of spin-off activity within a university context: (1) the attributes and the personality characteristics of academic entrepreneurs; (2) the resource endowments and capabilities of the university; (3) university structures and policies facilitating commercialization; (4) environmental factors influencing academic entrepreneurship. The remaining two factors focus on the consequences of spin-off activity: (5) the performance of spin-off businesses; and (6) studies that measure the economic impact of spin-offs on regional economies. We present each of these in more detail below.

For the purposes of this chapter, we define university spin-offs as the transfer of a core technology from an academic institution into a new company, where the founding member(s) may include the inventor academic(s) who may or may not be currently affiliated with the academic institution (Nicolaou and Birley, 2003).

Individual attributes as determinants of spin-off activity
A number of studies highlight the importance of entrepreneurial attributes in shaping the individual's behaviour and whether an academic will establish a spin-off business. Other researchers have stressed the role personality, motivation and disposition play in influencing academic entrepreneurship. Some studies have used psychological models to explain spin-off departure from universities. These studies emphasize the impact of individual

abilities and dispositions on the entrepreneurial behaviour of academics. This stream of research shares a common theme: that spin-off behaviour is a reflection of individual actions and therefore is largely due to the personality, ability or willingness of the individual to engage successfully in entrepreneurial behaviour.

Roberts (1991), for example, found that academic entrepreneurs with outgoing, extroverted personalities were more likely to engage in spin-off activity. Furthermore, from a study of almost 130 technical entrepreneurs and almost 300 scientists and engineers, he concluded that personal characteristics such as the need for achievement, the desire for independence and an internal locus of control were common in both groups. Tenure in universities and occupational and research skill levels amongst academics are also found to affect university spin-off behaviour. Audretsch's (2000) analysis of academic entrepreneurs found that university entrepreneurs tended to be older and more scientifically experienced than 'typical' high-technology entrepreneurs. Similarly, Zucker et al. (1998), using data on California biotechnology companies, found that scientific 'stars' collaborating with firms had substantially higher citation rates than pure academic 'stars'.

Organizational determinants of university spin-off activity
Social scientists operating at the organizational level have adopted a different approach to the study of spin-off activity. Organizational theories of university spin-off behaviour are generally concerned with the impact of environmental forces on academic entrepreneurship. But, rather than focusing on broad social or economic forces, such researchers have centred their attention on organizational and human resource aspects of the university. Specifically, researchers have sought to establish links between spin-off activity and the level and nature of research funding; the quality of the researchers, the nature of the research within the university; and the presence of technology incubators and technology transfer offices.

One factor that has received attention is the level and nature of funding for R&D activities within the university. For example, Lockett and Wright (2004) find that the number of spin-off companies created from UK universities is positively associated with R&D expenditure; the number of technology transfer staff; expenditure on intellectual property protection; and the business development capabilities of the university. Blumenthal et al. (1996) surveyed 2052 faculties at 50 universities in the life sciences field and found industry-funded faculty members to be more commercially productive (more patent applications and new products brought to the market) than those who are not industry-funded. Similarly, in a cross-sectional study of doctoral granting research universities, Powers and McDougall (2005) found a positive and statistically significant relationship between annual university-wide R&D expenditure and spin-off activity. Furthermore, Wright et al. (2004) found evidence to suggest that involvement of industry functioning as venture capitalists via joint venture spin-offs may facilitate the emergence of university spin-offs because they have the necessary financial resources and commercial expertise to transfer technologies successfully to the marketplace. The nature of this research engaged by the university also seems to be important in technology transfer as Shane (2004a) reports that the majority of MIT spin-off companies from 1980 to 1996 derived from life science research funding while the others originated from computer science research.

Faculty quality has also been cited as another factor that influences spin-off activity. Zucker et al. (1998) argue that 'star' scientists from higher-quality academic institutions create spin-off firms to capture the rents generated by their intellectual capital. Such capital is tacit and therefore it is difficult for lower-quality institutions to imitate. DiGregorio and Shane (2003) suggest faculty members who develop leading-edge innovations may wish to earn economic rents on valuable asymmetric information. They suggest it may be easier for academics from top-tier universities to assemble resources to create start-ups for reasons of credibility.

In recent years, the question of how universities are supporting the development of spin-offs is attracting increased attention. Tornatzky (1996) identified 50 best-practice incubator programmes in the US and highlighted the role technology incubators could play in accelerating technology transfer. In order to improve industry and commercial ties, some universities operate a Technology Transfer Office as a vehicle to support the creation of spin-off companies (Hague and Oakley, 2000). For example, Oxford University ISIS Innovation is a wholly owned subsidiary of the university and its task is to promote and support the commercialization of research ideas generated by Oxford academics. ISIS selects projects that it considers it should support and then uses its business network to attract investment into the spin-off business. According to Chugh (2004), the Technology Transfer Office plays a key role with respect to engendering academic entrepreneurship. The Technology Transfer Office achieves this by engineering synergistic networks between academics and venture capitalists, advisors and managers who provide the human and financial resources that are necessary to start a company; and by providing company formation expertise, as many technology transfer personnel have experience in evaluating markets, writing business plans, raising venture capital, assembling venture teams and obtaining space and equipment. From an organizational structure perspective, understanding the design and the development of productive TTO organizations has become another area of fruitful research. For example Debackere (2000), in a case analysis of K.U. Leuven Research & Development (LRD), found that having the right mix of governance structures (that is, matrix structures facilitating interdisciplinary research) processes (that is, seed capital fund, patent protection, business plan and new venture development services) and context (historic embeddedness of LRD) contributed to K.U. Leuven's success at generating 34 spin-off companies up to 1999.

Institutional determinants of spin-off activity
The central tenet of the third stream of research is that university spin-off activity is a reflection of institutional behaviour. This research suggests that universities that have cultures that support commercialization activity will have higher levels of commercialization and higher rates of spin-off activity. In contrast, university environments that do not encourage entrepreneurship will have less spin-off activity. Roberts (1991) argues that the social norms and expectations of the university are a key determinant of commercialization activity. He suggests that MIT's tacit approval of entrepreneurs was a key factor in explaining successful academic entrepreneurship at MIT. Golub (2003) supports this perspective and credits the growth in spin-off activity at Columbia University, at least in part, to the knowledge spillovers provided by academic inventors in life sciences who had established companies in the early 1990s.

By contrast, university environments that do not encourage entrepreneurship have been shown to inhibit spin-off activity. More specifically, an academic's reluctance to engage in spin-off behaviour may be exacerbated by the attitudes and behaviours of superiors such as professors or departmental heads. For example, Louis et al. (1989) found that local group norms were important in predicting active involvement in commercialization. They argue that this may be due to self-selection, which produces behavioural consensus, and behavioural socialization, where individuals are influenced by the behaviour of their immediate peers.

One reason why a university may not have a supporting culture is the issue of reward systems and the possible conflict between the institutional rewards for research publication and commercial rewards of ownership (Birley, 2003). For example, Thursby and Kemp (2002) found that less than half of faculty inventions with commercial potential are disclosed to the Technology Transfer Office. In some cases this may be because those involved do not realize the commercial potential of their ideas, but often it is due to the unwillingness to delay publication that results from the patent and licensing process. Restrictive leave of absence policies, whereby academics find it difficult to move between academia and the private sector, have been shown to have a negative impact on spin-off activity. According to Goldfarb and Henrekson (2003) the risk of forming inventor-led ventures is increased when leave of absence policies to start companies are restrictive. Furthermore, DiGregorio and Shane (2003) found evidence that university technology transfer policies that allocate a higher share of inventors' royalties decrease spin-off activity because the opportunity cost in engaging in firm formation (rather than licensing technology to an established firm) is increased. Other cultural factors such as the 'publish or perish' drive, the ambiguous relationship of researchers to money, and the 'disinterested' nature of academic research to industry are also seen as inhibitors to the valorization process of academic research (Ndonzuau et al., 2002).

Universities that lack a culture supportive of commercialization activity may take a number of actions. For example, studies in the UK suggest universities that are favourably disposed to the use of surrogate entrepreneurs are more likely to be effective at university spin-off activity (Franklin et al., 2001). Similarly, Siegel et al. (2004) propose that, in order to foster a climate of entrepreneurship within academic institutions, university administrators should focus on five organizational and managerial factors: reward systems for University Industry Technology Transfer (UITT); staffing practices in the Technology Transfer Office; university policies to facilitate university technology transfer; increasing the level of resources devoted to UITT; and working to eliminate cultural and informational barriers that impede the UITT process.

External determinants of spin-off activity

This stream of research emphasizes the impact of broader economic factors on academics within universities. Three factors that it could be argued will have an impact on spin-off activity are access to venture capital, the legal assignment of inventions (or, more specifically, in the US, the enactment of the Bayh–Dole Act) and the knowledge infrastructure in the region.

Florida and Kenney (1988) highlight the central role of the availability of venture capital in encouraging the formation of high-technology companies. Several studies have provided empirical support for the geographic localization of venture capital investments. Sorenson and Stuart (2001) found that the probability that a venture capital firm will invest in a start-up decreases with the geographical distance between the headquarters of the venture capital firm and the start-up firm: the rate of investment in companies ten miles from a venture capitalist's headquarters is double the rate of investment in companies located 100 miles away. However, more recently, DiGregorio and Shane (2003), using a data set collected from 101 universities between 1993 and 1998, found no evidence that the number of venture capital investments, the amount of venture capital invested, the number of venture capitalists, the amount of their capitalization or the presence of university venture capital funding are related to the amount of spin-off activity in a locale. In terms of seed capital, Franklin et al. (2001) found that those universities in the UK that generated a large number of spin-offs tended to provide their spin-offs with better access to sources of pre-seed stage capital than universities that did not generate a large number of spin-offs.

According to Shane (2004b) another significant impetus in the generation of university spin-offs in the US was the enactment of the Bayh–Dole Act whereby inventions were assigned to academic institutions rather than individual inventors. According to some European studies, national policies, which allow inventions to be assigned to academic inventors, have inhibited spin-off activity. In Sweden, for example (Wallmark, 1997), academic inventors are reluctant to bear the upfront costs and risks associated with patenting technology. Other researchers suggest that national policies of assigning inventions to individuals can lead to an anti-entrepreneurial attitude among faculty and university administrators who do not gain from inventors' entrepreneurial activity (Goldfarb and Henrekson, 2003).

The knowledge infrastructure of a region is also cited as a key factor determining spin-off activity. For example, Saxenian (1994) has shown that spin-off activity is more likely to occur in high-technology clusters because of ease of access to critical expertise, networks and knowledge.

The performance of university spin-offs
A small but growing number of studies deal with the performance of academic spin-offs. In terms of performance, the survival rate of university spin-off companies is extremely high. According to AUTM, of the 3376 university spin-offs founded between 1980 and 2000, 68 per cent remained operational in 2001. This number is much higher than the average survival rate of new firms in the US. Similar results have been found in other countries. Mustar (1997) found that only 16 per cent of the French spin-offs he studied failed over the six-year period that he tracked them. Dahlstrand (1997) found that only 13 per cent of the spin-offs from Chalmers Institute of Technology in Sweden, founded between 1960 and 1993, had failed by 1993. Furthermore, Nerkar and Shane (2003) analyse the entrepreneurial dimension of university technology transfer, based on an empirical analysis of 128 firms that were founded between 1980 and 1996 to commercialize inventions owned by MIT. Their findings suggest that new technology firms are more likely to survive if they exploit radical technologies and if they possess patents with a broad scope. Beyond this, Morray and Clarysse (2004), utilizing the case of a Belgian spin-off company, suggest that, instead of hiring a CEO at the start-up of the company, it might be a more efficient choice to 'coach' the start-up team and give them the time and freedom to learn. Similarly, Vohora et al. (2004) identify four critical junctures that spin-off management teams must pass in order to progress to the next phase of development: (1) opportunity recognition; (2) entrepreneurial commitment; (3) threshold of credibility; (4) threshold of sustainability. Shane and Stuart (2002) offered empirical evidence of the network–performance relationship, analysing how

social capital endowments of the founders affect the likelihood of three critical outcomes of spin-offs: attracting venture capital financing, experiencing initial public offerings (IPOs) and failure. Direct and indirect linkages to investors were found to be important determinants of whether the business received venture funding and in reducing the likelihood of spin-off failure.

The economic impact of spin-offs

University spin-offs are an important subset of start-up firms because they are an economically powerful group of high-technology companies (Shane and Stuart, 2002). According to the Association of University Technology Managers (AUTM, 2001), spin-offs from American academic institutions between 1980 and 1999 contributed 280 000 jobs to the US economy and $33.5 billion in economic value-added activity (Shane, 2004a). University spin-offs are also important economic entities because they create jobs, particularly for a highly educated workforce.

A Critique of Existing Research

University spin-offs have received increased attention from both scholars and policy makers during the last decade. While this research has provided many insights into reasons why some universities have higher levels of spin-off than others, there is still much we do not know about spin-offs. We outline seven limitations to extant research. The first four refer to the attempts to explain the determinants of spin-off activity; the next two refer to the policy context of the research; and the last refers to the research methods employed.

Explaining spin-off activity

1.   Many of the studies conducted to-date are based on theories that are actually atheoretical in nature (Nicolaou and Birley, 2003); for example, the research suggests relationships between events in the form of a model without providing a consistent explanation to account for those relationships. As a consequence, there is a need for more studies to explain systematically from an organizational perspective why some universities are more successful than others at generating technology-based spin-off companies (DiGregorio and Shane, 2003; Vohora et al., 2004).

2.   While existing research has sought to map out the dimensions of the patterning and rates of spin-off departure, it has only recently begun to explore the complex processes within institutions that give rise to these patterns. Research needs to address the different forms of spin-off companies and the complex causes that lead some, but not all, academics to engage in technology-based spin-off ventures.

3.   Past models and research of spin-offs have underestimated the role that the social setting of the institution plays in the spin-off process. This is despite evidence from, for example, Roberts (1991) who demonstrated that differences in spin-off rates can only be understood within the context of the social environment established by other faculty members in the university. Roberts argued that differences in spin-off rates in differing universities were a direct reflection of the degree to which the work peer culture made spin-off activity an important determinant of academic status. As such, differences in academic entrepreneurial intentionality seem to be a function of the ethos and culture which per-

vades the daily life of university and which informs the actions of academics alike. Therefore, research needs to investigate the behavioural and normative manifestations of academic entrepreneurship.

4. The question of the role of personality is still unresolved. Though it is obvious that individual personality may affect university spin-off rates, researchers have yet to discern anything resembling a 'personality of spin-off creation'. Although very insightful work has been carried out by Roberts (1991) and Shane (2004a) in an MIT context, constructs of personality have yet to capture in a reliable fashion specific attributes which underlie individual responses to experiences within different institutions of higher education.

The policy context of spin-off activity research

5. Many of the studies conducted to-date have not been particularly suited to the needs of institutional officials who seek to enhance spin-off activity on campus (Lockett and Wright, 2004; Shane, 2004a). Some researchers have tended to ignore and sometimes confuse the varying forms which spin-off activity takes in higher education and to play down the role the institution plays in the start-up activity.

6. There is insufficient research that addresses the (unintended) consequences of engaging in commercializing academic research. For example, authors such as Callon (1994), Nelson (2001) and McMillan et al. (2000) caution policy makers in other countries who wish to emulate the US experience in university technology transfer. They call for more reflection on the potential drawbacks to the US system of innovation regarding the tensions that may arise between departments and colleges within a university that are 'successful' and 'unsuccessful' at technology transfer. They also highlight a strong concern with the Bayh–Dole Act, suggesting that it may inhibit a long-standing tradition of 'open science and training'.

The research methods used

7. Much of the technology transfer literature is characterized by cross-sectional studies. Since the process of spin-off creation is longitudinal in character, more studies need to be longitudinal in structure. From a methodological perspective, to be effective in assessing university spin-off programmes, researchers must employ multiple methods for collecting data. In addition to the need to record, document and explain interinstitutional variations of spin-off rates accurately, research must also capture the complexity and richness of the dynamics of academic entrepreneurship. For that reason, assessment systems in the literature should employ more combined quantitative and qualitative methods to understand the nature of spin-off activity. However designed, survey methods are not able to tap fully the complexity of academics' views and the character of their understanding of the quality of their entrepreneurial experiences. Therefore there is a need for the use of a variety of qualitative methods, ranging from focus-group interviews to qualitative interview techniques to explain academics' perceptions of their experiences within their institutional context. Though such methods are typically unable to demonstrate a representative picture of academic entrepreneurial intentionality, they enable research scientists to uncover how academics make sense of their decisions. And they do so in ways not constrained by prior judgments that sometimes frame the questions of survey questionnaires.

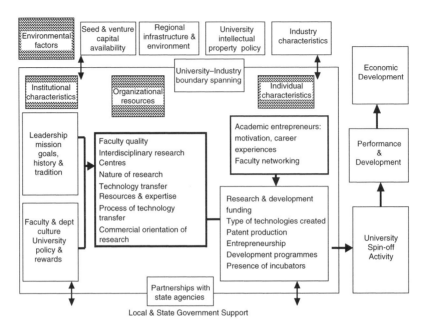

Figure 9.1   University spin-off framework

Developing a Conceptual Framework for the Study of Spin-offs

We have identified a number of streams of research within the domain of academic entre-preneurship. We have specifically focused on research that has sought to identify the deter-minants of spin-off activity within universities and the consequences of such activity. We now seek to integrate these perspectives into a university spin-off framework. We believe this framework provides a useful organizing scheme for understanding existing literature on academic research and for explaining the determinants and consequences of spin-off activity.

This framework (see Figure 9.1) represents a conceptual integration of elements found in the academic entrepreneurship literature. The framework assumes a social–psychological perspective, in that we suggest that spin-off creation not only varies owing to variation in the characteristics of individual academics but also because of variation in environments and university contexts. The framework suggests that four factors influ-ence the rate of spin-off activity: (1) engaging in entrepreneurial activity (individual char-acteristics studies); (2) the attributes of universities such as human capital, commercial resources and institutional activities (organizational-focused studies); (3) the broader social context of the university, including the 'barriers' or 'deterrents' to spin-offs (insti-tutional and cultural studies); (4) the external characteristics such as regional infrastruc-ture that have an impact on spin-off activity (external environment studies). In addition, we incorporate two further streams of research that deal with the consequences of spin-off activity by suggesting that the consequences of spin-off activity can be considered in terms of (5) the development and performance of spin-offs, and (6) the spillover effect of spin-offs on the regional economy.

Conclusion

In this chapter we organize the growing body of theory and research on university entrepreneurship into six different research streams. Specifically, we argue for the existence of an underlying set of individual and contextual factors that need to be recognized by universities implementing technology transfer policies. In addition, the two other primary streams of research identified (that is, development and performance of spin-offs and the economic impact of spin-off activity) provide a parsimonious description of the outcomes of spin-off activity. We provide an overview of the limitations of the university spin-off literature. We argue that a theoretical void exists in the research on university entrepreneurship. The literature on this subject is primarily subjective, in that most writers develop conceptual models that are not empirically tested.

Furthermore, much research in the spin-off literature has focused on a single university or on a very small number of institutions, making it hard to draw any generalizations (Nicolaou and Birley, 2003). As a result, the conclusions of much of the current research concerning university spin-out performance may not be generalizable to other settings. Therefore, empirical studies that provide a more fine-grained analysis of the nomological influences surrounding academic entrepreneurship are needed. We suggest that researchers need to test models of university spin-off activity. This should allow researchers to assess the relative influence of previously identified variables on spin-off activity.

To conclude, we argue that spin-offs are increasingly important for economic development. Policy makers and universities will increasingly seek to understand how best higher educational institutions can contribute to both their traditional functions and the added function of making the regional or national economy more competitive. In this chapter we suggest a conceptual framework that should aid researchers in completing a much-needed assessment of the impact of organizational policies, practices and structures on university entrepreneurship. Specifically, our framework should lead to the development of organizational interventions that facilitate technology transfer and spin-off activity. The integrative framework we present suggests that university heads and policy makers can encourage and develop university entrepreneurship by using a comprehensive systems approach for the identification, protection and commercialization of university intellectual property.

Notes

1. For example, *Management Science* and *Research Policy* have both devoted special issues to the topic.
2. For example, Frank Ryan, Chief Executive, Enterprise Ireland stated, 'In order to advance indigenous Irish industry, it is vitally important that we commercialise the knowledge we have emanating from third level colleges and create in greater numbers, new, ambitious and globally competitive companies' (*Irish Independent*, 6 February 2004).

References

Allen, T.J. (1977), *Managing the Flow of Technology: Technology Transfer and the Dissemination of Technological Information within the R&D Organization*, Cambridge, MA: MIT Press.
Allen, T.J. (1997), 'Distinguishing science from technology', in Ralph Katz (ed.), *The Human Side of Managing Technological Innovation*, New York: Oxford University Press.
Association of University Technology Managers (2001), 'The AUTM licensing surveys: university start-up data', AUTM Inc., Norwalk, Connecticut.

Audretsch, D. (2000), 'Is university entrepreneurship different?', working paper, mimeo, Indiana University.

Bank of Boston (1997), 'The impact of innovation', Economics Department, MIT, Boston, MA.

Birley, S. (2003), 'Universities, academics and spinout companies: lessons from imperial', *International Journal of Entrepreneurship Education*, **1** (1), 1–21.

Blumenthal, D., E.G. Campbell, N. Causino and K.S. Louis (1996), 'Participation of life-science faculty in research relationships with industry', *New England Journal of Medicine*, **335** (23), 1734–9.

Bok, D. (2003), *Universities in the Marketplace: The Commercialisation of Higher Education*, Princeton, NJ: Princeton University Press.

Callon, M. (1994), 'Is science a public good?', *Science, Technology and Human Values*, **19**, 395–424.

Chiesa, V. and A. Piccaluga (2000), 'Exploitation and diffusion of public research: the case of academic spin-offs in Italy', *R&D Management*, **30** (4), 329–40.

Chugh, H. (2004), 'New academic venture development: exploring the influence of the Technology Transfer Office on university spinouts', working paper, Tanaka Business School, Imperial College London.

Clark, B.R. (1998), *Creating Entrepreneurial Universities; Organisational Pathways of Transformation*, New York: IAU Press.

Dahlstrand, A. (1997), 'Growth and inventiveness in technology-based spinoffs firms', *Research Policy*, **26** (3).

Debackere, K. (2000), 'Managing academic R&D as business at K.U. Leuven: context, structure and process', *R&D Management*, **30** (4), 323–8.

DiGregorio, D. and S. Shane (2003), 'Why some universities generate more start-ups than others?', *Research Policy*, **32** (2), 209–27.

Doutriaux, J. (1987), 'Growth patterns of academic entrepreneurial firms', *Journal of Business Venturing*, **2**, 285–97.

Etzkowitz, H. (1998), 'The norms of entrepreneurial science: cognitive effects of the new university–industry linkages', *Research Policy*, **27**, 823–33.

Etzkowitz, H. (2000), 'The future of the university and the university of the future: evolution of ivory tower to entrepreneurial paradigm', *Research Policy*, **29**, 313–30.

Etzkowitz, H. (2002), *MIT and the Rise of Entrepreneurial Science*, London: Routledge.

Florida, R. and M. Kenney (1988), 'Venture capital financed innovation and technological change in the United States', *Research Policy*, **17**, 119–37.

Franklin, S., M. Wright and A. Lockett (2001), 'Academic and surrogate entrepreneurs in university spin-out companies', *Journal of Technology Transfer*, **26** (1/2), 127–41.

Geiger, R.L. (1993), *Research and Relevant Knowledge: American Research Universities since World War II*, Oxford: Oxford University Press.

Gibson, D. and R. Smilor (1991), 'The role of the research university in creating and sustaining the US technopolis', in A. Brett, D. Gibson and V. Smilor (eds), *University Spin-off Companies*, Savage, MD: Rowan & Littlefield.

Goldfarb, B. and M. Henrekson (2003), 'Bottom-up vs. top-down policies towards the commercialization of university intellectual property', *Research Policy*, **32** (4), 639–58.

Golub, E. (2003), 'Generating spin-offs from university based research: the potential of technology transfer', PhD dissertation, Columbia University.

Hague, D. and K. Oakley (2000), 'Spin-offs and start-ups in UK universities', Committee of Vice-Chancellors and Principals (CVCP) Report.

Jones-Evans, D., M. Klofsten, E. Andersson and D. Pandaya (1999), 'Creating a bridge between university and industry in small European countries: the role of the Industrial Liaison Office', *R&D Management*, **29**, 7–56.

Kenney, M. (2000), *Understanding Silicon Valley: The Anatomy of an Entrepreneurial Region*, Stanford: Stanford University Press.

Lockett, A. and M. Wright (2004), 'Resources, capabilities, risk capital and the creation of university spin-out companies: technology transfer and universities' spin-out strategies', paper presented at the Technology Transfer Society Meetings, Albany, NY, 30 September.

Louis, K.S., D. Blumenthal, M.E. Gluck and M.A. Stoto (1989), 'Entrepreneurs in academe: an exploration of behaviors among life scientists', *Administrative Science Quarterly*, **34** (1), 110–31.

Mansfield, E. and Y. Lee (1996), 'The modern university: contributor to industrial innovation and recipient of industrial R&D support', *Research Policy*, **25**, 1027–58.

McMillan, G.S., F. Narin and D.L. Deeds (2000), 'An analysis of the critical role of public science in innovation: the case of biotechnology', *Research Policy*, **29** (1), 1–8.

Morray, N. and B. Clarysse (2004), 'A process study of entrepreneurial team formation: the case of a research-based spin-off', *Journal of Business Venturing*, **19**, 55–79.

Mustar, P. (1997), 'Spin-off enterprises: how French academics create hi-tech companies: the conditions for success or failure', *Science and Public Policy*, **24** (1), 37–43.

Ndonzuau, F.N., F. Pirnay and B. Surlemont (2002), 'A stage model of academic spin-off creation', *Technovation*, **22** (5), 281–9.

Nelson, R. (2001), 'Observations of the post-Bayh–Dole rise of patenting at American universities', *Journal of Technology Transfer*, **26**, 13–19.

Nerkar, A. and S. Shane (2003), 'When do startups that exploit academic knowledge survive?', *International Journal of Industrial Organization*, **21** (9).

Newman, J.H. (1996), *The Idea of a University: Rethinking the Western Tradition*, edited by Frank M. Turner, New Haven, CT: Yale University Press.

Nicolaou, N. and S. Birley (2003), 'Academic networks in a trichotomous categorisation of university spin-outs', *Journal of Business Venturing*, **18** (3), 333–59.

OECD (1998), *Fostering Entrepreneurship*, Paris: OECD.

Powers, J. and P. McDougall (2005), 'University start-up formation and technology licensing with firms that go public: a resource based view of academic entrepreneurship', *Journal of Business Venturing*, **20** (3), 291–311.

Roberts, E. (1991), *Entrepreneurs in High Technology, Lessons from MIT and Beyond*, Oxford: Oxford University Press.

Roberts, E. and D.E. Malone (1996), 'Policies and structures for spinning off new companies from research and development organizations', *R&D Management*, **26**, 17–48.

Rogers, E.M. (1986), 'The role of the research university in the spinoff of high technology companies', *Technovation*, **4**, 169–81.

Saxenian, A. (1994), *Regional Advantage: Culture and Competition in Silicon Valley and Route 128*, Cambridge, MA: Harvard University Press.

Segal, N.S. (1986), 'Universities and technological entrepreneurship in Britain: some implications of the Cambridge phenomenon', *Technovation*, **4** (3), 189–205.

Shane, S. (2004a), *Academic Entrepreneurship: University Spin-offs and Wealth Creation*, Cheltenham, UK and Northampton, MA, USA: Edward Elgar.

Shane, S. (2004b), 'Encouraging university entrepreneurship: the effect of the Bayh–Dole Act on university patenting in the United States', *Journal of Business Venturing*, **19** (1), 127–51.

Shane, S. and T. Stuart (2002), 'Organisational endowments and the performance of university start-ups', *Management Science*, **48** (1).

Siegel, D., D. Waldman, L. Atwater and A. Link (2004), 'Toward a model of the effective transfer of scientific knowledge from academicians to practitioners: qualitative evidence from the commercialization of university technologies', *Journal of Engineering and Technology Management*, **21**, 115–42.

Smilor, R.W., D.V. Gibson and G.B. Dietrich (1990), 'University spinout companies: technology start-ups from UT-Austin', *Journal of Business Venturing*, **5**, 63–76.

Sorenson, O. and T.E. Stuart (2001), 'Syndication networks and the spatial distribution of venture capital financing', *American Journal of Sociology*, **106**, 1546–88.

Thursby, J. and S. Kemp (2002), 'Growth and productive efficiency of university intellectual property licensing', *Research Policy*, **31**, 109–24.

Tornatzky, G. (1996), 'The art and craft of technology business incubation: best practices, strategies, and tools from more than 50 programs', Research Triangle Park, NC: Southern Technology Council, Athens, OH: National Business Incubation Association.

Vohora, A., M. Wright and A. Lockett (2004), 'Critical junctures in the development of university high-tech spin-out companies', *Research Policy*, **33**, 147–75.

Wallmark, J.T. (1997), 'Inventions and patents at universities: the case of Chalmers University of Technology Technovation', **17** (3), 127–39.

World Economic Forum (2003), 'Global Competitiveness Report', ch. 1.

Wright, M., A. Vohora and A. Lockett (2004), 'The formation of high-tech university spinouts: the role of joint ventures and venture capital investors', *Journal of Technology Transfer*, **29** (3/4), 287–310.

Zucker, L.G., M.R. Darby and J. Armstrong (1998), 'Geographically localized knowledge: spillovers or markets?', *Economic Inquiry*, **36**, 65–86.

10 The size and the characteristics of the high-tech spin-off phenomenon in Sophia Antipolis

Michael Bernasconi and Dominique Jolly

The creation of new companies from existing organizations, termed 'spin-offs', is a phenomenon which has been observed and described over a large number of years. In the specific area of high-technology, spin-offs are considered an important source of new companies (Cooper, 1972). The internal dynamic of Silicon Valley comes from the continuous emergence of new spin-off companies set up by former executives of big companies (Storper, 1993). For example, the majority of the 31 semiconductor firms started in Silicon Valley in the 1960s traced their lineage to Fairchild (Saxenian, 1994). Spin-off activity is therefore considered a key factor in the technology transfer and collective learning process within an innovative milieu (Camagni, 1991).

Our aim is to shed light on the spin-off phenomenon in a high-tech park where it has not previously been analysed in detail. The objective of this research is to complement former research by describing the spin-offs, academic and non-academic, in relation to the development of Sophia Antipolis. At present we lack a global understanding of the spin-off activity within Sophia Antipolis. No research has been carried out to date to give a clear overview of the dimensions of the global phenomenon on a quantitative basis, through either a comparative analysis of academic and non-academic spin-offs or an assessment of the economic characteristic of those companies. This research is, therefore, the first step of a more ambitious research project.

The research field is the Sophia Antipolis Science Park, which is located 25 km west of Nice. It is considered one of the most active technopoles in Europe, in particular in the information technologies sphere. The geographical reach of the research is not only the science park itself but the whole Alpes-Maritimes region of France within which it is located. In the same way as Silicon Valley is not strictly geographically delineated because it has been continuously expanding in the San Francisco Bay area, Sophia Antipolis is the catalyser of the development of its region and companies are expanding outside the park itself. This is especially the case of big companies such as Alcatel Space, IBM or Texas Instruments. Nevertheless the park still contains more than 70 per cent of the high-tech companies of the region. Thus the term 'Sophia Antipolis' will be used to denote the Alpes-Maritimes high-tech economic region.

The research was conducted using mainly historical data, relying on a unique in-house database of companies located in the Sophia Antipolis area, called Dynamis. The database, which is composed of more than 600 companies, was set up in 1999 in order to analyse the endogenous development of the technopole. Topics analysed include the creations, failures, takeovers and mergers of locally created independent technology-based ventures. Variables also include figures such as turnover, employment and venture capitalist funding. The database has been built using data from Sirius, the economic database of the Chamber of Commerce of Nice Côte d'Azur. Private economic databases and secondary sources, as well as primary data collections, are used to feed and improve the database. The use of these diverse sources allows increasing the quality of the data collected. The database is used to produce a published continuing assessment of the high-tech entrepreneurial dynamic of the area.

To identify and document the information on the spin-offs, prior research and surveys a's well as other secondary sources were reviewed. The information has been carefully controlled for companies taken into account in our research thanks to complementary interviews conducted with key entrepreneurs and observers. The database identifies more than 50 academic and non-academic high-tech spin-offs established between 1981 and 2001. However, it is not possible to assume that the database contains the total population of spins-offs, because the information was not carefully gathered during the initial years of the inception of Sophia Antipolis as a technopole. For that reason the size of the spin-off phenomenon is likely to be underestimated. This is a limitation in our work.

For our research, we will take a definition of spin-offs inspired by Garvin (1983) which considers them to be new firms created by individuals who break away from existing firms, or university and research labs, to create companies of their own, using technology or knowledge from the former organization. This broad definition is appropriate to our aim which is to observe the spin-off phenomenon in an innovative milieu. This broad definition is better able to capture the whole phenomenon. Two different facets of the spin-off phenomena were analysed: the role of the innovative milieu in new venture creation, and the differences between academic spin-offs and company spin-offs.

The Role of the Innovative Milieu in New Venture Creation

A well established body of literature

The role and importance of the milieu in the development of firms have been explored by the pioneering analysis of Marshall (1920) on industrial districts. Since that time, the concepts employed to define a favourable milieu for business development and innovation have been significantly enriched: Industrial and Technology District (Castells and Hall, 1994; Storper, 1993, 1995), Silicon Valley model (Storper and Walker, 1989; Arthur, 1990; Saxenian, 1994), clusters (Porter, 1990) and innovative milieu (Aydalot, 1986; GREMI[1]). The dynamic and characteristics of such milieu have been abundantly analysed in the literature.

Venture creation is at the heart of the literature on industrial districts and innovative milieus. Since Marshall (1920) and Cooper (1972), authors have emphasized the importance and characteristics of the phenomenon of new company creation. In the high-tech sphere, Silicon Valley and its tremendous business creation capacity became the reference. The Silicon Valley model became the benchmark internationally. In a district or milieu, the diffusion of technologies from laboratories or companies, otherwise known as 'spillover', is the cornerstone of the phenomenon. A continuous flow of new companies, or spin-offs, is constantly created by former executives of big companies or researchers of laboratories. But this phenomenon, to a lesser extent, has been observed elsewhere. Carayanis et al. (1998) quote a Bank of Boston survey (1997) which observed that MIT had spun-off some 4000 companies, employing 1.1 million people and generating a turnover of 232 billion US dollars.

Our interest in the literature of innovative milieu is restricted to the advantages that such a milieu offer companies and new firms, and how it favours the spin-off process.

Everyone knows that high-tech parks give a straightforward access to a valuable base of resources – including highly qualified staff. In a district, spin-offs benefit from external economies (Marshall, 1920) or more broadly from untraded externalities represented by numerous informal elements offered by the territory (Storper, 1995). According to Camagni (1991), spin-offs benefit from the advantages of the collective learning of the territory constituted by tacit functions, which are not necessarily apparent, shared by the actors. At the same time those spin-offs contribute to the collective learning by the diffusion of technology, management practices, and informal networking activities. For researchers, spin-off creation is the result of a set of interactions, often complex, between people and their specific environment (Gartner, 1985; Bird, 1988; Greenberger and Sexton, 1988; Bygrave, 1989).

The European case
The Silicon Valley model cannot be considered as relevant elsewhere. Because of different cultures, governmental policies, expertises, technical fields and the rest, each district is unique. For example, many companies are headquartered in Silicon Valley while most of the big employers in the Sophia Antipolis area are subsidiaries. The research conducted in selected European regional clusters of innovative high-technology SMEs, coordinated by Keeble and Wilkinson (1999) is a significant input in the field. As quoted above, the start-up phenomenon is considered a key element of the collective learning process, and for that reason is studied in selected research projects. The analysis of Cambridge is based on an empirical survey of the new firms, including spin-offs, whereas the methodology is purely qualitative in the cases of Grenoble and Sophia Antipolis. Nevertheless, a comparison of the results of this research is valuable for the purposes of the current study. The importance of the spin-off phenomenon and the methodologies are different, but the three studies add significantly to the specificities of the roots of the spin-off movement, its importance and its particular characteristics in their respective milieu.

   The evolution of the spin-off phenomenon differs significantly in the three locations. In Cambridge the spin-offs are a founding component of the 'Cambridge phenomenon' (Segal, Quince and Wicksteed, 1985) and 'a high proportion of those operating owed their existence to the University of Cambridge, either directly or indirectly by spin-off from firms themselves originally spinning-off from the University'. Keeble et al. (1999) call it 'a cumulative and mushrooming process'. In that latest category are included the large local R&D consultancies (Cambridge consultants, PA Technology, Scientific Generic and the Technology Partnership). In Grenoble, the existence of the spin-off phenomenon has its roots in the 1940s, in particular with the technology transfer of the work of Nobel Prize winner Louis Neel (Lanciano-Morandat and Nohara, 2001). This movement has been continuously reinforced by research centres and the university. The non-academic spin-offs are more recent and linked to the restructuring of large corporates.

The development of Sophia Antipolis
In Sophia Antipolis the pattern is different and has to be observed in relation to the phases of development of the technopole (Longhi, 1999; Boucand, 2000). In the first period (1974–90), the development of Sophia Antipolis, which was then essentially an empty space, was exogenous through successfully attracting French public research laboratories as well as subsidiaries of international companies. The accumulation of research and

development activities made endogenous development possible. The accumulation of technological activities has been significant in two main areas. The first and most important relates to computers, electronics and telecommunications which have been at the origin of the development of the technopole. The second area encompasses activities in life sciences and health. A continuous stream of SMEs has been set up, most of them arising from a close relationship with companies or labs, acting as subcontractors in either services or research activities. At the same time this trend of new business creation has been impeded by a reverse spin-off effect, due to the substantial human resources and technological skills demands of big companies already installed or arriving. However, a significant flow of academic spin-offs emerged from the research bodies located in Sophia Antipolis and particularly INRIA (*Institut National de Recherche en Informatique et en Automatisme*).

In the second period (1991–94), the model of building up the technopole through attracting companies no longer worked. A slowdown in the economy and in the computer industries forced big companies to restructure, to reduce staff, and even to leave the technopole. A new spin-off wave was observed, which arose from engineers who had been made redundant from big companies externalizing technologies or business know-how from their former employers. 'The non-academic spin-offs did not represent a positive process but were the result of a process of restructuring and outsourcing of activities, and many were established to carry out subcontracting for their parents' (Longhi, 1999).

In the third period (1995–2001), the development of the technopole was driven by a double dynamic process: the investment in development by local companies and the attraction of companies in software and telecommunications activities, as well as a strong flow of new business creation driven by the new economy phenomenon. In that period, and particularly since 1997, the number of new ventures increased significantly (Bernasconi and Moreau, 2003). More than 90 per cent of the new company creations were in information technologies, and less than 5 per cent in the life and health sciences. In that period a significant change occurred in the local environment with the launch of the International Venture Capital Summit (IVCS). This gave promising start-up companies better access to international venture capital financing. In that period new incubation initiatives were undertaken by research labs and universities (Eurecom, Incubateur Paca Est) to facilitate the creation and the development of academic spin-offs. The cumulative impact of these boosters might be even stronger in the future.

The spin-off history in Sophia Antipolis
The presentation of the three development periods of Sophia Antipolis highlights the significant differences in the importance and characteristics of the spin-off phenomenon over the economic life of the technopole. Table 10.1 and Figure 10.1 show the number of spin-offs created over the period 1981–2001 in the Sophia Antipolis area. The data, especially those relating to the early periods, should be analysed with caution, as part of them have been reconstructed *a posteriori*, with the result that there are probably some missing data. It should also be mentioned that the flow of spin-offs that left Sophia Antipolis is balanced by the spin-off companies established in Sophia Antipolis which were originally spun off from other regions.

The number of creations annually is very irregular. Nevertheless, a few patterns can be inferred. First, there is a clear relationship between the periods identified in previous

Table 10.1   Spin-off creations in Sophia Antipolis (1981–2001)

Year	Academic spin-offs	Company spin-offs	Total spin-offs
1981	1		1
1982			0
1983	1	1	2
1884	2		2
1985	1	1	2
1986	1		1
1987	1	1	2
1988	1	2	3
1989	3	3	6
1990			0
1991	1	1	2
1992	1	2	3
1993			0
1994	2	2	4
1995		1	1
1996	1	1	2
1997	1		1
1998	3	2	5
1999	3	2	5
2000	6	5	11
2001	3	2	5
Total	32	26	58

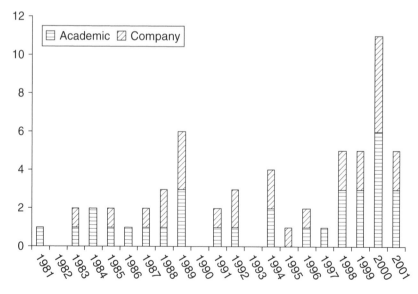

Figure 10.1   Evolution of spin-off creations in Sophia Antipolis (1981–2001)

Table 10.2   Three periods of spin-off creation

	Period 1 1981–1990	Period 2 1991–1994	Period 3 1995–2001	Total
Academic	11	4	17	32
Company	8	5	13	26
Total	19	9	30	58
% of all spin-off creations over whole period	33	16	52	100
Mean per year	1.9	2.3	4.3	

sections and the waves of spin-off creation. Second, there are differences between academic and company spin-offs. This second point will be analysed in the next section. The first period cannot be analysed in depth owing to the mediocre quality of data over the period. It is therefore not possible to confirm the reverse spin-off effect identified by Longhi. We can, however, observe an acceleration in spin-off creation at the end of the period. But this growth is suddenly interrupted in 1990, when no spin-off creation at all was identified. This was a forerunner to a slowdown in the economy. In the second period (1991–94), one possible explanation is that spin-off creation may have resulted from the social situation arising from staff lay-offs mentioned previously. Finally, a new cycle of creation started in 1995, with an active peak in 2000.

The average number of spin-off creations per year is an interesting indicator. As set out in Table 10.2, there is an overall increase in the spin-off phenomena over the last 20 years in Sophia Antipolis: 1.9 spin-offs on average were created each year between 1981 and 1990; 2.3 over the period 1991–94; and finally, 4.3 between 1995 and 2001. Data in Tables 10.1 and 10.2 tend also to show an acceleration of the process over the last four years. The rate of spin-off creation over this period is twice the rate of the second period. How do we compare the level of spin-off creation with total venture creation? The spin-off creation cannot be isolated from the new venture creation in the Sophia Antipolis area during the same period. Data extracted from the Dynamis database allows us to shed light on this issue. Table 10.3 gives data on the evolution of venture creation over periods 2 and 3 (data for period 1 was, unfortunately, not available). The numbers of spin-off creations was extracted from the total number of venture creations (percentages are given in the last column).

A total of 600 creations were identified. The number of creations per year varies according to economic conditions. Obviously, the number of spin-off creations is significantly less than the number of non-spin-off creations. Over period 2 (1991–94), few ventures were created (22 to 40 per year). Period three (1995–2001) exhibits much higher figures, with a peak in 2000. For the two periods 2 and 3, it is striking that the percentage of spin-offs is, on average, the same (6 per cent). Except for 1993, there was a little more activity during the period 1991–94; this might be explained by social spin-offs. Period 3 exhibits a trend towards an increase in the percentage of spin-offs relative to total venture creations.

These results show the positive dynamic created by the development of the science park. The model of new venture creation through spinning off observed elsewhere is in action,

Table 10.3   Spin-off and non-spin-off creations

Year	New ventures	Spin-offs	% Spin-offs
1991	22	2	9
1992	36	3	8
1993	34	0	0
1994	40	4	10
Total period 2	132	9	7
1995	41	1	2
1996	39	2	5
1997	39	1	3
1998	52	5	10
1999	95	5	5
2000	115	11	10
2001	88	5	6
Total period 3	469	30	6
Phase 2+3	601	39	6

Table 10.4   Activities carried out by spin-offs in Sophia Antipolis (1981–2001)

	Academic spin-offs	Company spin-offs	Total
IT software	7	9	16
Multimedia – internet	6	4	10
Technical counselling	5	3	8
Electronic	1	4	5
Telecommunications	4	1	5
Instruments and technical products	1	3	4
Medical/pharmacy	4		4
Computer hardware	1	1	2
Energy	2		2
Chemicals		1	1
Other	1		1
Total	32	26	58

creating new companies. But the proportion of spin-offs to total new venture creation (6 per cent) does not significantly increase over the period. This result raises questions about the origins of the other ventures and their relationship with existing companies. It can be assumed that many natural spin-offs are not taken into account owing to the difficulty of identifying them. Complementary survey analysis and comparative studies with other milieu would be helpful in addressing this issue.

The literature on innovative milieus stresses the spillover effect, which allows innovation and skills to diffuse from existing companies and labs to new companies. Table 10.4 offers some interesting insights into the activities carried out by the spin-offs created over the period 1981–2001 in Sophia Antipolis. It shows that there are a significant number of spin-offs created in the information technology sector as well as another more limited set of spin-offs, in activities related to biosciences and bioindustries. These results are in line with the relative importance of these activities in the region. In particular, the strength of Sophia Antipolis in information technologies made a significant flow of new companies in those industries possible. This shows how the spillover effect has been influential in the region.

Differences between Academic Spin-offs and Company Spin-offs

An unbalanced literature
Garvin (1983) gave one of the first definitions of spin-offs: 'Spin-offs are new firms created by individuals breaking off from existing ones to create competing companies of their own. A spin-off normally occurs when a firm is formed by individuals leaving an existing firm in the same industry.' Later on, literature considered a spin-off to be a new company based on (1) new knowledge or a new or improved technology coming from research from university, public or private laboratories, and (2) established by entrepreneurs who were researchers or employees with the former organization (Smilor et al., 1990), or by students or graduates (Rogers and Larsen, 1894; Roberts, 1991). Spin-offs linked to universities and laboratories are called academic or university spin-offs, whereas those coming from existing companies are called non-academic, company or non-university spin-offs. These two different categories have been analysed, in particular, by Klofsten et al. (1988).

The academic spin-off phenomenon has been described in detail. In particular, emphasis has been put on the importance of technology transfer from universities to private companies. Cooper first described the role of Stanford in the development of Silicon Valley. Similar phenomena have been observed elsewhere: Rogers and Larsen (1984) have extended the observation to the other US 'Silicon Valleys', showing the importance of universities in the development of new companies; Olofson and Wahlbin (1984) described the same phenomenon in Sweden, as Segal, Quince and Wicksteed (1985) did in the 'Cambridge phenomenon'. In France, Mustar's (1997) studies on academic spin-offs showed that such companies have a significant durability but a weak growth.

The non-academic spin-off appears to be close to what Johnson and Hägg (1987) call 'extrapreneurship'. In this situation, where a mother company is externalizing activities, relationships between the two companies are well defined through cooperation agreements, in intellectual property, business matters and sometimes financial support. Gemplus, which was spun off from Thomson CSF,[2] is a perfect example of this. The smart card developed by Thomson CSF was not considered a key business by the company, which was primarily involved in defence and control. A spin-off was organized with the management team of the department, which subsequently became the world leader in this new smart card activity (Humbert, Jolly and Thérin, 1997). If spin-off creation is part of a long-term organized process it is considered 'cold', whereas, when it results from a short-term brutal initiative, it is termed 'hot' (Lloyd and Seaford, 1987) or 'dynamic' or 'curative' (Daval, 2000).

Many authors have observed and described non-academic spin-offs over the last twenty years, establishing categories or typologies (Klofsten et al., 1988; Pirnay, 1998; Brenet, 2000; Daval, 2000, 2002). These categories have been based on two distinct scenarios:

either the spin-off is sponsored by the mother company or it is the result of an initiative by an employee. In the first scenario, spin-offs are defined and analysed from the perspective of the strategic rationality of the parent companies to favour the creation of a new venture by employees. Rationale for such decisions has been found in the strategic refocusing of business activities and repositioning around specific components of the value chain. Either objective can involve a decision between selling the activity to an existing company or stimulating entrepreneurship within the company by creating a new one. For a high-tech company a basic strategic decision is whether or not a new technology is crucial for its development and, if not, how to transfer and realize some value from it. Spin-off creation by research team members or managers is one of the possibilities proposed. Spin-offs are also generated by companies to solve overstaffing problems. In that specific situation, the purpose of the mother company is to stimulate employees to set up new ventures in areas close to or far from its businesses, giving support to the creation process. This kind of spin-off was significantly developed in France in the 1980s and has been analysed by a number of researchers (Belley et al., 1997; Queniet, 1997; Brenet, 2000).

The second company spin-off scenario arises when the venture project is due to an initiative of an employee. This type corresponds more closely to the main stream of research in the Anglo-Saxon literature (Garvin, 1983; Scheutz, 1986; Johnson and Hägg, 1987; Knight, 1988). For French researchers this type of spin-off is considered 'savage' (Sire, 1988) or 'natural' (Brenet, 2000). In these natural spin-offs, there is no direct help or support from the mother company, but the employee builds their own company on the basis of knowledge and skills acquired in the former company. This type of spin-off is not considered a threat by the mother company as long as the business of the new company does not compete directly with it. If it does, the spin-off is considered *competitive* (Lloyd and Seaford, 1987) or *illegitimate* (Johannison and Johnson, 1994). In technological activities, intellectual property makes these situations easier to control, even though it is still possible to bypass patents or to copy. This occurs in places such as Silicon Valley. When looking at the literature on spin-offs we observe a huge difference in the number of studies on academic and non-academic spin-offs. Academic spin-offs have been closely analysed, often highlighting the importance of universities and research labs in the development of new companies in their respective regions. Non-academic spin-offs have been less studied so far.

The case of Sophia Antipolis
The academic spin-off dynamic emerged slowly in the absence of any real policy from research labs, with the notable exception of INRIA and its national spin-off policy, which has been actively implemented at the heart of Sophia Antipolis. Lanciano-Morandat and Nohara (2001), who did a comparative study on INRIA spin-offs in Sophia Antipolis and Grenoble, noticed some significant differences: in Sophia Antipolis there was less direct access to the industrial companies, no real incubator available outside INRIA and an important technological irreversibility due to the relative weakness of the local innovation system. Incubators and spin-off policies have been developed only recently in universities and research labs owing, on the one hand, to the development of those labs, and, on the other, the importance attributed to technology transfer policies. As previously shown, in the case of company spin-offs, initiatives were more 'social' to reduce unemployment than 'industrial' to develop new businesses or transfer new technologies. In this category,

Table 10.5   Parent organizations of academic spin-offs

Academic institutions	1974–1990	1991–1994	1995–2001	Total
INRIA	2	1	5	8
CERAM	1	1	4	6
UNSA	4		2	6
MINES	3	1	0	4
EURECOM	0	0	4	4
INRA		1		1
CNRS			2	2
THESEUS			1	1
Total	10	4	18	32
Percentage	31	13	56	100

Thomson, with its GERIS, and France Télécom with its 'Ecole des Entrepreneurs' were the exceptions. No specific research has been conducted so far on these spin-offs.

Data extracted from the Dynamis database
Tables 10.1 and 10.2 show a larger proportion of academic spin-offs than non-academic ones (32 versus 26), but the evolution of the creation of academic spin-offs and company spin-offs seems to be the same; that is, it follows the same pattern (see Figure 10.1). It even seems to show the same three phases as described in the previous section. Nevertheless, some differences may be inferred in the nature of the businesses undertaken (see Table 10.4). For example, there seem to be more academic spin-offs in telecoms and pharmaceuticals but more company spin-offs in electronics.

Table 10.5 allows us to identify the parent organizations of the academic spin-offs. These are the principal stakeholders. They represent public research centres, business schools and engineering schools. INRIA, referred to earlier, is at the top of the list. The number of cases is unfortunately too limited to infer any patterns over the years. Surprisingly, the engineering school, Les Mines, has not been active in period 3, which was, as indicated earlier, the most flourishing period.

With regard to the creation of company spin-offs, Table 10.6 shows that two groups can be identified. The first group encompasses five highly active companies. This set includes national champions, as well as foreign companies (DEC-Compaq and Texas). Interestingly, the most active French companies are state-owned companies: Aérospatiale, Thomson/Thalès and France Télécoms. All these companies are large corporates with very large staff numbers; this indicates that non-academic spillover is related to the size of the parent company. The second group of companies have only had a single spin-off each in the period analysed here. It includes large as well as smaller companies. Surprisingly, this group includes companies such as IBM.

Comparing the efficiency of academic and non-academic spin-offs is not the purpose of this exploratory survey. Nevertheless, data on funding of new ventures by venture capitalists give an interesting insight on this issue (Table 10.7). Firstly, we observe that 64 per cent of the funded companies are not identified as spin-offs. This raises the question of where

Table 10.6   Parent organizations of company spin-offs

Parent company	1974–1990	1991–1994	1995–2001	Total
Thomson/Thalès	1	3		4
DEC/Compaq		1	2	3
Aerospatiale	2	0	1	3
Texas Instruments	1	1	1	3
France Telecom			2	2
Rhone-Poulenc	1			1
Philips			1	1
IBM	1			1
Siemens			1	1
ATT			1	1
DECOBECQ	1			1
Small companies	1		4	5
Total	8	5	13	26
%	31	19	50	100

Table 10.7   Money raised by spin-offs (1995–2001)

	Number	%	Equity raised (million €)	%	Equity raised per company (million €)
Academic spin-offs	9	23	40	18	4.5
Company spin-offs	5	13	76	35	15.3
Others	25	64	104	47	4.2
Total	39	100	221	100	

the innovation comes from, and the limit of the spillover through spinning off. A part of the answer is that such companies are coming from outside the territory, from other French regions or from abroad. When looking at the spin-offs, we observe that almost double the number of academic spin-offs are funded relative to non-academic spin-offs (nine as against five), but they raised only half as much money as non-academic spin-offs (€40 million against €76 million). Furthermore, the mean amount of money raised by non-academic spin-offs is nearly four times greater than the mean amount raised by academic spin-offs (€15.3 million compared to €4.5 million). To explain these figures, we can hypothesize that either non-academic spin-offs are better designed for growth or they are more advanced in the funding phases than their academic counterparts.

Conclusion

Summary of main findings
This research represents a unique attempt to offer a longitudinal study of spin-off phenomena in the technopark of Sophia Antipolis. It gives a first quantitative appreciation

of the global phenomenon and better understanding of the spin-off development. Three phases were distinguished: the creation of the science park (prior to 1990) which resulted in a positive dynamic and spillover effect; the economic turnaround (1991–94), which produced social spin-offs, and finally, the relaunch (1995–2001), which created a new dynamic.

With regard to the relative importance of academic and non-academic spin-offs, academic spin-off creations outpaced company spin-off creations in Sophia Antipolis. They followed a similar pattern over the three periods previously mentioned, but they did not relate to exactly the same economic activities.

The research also investigated the profile of the organizations which have been the source of these spin-offs. Parent organizations of academic spin-offs encompass public research centres as well as engineering and business schools. Parent organizations of company spin-offs cover an ever larger variety of firms: national/foreign, private/public, large/small, and there seems to be a relationship between the size of the parent organization and the number of spin-offs. The difference in attractiveness between the two different categories of spin-offs to venture capitalists raises questions as to differences between the dynamic of the projects.

Limitations of the study

The first limitation of this study relates to the way the Dynamis database was built. In order to develop a long-term perspective, historical data were reconstructed. This means that some companies may not have been identified. The Dynamis database probably does not represent the total set of spin-offs established in Sophia Antipolis. Secondly, we have not been able to distinguish between company spin-offs resulting from a strategic decision of the company and spin-offs arising from the sole initiative of one given employee.

Future research

This research is a first overview. More in-depth research on these companies will be necessary. Issues which merit further attention include the following. Why and how have entrepreneurs set up and developed their company in Sophia Antipolis? Which types of advantages and disadvantages did they find? Who are the spin-off entrepreneurs? Why did they become entrepreneurs? How did they recognize and build the business opportunity? Which types of relationship exist between the spin-off and the parent organization? How is technology transfer implemented in a spin-off? How can the importance of technology transfer through the spin-off phenomenon be evaluated in Sophia? How does the Sophia Antipolis spin-off phenomenon compare with other innovative milieus such as Grenoble or Cambridge?

Notes

1. *Groupe de Recherche Européen sur les Milieux Innovants (Group for European Research on Innovative Milieus)*. This network, funded by DG XII of the European Union, has been studying the role and importance of research and technology linkages in the evolution and competitiveness of selected European regional clusters of innovative high-tech SMEs.
2. *Thomson-CSF* has since changed its name to *Thalès*.

Bibliography

Arthur, W.B. (1990), 'Silicon Valley locational clusters: when do increasing returns imply monopoly?', *Mathematical Social Sciences*, **19**.

Aydalot, Ph. (1986), 'Présentation', in Ph. Aydalot (ed.), *Les milieux innovants*, Paris: GREMI.

Belley, A., L. Dussault and J. Lorrain (1997), 'L'essaimage: une stratégie délibérée de développement économique', Fondation de l'Entrepreneurship, ANCE.

Bernasconi, M. and F. Moreau (2003), 'Le développement endogène de Sophia Antipolis: dynamique des entreprises technologiques pour la période 1995–2000', *Les Cahiers du Management Technologique*.

Bird, B. (1988), 'Implementing entrepreneurial ideas, the case for intention', *Academy of Management Review*, **13**, 442–53.

Boucand, F.-X. (2000), 'Développement de start-up high-tech: exemple de Sophia Antipolis', in M. Bernasconi and M. Monsted (eds), *Les Start-Up High-Tech, Création et Développement des Entreprises Technologiques*, Paris: Editions Dunod.

Brenet, P. (2000), 'Stratégie d'essaimage des grandes entreprises et création de PME', Actes du 5ème Congrès International Francophone sur la PME, 25, 26 et 27 octobre, Lille.

Bygrave, W.D. (1989), 'The entrepreneurship paradigm (I); a philosophical look at its research methodologies', *Entrepreneurship Theory and Practice*, **14**(1), 1–26.

Camagni, R. (1991), 'Local milieu, uncertainty and innovation networks: toward a new dynamic theory of economic space', in R. Camagni (ed.), *Innovation Networks: Spatial Perspectives*, London: Belhaven.

Carayanis, E.G., E.M. Rogers, K. Kurihara and M.M. Allbritton (1998), 'High-technology spin-offs from government R&D laboratories and research universities', *Technovation*, **18**(1), 1–11.

Castells, M. and P. Hall (1994), *Technopoles of the World; the Making of 21st Century Industrial Complexes*, London: Routledge.

Cooper, A.C. (1972), 'Incubator organizations and technical entrepreneurship', in A.C. Cooper and J.J. Komives (eds), *Technical Entrepreneurship: A Symposium*, Milwaukee, WI: Centre for Venture Management, pp. 108–25.

Daval, H. (2000), 'La valorisation de compétences au sein de PMI essaimées: le cas du C.E.A.', Actes du 5ème Congrès International Francophone sur la PME, 25,26 et 27 octobre, Lille.

Daval, H. (2002), 'L'essaimage: vers une nouvelle rationalité entrepreneuriale', *Revue Française de Gestion*, **138**, avril–juin.

Gartner, W.B. (1985), 'A framework for describing the phenomenon of new venture creation', *Academy of Management Review*, **10**, 696–706.

Garvin, D.A. (1983), 'Spin-offs and the new formation process', *California Management Review*, **25**(2), 3–20.

Greenberger, D.B. and D.L. Sexton (1988), 'An interactive model of new venture creation', *Journal of Small Business Management*, **26**, 1–7

Humbert, M., D. Jolly and F. Thérin (1997), 'Building strategy on technological resources and commercial proactiveness: the Gemplus case', *European Management Journal*, December.

Johannison, B. and T. Johnson (1994), 'Radical ventures strategies on industrial markets – extrapreneurship and illegitimate spinoffs', SIRE – Scandinavian Institute for Research in Entrepreneurship, working paper 2. 22.

Johnson, T. and I. Hägg (1987), 'Extrapreneurs – between markets and hierarchies', *International Studies of Management and Organisation*, **17**(1), 64–74.

Keeble, D. and F. Wilkinson (1999), 'Collective learning and knowledge development in the evolution of regional clusters of high-tech SMEs in Europe', *Regional Studies*, Cambridge, June.

Keeble, D., C. Lawson, B. Moore and F. Wilkinson (1999), 'Collective learning process, networking and "institutional thickness" in the Cambridge region', *Regional Studies*, Cambridge, June.

Klofsten, M., P. Lindell, C. Olofsson and C. Wahlbin (1988), 'Internal and external resources in technology-based spin-offs: a survey', in B.A. Kirchhoh, W.A. Long, E.W. McMullan, K.H. Vesper and W.E. Wetzel (eds), *Frontiers of Entrepreneurship Research*, Wellesley, MA: Babson College, pp. 430–43.

Knight, R.M. (1988), 'Spinoff entrepreneurs: how corporations really create entrepreneurs', in B.A. Kirchhoh, W.A. Long, E.W. McMullan, K.H. Vesper and W.E. Wetzel (eds), *Frontiers of Entrepreneurship Research*, Wellesley, MA: Babson College, pp. 134–49.

Lanciano-Morandat, C. and H. Nohara (2001), 'Les spin-offs académiques dans le secteur de l'informatique en France: effets institutionnels ou effets de territoire?', contribution to the Colloquium SASE 2001, Amsterdam.

Lloyd, S. and C. Seaford (1987), 'New forms of enterprise: from intrapreneurship to spin-off', London: Small Business Research Trust.

Longhi, C. (1999), 'Networks, collective learning and technology development in innovative high-tech regions: the case of Sophia Antipolis', *Regional Studies*, **33**(4), 333–42.

Marshall, A. (1920), Industry and Trade, London: Macmillan.

Mustar, P. (1997), 'Spin-off enterprises. How French academics create high-tech companies: the conditions for success or failure', *Science and Public Policy*, **24**(1), February, 37–43.

Olofson, C. and C. Wahlbin (1984), 'Technology based new ventures from technical universities: a Swedish case', *Frontiers of Entrepreneurship Research*, 192–211.

Pirnay, F. (1998), 'Spin-off et essaimage: de quoi s'agit-il? Une revue de la littérature', Actes du 4ème Congrès International Francophone sur la PME, 22 au 24 octobre, Metz et Nancy.

Porter, M.E. (1990), 'The competitive advantage of nations', New York: Free Press.

Queniet, V. (1997), 'Essaimage: les clefs de la réussite', *Défis*, **151**, 61–4.

Roberts, E.B. (1991), *Entrepreneurs in High-Technology: Lessons from MIT and Beyond*, New York: Oxford University Press.

Rogers, E.M. and J.K. Larsen (1984), *Silicon Valley Fever: Growth of High-Technology Culture*, New York: Basic Books.

Saxenian, A. (1994), *Regional Advantage, Culture and Competition in Silicon Valley and Route 128*, Cambridge, MA: Harvard University Press.

Scheutz, C. (1986), 'Critical events for Swedish entrepreneurial spin-offs', *Technovation*, **5**, 169–82.

Segal, N.S. (1986), 'Universities and technological entrepreneurship in Britain: some implications of the Cambridge phenomenon', *Technovation*, **4**, 189–204.

Segal Quince Wicksteed (1985), 'The Cambridge phenomenon: the growth of high-technology industry in a university town', SQW, Swacesey, Cambridge.

Sire, B. (1988), 'L'essaimage: facteur d'émergence et de développement de la petite entreprise, l'exemple de la région Midi-Pyrénées', *Cahier de recherche de l'IAE de Toulouse*, 83.

Smilor, R.W., D.V. Gibson and G.B. Dietrich (1990), 'Universities spin-out companies: technology start-ups from UT-Austin', *Journal of Business Venturing*, **5**, 63–76.

Storper, M. (1993), 'Regional "Worlds" of production: learnings and innovation in the technology district of France, Italy and the USA', *Regional Studies*, **25**(5).

Storper, M. (1995), 'The resurgence of regional economies, ten years later: the region as a nexus of untraded interdependencies', *European Urban & Regional Studies*, **2**, 191–221.

Storper, M. and R. Walker (1989), *The Capitalist Imperative. Territory, Technology and Industrial Growth*, New York: Basil Blackwell.

PART 4

INDUSTRY SPECIFICS: E-ENTREPRENEURSHIP

11 What is e-entrepreneurship? Fundamentals of company founding in the net economy
Tobias Kollmann

Over recent years internal and external information and communication processes at enterprises across almost every industry sector have been increasingly supported by electronic information technologies. The fundamental advantages of technologies such as these (for example, the Internet), especially in regard to their efficiency and effectiveness, ensure that this trend continues into the future. The constant and rapid development of technology in the accompanying net economy has inevitably had a significant influence on various possibilities for developing innovative business concepts based on electronic information and communication networks and realizing these by establishing a new company (hence e-ventures). Against this background the term 'e-entrepreneurship' describes the act of establishing new companies specifically in the net economy (Matlay, 2004). The expansion of the classical use of the term 'entrepreneurship' raises, however, several questions that will be answered by this chapter. Which environment and which possibilities does the net economy offer for new and innovative entrepreneurial activities? What is different or what unusual features can be found in establishing companies in the net economy? What are the building blocks and phases of development involved in setting up a company in the net economy?

Answering these questions should help to define clearly the area of 'e-entrepreneurship' and the proof should be provided that this is worthy of special consideration in the context of research on entrepreneurship.

1 The Net Economy

The basis of the net economy is formed by four technological innovations: telecommunication, information technology, media technology and entertainment (the so-called 'TIME' markets). These innovations have affected and continue to have a significant impact on the possible ways in which information, communication and transactions are managed (Kollmann, 2001, p. 5). The increased support of business processes using electronic systems takes centre stage here. There are a number of terms for this that can be identified (for example e-business, e-commerce, information economics, network economics), which can, to some degree, be used synonymously (Jelassi and Enders, 2005, p. 3). It is easiest to structure and clarify the terms, define their boundaries and field of application by using the Shell Model of the net economy which will subsequently be described in more detail (Figure 11.1).

The initial assumption in the Shell Model is the general development towards an information society (see Figure 11.1). Beginning in the 1990s, innovative information technology induced a structural change in both social and economic spheres, especially through the digitalization of information and the networking of computers (Hagel and Singer,

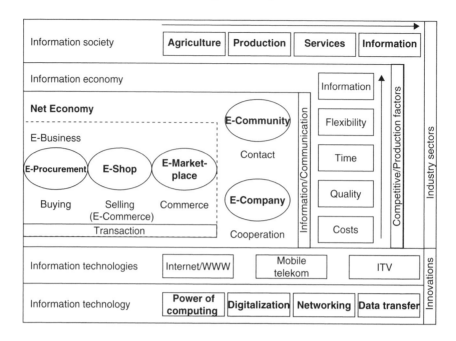

Figure 11.1   The Shell Model of the net economy

1997, p. 35; Tapscott, 1996, p. 17). Whereas just a few years ago computers and networks were reserved for only a few specialists, today they are already an integral part of daily life: digital technologies and their influence on the transfer of information are ubiquitous. The results of this development are clear: innovative information technologies such as the Internet/WWW, mobile telecommunications and interactive television (ITV). These technologies are changing the world as radically as the steam engine, loom, railways and tractor once did (Pruden, 1978). The digitalization and spread of information via electronic data pathways or networks serve as a pace maker for future economic growth that is comparable with the significance of the printing press in the fifteenth century or motorization in the twentieth century. The information society is characterized by the intensive use of information technologies and the resulting change from an industrial to a knowledge society (Evans and Wurster [1997], p. 51). Analogously from a global economic point of view there is an obvious shifting from the traditional economic sectors of agriculture, production and (non-virtual or rendered) services towards the information industry sector.

Against this background one of the central characteristics of the post-industrial computer society is the systematic use of information technology (IT) as well as the acquisition and application of information that complements work-life and capital as an exclusive source of value, production and profit. Information becomes an independent factor of production (Porter and Millar, 1985; Weiber and Kollmann, 1998) and thus establishes the information economy (see Figure 11.1). From a historical perspective, initially only the product characteristics (quality) and corresponding product conditions (for example price, discount) determined whether a product was successful (Porter, 1985; Kirzner, 1973). At that point it was important either to offer products or services to the customer that were cheaper than (cost leadership) or qualitatively superior to (quality leadership) the competitor's product. After the first major successes, two additional factors joined the scene: time (speed) and flexibility (Stalk, 1988; Meyer, 2001). At this point it was important to offer products/services at a certain point in time at a certain place (availability leadership). Additionally it became crucial to allow for customer-oriented product differentiation of important product characteristics (demand leadership). Information technologies have now created an environment in which information is more easily accessible and can be increasingly used for commercial purposes. The source of a competitive advantage will be determined in the future, as a result of the technological development presented here, by achieving knowledge and information superiority over the competition (information leadership). Those who possess better information about the market and their customers (potential customers) will be more successful than the competition. Whereas information previously held merely a supporting function for physical production processes, in the future it will become an independent factor for production and competitiveness (Weiber and Kollmann, 1998).

The growing relevance of information technology and the expansion of electronic data networks have created a new commercial/business dimension that can be called the network economy or the net economy (see Figure 11.1). It is especially influenced by the area of electronic business processes that are concluded over digital data pathways (Kollmann, 2001, p. 11; Zwass, 2003; Taylor and Murphy, 2004). Because of the importance of information as a supporting and independent competitive factor, as well as the increase in digital data networks, it must be assumed that there will be a division of the relevant trade levels on which the world does business in the future (Weiber and Kollmann, 1998, p. 603). In addition to the real level of physical products and/or services (real economy) an electronic level for digital data and communication networks (net economy) will evolve. The commercial possibilities resulting from this development may be called in this context e-business (see Figure 11.1), which means the use of digital information technologies for supporting business processes in the preparation, negotiation and conclusion phases (Kollmann, 2001, p. 64). The necessary building blocks including information, communication and transaction are in this case transferred and concluded between the participating trade partners over digital networks (Kollmann, 2004a).

Three central platforms have been formed which serve as a basis for these electronic business processes in e-business that include the exchange of all three building blocks (information, communication and transaction). E-procurement enables the electronic purchasing of products and services from a company via digital networks. This uses the integration of innovative information and communication technologies to support and conclude both operative and strategic tasks in the area of procurement. An e-shop allows the electronic sales of products and services by a company using digital networks. This allows innovative information and communication technologies to be used in supporting and concluding the operative and strategic tasks for the area of sales. Finally, an e-marketplace allows electronic trade with products and/or services via digital networks. This represents the integration of innovative information and communication technologies to support and conclude the matching process of the supply and demand sides.

Certainly, it must be understood that these terms are subject to overlapping. As a result of this, electronic procurement can most certainly be offered as a marketplace solution. In addition to this, two further platforms exist that are also attributed to the net economy, which, however, do not emphasize all three building blocks equally, concentrating rather more heavily on information and communication. An e-community enables electronic contact between persons and/or institutions using digital networks. What occurs here is an integration of innovative information and communication technologies to support the exchange of data and knowledge. An e-company enables electronic cooperation between companies using digital networks. This involves an integration of innovative information and communication technologies to link together individual business activities to form a virtual company that presents a bundled offer.

In view of the topic area of establishing a company it appears suitable hereafter to view the entire field of the net economy and, thus, all platforms as a basis for new business ideas. This builds upon the fact that website operators in the Internet can generate income with all platforms and, in doing this, establish new companies. Against this background the following definition may be proposed:

> *The 'net economy' refers to the commercial use of electronic data networks, that is to say, a digital network economy, which, via various electronic platforms, allows the conclusion of information, communication and transaction processes.*

The electronic value chain
With the establishment of the net economy and the heightened importance of the factor 'information', new possibilities resulted with respect to the way in which enterprises create value (Amit and Zott, 2001; Lumpkin and Dess, 2004). An enterprise can create customer value not only through physical activities on the real level but also through the creation of value on the electronic level. The value chain of the real economy, represented by the first case, is based upon the approach used by Porter (1985): the value chain divides a company into strategically relevant activities and identifies physically and technologically differentiable value activities (see Figure 11.2), for which the customer is prepared to pay. Value activities are, according to this, those basic building blocks from which the company produces a 'valuable product' in the eyes of the customer. This product can then form the basis for establishing an enterprise in the real economy. In this model – a sequence of value-generating or value-increasing activities – the individual steps are analysed in order to structure and develop efficiently and effectively primary and supporting processes. Even here information is extremely important when striving to be more successful than the competition. Information can be used to better analyse and monitor existing processes. The crucial point here is that information has previously been regarded only as a supporting element, not as an independent 'source of customer and/or corporate value'.

The value chain of the net economy presented in the second example is based on the approach proposed by Weiber and Kollmann (1998): through the newly created dimension of information as an independent source of competitive advantage, value can be created through electronic business activities in digital data networks independent from a physical value chain. These electronic value added activities, however, are not comparable to the physical value creation activities presented by Porter (1985); rather they are characterized by the way in which information is used. Such value activities might include, for example, the collection, systemization, selection, composing and distribution of information (see Figure 11.2). An 'electronic value chain' manifests itself through these specific activities of creating value within digital data networks that originate in and affect only the net

Value Chain of the Real Economy

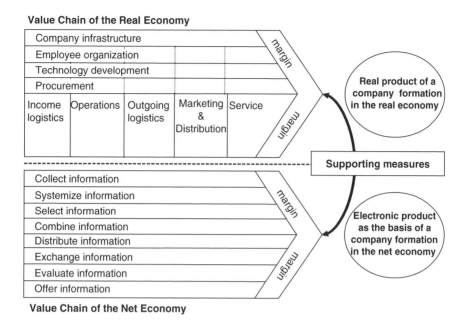

Value Chain of the Net Economy

Figure 11.2   The concept of the electronic value chain in the net economy

economy. The result is that, based on this new value creation level, innovative business ideas evolve through the use of the various platforms, and new 'electronic products' are created. Customers are willing to pay for the value created by this product and the product can form the basis for establishing a company in the net economy (see Figure 11.2).

An example of the electronic value chain can be seen in Autoscout24.de. In an electronic marketplace, car sellers and buyers deal in used cars offered over the Internet (e-marketplace). User value is not necessarily just the used car. Value also rests in the provided overview, selection and mediation functions of the information related to the car and its availability regardless of temporal and spatial restrictions. This 'electronic product' is made possible only through the use of information technologies. The website Autoscout24.de is therefore a company of the net economy, as the creation of customer value only occurs at the electronic level. Amazon.com is another example where the book as an object does not create value but where the electronic selection and ordering processes are made online. However, this is an information product (overview, mediation, transaction) and thus Amazon.com is a net economy company with its e-shop. This does not mean that companies such as Autoscout24.de and Amazon.com do not require real resources (personnel, logistics and so on). They also possess a real value chain, but it has a supporting role in order to offer successfully the electronic creation of value. These correlations do not apply to an offer such as the one at Seat.com. In this case, value is created for the customer through the real product 'car' and the shop in the Internet is 'merely' an additional distribution channel. This simplifies the ordering process yet there is no independent value created for which the customer would be willing to pay extra. The car is not purchased because of the company's website. Its Internet presentation plays a supporting role for sales as a part of the real value chain (Figure 11.2). Thus Seat.com is not a company of the net economy.

The electronic creation of value

Building upon the underlying value chain in the net economy (see Figure 11.2), it must also be determined what form of electronic value is 'created' in the eyes of the customer for which he would be prepared to pay; that is, what makes an online offer attractive in the first place (from the customer's point of view). The most pertinent question for the company in the net economy (e-ventures) is the question: what value is created for the customer within the net economy (see Figure 11.3)? In the example of the electronic creation of value, this might include the following aspects.

1. Overview: the aspect that an online offer provides an overview of a large amount of information that would otherwise involve the arduous gathering of information. By offering an overview, the e-venture creates value through structuring.
2. Selection: by submitting database queries, consumers can located exactly the desired information/products/services more quickly with an online offer and, thus, do so more efficiently. By offering this function, the e-venture creates selection value.
3. Concluding transactions: this aspect refers to the possibility created by an online offer to design and structure business activities more efficiently and effectively (for example as regards the cost aspect or payment possibilities). The e-venture in this way creates transaction value.
4. Cooperation: this aspect deals with the ability, using an online offer, for various vendors or companies to interlink more efficiently and effectively their service or product offers with each other. By doing this, the e-venture creates matching value.
5. Exchange: in this case, an online offer allows different consumers to communicate more efficiently and effectively with each other. Through this the e-venture creates communication value.

Considering these aspects, it is certainly possible that an e-venture creates several different types of value and that both structuring value and selection and mediation value are created. After the identification of the creation of value, the perspective changes to the entrepreneur's point of view. The question then remains: how is this value created? For the purpose of answering this question, the previously presented electronic value chain can once again be applied (see Figure 11.2). The electronic value chain separates an e-venture into strategically-relevant activities in order to better understand cost behaviour and recognize present and potential sources of differentiation. Thus the electronic value chain represents respectively those value activities which, for example, involve collecting, systemizing and distributing information. Through specific value activities such as these within digital data networks, an 'electronic information product' is created that presents value for which the customer (hopefully) is willing to pay. The electronic value chain embodies, therefore, the total value that is generated by the individual electronic value activities plus the profit margin. Now those value activities within the value chain will be identified that are especially relevant for the creation of value. These value activities, once identified, form in turn the basis of an electronic value creation process within a company (Figure 11.3). Thereafter, real work processes must be conceptualized to realize the electronic process of value creation.

Should an idea be based upon, for example, dealing in used photo cameras in an e-marketplace in the Internet (founder's point of view), there is a typical way in which value can be electronically created (see Figure 11.3). This value creation is directly reflected in

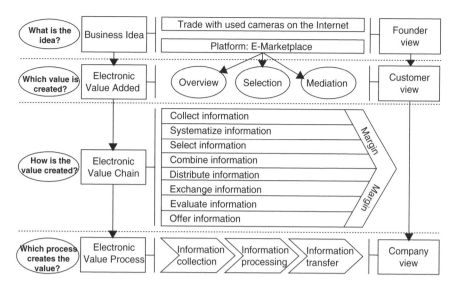

Figure 11.3   The electronic creation of value

the resulting added value for the user (customer's view) and refers centrally, in the example presented here, to the overview, selection and mediation functions. An example: a supplier would be prepared to pay, especially for the mediation function, whereas the customer would eventually be willing to pay a fee for the overview function. In order to realize this creation of value, companies use the value chain to identify particularly those value activities that form the core of value creation (see Figure 11.3). In order to do this, information on the object must first be collected; secondly, the location and the seller of the used camera must be determined and, in the third step, systematically stored in a database. Using this database, information is then offered to the potential buyers who can formulate a query using appropriate search mechanisms. If a match is found through the query process, then the accompanying information pertinent to the request is exchanged. If all of this occurs, the final product is a transaction. The electronic process of creating value, from the company's point of view, is thus collecting information, processing and transferring it.

The electronic value creation process
The electronic value creation process describes especially those information activities and/or the sequence of information activities which in total create added value for the customer. This involves both the core and service processes. Core processes hold a true function in the creation of value, whereas service processes support the business processes along the value chain. As a general rule, the electronic value chain process begins with the input of information for the e-venture. In order to provide the target added value (for example overview function), the required information must first be gathered (for example who demands what at which level of quality and who offers this). In the next step, the information is processed internally so that it can then be transferred to the customer in the desired form as information output and in a way that specifically adds value for that customer. This process may be called the 'electronic value creation process' and describes thus

the core processes of most e-ventures. When considering e-ventures, it is therefore possible to formulate a representatively typical electronic value creation process (Kollmann, 1998).

The first step is the acquisition of information which involves gathering relevant data that serve as information input for the additional creation of value. This results in the collection of useful data stores. This step in the value creation may also be called information collection (see Figure 11.3).

The second step involves information processing, which means the conversion of the collected data stores into an information product for the customer. This step along the value creation process may also be called 'information processing'.

The third step involves the information transfer. This means actually implementing the newly acquired or confirmed knowledge obtained from collected, saved, processed and evaluated data for the benefit of the customer. The result is an output of information which creates value. This step in the value creation can also be described as the information transfer.

It is important to recognize that it is not sufficient to go through the sequence of this (here presented in its most ideal form) electronic value creation process just once. Rather, it is the continual process of acquiring, processing and transferring information which is necessary. This is even more essential, when the data, from which information is created, are constantly subject to change. Thus the data must be continually checked so that they remain current. Against this background, several examples of the electronic value creation process in the net economy are presented in Figure 11.4.

	Information collection	Information processing	Information transfer	Value added
google.com	Information about websites and search queries (=input)	Matching of search strings and web content	List of appropriate websites (=output)	Overview Selection
webmiles.de	Information about products,customer and web offers (=input)	Allocation of incentive points for the usage of web content	Information about points, options for exchange, customer information (=output)	Transaction Cooperation
delticom.de	Information about tyres and customer requests (=input)	Matching of demand and supply	List of adequate offers and their possibility for online ordering (=output)	Overview Selection Transaction
guenstiger.de	Information about product prices and customer requests(=input)	Structuring of product prices, matching of demand and supply	Product information, price information, customer information (=output)	Overview Selection Mediation
travelchannel.de	Facts about destinations, online booking and travel reports (=input)	Matching of demands and supply, structuring of travel offers and travel reports	Travel offers, destination information, travel reports (=output)	Overview Selection Transaction Exchange

Figure 11.4   Examples of the electronic process supporting the creation of value in the net economy

2 Establishing a Company in the Net Economy

If one takes a closer look at the new companies in the net economy (e-ventures) equipped with electronic value chains and electronic processes of value creation (see Figure 11.4), there are a number of noticeable, common traits with regard to the way the company was established. Most often it is a so-called 'original company founding', meaning that a completely new company is established without relying on any previously existing or available company structures. Additionally, one observes that these cases were most often so-called 'independently established' companies initiated independently by the company founders seeking self-employed/full-time employment in the newly established company. Furthermore, establishing the company was a means to securing one's independent, entrepreneurial existence. Finally, it can be seen that established e-ventures were most often innovative companies, that is, not established to imitate an existing company. An innovative start-up presents a situation in which the initiating factors, in the classical sense proposed by Schumpeter (1911, p. 100), are combined in a new way. This new combination may involve material or immaterial factors. The increasing importance of 'information' as a significant factor in the competitive advantage has recently increased, particularly the significance of the immaterial factors (for example knowledge and know-how). Because of this, a number of newly formed companies in the net economy are established consistently upon new knowledge-based and conceptually creative factors (the way in which information is dealt with and processed in the context of electronic value creation to form an electronic product; see Figure 11.3).

In addition to having an electronic product when establishing an e-venture, it was and still is necessary to have an e-management, that is, members of management who have specific knowledge about the correlating factors within the network economy. In this case, special emphasis is placed on the combination of management and computer science (informatics), to establish the company and guarantee the necessary technical processes. This is particularly important considering that information can change very quickly and along with it the company's basis for the value creation activities in digital data networks. There is a further special characteristic trait of the net economy in addition to the electronic value chain, namely that this is a considerably new area of business and lacks the years of experience on which established business sectors can rely. Accordingly, the electronic creation of value and the business which is based upon it are oriented especially towards future innovations and developments. Furthermore, there is a high level of uncertainty on the customer side with respect to the amount and the timely presence regarding acceptance of innovative information technologies (for example, Internet start-ups' use of electronic procurement; see Kollmann, 2004b). The conditions outlined in such cases, as presented here, underline the high level of risk involved with the development of the net economy and the influence this has over investments in this area.

This risk is countered, however, by the fact that the net economy and its underlying technologies represent a central growth sector and are therefore linked to numerous opportunities. This is seen in the continuing, rapid expansion and use of the Internet in the USA and Europe. Further, the level of investments in information technologies is still quite high and, consequently, two aspects that are particularly pertinent for new companies become very clear: (1) information technologies require a certain amount of capital or funding for the initial development and/or company; and (2) information technologies

	Type of company established	Establishment environment
Establishing the company	Original Independent Innovative	Growth potential Risk Capital
	Reference for establishing the company	**Basis for establishing the company**
Net Economy	Information technology Information economy Net economy	E-value creation (concept) E-platform (realization) E-management (operation)
	Establishing the company in the net economy (e-venture)	

Figure 11.5   The distinguishing characteristics of companies established in the net economy

are subject to continual change and constant development, thus requiring subsequent investments. In addition to the need for capital to develop the technology, additional investments for the establishment of the new company in the net economy are necessary (for example, personnel, organization, establishing a brand, sales, production and the rest).

   This concludes the description of the basic conditions and requirements for establishing a company in the net economy. In particular, four central characteristic traits can be identified that clearly distinguish the process of establishing a business in the net economy from the 'classical' company establishment in the real economy (Figure 11.5).

1. Type of company established: an e-venture is often an independent, original and innovative company established within the net economy.
2. Establishing environment: an e-venture is characterized by enormous growth potential and yet is also marked by uncertainty of its future development concerning the true success of its information technology – technology that requires significant investments.
3. Reference for establishing the company: an e-venture is based on a business idea that is first made possible through the use of innovative information technologies. The idea itself focuses strongly on 'information' as a competitive factor within the network economy.
4. Basis for establishing the company: an e-venture is based upon a business concept that involves the electronic creation of customer value offered on an electronic platform of the net economy. It requires continual, further development and administration.

In view of these conclusions, and on the basis of the circumstances, the following questions arise from the company founder's point of view. What information do I need in order to create value for a customer? What type of platform should I use to present this information? How can I guarantee that my information product will remain attractive for the customer also in the future? How do I achieve this in such a way that my innovative company can grow independently? Due to these questions, companies established in the net economy tend to be heterogeneous and more complex. They differ from companies established in the real economy in many respects. This justifies an isolated and separate approach to researching how companies are established in the net economy (e-venture). Against this background, the term 'e-entrepreneurship' can be defined as follows:

> *'E-entrepreneurship' refers to establishing a new company with an innovative business idea within the net economy, which, using an electronic platform in data networks, offers its products and/or services, based upon a purely electronic creation of value. What is essential is the fact that this value offer was only made possible through the development of information technology.*

The success factors
A number of studies have shown that, at first glance, success factors for establishing a company in the net economy do not particularly differ from those in the real economy, although one does find specific differences in the realization and development of these success factors that are directly dependent upon the particular conditions in the net economy. These differences will be presented in the following section and cover the areas of management, product, market access, process and finance.

The building block of 'management' (see Figure 11.6) puts emphasis on founders of the company, who, through their personality and motivation, strongly determine the activities of an e-venture. Studies on the influence of technical, social and methodical skills and capabilities possessed by business founders determined that these have a positive influence on the successful realization of the activities involved with establishing a company (Walter, Auer and Gemünden, 2002, p. 268). This also holds true with respect to the motivation of the founder or the team of founders. High stress limit, pressure to succeed, self-confidence and awareness of risk influence and characterize the actions during the sustainable phase of conception and thereafter in the realization phase. Whereas creativity on the one hand and analytical and conceptual thinking on the other dominate the first development phases of a new company, experience in the net industry, knowledge of the interrelated aspects of the net economy and real experience in operative management are increasingly the points that truly matter when establishing an e-venture. In view of this, establishing a company in the net economy is very complex and the knowledge required to achieve this must be drawn similarly from the areas of computer science, information management (study of information systems), business administration and entrepreneurship. Accordingly, the founders must to a certain extent possess competence and know-how in all three of the following areas:

1. Computer science: The technological aspect of the net economy makes it necessary to have a substantial understanding and knowledge of technologies, systems, databases, programming and the architecture of the Internet.
2. Information management: The technological basis, provided by computer science, must be assessable with respect to its content and relevance for business issues. For this reason it is important to have knowledge in the areas of management information

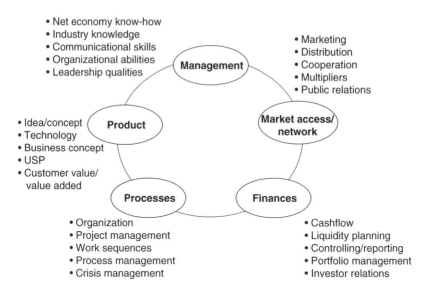

Figure 11.6   Success factors of establishing a company in the net economy

systems, IT security, data warehousing and data mining or even electronic payment systems. It is just as important to understand fundamental platforms in the net economy as it is to have a sound overview of current existing business models and possibilities of creating value electronically.

3. Business administration: At the business administration level, it is essential to have solid business knowledge. Topics which should be especially emphasized here in connection with this aspect include marketing, business organization, management, financing or investments.

Seldom does one person possess all of these skills, so that it is more often the case that an e-venture is established by a team of founders.

The building block 'product' (Figure 11.6) refers to the configuration of the services and offers of an e-venture. In this respect, the electronic product and/or service offer must be specified and communicated, according to its electronic added value. Thus the essential question is whether or not the customer needs the electronic offer/service provided by the e-ventures based on information technology and, if so, whether the customer is willing to pay. Further, it is the aim of the company to achieve added value for the customer through the output realized with electronically created value. But it is also the company's aim to ensure that its offer possesses a unique characteristic which differentiates it from the other competitors. In addition to this, most e-ventures are dealing in new forms of business ideas and/or business models. From the customer side, initially it takes some time to get acquainted or to acknowledge the effect provided as value added that results from such new ideas and models. For this reason, a regular reconnection with customers and users must take place because it is, in the end, customer acceptance that determines whether the electronic business idea is a success or not (Kollmann, 2004a). Establishing a business in the net economy is, apart from the aforementioned, additionally singled out by the fact that an e-venture and its electronic business idea must not only satisfy a need but also do this in a superior way compared to existing solutions in the real economy. Thus the need for books is already fulfilled through real book shops, however, Amazon.com with its e-shop, can offer overview, selection and transaction functions creating additional electronic value in the market space (see Figure 11.4).

The building block 'processes' (Figure 11.6) refers particularly to the need for a newly established company to move quickly out of that critical stage, where its activities are informal and uncontrolled. This applies especially to work, finance and organizational processes which form a solid operative foundation in a newly established company. This essentially means that core processes must be firmly established and must also harmonize with the evolving company organization. Further, in this context, it is also important that not too many activities are initiated simultaneously. Otherwise, there is an ensuing danger that some of these activities may not receive the full attention they require. Therefore it is necessary to have a logical and effective project and process management. When dealing with an e-venture, sophisticated development and presentation of concrete work flows should be based on a model example of the value creation process that was previously determined (see Figure 11.3). The company's business processes can then be conceptualized in parallel with the electronic process of value creation. These business processes should be understood as activity bundles necessary for realizing the value offer. They can be described as those target activities which are performed in a timely and logical sequence and whose aim is directly determined by the company strategy (Hammer and Champy, 1993). Business processes thus describe the realization of the electronic process of creating value with the help of electronic resources within an e-venture.

Particularly in the net economy, which is characterized by a high degree of virtualization, the knowledge of concrete process flows is extremely important. Many business models in the net economy are based upon taking advantage of the 'effects of economies of scale'. This is possible only when a large number of users can be serviced by either very few or even with just one basic process (for example at online auction houses). The complexity of value creation, especially if the creation of this value involves the participation of multiple companies, requires reducing the process down to the most essential steps. Weaknesses in core processes can then be more easily recognized. Especially regarding steps of the process which are electronic and thus automatic, mistakes can significantly impair the success of a company. Moreover, the process is externally visible to customers. The quality of process flows influences, therefore, the customer's use behaviour. Supported by the virtual quality of information products, process flows become representatives of the quality image. The customer rates a company according to the functionality and security of its processes.

The 'market access' building block (see Figure 11.6) in an e-venture means not only assuring market entrance and establishing a product and/or brand, but also reaching the customer via an electronic communication channel (for example online/viral marketing). The focus here is the question: how do I reach the customer with my information product? Here, it is possible to achieve market access through company-initiated marketing and sales activities. However, this seems to pose a signification problem considering the lack of resources at start-up companies. Market entrance in the net economy is – in most cases – characterized by the fact that most e-ventures are unknown, have limited capital, for the most part lack resources and do not have an established network. In particular, the lack of financial means often leads to deficits for a newly established company in the area of service or product performance, communication/sales and market positioning. In order to eliminate these deficits, especially when dealing with e-ventures, potential cooperation plays an elementary role in supporting market entrance and positively steering the company's further development (Kollmann, 2004a). In view of the current state of the Internet's development and other online media, the idea of capturing a market alone with the existing limitations is unfathomable. Examples of such cooperation are the so-called 'affiliate programmes', which have developed alongside the establishment of electronic business ventures. This is predominantly understood to be marketing and sales concepts that are directly based upon a partnership-like relationship and profit-scheme compensation. The e-venture (merchant) concludes an advertisement and/or sales agreement with a cooperation partner (affiliate), who in turn integrates the merchant's service/product offer on their Internet presence or website. If this results in a successful transaction, the affiliate receives a commission on sales which is normally somewhere between 5 and 15 per cent (Rayport and Jaworski, 2002, p. 245). In this way, a newly established company can reach, from the very beginning, a wide range of customer segments and establish a comprehensive sales network.

The building block 'Finance' (see Figure 11.6) is concerned with guaranteeing the activities from a liquidity point of view. There are two essential aspects which are of importance here. On the one hand, there is a significant need for investing in technology and in establishing the company in the beginning phase; on the other hand, the free cash-flow cannot be too negatively influenced. The financing and cash planning is often a significant weak point at companies in the net economy. Often there is a lack of necessary realism, if investors or financers are to be convinced by euphoric turnover forecasts or make decisions based upon underestimated investment requirements. Hence there should be a continually updated finance planning that can provide, at any given point in time, a realistic estimate of the financial situation of the company and also present the actual financing requirement. The financing of a company in this case becomes increasingly a mixture of equity (own capital) and various forms of participations. In situations such as these, risk capital should be used strategically for investments (for example sales), that is, for generating cash flow. Furthermore, the financing of the company requires proof of solid controlling, especially of the cost side of the business. A further aspect concerns the communication with investors (investor relations), who want to be informed on a regular basis about the development of the company (Kollmann, 2004a).

The phases of development
The future development of a company in the net economy can be outlined by just one simple question: what will happen to the idea with the passing of time? At the very core, when a new company is to be founded, there is an idea for a possible business concept. This idea must first be discerned and then assessed for its probability and potential for success (phase of idea finding). In a subsequent step, the idea must be transferred to a plausible and sustainable foundation and a corresponding business plan for the idea must be prepared (phase of idea formulation). This must be done in order to actually realize the idea in the next step (phase of idea realization). Success of the e-venture, however, is not only dependent upon the initial realization of the business model, but especially depends upon the continued development and appropriate adjustment to market

demands (phase of idea intensification). Finally, the idea must be capable of continually growing with the market and developing into a long-term business (phase of idea continuation). In each of these phases, it is essential that certain tasks along the previously outlined building blocks for establishing a company be fulfilled (see Figure 11.7). The individual phases and specific questions, which are of significant importance throughout the development of a company in the net economy, will be described in more detail in the following section (Ruhnka and Young, 1987).

The phases of finding, formulating and realizing the idea are considered, in the context of the financing of a new company or start-up, to be the early stage. Generally, they are divided up into the pre-seed, seed and a start-up phase. In the pre-seed and seed-phase the company has not yet been founded. These phases reflect more specifically the time during which the future founders of a company are searching for the idea and planning the realization of their business model. Even if there is no company and no marketable product in existence at this phase, there is nevertheless a need for capital as, for instance, market studies or acceptance and feasibility studies must be performed (costs for preparation). If the company is to be established, based upon a business plan (idea formulation), then the start-up phase begins, in which production capacities are established, personnel is sought and the market entrance is prepared. For an e-venture, this most often means the programming of the Internet platform and its functionalities (development costs). When a successful online start can take place and the product/service offer is introduced into the market, the start-up phase ends. Following this comes the time when the idea must be intensified and the expansion stage begins. Especially during the 'early stage', the building blocks 'product' and 'management' play an essential role as there will surely be no further progress without them.

If the start-up phase is completed, the actual online start of the e-venture can occur with a market introduction or launch of the product or service (see Figure 11.7). Beginning here, one of the central, strategic targets of the company is to expand the presence of its product/service on the market and achieve constant turnover growth. The newly formed company then enters the expansion stage and the first stable income is earned. In this phase, it is absolutely necessary to expand production and sales capacities. In order to achieve this, it is possible to form cooperative blocks. As a general rule, the further expansion of the company cannot be solely financed through its cash flow. The company is thus confronted with additional capital requirements. At this stage, potential investors can be offered far more security for their investment as compared to the early phase of the business development. Considering this, the management is nevertheless then challenged by an entirely new problem, that of properly steering the growth of the company. This is the point where internal processes must be established. Within the expansion stage, the building blocks of 'market access' and 'processes' are particularly important as, without them, further growth can most certainly not be achieved.

As soon as a company can rely upon an ever-increasing growth rate and guaranteed business income, the later stage of the company's development has been achieved. From a turnover perspective, the company is stable in its business development and there is eventually the opportunity to consider a diversification of the original idea. The company has established unique selling aspects for its product or service that separate it from the competitors and has achieved a significant market penetration. This means that even the future growth of the e-venture can be calculated and risks can be much better defined than

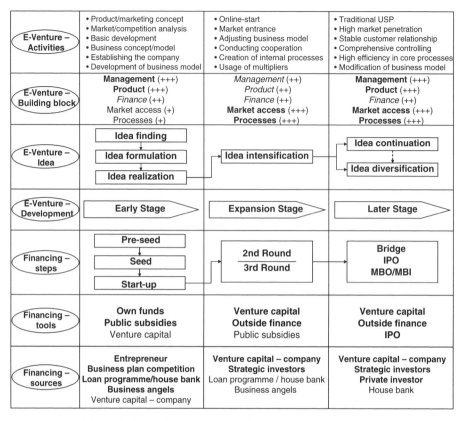

Figure 11.7   Building blocks and phases of development for companies in the net economy

in the previous phases of the business development. When there is a significantly high level of growth potential, the break-even point can be achieved through 'bridge financing', or possibly an IPO can be prepared. Investors from the previous financing rounds also have the option of a 'trade sale' to a strategic investor as well as selling their shares back to the founders or the management in a management buy-out, or a management buy-in. During the later stage, all of the building blocks play a significant role, owing to the fact that, generally, growth can only be obtained when all of these elements are functioning seamlessly.

3   Summary

The creation of new ventures plays a decisive role in the social and economic development of every country. This is due to the fact that, with each new venture created, a market participant comes into existence which potentially stimulates competition and drives the economy further. The formation of new companies within the net economy (e-entrepreneurship) is therefore – in spite of the current market turbulence – a key topic for every national industry. Consequently, e-business must not be ignored by decision makers; its technological advantages are obvious and therefore will most certainly lead to new business processes and business concepts as well. Because of these circumstances there will be

Table 11.1 Example of business processes for an electronic platform

Platform	Function	Information	Communication	Transaction
E-Shop	Selling	Yes, by product choice	Yes, between vendor and buyer	Yes, by product selling

a solid basis for new venture creation within the net economy in the future, too. As this chapter has shown, the competent processing of information has to be the foundation of such entrepreneurial attempts. The electronic value chain and the value-oriented processing of information thus serve as the starting point for every net economy venture. Below, questions are proposed to which the reader might apply the theory of 'e-entrepreneurship' in the practical field.

What is the difference between the real economy and the net economy? Give an argumentation in respect to the different approaches for conducting business processes. Which central platforms exist within the net economy and how do they differ in terms of 'information', 'communication' and 'transaction'? Use the given scheme as a basis for your answer and provide three examples for each platform.

Describe the value chain approach in the real economy and explain the possibilities given in the real economy. Identify the differences compared to an electronic value creation based on the value chain approach introduced by Weiber and Kollmann. Find three examples for an electronic value creation within the Internet.

Characterize the specific aspects of a business venture within the net economy (e-venture). Name the essential differences between a new venture and the real economy. What are the criteria of a new venture within the net economy from the founder's point of view and what role is taken over by the investors?

References

Amit, R. and C. Zott (2001), 'Value creation in e-business', *Strategic Management Journal*, **22**(6/7), 493–520.

Evans, P.B. and T.S. Wurster (1997), 'Strategy and the new economics of information', *Harvard Business Review*, **75**(5), 71–82.

Hagel, J. and M. Singer (1997), *Net Gain*, Boston, MA: Harvard Business School Press.

Hammer, M. and J.A. Champy (1993), *Reengineering The Corporation: A Manifesto for Business Revolution*, New York: Harper Business.

Jelassi, T. and A. Enders (2005), *Strategies for e-Business. Creating Value through Electronic and Mobile Commerce*, Edinburgh, UK: Prentice-Hall.

Kirzner, I.M. (1973), *Competition and Entrepreneurship*, Chicago: University of Chicago Press.

Kollmann, T. (1998), 'The information triple jump as the measure of success in electronic commerce', *Electronic Markets*, **8**(4), 44–9.

Kollmann, T. (2001), 'Measuring the acceptance of electronic marketplaces', *Journal of Computer Mediated Communication*, **6**(2).

Kollmann, Tobias (2004a), *E-Venture: Grundlagen der Unternehmensgründung in der Net Economy*, Wiesbaden: Gabler.

Kollmann, T. (2004b), 'Attitude, adoption or acceptance? Measuring the market success of telecommunication and multimedia technology', *International Journal of Business Performance Management*, **6**(2), 133–52.

Lumpkin, G.T. and G.G. Dess (2004), 'E-business strategies and Internet business models: how the Internet adds value', *Organizational Dynamics*, **33**(2), 161–73.

Matlay, H. (2004), 'E-entrepreneurship and small e-business development: towards a comparative research agenda', *Journal of Small Business and Enterprise Development*, **11**(3), 408–14.

Meyer, C. (2001), 'The second generation of speed', *Harvard Business Review*, **79**(4), 24–6.

Porter, M.E. (1985), *Competitive Advantage*, New York: Free Press.

Porter, M.E and V.E. Millar (1985), 'How information gives you competitive advantage', *Harvard Business Review*, **63**(4), 149–60.

Pruden, H.O. (1978), 'The Kondratieff wave', *Journal of Marketing*, **42**(2), 63–70.

Rayport, J.F. and B.J. Jaworski (2002), *Introduction to E-commerce*, Boston, MA: McGraw-Hill.

Ruhnka, J.C. and J.E. Young (1987), 'A venture capital model of the development process for new ventures', *Journal of Business Venturing*, **2**(2), 167–84.

Schumpeter, J.A. (1911), *The Theory of Economic Development: an Inquiry into Profits, Capital, Credit, Interest and the Business Cycle*, trans. 1934, Cambridge, MA: Harvard University Press.

Stalk, Jr., G. (1988), 'Time – the next source of competitive advantage', *Harvard Business Review*, **66**(4), 28–60.

Tapscott, Don (1996), *The Digital Economy. Promise and Peril in the Age of Networked Intelligence*, New York: McGraw-Hill.

Taylor, M. and A. Murphy (2004), 'SMEs and e-business', *Journal of Small Business and Enterprise Development*, **11**(3), 280–89.

Walter, A., M. Auer and H.G. Gemünden (2002), 'The impact of personality, competence, and activities of academic entrepreneurs on technology transfer success', *International Journal of Entrepreneurship and Innovation Management*, **2**(2/3), 268–89.

Weiber, R. and T. Kollmann (1998), 'Competitive advantages in virtual markets – perspectives of "Information-based-marketing" in cyberspace', *European Journal of Marketing*, **32**(7/8), 603–15.

Zwass, V. (2003), 'Electronic commerce and organizational innovation: aspects and opportunities', *International Journal of Electronic Commerce*, **7**(3), 7–37.

12 Exploring the socio-demographic characteristics of the e-entrepreneur: an empirical study of Spanish ventures

Antonio Padilla-Meléndez, Christian Serarols-Tarres and Ana Rosa del Águila-Obra

Introduction

Nowadays, the Internet is a framework where people can exchange information at a speed never seen before (Schwartz, 1997). In this network, pure dotcoms, Internet start-ups or cyber-traders arise as companies specifically conceived to operate in this new environment. In the context of the development of electronic commerce, these firms are taking on a significant role in the Internet in Europe. According to a study by the Spanish Association of Electronic Commerce (AECE–FECEMD, 2004), e-commerce in Spain moved 1.53 billion euros in 2003, 31.5 per cent more than in the previous year. Almost 40 per cent of the Spanish population is an Internet user, but only 20 per cent bought online products or services in 2002, which scarcely represents 7.3 per cent of the Spanish population. In Spain, the most active sectors are travel, electronics (including hardware and software) and food. However, the situation in Spain trails that of other European countries, not to mention the US. According to the Census Bureau of the US Department of Commerce (US Department of Commerce, 2004) the estimate of US retail e-commerce sales for the second quarter of 2004, not adjusted for seasonal, holiday or trading-day differences, was $15.7 billion, an increase of 23.1 per cent (±3.5 per cent) on the second quarter of 2003. In the US, online sales reached $114 billion in 2003, according to a Forrester Research (2004) study of retailing online. This study also reveals that 79 per cent of online stores in the US are profitable.

The entrepreneurship literature suggests two approaches to measure the success of start-ups (Chandler and Hanks, 1993): objective measures and subjective measures. Although entrepreneur characteristics have been very widely studied in general terms (Morel d'Arleux, 1999; Sandberg and Hofer, 1987), there are no studies that focus on the characteristics of the digital related entrepreneurs (e-entrepreneurs). There are some studies comparing entrepreneurs from the IT sector with those starting up dotcoms (Colombo and Delmastro, 2001), but there is very little research referring specifically to the Internet start-ups.

The main objectives of this chapter are to describe the main socio-demographic characteristics of the e-entrepreneur, its motivations to create its own companies, and to explore how its characteristics may affect the success of Internet start-ups. In addition, we compare the e-entrepreneur's profile to the common entrepreneur's profile in Spain. The chapter is organized as follows. After a literature review on entrepreneur characteristics and the success of start-ups, the methodology of the empirical study is explained. The chapter continues with the analysis of results and discussion, and finishes with some final remarks.

Table 12.1   Main variables used in the studies on success factors

Variables	Authors
Market	Cooper (1979, 1981); Stuart and Abetti (1987)
Market and product strategy	Rothwell et al. (1974); Cooper (1979, 1981); McDougall, Robinson and De Nisi (1992); Stuart and Abetti (1987, 1990); Sandberg and Hofer (1987); Keeley and Roure (1990); Cooper (1984)
Industrial structure	McDougall, Robinson and De Nisi (1992); Stuart and Abetti (1987); Sandberg and Hofer (1987); Keeley and Roure (1990); Kunkel (1991)
Type of organization	Rothwell et al. (1974); Maidique and Zirger (1985)
Entrepreneur characteristics (entrepreneurship)	Rothwell et al. (1974); Lussier and Corman (1995); Stuart and Abetti (1987); Sandberg and Hofer (1987); Cooper, Woo and Gimeno-Gascon (1994); Planellas (1999)
Financial aspects	Lussier and Corman (1995); Keeley and Roure (1990); Bruno, Leidecker and Harder (1987); Cressy (1996); Cooper, Woo and Gimeno-Gascon (1994)
Human capital, team and management	Lussier and Corman (1995); Keeley and Roure (1990)

Literature Review

Many studies, including descriptive studies, conceptual models, case studies, surveys, longitudinal studies, and so on, have attempted to examine the factors causing firms to succeed or fail. Table 12.1 summarizes the main variables used in the studies on success factors. This table is not intended to go into great detail about the various techniques employed to measure the success variables, or the different analytical techniques used, since this is not the objective of the current work.

These variables should be considered as some of the factors that may be relevant in the success of new firms, but the list does not end there. In addition, most of these variables differ in their degree of importance according to the study or author. The specific factors of the main success variables that have been examined most in the literature are shown in Table 12.2.

It could be stressed that the entrepreneur's characteristics are among the factors most studied related to the firm success.

Entrepreneur's characteristics
The literature on the entrepreneur's background as success factor has analysed the following: the entrepreneur's personality, the entrepreneur's biographical background and the type of firm created. As regards the entrepreneur background, the literature stresses the following aspects: gender, age, education, incubator organization, experience in the sector, and experience in starting up firms, motivations, planning capacity and managerial skills.

Table 12.2   Most studied factors of the main variables affecting firm success

Variables	Factors studied
Entrepreneur characteristics (entrepreneurship)	Leadership capacity Ability to delegate and form good team Ability to work in team (networking) Ability to assume risks and take decisions Have ambition of economic and professional independence Be confident about the business Be right age (not be too young) and have entrepreneurial parents Have right creative and marketing skills Ability to select right colleagues (team of entrepreneurs is better than one) Be highly tolerant of ambiguity and persistent Be dynamic and enthusiastic Have experience and knowledge about the industry, products and market Be trained in starting up firms
Market and product strategy	Thoroughly study market from client's perspective (specifications, design, distribution channels) Be oriented to market needs (niches well identified and big enough to be profitable) Have unique and differentiating innovation Have defensive and offensive strategies allowing firm to survive Choose right market for product (should be dynamic and attractive) Compatibility of new venture with entrepreneur's image, culture and product experience Continuously innovate product
Industrial structure	Choose right strategy in function of industry Maintain good relations between strategy and industrial structure in function of stage of industry and firm's objectives
Financial aspects	Accept firm needs to make minimum investment possible in assets Stock control Obtain payments from clients as soon as possible Negotiate payments with suppliers Achieve right level of financial independence Get right funding, taking into account delayed client payments and financial costs Design financial structure that minimizes fixed costs Promote high-margin products

Source: Adapted from Lussier and Corman (1995, 1996) and Magaña (1998).

Gender

Women could be expected to have had fewer opportunities to develop the necessary experience, more difficulty gathering the resources required or fewer contacts with other people able to help them to create their firm (Sexton and Robinson, 1989).

Age
Lussier and Corman (1996) said that younger people who start a business have a greater chance of failure than older people. In a dynamic market like the Internet, 'knowledge' is a basic requirement and young entrepreneurs may have the skill to adapt better to the environment. The Internet entrepreneurs are generally younger than other types of entrepreneur (Colombo and Delmastro, 2001).

Educational level
This is one of the most studied variables and relates to knowledge, skills, problem solving, discipline, motivation and self-confidence. All this provides the entrepreneur with the ability to face numerous problems, hence influencing the success of the company (Cooper, Woo and Gimeno-Gascon, 1994).

Incubator organization
These organizations (firms, universities or research centres) determine not only the number of new firms generated, but also their characteristics (Veciana, 1999). This organization seems to play an important role in the success of high-technology firms (Cooper, 1981; Feeser and Willard, 1988), because it provides the expertise needed to produce the firm's products and services efficiently, the contacts with potential partner-founders, and the experience (Cooper, 1981).

Knowledge of the industry
This is vital for the entrepreneurs' success in their ventures (Kotha, 1998).

Experience in the firm's creation
This measures the number of companies created previously by the entrepreneur. This variable has been studied in a broad number of models of success and failure. It integrates the psychological approach with the institutional, the socio-cultural, and other perspectives. This experience provides the entrepreneur with advanced managerial skills and problem-solving capacity. McMillan (1986) cited in Starr and Bygrave (1991) suggests that there is an experience curve of entrepreneurship, which allows start-up firms to overcome obstacles in their early stages.

Motivations
Most businesses founded are motivated by negative inducements (for example, loss of employment, conflicts in the workplace and so on), and not because of opportunities detected (Sapienza and Curtis, 1997). From this perspective, there are two different types of precipitating condition (Alstete, 2002; Watson et al., 1998): push factors (negative inducements) and pull factors (perceived opportunity and other positive inducements). According to Alstete (2002) and Littunen (2000), personal relationships and the entrepreneur's personality itself appear to be changing in the wake of the Internet boom, and this should be studied. In this context, the motivations of entrepreneurs in creating their own businesses take on particular importance. A significant proportion of the entrepreneurs who have been successful on the Internet founded their firms after detecting a business opportunity, a characteristic that does not appear to be so common in the physical world.

Planning capacity and managerial skills

These managerial skills have been amply studied with respect to the managerial approach of the business function and firm creation (Argenti, 1976; Cooper, 1979; Houston, 1972; Keeley and Roure, 1990). The theories of this approach start from the assumption that founding a business is the result of a rational decision-making process in which the knowledge and techniques employed in the fields of economics and business administration are decisive (Veciana, 1999).

Indicators to measure the success of pure dotcom firms

The entrepreneur literature suggests two approaches to measure the success of new ventures: objective and subjective measures. Objective measures refer to indicators that can be measured quantitatively, such as rate of interest (ROI), cash flow, profits, sales, and so on. Brush and Vanderwerf (1992) detected more than 35 different objective indicators to evaluate the success of a start-up. These indicators sacrifice the precision of other measures to some extent, but at the same time they resolve problems such as the difficulty in gaining access to the founder, and his reluctance to offer information about his businesses.

The subjective measures have followed two tendencies. The first approach is to measure the satisfaction of the entrepreneur/manager with the firm's performance (Cooper, 1984; Dess and Robinson, 1984; Gupta and Govindarajan, 1984). In addition, satisfaction with the results of the firm may be influenced by the entrepreneur's expectations, which may diverge substantially from the objective results. The second tendency is to measure the results of the firm with respect to the competitors (Brush and Vanderwerf, 1992; Dess and Robinson, 1984; Sapienza, Smith and Gannon, 1988; Stuart and Abetti, 1987). In these studies, the information entrepreneurs have about their rivals may distort their responses and so cast doubt on the findings. On the other hand, Morel d'Arleux (1998) defined, using a combination of subjective and objective measures, three dimensions to cover all aspects of entrepreneurs' success. These were professional success (PRS, which refers to the business results and the growth of the firm); personal success (PS, which refers to aspects of the entrepreneur's personal life, the achievement of individual happiness); and family success (FS, which refers to the implications that the firm has for the entrepreneur's family life). Thus the author concludes that success is a global concept (total success, TS) that should be studied at the individual level, and that it comprises three dimensions.

Methodology

The variables analysed in this study, according to the previously mentioned propositions, were age (AG), gender (GE), education (ED), incubator organization (IO), experience in the sector of operation (EXS), experience in founding companies (EXF), motivations or triggering events to create the venture (MOT), and planning capacity (PC). This combination of measures was used in the study.

Owing to the current stage of development of e-commerce in Spain, it is practically impossible to determine the total population of firms that operate exclusively on the Internet. This is because (a) there is no specific CNAE (Spanish industrial classification system) classification for this type of firm, (b) there is no special file where they are

Table 12.3   Technical specifications of the study

Technical specifications	
Type of study	Exploratory, qualitative, using 'grounded theory' and 'case study' techniques
Number of entrepreneurs interviewed	23
Sources of information	Primary and secondary
Mean duration of interviews	95.74 minutes
Sample segmentation criteria	1. Proportion of sales turned over on internet >95%
	2. Geographic situation: Barcelona, Girona and Malaga
	3. Age of operation:< 5 years
	4. Belongs to already existing business group: subsidiaries of already existing groups eliminated
	5. Main activity of firm: attempt to include widest range of activities, at most 2 firms from each activity
Subsamples of analysis	Group 1: 7 firms from Girona province and Barcelona, to test research protocol
	Group 2: 6 firms from Malaga province
	Group 3: 10 firms from Girona province and Barcelona

required to register, and (c) this study focused on firms in the Catalonia and Malaga region because of its high concentration of Internet start-ups in comparison to the rest of Spain and because of the resources available for doing this work. There is only one database of Spanish cyber-traders, which is edited by the magazine *Ganar.com* (Recoletos Group), with around 1200 entries. Access to the database of technological firms located in the Andalusian Technology Park, in Malaga, was also useful (see Table 12.3).

Guided by the above mentioned Morel d'Arleux (1998) proposal, the following subjective estimators of total success (TS) were used: professional success (PRS), personal success (PS) and family success (FS).

To compare the digital entrepreneur's profile with the common entrepreneur's profile in Spain we used the study conducted by Urbano (2001) which analyses the main characteristics of the entrepreneur in Spain. This work focuses on the following:

1. *Current entrepreneurs*, those who have created a venture in Spain, between 1994 and 1998. Urbano conducted 64 personal interviews from a sample of 1352 entrepreneurs.
2. *Potential entrepreneurs*, those who have contacted CIDEM (Managerial Innovation and Development Center), between 1997 and 1999, to request information related to venture creation. Among a sample of 2452 potential entrepreneurs, 346 telephone interviews were conducted.
3. *New entrepreneurs*, a subsample of 'potential entrepreneurs' characterized those entrepreneurs who created their firm. This subsample consists of 107 individuals.

Table 12.4   Success of the businesswomen of the study

Variables	Case 3	Case 23	Mean	The others (Mean)
Total success	7.57	8	7.79	6.61
Professional success	7	7	7	6.14
Personal success	8.5	9	8.75	7.24
Family success	8	10	9	7.26
Total employees	53	26	39.5	20.35

Table 12.5   Entrepreneurs' gender in Spain

[GE] Gender	Present entrepreneurs	Potential entrepreneurs	New entrepreneurs	Digital entrepreneurs
Male	93.7	57.7	66.3	91.3
Female	6.3	42.3	33.7	8.7

Results and Discussion

The descriptive analysis of the entrepreneur dimension of our model was based on the data and transcriptions of the interviews with the founders. In our sample, female entrepreneurs have been more successful and employ many more workers than the average; they have been able to attract funding rounds and come from prestigious incubator organizations (see Table 12.4).

Nevertheless, very few women decide to start up their own pure dotcom firms (8.7 per cent of the sample), perhaps because of the educational background required to undertake a project with these characteristics. A large part of our sample of entrepreneurs had a markedly technical profile and mainly men in Spain historically demand these technical qualifications. Although the sample of e-entrepreneurs may not be statistically representative, we observe significant differences among gender between digital entrepreneurs and new entrepreneurs. Only 8.7 per cent of digital entrepreneurs are female, in comparison to 33.7 per cent of the new entrepreneurs (see Table 12.5). Thus, as regards gender, digital entrepreneurs are similar to the present entrepreneurs.

With respect to age, 91.3 per cent of the entrepreneurs participating in this study were between 20 and 40 years old (see Table 12.6).

According to Urbano (2001), the present and new entrepreneur's average age is 43.5 and 35.6 years old, respectively. We observe significant differences among the digital entrepreneur's age range with respect to the rest of entrepreneurs. Only 4.3 per cent of the digital entrepreneurs are over 45 years old, in comparison to 53.3 per cent of present entrepreneurs and 26.1 per cent of new entrepreneurs. This phenomenon may be related to the capacity of adaptation to technology. In the Internet, where the technology is a barrier to entry, young entrepreneurs adapt better to technology than the older ones.

With regard to educational level, 82.6 per cent have at least a university education. About 52.17 per cent of the entrepreneurs interviewed have reached postgraduate level.

Table 12.6   Digital entrepreneurs' age in Spain

[AG] Digital entrepreneur's age		Absolute frequency	Relative frequency (%)
Average age		33.65 (average)	33 (median)
Age	Under 20	0	0.00
	From 20 to 29	5	21.74
	From 30 to 39	16	69.57
	Over 40	2	8.70

Table 12.7   Entrepreneurs' age in Spain

[AG] Age	Present entrepreneurs	Potential entrepreneurs	New entrepreneurs	Digital entrepreneurs
Average age	43.5	33.8	35.6	33.65
Under 25	0.0	5.2	2.8	4.4
From 25 to 34	20.0	41.4	32.7	56.5
From 35 to 44	26.7	30.3	38.3	34.8
Over 45	53.3	23.1	26.1	4.3

Table 12.8   Educational level of the digital entrepreneur in Spain

[ED] Digital entrepreneur		Absolute frequency	Relative frequency (%)
Educational level	Without	0	0.00
	Primary school	1	4.35
	Secondary school	3	13.04
	Graduate	7	30.43
	Postgraduate	12	52.17

Table 12.9   University degrees of the digital entrepreneur in Spain

[ED] Educational level: university degrees	Absolute frequency	Relative frequency (%)
Technical and engineering degrees (computer science, industrial, telecommunication and electric)	8	42.11
Business administration and economics (management, economy and public relations)	5	26.32
Law	4	21.05
Other degrees (geography and literature)	2	10.53

Only 17.39 per cent have primary or secondary-level educations only. Tables 12.8, 12.9 and 12.10 show the different educational degrees from the sample of e-entrepreneurs.

These data indicate that the entrepreneurs who have started Internet start-ups have a very superior educational level to that of the rest of the population of entrepreneurs (only 2 to 5 per cent of these tend to have postgraduate qualifications, as can be seen in Table

Table 12.10   Postgraduate degrees of the digital entrepreneur in Spain

[ED] Educational level: postgraduate degrees	Absolute frequency	Relative frequency (%)
Master degree (6 MBA; 2 Law; 1 Geography; 1 Politics; 1 New Technologies)	11	73.33
PhD (2 Computer Science; 1 Geography; 1 Information Technologies)	4	26.67

Table 12.11   Educational level of the entrepreneur in Spain

[ED] Educational level	Present entrepreneurs	Potential entrepreneurs	New entrepreneurs	Digital entrepreneurs
Without	5.0	1.0	0.3	0.0
Primary school	20.0	14.0	8.4	4.35
Secondary school	38.3	25.1	37.4	13.04
Graduate	18.3	42.7	37.1	30.43
Postgraduate	1.7	4.5	5.6	52.17
Others	16.7	12.7	11.2	0.0

Table 12.12   Experience in start-ups of the entrepreneur in Spain

[EXF] Had started up a venture previously?	Present entrepreneurs	Potential entrepreneurs	New entrepreneurs	Digital entrepreneurs
Yes	75	12.4	27.1	52.17
No	25	87.6	72.9	47.83

12.11). However, the study has not been able to detect a direct statistical relationship between the variable educational level and firm success.

More than half of the entrepreneurs had started up a venture previously. It is noteworthy that the dotcom entrepreneurs, although they are a very young sample, have been very enterprising in the sense of creating firms.

The survival rate of these companies is, however, only 25 per cent. It would be interesting to analyse the survival rate of traditional non-dotcom start-ups and compare than with the results of this study. Table 12.13 explains the digital entrepreneur's experience in creating new ventures.

Almost 70 per cent of the entrepreneurs have had previous experience of the sector in which they are currently operating, with an average of 7.16 years and a median of five years of experience. The study has not been able to determine whether this variable individually affects firm success. However, it was determined that this variable, along with experience in Internet start-up creation and triggering events, does affect success. More than 82 per cent of the entrepreneurs interviewed affirmed that their incubator organization had positively affected their project of starting up a dotcom. The main incubator organizations of the sample entrepreneurs are traditional firms (40 per cent), followed by

Table 12.13   Experience in start-ups of the digital entrepreneur in Spain

[EXF] Previous experience in start-ups	
Case 1	The entrepreneur founded a firm that commercializes computer memories and it had to shut down because it could not compete in costs with big computer memories manufacturing firms
Case 2	The entrepreneur founded a book shop that still exists but he had to leave because he did not have the same business vision as the rest of the stakeholders
Case 3	The entrepreneur founded a new born gift venture. The firm is still operating and a second gift venture was also founded
Case 4	The entrepreneur founded a music services firm that had to close because of financial problems
Case 7	The entrepreneur created a digital real-state management application to buy, hire and sell flats that did not work because he left the project and started his present venture
Case 9	The entrepreneur has created several firms; however, none of them is still operating. He has been working on those firms parallel to his job in a big enterprise
Case 11	The entrepreneur founded a technological firm six years ago and it has been the core of his present firm
Case 13	The entrepreneur created a spin-off in his previous job; it is still operating
Case 14	The entrepreneur founded several firms (car import, sea bikes, etc.) but none of them is still operating
Case 15	The entrepreneur created his first firm when he was 16, in the publicity business. When he was 20, he founded a TV producer company and both closed down
Case 16	The entrepreneur had created two firms previously; the first one was a language school that closed down owing to lack of demand and the second was a record study that had to shut down because of personal problems with his associate
Case 19	The entrepreneur created a consultancy firm, but left the project to start up his present venture. The firm is still operating

technological firms (36 per cent) and universities and research centres (24 per cent). Among the technology firms, Intercom (http://www.grupointercom.com) is of note, because it has helped to produce 44 per cent of the entrepreneurs coming from this firm. The main benefits that the entrepreneurs have obtained from their incubator organizations have been 'experience in management and in founding firms' (32.5 per cent), followed by 'contacts and clients' (25 per cent). 'Experience in the technology and in Internet projects' (15 per cent) and 'sector knowledge' (15 per cent) were considered less important. Some other interesting contributions of these incubator organizations to the entrepreneurs, from the statements of some interviewees were

(Entrepreneur 11): 'Above all vision, a bit of training, some contacts.';

(Entrepreneur 20): 'Intercom taught me to listen, organize and present a project that is meaningful to the client.' The Incubator Organization provided experience in Internet projects. (Entrepreneur 23): 'Sitting next to the CEOs of the biggest companies in Spain and you learn a lot. Perhaps not technical stuff, very little of that, but you do learn management skills or how to run a company, that's what I learnt.' The Incubator Organization provided management skills.

Some 73.91 per cent of the entrepreneurs decided to create their own company because of positive inducements. Only 13.04 per cent were forced to undertake the venture. It is also worth pointing out that 13.04 per cent of entrepreneurs were motivated to start up their own pure dotcoms without distinction for the push or pull factors. The main pull aspects detected were desire to do something and/or work for themselves (37.14 per cent), perceiving a market opportunity (22.86 per cent), and doing something new/something I like (22.86 per cent). The main push factors on the other hand were to find a job for my spouse, find work while doing my doctorate, have more time for my family, and my family pushed me into it.

From the transcriptions of the interviews, it was observed that various entrepreneurs already had the idea of creating their own firm, and the Internet was simply a catalyst. Perhaps this was due to the euphoria of the moment, or to the fact that creating a dotcom required so few initial resources compared to creating a traditional company in the real world. Some other interesting contributions to the idea of the Internet as simply a catalyst were found in the interviews:

(Entrepreneur 2): 'I had been wanting to do something on my own for some time. But I couldn't think what, [. . .] until one day the net came to Spain and I began to think that perhaps [the Internet] would be a good channel. With Julia [his wife] we thought we had found the channel that would allow us to start without investing very much, without having to have business premises.'
(Entrepreneur 5): 'And it was 1996 when the Internet appeared and I thought that it fitted in very well with what I had been doing up till then. Since it wouldn't mean printing catalogues, or fixed costs, and I would be able to have a much bigger public.'

Finally, with regard to planning capacity, 82.61 per cent of the entrepreneurs had made efforts to plan, which eventually resulted in the elaboration of a business plan. These plans were very varied in terms of their level of detail. Entrepreneurs who have had external help (26.09 per cent of the total number of entrepreneurs, or 31.58 per cent of those who have produced business plans), or who have needed a plan to close a funding round, produced more detailed business plans and dedicated much more time to preparing them. The entrepreneurs' comments with respect to this question included the following:

(Entrepreneur 5): initially this entrepreneur did not write the business plan, until the entry of a capitalist partner forced him to do so.
(Entrepreneur 8): this entrepreneur was forced to write down a business plan in order to win a space in a business incubator: '. . .we needed it to come here, we had to do it, it was as simple as that. Because this place is a business incubator, so they demand a number of things.' (Entrepreneur 17): 'Personally, I think that these plans help you to

organize the agenda, but you must then be able to react to events. Until you have decided the 10 things you need to satisfy the market, which is first, second etc. . .'

After analysing all the interviews' transcriptions, we found some common aspects that are repeated among the entrepreneurs: (a) difficulty in planning, especially related to the sales plan, (b) BP (a business plan) is helpful in evaluating the costs of the project, (c) BP is compulsory whether you want to obtain financing or want to get a place in a business incubator, and (d) BP helps you to 'organize your agenda' but is not as useful for producing good plans owing to the lack of historical information.

Final Remarks

The results of the study show that the Spanish e-entrepreneur is on average a male about 33 years old with a university degree and a postgraduate qualification. The entrepreneur has had previous experience in the industrial sector where the firm operates, and has created another firm previously.

The incubator organization from which the entrepreneur comes has provided him with experience in management and firm creation as well as access to contacts and clients. In contrast to what is found in most studies on traditional entrepreneurs, this study found that the e-entrepreneurs created their new ventures, motivated by positive pull factors such as a desire to work for themselves and the perception of a market opportunity. It was noticeable that various sample entrepreneurs had had the idea of starting up their own company some time before actually doing so, and that the Internet was simply a catalyst.

It was observed that younger entrepreneurs with university studies, who had created their own firm with external help and motivated by push factors, tended to be personally very unsuccessful (very low PS), and to a lesser extent very unsuccessful as a whole (very low TS). Other characteristics of the e-entrepreneur are summarized in Table 12.14.

Although this qualitative study has not been conducted with the aim of confirming any propositions, it builds theory in the sense of Eisenhardt (1989), and some evidence was found. The study has two main limitations. First, the researchers found it difficult to detect and select Internet start-ups. For this reason, this sample may not fully represent the entire population of Internet start-ups in Spain. Second, the methodology used helped the researchers only to explore the initial explanation of the phenomenon, but more in-depth and quantitative studies are necessary in order to find valuable statistical evidence about our propositions.

The implications of this study for future research in entrepreneurship are to a certain extent exploratory, and aimed at opening up new lines of research for the study of the success factors of firms operating exclusively on the Internet. This chapter suggests that the entrepreneurs' characteristics and their motivations for creating their firms play an important role in the success of pure dotcoms. However, the literature on the success factors for traditional firms suggests that success may also have something to do with the market, the type of product and product strategy, the industrial structure and the human capital and financial aspects, among other factors. Future research should amplify these socio-demographic characteristics of the e-entrepreneur, as well as being able to analyse differences between e-entrepreneurs and traditional entrepreneurs.

Table 12.14   E-entrepreneur characteristics

Summary	
Age	There is no direct relation between the age of the entrepreneur and the success of the digital company
	Age can be related to the technological adaptation. Younger entrepreneurs have greater adaptation capacity than others, nevertheless their companies present/display minor success
	The age of the entrepreneur is much lower than that of the rest of Spanish entrepreneurs
Gender	It has been found that the digital companies created by women are more successful than the average
	There is a very small proportion of women e-entrepreneurs, which could be explained by the technical education that is necessary
Education	The level of studies of the e-entrepreneur is much higher than that of the rest of the entrepreneurs
	There seems to be a tendency of the greater the education, the greater the success. At a higher level of studies and especially MBAs, the companies present/display greater success
Incubator organization	82% of the entrepreneurs interviewed point out that the incubator organization has affected them positively
	The entrepreneurs who create a digital company are influenced strongly by the incubator organization where they have worked previously
	The e-entrepreneurs come mainly from traditional companies. One of the incubator organizations which has had greater influence on the sample of entrepreneurs interviewed has been Intercom
	The main assets which entrepreneurs have obtained from the incubators have been 'experience in management and creation of companies' and 'contacts and clients'
Experience in the sector	Most of the e-entrepreneurs had previous experience in the sector
	This variable, together with the experience of creating companies, affects the success of the e-entrepreneur
Experience in founding companies	More than half of the entrepreneurs had created a company prior to the present one
	It has not been possible to determine whether this variable individually affects the success of the new company
	Important differences between the traditional entrepreneurs and the e-entrepreneurs have been detected
	The index of survival of these companies has been relatively low
Motivations	Most of the e-entrepreneurs have decided to create their company as a result of 'positive inducements'
	The main reason to create these companies has been the 'desire to do something and/or to work by oneself'
	It has been detected that this variable ('pull') tends to affect success rate positively
	On the other hand, it has not been possible to determine that the aspects 'push' negatively affect the success of companies
	Several of the entrepreneurs of the sample already had the idea to create a company and the appearance of the Internet was a catalyst for them

Table 12.14   (continued)

Summary	
Planning capacity	Most of the entrepreneurs have made planning efforts that have been translated into company plans
	The entrepreneurs who have had financial support present more detailed business plans and have given much more time to their planning activities
	Not having a business plan tends to affect negatively the success of companies
	It is difficult to plan activities on the Internet (mainly the sales plan)
	Entrepreneurs said that the business plan is not used for anything other than to help to organize ideas

References

AECE; FECEMD (2004), 'Estudio Comercio Electrónico', retrieved 15 May 2004 from http://www.aece.org/recursosclasifica.asp.

Alstete, J.W. (2002), 'On becoming an entrepreneur: an evolving typology', *International Journal of Entrepreneurial Behaviour & Research*, **8**(4), 222–34.

Argenti, J. (1976), *Corporate Collapse: the Causes and Symptoms*, London and New York: McGraw-Hill.

Bruno, A.V., J.K. Leidecker and J.W. Harder (1987), 'Why firms fail', *Business Horizons*, **30**(2), 50–58.

Brush, C.G. and P.A. Vanderwerf (1992), 'A comparison of methods and sources for obtaining estimates of new venture performance', *Journal of Business Venturing*, **7**, 157–70.

Chandler, G.N. and S.H. Hanks (1993), 'Measuring the performance of emerging businesses: a validation study', *Journal of Business Venturing*, **8**, 391–408.

Colombo, M.G. and M. Delmastro (2001), 'Technology-based entrepreneurs: does internet make a difference?', *Small Business Economics*, **16**, 177–90.

Cooper, A. (1981), 'Strategic management: new ventures and small business', *Long Range Planning*, **14**(5), 39–45.

Cooper, A., C.Y. Woo and F.J. Gimeno-Gascon (1994), 'Initial human and financial capital as predictors of new venture performance', *Journal of Business Venturing*, **9**(5), 351–95.

Cooper, R.G. (1979), 'The dimensions of industrial new product success and failure', *Journal of Marketing*, **43**, 93–103.

Cooper, R.G. (1984), 'How new product strategies impact on performance', *Journal of Product Innovation Management*, **1**, 5–18.

Cressy, R. (1996), 'Small firm failure: failure to fund or failure to learn by doing', *Electronic Proceedings of the International Council on Small Business Conference*, Stockholm, 16–19 June, 1–7.

Dess, G.G. and R.B. Robinson (1984), 'Measuring organizational performance in the absence of objectives measures: the case of privately held firm and conglomerate business unit', *Strategic Management Journal*, **5**, 265–74.

Eisenhardt, K. (1989), 'Building theories from case studies research', *Academy of Management Review*, **14**(4), 532–50.

Feeser, H.R. and G.E. Willard (1988), 'Incubators and performance: a comparison of high and low growth high tech firms', *Frontiers of Entrepreneurship Research*, 549–63.

Forrester Research (2004), 'The state of retailing online 7.0. A Shop.org study by Forrester Research', retrieved 19 October 2004 from http://www.shop.org/research/SRO7/SRO7main.asp.

Gupta, A.K. and V. Govindarajan (1984), 'Business unit strategy, managerial characteristics, and business unit effectiveness at strategy implementation', *Academy of Management Journal*, **27**, 25–41.

Houston, B. (1972), 'Let's put more spirit in the corporation', *Harvard Business Review*, **70**, 25–42.

Keeley, R.H. and J.B. Roure (1990), 'Management strategy and industrial structure as influences on the success of new firms: a structural model', *Management Science*, **36**(10), 1256–67.

Kotha, S. (1998), 'Competing on the internet: the case of Amazon.com', *European Management Journal*, **16**(2), 212–22.

Kunkel, S.W. (1991), 'The impact of strategy and industry structure on new venture performance', unpublished doctoral dissertation, The University of Georgia, Athens.

Littunen, H. (2000), 'Entrepreneurship and the characteristics of the entrepreneurial personality', *International Journal of Entrepreneurial Behaviour & Research*, **6**(6), 295–309.

Lussier, R.N. and J. Corman (1995), 'There are few differences between successful and failed small businesses', *Journal of Small Business Strategy*, **6**(1), 21–33.

Lussier, R.N. and J. Corman (1996), 'A business success versus failure prediction model for entrepreneurs with 0–10 employees', *Journal of Small Business Strategy*, **7**(1), 21–35.

Magaña, M. (1998), 'Factors affecting success and failure of new firms', *European Doctoral Programme on Entrepreneurship and Small Business Management (97/98)*, Barcelona.

Maidique, M.A. and B.J. Zirger (1985), 'The new product learning cycle', *Research Policy*, **14**, 299–313.

McDougall, P., R.B. Robinson and A.S. De Nisi (1992), 'Modeling new venture performance: an analysis of new venture strategy, industry structure and venture origin', *Journal of Business Venturing*, **7**(4), 267–89.

McMillan, I. (1986), 'Executive forum: to really learn about entrepreneurship, let's study habitual entrepreneurs', *Journal of Business Venturing*, **1**, 241–3.

Morel d'Arleux, C. (1998), 'Proposition of a conceptual framework for a better distinction between the notions of performance, growth and success', *Rent XII*, Lyon, France.

Morel d'Arleux, C. (1999), 'Proposition of a conceptual framework for a better distinction between the notions of performance, growth and success', paper presented at the Kauffman-Babson Entrepreneurship Research Conference, Columbia, SC.

Planellas, M. (1999), 'Influencias de las características del empresario, la estructura del sector y la estrategia empresarial en el éxito inicial de las nuevas empresas', *Paper ESADE*, 167.

Rothwell, R., C. Freeman, A. Horsley, V.T.P. Jervis, A.B. Robertson and J. Townsend (1974), 'SAPPHO updated: Project SAPPHO phase II', *Research Policy*, **3**(3), 258–91.

Sandberg, W.R. and C.W. Hofer (1987), 'Improving new venture performance: the role of strategy, industry structure and the entrepreneur', *Journal of Business Venturing*, **2**, 5–28.

Sapienza, H.J. and G. Curtis (1997), 'The founder, start-up process, strategy/structure variables as predictors of shorttime railroad performance', *Entrepreneurship: Theory and Practice*, **22**(1), 5–24.

Sapienza, H.J., K.J. Smith and M.J. Gannon (1988), 'Using subjective evaluations of organizational performance in small business research', *American Journal of Small Business*, **12**(2), 45–53.

Schwartz, E. (1997), 'Webonomics: nine essential principles for growing your business on the World Wide Web', New York: Broadway Books.

Sexton, E.A. and P.B. Robinson (1989), 'The economic and demographic determinants of self-employment', in R.H. Brockhaus, W.D. Bygrave and N.C. Churchill (eds), *Frontiers of Entrepreneurship Research*, Wellesley, MA: Babson College, pp. 28–42.

Starr, J.A. and W.D. Bygrave (1991), 'The assets and liabilities of prior start-up experience: an exploratory study of multiple venture entrepreneurs', *Frontiers of Entrepreneurship Research*, 213–27.

Stuart, R.W. and P.A. Abetti (1987), 'Start-up ventures: towards the prediction of initial success', *Journal of Business Venturing*, **2**, 215–30.

Stuart, R.W. and P.A. Abetti (1990), 'Impact of entrepreneurial and management experience on early performance', *Journal of Business Venturing*, **5**(3), 151–62.

Urbano, D. (2001), 'Marco Institucional Formal de la Creación de Empresas en Catalunya', *Trabajo de Investigación (European Doctoral Programme)* dirigido por el Dr. José María Veciana, Septiembre 2001, Departament d'Economia de l'Empresa-UAB.

US Department of Commerce (2004), 'US department of commerce news', 20 August, retrieved from http://www.census.gov/mrts/www/current.html.

Veciana, J.M. (1999), 'Creación de empresas como programa de investigación científica', *Revista Europea de Dirección y Economía de la Empresa*, **8**(3), 11–36.

Watson, K., S. Hogarth-Scott and N. Wilson (1998), 'Small business start-ups: success factors and support implications', *International Journal of Entrepreneurial Behaviour & Research*, **4**(3), 217–38.

13 Virtual alliances as coordination and influence mechanisms in the Internet context: evidence from a cross-section of Internet-based firms
Lalit Manral

Virtual alliances are options to use tangible or intangible assets owned or controlled by partner firms to provide services. They differ from other alliances in their virtuality (control). Since no partner commits specialized assets to the relationship, their flexibility and ease of switching differs from other forms of inter-firm cooperation. Not confined to virtual firms alone, virtual alliances have been used by a variety of firms to build legitimacy, propagate standards, reach new customers, coordinate with stakeholders and potential partners, and accomplish other purposes. As competitive and organizational phenomena evocative of their era, virtual alliances present novel issues of interest to strategic management research.

Virtual alliances should not be confused with conventional strategic alliances or with firms' outsourcing arrangements in which virtuality replaces ownership of vertically related value-adding operations (Chesbrough and Teece, 1996), a 1980s practice castigated as the hollowing-out of an industrial firm (Jonas, 1985; Bettis, Bradley and Hamel, 1992). Virtual alliances can be horizontal in scope, as well as vertical, and differ from conventional 'strategic alliances' in three salient ways: (1) they have no specific partnership commitments to duration and exclusivity, (2) they use partners' general-use assets, but neither own assets in their own right nor commit themselves to owning them in the future; that is, they are characterized by lack of asset specificity, and (3) they are at best viewed as options to form strategic alliances in future by the parties to the virtual alliance.

Two explanations for the formation of virtual alliances may be posited (Manral and Harrigan, 2005). One view holds that virtual alliances exist to create legitimacy for ideas, practices, software and other innovations by influencing the expectations of consumers and stakeholders. The other explanation (the 'coordination' perspective) is concerned less with the form by which the task is accomplished and more concerned with the systemic process underlying the mechanism by which virtual alliances increase overall returns through compatibility and complementarity. These intertwined arguments will be dissected herein to explain why virtual alliances have been formed at this time in economic history and assess their efficacy in attaining their objectives. The virtual alliances analysed below involve single-business firms that make transactions via the Internet (or offer services specifically designed to be used for Internet activities).

Literature Review

Inter-firm alliances
Since the early 1980s, an inter-firm alliance has gained legitimacy as an organizational arrangement and high comfort levels among corporations as a way to achieve objectives

beyond the reach of a single firm's capabilities. Spanning almost the entire range of activities that comprise a typical firm's value chain, alliances can be horizontal, as well as vertical, in scope (Harrigan, 1985b). As an organizational form that lies between the two extremes of 'market' and 'hierarchy', a typical inter-firm alliance can take on diverse forms: equity joint ventures, joint-marketing, -promotion, -selling, -distribution, and -product development arrangements, technology licenses, R&D contracts, design collaborations, production arrangements, outsourcing functions, et cetera, to achieve its objectives (Harrigan, 1985a).

In Table 13.1, the 'strategic behaviour' perspective literature (Table 13.1a) addresses the strategic concern of a firm to join with allies. In it, the decision to form an inter-firm alliance is often the outcome of the make-or-buy decision arising for various reasons, such as the need to acquire complementary assets, risk reduction and so on (Williamson, 1975, 1991; Teece, 1986). The 'structural sociology' perspective literature (Table 13.1b) addresses the choice of partners (Gulati, 1999; Ahuja, 2000) by focusing on the firm's social context (Gulati, 1995b, 1999; Gulati and Gargiulo, 1999; Walker, Kogut and Shan, 1997). In it, the alliances formed are influenced by interdependence and network embeddedness, contingent on the level of structural differentiation of the social system in which the firms are embedded (Gulati and Gargiulo, 1999).

Because virtual alliances lack asset specificity, finite duration and mutual exclusivity, their formation and efficacy are at odds with literature that evaluates alliances according to their (a) duration (Levinthal and Fichman, 1988), (b) exclusivity (Cook, 1977; Cook and Emerson, 1978), and (c) exploitation of substantial relationship-specific investments that lose their value when applied to another relationship (Blau, 1964; Williamson, 1975). My theory explaining the enabling conditions that facilitate the formation of virtual alliances and their effect on firm performance draws upon insights from network economics.

Network externalities and market outcomes

Virtual alliances are short-term opportunistic *quasi* structures that link virtual networks of components. A number of components combine to form a technological system and are offered by different firms. Virtual alliances influence market outcomes in favour of firms who form such alliances. The theoretical rationale underlying this behaviour is that such association fosters adoption of particular combinations of components as a system, thereby benefiting individual firms that supply different components. Hence the competitive value of the individual component supplier arises from their ability to influence market outcome by exploiting indirect network externalities to their advantage.

In markets subject to network effects, where one firm's investment is complementary to another's, start-up firms either create new networks through extension, or join pre-existing networks. They do so to exploit inherent network effects to influence the market outcome in their favour. Market outcome is defined as the outcome of competition for adoption of a product or technology by potential users. It is also influenced by various other factors, such as ex-ante knowledge of consumers' preferences and the future potential of the economic object being considered (Arthur, 1989). I explain below the relationship among virtual alliances formed by start-up firms, the network effects they exploit and the market outcomes they seek in such settings. I explain the above relationship in terms of the 'increasing returns' properties of networks. A fundamental property of networks is that they exhibit *network externalities,* that is, a product derives much of its value from

Table 13.1   Diverse perspectives on determinants of inter-firm alliances[1]

Area	Determinant of inter-firm alliance
Transaction cost economics	Make-or-buy; reduction of transaction costs: Williamson, 1975, 1991; Teece, 1986
Resource-based view	Access complementary resources: Kogut, 1989; Kleinknecht and Reijnen, 1992; Hagedoorn, 1993; Mowery and Teece, 1993; Eisenhardt and Schoonhoven, 1996; Galaskiewicz and Zaheer, 1999; Wernerfelt, 1984
	Sharing marketing assets or brand names: Hagedoorn and Schakenraad, 1994; Singh and Mitchell, 1996
	Joint manufacturing or sharing a manufacturing process: Ahuja, 2000
Risk management	
Strategic flexibility	Manage strategic flexibility: Harrigan, 1988
Resource dependence	Manage mutual interdependence to reduce uncertainty: Pfeffer and Salancik, 1978; Galasckiewicz, 1985
International management	Mechanisms to reduce net costs of conducting international business: Buckley and Casson, 1989; Dunning, 1993
	Coping with national political restrictions: Mowery, 1988
	Geographic expansion: Chang, 1995
	Capitalizing on a combination of firm-specific, industry-specific and alliance-specific advantages: Dunning, 1993
Organizational learning	Access to sources of innovation: Shan, Walker and Kogut, 1994; Podolny and Stuart, 1995; Powell, Koput and Smith-Doerr, 1996
	Learn new skills: Baum, Calabrese and Silverman, 2000; Hennart, 1988; Kogut, 1988
Social network or interorganizational embeddedness[2]	Advantages from network of prior alliances or relational, structural, positional embeddedness such as board interlocks, trade associations, R&D ventures, etc.: Baker, 1990; Kogut et al., 1992; Podolny, 1993, 1994; Han, 1994; Podolny and Stuart, 1995; Burt and Knez, 1995; Gulati, 1995a, 1995b; Gulati and Gargiulo, 1999
	Informational advantage on the availability, competence and reliability of prospective partners: Kogut, Shan and Walker, 1992; Burt, 1992; Gulati, 1995b
	Alliance formation and management capabilities, alliance–network centrality: Lyles, 1988; Amburgey, Dacin and Singh, 1996; Dyer and Singh, 1998; Anand and Khanna, 1997; Arregle, Amburgey and Dacin, 1997
	Personal ties among key individuals: Ring and Van de Ven, 1992; Doz, 1996
	Social structure of resource dependence: Pfeffer and Salancik, 1978; Burt, 1983
Interdependence	Environmental contingencies; legitimacy, asymmetry, reciprocity, efficiency, stability, necessity: Hannan and Freeman, 1989; Oliver, 1990; Scott, 1995

Notes:
1.   Strategic behaviour perspective.
2.   Structural sociology perspective.

the size of its network (Katz and Shapiro, 1985). The role of network externalities is critical in the success of firms competing in industries like railroads, airlines, highways, satellite television, fax machines and telephones, where a large number of economic objects – technologies, products, firms or even systems – compete for adoption. However, the market outcome may not always favour the most efficient or superior performance (for example, Arthur, 1989; Shapiro and Varian, 1999; Katz and Shapiro, 1985, 1986, 1992, 1994).

In these markets, where one network can dramatically increase its value by interconnecting with other networks, firms compete by expanding the reach of their networks. A firm with a small initial advantage in a network market may be able to parlay its small initial advantage into a larger and lasting one. This enables them to influence the outcome favourably through economies of scale on the demand side.

Network externalities influence the dynamics of market outcome by generating increasing returns to adoption – scale economies that result in a sharp decline in factor prices. Internet industries are highly susceptible to the effects of network externalities. Internet economics exploited the higher value derived by consumers from (a) the larger installed base or size of the existing network of an economic object, and (b) consumers' expectations regarding the larger size of that network in the future (Katz and Shapiro, 1986).

Market outcome
The market outcome in any industry is influenced by market power, which is usually associated with the ability to set prices at levels that drive out marginal competitors. In general, competitive market outcomes result in a number of surviving firms with varying market shares, pursuing diverse standards, and aiming at different customers. However, industries with network externalities are often subject to market failure; that is, the market may tip in favour of a particular firm (or technology) owing to the presence of inertia in customers' purchases and in complementary systems (Katz and Shapiro, 1985; Besen and Farrell, 1994).

Network effects exacerbate inertia; that is, once a firm establishes a substantial lead in its installed base, it is difficult for legitimate transactional relationships to be displaced by a superior alternative. Where network externalities are strong, start-up firms race to establish a large installed base, as in the example of the free e-mails or instant-messaging services that are offered by various Internet-based firms (Besen and Farrell, 1994). For instance, AOL accumulated substantial losses to build its brand and infrastructure by continually buying market shares until it had a larger installed base than competitors like Microsoft and AT&T, among others. AOL retained these customers through a clutch of free services, thus exploiting systemic switching cost barriers.

Forming systems, consumer adoption and network effects
If a large number of products possessing low or no value in isolation generate higher consumer value when combined with others, a gestalt of such products constitutes 'forming systems' (Katz and Shapiro, 1994). More specifically, a forming system is a system of complementary and interoperable components. Hence, the bundled components of a forming system embody a core technology and perform a well-defined user function. The components can be considered as analogous to value chain components, but a forming system more likely creates *horizontal* synergies in linking necessary

services that are used simultaneously to produce value. For example, the simple transaction of enabling a consumer to purchase a book from an Internet-based retailer involves the coordination of a large number of complementary activities (services) performed by different firms: the credit card company coordinates with the retailer to offer its service for the transaction (while another company validates the authenticity of the payment process) every time a transaction takes place. Each of these companies provides a single and complementary service that together constitutes a system for providing retailing service to the customer.

The effect of 'forming systems' further exacerbates transactional inertia during the race for consumer adoptions within industries where network externalities are pronounced. This is a typical characteristic of such industries during their formative stage and sometimes even later until their context is malleable. Where path dependencies make the replication of a particular forming system difficult (with costly switching costs for consumers), legitimized systems become popular, and components compatible with that system become widely available (with several interchangeable components that could be mixed and matched to provide customized solutions to a user). Network benefits accrue to participants indirectly through consumers' adoption decisions; their impact influences the future variety, availability and prices of components used in legitimate systems. Cooperation is vital in this context because ownership of entire forming systems by single firms is unlikely in embryonic industry settings where market outcome uncertainties are so high. No single firm would have all the internal capabilities necessary for success (Powell et al., 1996) and no investors would underwrite such high risks. The presence of strong partners legitimizes the system and enhances its development.

Theory and Hypotheses

Virtual networks and virtual alliances
Virtual networks refer to the installed base of the group of firms supplying the potential components of forming systems. This is different from forming systems, which indicate the group of tangible products or services that need to be used together to generate consumer value (basic recipe). A virtual network is tied together by means of virtual alliances. Start-up firms exploit the network effects at the system level to gain market share at the firm level. Through virtual alliances, start-up firms can build a large installed base or virtual network rapidly, by interconnecting with the virtual networks of other firms. Thus virtual alliances are *quasi*-structures that connect virtual networks of component firms and allow nascent industries to develop through joint risk taking among well-regarded participants.

Where network externalities are strong and diverse firms compete to provide complementary products within various forming systems, questions of interconnection, compatibility, interoperability and coordination of quality of services become important for coordinating suppliers' activities (Economides and White, 1994). Virtual networks are susceptible to underutilization (Spence, 1976; Dixit and Stiglitz, 1977). To avoid excess capacity costs, start-up component firms enter as many virtual alliances as possible to increase the size and scope of their virtual networks, driven by *compatibility* (whether products offered by sponsoring firms can be used together) and *complementarity* (whether add-on products increase a network's utility for consumers).

Complementarity and virtual alliances

Figure 13.1 illustrates the various permutations and combinations of alliance that are possible in terms of a network's complementary offerings, and each single-business firm is assumed to supply only one component (narrow product line). In this figure, a large number of start-up firms supply differentiated variants of complementary component classes A, B, C and L. Each class of components provides a specific function, is compatible with, and complementary to the others. Figure 13.1 depicts two variations of $L - L_1$

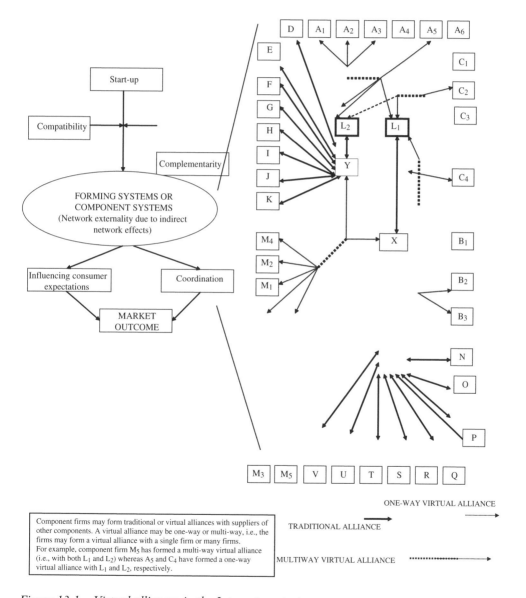

Figure 13.1   Virtual alliances in the Internet context

and L_2 – and six, three and four respective variations of A, B and C (components that are compatible with both L_1 and L_2). Each of these components is assumed to have little or no value independently, and subsystems (X and Y) are formed by mixing only specified components in fixed proportions. Only component M can be chosen by consumers for themselves, since X is compatible only with L_1 and Y is compatible only with L_2.

In Figure 13.1, there exist two possible systems that a consumer might choose: ALPHA and BETA. In order to form system ALPHA, the provider needs to combine one unit of L_1 with one unit each of components A, B and C and the subsystem X (which itself is an assemblage of several components: N, O, P, Q, R, S, T, U, V and any variant of M). Similarly one unit of L_2 needs to be combined with one unit each of components A, B and C and the subsystem Y (a bundle of D, E, F, G, H, I, J, K and any variant of M) to form system BETA. The focal firm has multiple options for horizontal partnering with suppliers of complementary components and can enter into parallel virtual alliances simultaneously. The product offered by the focal firm must be both complementary and compatible with the product of prospective partners for them to form a virtual alliance.

Compatibility and virtual alliances

A component firm expands the size of its virtual network by linking it with the virtual network of another firm which offers a complementary component. It may also link its virtual network to the virtual network of a pre-existing forming system. However, the link is possible only if its component is compatible with the other firms' (or forming systems') components. Compatibility enhances adoption because it increases legitimacy; consumers are not afraid that the new system they select will end up a loser, forcing them to reinvest in an alternative system (Berg, 1984) and the benefits of compatibility are augmented in markets where network externalities are substantial.

Within systems of compatible components, there are greater opportunities to take advantage of economies of scale, learning effects and technological spillovers in the development and production of specific components if many complements are available to increase usage. Compatibility between different systems leads to a greater choice for the consumers by allowing them to mix and match the complementary components that constitute the systems (Matutes and Regibeau, 1988). Complementary component suppliers can work together, as would an Internet-based florist, greetings card company, and a gift retailer to create a service for the 'romance' market, to increase sales volumes for the whole team.

> *Hypothesis 1: the probability of virtual alliances forming increases with the level of compatibility between firms.*
> *Hypothesis 2: the probability of virtual alliances forming increases with the level of complementarity between the products offered by the firms.*

Effects of Virtual Alliances on Firm Performance

The type of virtual alliance formed depends on the nature of markets served by component firms, whether they cater to business firms or individual consumers, respectively. Firms that sell to other firms as customers use virtual alliances as a coordinating mechanism (to ensure compatibility), whereas firms that sell to residential consumers use virtual alliances to increase complementarity, which influences consumers' perceptions of utility. The mediating variable in both cases is the same: organizational legitimacy due to either

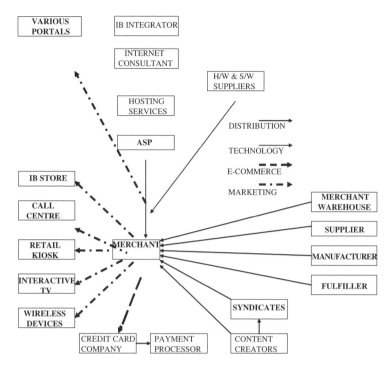

Figure 13.2   A typical Internet commerce network

type of virtual alliance. The desired market outcomes are similar (inclusion in a dominant standard) but the paths to survival and prosperity exploit network externalities in different ways (see Figure 13.2).

Virtual alliances as coordinating mechanisms
When component firms sell to other firms as customers, introductions (or upgrading) of system components force component firms to innovate to maintain the interoperability of their respective components with the upgraded system. Thus AOL's transition from dial-up Internet access service to broadband Internet access required it to roll out new platforms and service, while simultaneously supporting the interoperability of all previous platforms with extant software components, and AT&T supported four extant communications protocols as it upgraded to Generation Three (G3) services.

To manage risks of redundancy in rapidly evolving markets facing architecture changes (Henderson and Clark, 1990), component firms continuously develop new relationships, while maintaining existing relationships with customers, business and technology partners, and other third parties. Promiscuity in partnering is crucial to avoid the inflexibility of being compatible only with systems that are losing marketplace legitimacy (Harrigan, 2001).

Yet virtual alliances guarantee no obligations by partners. When a system loses legitimacy, linkages dissolve quickly. The objective of a start-up firm is to maintain compatibility with as many suppliers of complementary products as possible by forming multiple, virtual alliances with diverse types of firms – both corporate consumers and suppliers of technology. By renewing its survival options frequently and linking with as many diverse but legitimate buyers and suppliers of technology as possible, the start-up firm should enjoy a higher performance potential because it is in the thick of so many technological alternatives, one of which may catch on with ultimate consumers.

Hypothesis 3: firms (selling to other firms) that have higher proportions of technology-oriented virtual alliances (than other types of virtual alliances) will enjoy higher compounded growth.

Influencing consumer expectations
Individual consumers are often so risk-averse when adopting new technologies that they flock to legitimized products like lemmings. In extreme cases, a single system protocol may corner the entire market temporarily, for example the 'wintel' standards of Microsoft's Windows® and Intel's processors. Thanks to network externalities, consumer utility increases as more and more applications are devised that use a platform technology. Adoptions by trendsetters increase product legitimacy for followers, who encourage additional uses for the products. Responsive firms enlarge their installed bases of consumers through virtual alliances with diverse firms that offer complementary products to extend system functionality. Such partnerships are often marketing and distribution programmes to reach underserved customers and quickly add them to the installed base. Joint promotion or distribution of a start-up firm's product with those of existing firms sends out a strong legitimating signal to consumers to adopt the products jointly, thereby increasing the leveraging powers of network externalities on firms' performance.

Hypothesis 4: firms selling to individual consumers with higher proportions of marketing and distribution-oriented virtual alliances (than other types of virtual alliances) will enjoy higher compounded growth.

Increases in start-up firms adopting virtual alliances, either for short-term gain (quest for legitimacy) or for long-term objectives (influence of market outcomes), resulted in a plethora of virtual alliances being formed in the internet industries. Contextually, the 'Internet bubble' environment suspended reliance on traditional evaluation rules. The virtual alliance that start-up firms used in associating themselves with large or successful incumbents was symptomatic of the Internet context. While reality was suspended, success could breed success through extension of press release alliances and other means of amassing social capital, especially where track records were thin.

Methodology

This study seeks to demonstrate the enabling conditions, typical patterns and effect of virtual alliances on market outcome. Although these alliances are formal ties, they rarely involve expensive relation-specific investments by both parties in the majority of the cases. In addition, they are not mutually exclusive in the sense that an Internet-based firm may replicate a virtual alliance with many other firms. These alliances may also be specifically announced for a short duration. I built a relational database that contains separate files for (1) Internet-based firms, (2) the formal contractual, interorganizational alliances involving Internet-based firms, (3) the partners to these alliances, and (4) the six-digit NAICS code of both the Internet-based firms and the partners. The information gathered for each Internet-based firm (IBF) includes date of incorporation, employment levels, sales turnover, date of commencement of public trading, collaborative agreements and major competitors.

The main sources of data used in this study are Hoover's online, Inc., (www.hoovers. com), Interactive iWeek (www.zdnet.com/intweek), and the respective websites of each of the sample firm. Interactive iWeek publishes annually a list of top 500 Internet-based firms (the Internet 500) ranked in order of their online revenues. Apart from the online revenues, the list also contains the total revenues, online profits and total profits along with the name of the chief executive officer and the line of business of each company. Hoover's online database offers information on some 14000 public and private companies (and access to 37000 additional companies).

Sample

I focused on publicly traded Internet-based firms that generated all of their sales online, that is, publicly traded purely Internet-based firms. The sample of Internet-based firms was culled from the Internet 500 (for fiscal year 2000, updated in November 1999) that ranks the Internet-based firms based on their online revenues for the four quarters ending 30 June 1999. Starting with the Internet 500 firms, I short-listed firms that carried out their entire transaction online (dividing online revenues by total revenues and retaining only the firms that gave a value of 1.0). Using Hoover's Online to verify for company type (public or private), I eliminated all the firms that were not publicly traded. Of the total firms in the Internet 500, only 98 qualified as publicly traded, purely Internet-based enterprises; their industries are shown in Table 13.2.

The data on alliances developed by these 98 firms were collected by content analysis of their respective websites. Many Internet-based firms prominently display information about their alliance partners in their websites. In cases where a list of partners was not explicitly displayed, I analysed the content of the archival press releases of the respective Internet-based firm from the time of incorporation to May 2001. In very few cases where the information on partners is neither displayed on the website nor exists in the press releases, I contacted the concerned Internet-based firms for specific information. (Some single-business, Internet-based firms had gone out of business by May 2001 and were dropped from the lists, resulting in the sample of 89 firms.)

I coded each alliance for its purpose, into categories as described in Table 13.3: marketing, distribution, technology, R&D and so on. To minimize subjectivity in coding the alliances, I coded each alliance according to the description provided in the website of the respective companies and cross checked the same with the press release archived in the website. For example, an alliance of the type described by a typical headline in the press release, '24/7 Media, EarthLink Announce Multi-Year Strategic Marketing Relationship', is coded as a marketing alliance. I focused only on contractual arrangements that have been publicized by either of the partnering firms through press releases or displayed on the websites of either of the partners or have received direct information from the company upon request. There may be various other alliances entered into by the Internet-based firms in the sample but have been left out from the data file because neither of the partners publicly announced their formation.

The 'partner' data file for all organizations that appear as partners on any alliance with an Internet-based firm (IBF) is large and exceptionally diverse in both forms and

Table 13.2   Sectoral distribution of the sample firms

Sector	Industry	Number of Firms
Computer software & services	Educational software	2
	Internet & intranet software & services	6
	Networking & connectivity software	1
	Security software & services	1
Computer hardware	Computer peripherals	1
Consumer products (non-durables)	Luxury goods	1
Diversified services	Advertising	3
	Market & business research services	1
	Marketing & public relations services	4
	Miscellaneous business services	9
	Printing, photocopying & graphic design	2
	Telemarketing, call centres & other direct marketing	2
	Staffing, outsourcing & other human resources	1
Financial services	Consumer loans	1
	Investment banking & brokerage	1
	Miscellaneous financial services	1
	Mortgage banking & related services	1
	Services to financial companies	1
Health products & services	Medical products distribution	1
Insurance	Accident & health insurance	1
	Insurance brokers	2
Leisure	Miscellaneous entertainment	2
	Travel agencies, tour operators & other travel services	2
Media	Information collection & delivery services	5
	Internet & online content providers	19
Retail	Consumer electronics & appliance retailing	1
	Drug, health & beauty product retailing	2
	Grocery retailing	1
	Non-store retailing	1
Schools & educational services	Education & training services	1
Speciality retail	Computer & software retailing	3
	Miscellaneous retail	2
	Music, video, book & entertainment	4
Telecommunications	Internet & online service providers	3

industry of operation, as is evident from the wide range of the six-digit NAICS code assigned to each of the partners. The 89 pure Internet-based firms considered in this study formed a total of 2455 alliances, of which 2144 were either marketing, distribution or technological alliances.

Table 13.3   *Typical alliances formed by Internet-based firms*

	Typology	Criterion for coding	Number
1	Joint marketing or promotional agreements	Joint creation of new services or new product offerings, co-branded Ib-sites, promotional offers of complementary products, cross-advertising, customer referral programmes, etc.	513
2	Joint selling or distribution agreements	Cross-distribution of content, products and services and cross-sales of products and services	1178
3	Technology agreements	Internet technology licensing or technology sharing through any other mode that does not include joint development of the technologies per se	453
4	R&D contracts	Joint development of Internet technologies	6
5	E-commerce agreements	E-business development that involves monetary transactions over the Internet	44
6	Outside investors	Minority equity investment by other firms	138
7	OEM/supplier agreements	Agreement for outsourcing of products/services distributed through the websites of the client firm	46
8	Other alliances (miscellaneous)	Any other form of alliance that is not covered by the above types	77

Dependent variables
Probability of virtual alliances   This variable takes a value of 1.0 if there was a virtual alliance between a sample firm and the partner firms, and 0 otherwise.

Compounded annual growth rate   The performance measure was compounded annual growth, and I considered the compounded annual growth rate ($CAGR$) in reported revenues from the first year of operation to the completed financial year immediately preceding the period of the study, that is, the financial year 2000.

Independent variables
I seek to predict the effects of the different types of virtual alliances, fundamental conditions that govern the formation of these virtual alliances and the causal factors that may be responsible for the difference in particular observed patterns of virtual alliances formed by firms in the sample.

Level of compatibility   I predict that the probability of formation of a virtual alliance increases with the level of compatibility between two firms. Compatibility is defined as whether two products can be used together. For example, one way to see whether a range of complementary home entertainment products (audio player, video player, speakers and so on) is compatible is (say) whether all of them run on 220V of electricity or 110V. Another way would be to determine whether the speakers and the audio player could be plugged into the video player and played together. Similarly, I define compatibility

Table 13.4 (a)   Coding pattern for level of compatibility of a potential dyad

State	Dyad d	Sample firm i	(T_i, D_i)	(T_j, D_j)	Partner firm j	Total $(T_i + D_i + T_j + D_j)$	Level of compatibility
1	$Dyad_{ij}$	Firm i	(0, 0)	(0, 0)	Firm j	0	Incompatible
2	$Dyad_{ij}$	Firm i	(1, 0)	(0, 0)	Firm j	1	Incompatible
3	$Dyad_{ij}$	Firm i	(1, 1)	(0, 0)	Firm j	2	Incompatible
4	$Dyad_{ij}$	Firm i	(0, 0)	(1, 0)	Firm j	1	Incompatible
5	$Dyad_{ij}$	Firm i	(0, 0)	(1, 1)	Firm j	2	Incompatible
6	$Dyad_{ij}$	Firm i	(1, 0)	(1, 0)	Firm j	2	Low
7	$Dyad_{ij}$	Firm i	(1, 0)	(1, 1)	Firm j	3	Medium
8	$Dyad_{ij}$	Firm i	(1, 1)	(1, 0)	Firm j	3	Medium
9	$Dyad_{ij}$	Firm i	(1, 1)	(1, 1)	Firm j	4	High

Note: i = 1 to 89, j = 1 to 1624.

between two Internet-based firms as whether both of them carry out transactions or distribute their respective products over the Internet, that is, use the same TCP/IP protocol (a standard Internet protocol) to transact and distribute over the Internet.

Table 13.4 (a) provides the pattern adopted to code the level of compatibility between two potential partner firms. I created four dummy variables, T_i, D_i, T_j and D_j. The variable T_i takes on a value of 1.0 if the sample firm transacts online and 0 otherwise; similarly T_j takes on a value of 1.0 if the partner firm transacts online and 0 otherwise, because the sample comprises only firms that transact online and hence by default the value of T_i will always be 1.0. The variable D_i takes on a value of 1.0 if the sample firm distributes its products online and 0 otherwise; similarly the variable D_j takes on a value of 1 if the partner firm distributes online. D_i and D_j can assume a value of 1.0 only if the value of corresponding T_i and $T_j = 1.0$, because a firm cannot distribute on the Internet if it does not transact on the Internet. State 1 and 4 are ruled out in the sample as all the firms have a default value of $T_i = 1.0$.

I then created a matrix by matching the set of sample firms (89 Internet-based firms) to the entire set of partner firms (1624 firms) to obtain the maximum number of dyadic virtual alliances that could have been possible if each sample firm had a virtual alliance with each of the partner firms. The dummy variables are then added to give a variable for each potential dyad; total = $T_i + D_i + T_j + D_j$. The variable, level of compatibility, is coded as a categorical variable, with four categories, each based on the respective state of the dyad. The four categories of level of compatibility are *incompatible, low compatibility, medium compatibility* and *high compatibility*. If the total for a particular dyad falls within state 1 to 5 it is coded as incompatible, and so on as depicted in Table 13.4 (a).

The level of compatibility is highest when both the firms transact as well as distribute over the Internet. Hence a firm involved in online securities dealing has a higher level of compatibility with a firm that distributes antivirus software over the Internet than with a firm that transacts over the Internet to sell flowers, since the first two companies not only transact but also distribute over the Internet, whereas the third company only transacts over the Internet. Hence compatibility is viewed as an ability to use the two components together, that is, it provides a greater opportunity to mix and match the components.

Table 13.4(b)   *Coding pattern for level of complementarity of products of a potential dyad*

State	Dyad d	$NAICS_i$	$NAICS_j$	abs | $NAICS_i$ − $NAICS_j$ |	Level of complementarity
1	$Dyad_{ij}$			abs | $NAICS_i$ − $NAICS_j$ | < 10000	High
2	$Dyad_{ij}$			10000 < = abs | $NAICS_i$ − $NAICS_j$ | < 100000	Medium
3	$Dyad_{ij}$			100000 < = abs | $NAICS_i$ − $NAICS_j$ |	Low

Level of complementarity   I create a categorical variable at the dyadic level, *level of complementarity*, based on the magnitude of the Euclidian distance between the two firms calculated as the difference in their respective North American Industrial Classification System (NAICS) code. The three categories are *low complementarity*, *medium complementarity* and *high complementarity*. The products of two firms are complementary if their combined value (to a consumer) as a package is more than the sum of their individual values. Hence the basic criterion to decide whether a pair of products (offered by two different companies) is complementary is whether they can be offered together as a package. To code the products of two hypothetical firms in a dyad as complementary or not complementary would have been quite subjective. Although researchers in the past have used a panel of experts to code such variables, I felt it was pragmatic to find an alternative measure that would be both objective and a true measure of complementarity. To eliminate the subjectivity involved in deciding whether the respective products of a dyad are complementary or not, I decided to code complementarity as a categorical variable. I therefore started with the basic assumption that any two products having a different NAICS code are complementary; they may differ from another pair of products in their level of complementarity. This seems to be quite practical too because, if we look around us, we will find numerous examples of products as unrelated as chalk and cheese being bundled together by marketers. For example, a pack of French fries at a fast food joint is offered with a free 10-hour access to the Internet through a particular Internet service provider. French fries and Internet usage, a combination of a product and a service, may not sound complementary, but they are indeed so.

In order to strike a balance between maintaining objectivity of coding and construct validity, I used the hierarchy implicit in the NAICS code to code the level of complementarity as a distance between two firms, albeit with a boundary condition. Two firms would have the highest level of complementarity if the magnitude of their distance in terms of NAICS code was less than or equal to four digits and thus the level of complementarity of the dyad is *high complementarity*. The level of complementarity is considered as *medium complementarity* if the magnitude of the distance between two firms has five digits and *low complementarity* if it has six digits (Table 13.4(b)). I assumed the magnitude of distance, four digits or less, as the highest level because the largest theoretical distance between two firms in the same sector, say Information (NAICS code 51) is four digits. Two information products would have a higher level of complementarity than an agricultural product and an information product.

A weakness of this measure, although rectifiable, is that two firms with the same six-digit NAICS code could also offer complementary products. I am constrained by the non-availability of further classification of firms in terms of a seven or eight-digit NAICS code.

Proportion of marketing, distribution and technological alliances   The proportions of marketing and distribution alliances a firm develops capture the firms' attempt at seeking to exploit the inherent network externality in its market. A firm may wish to join the networks of as many other firms as possible to increase the size of its own network (installed base). This trend would be seen mostly in Internet-based firms that cater to consumers (B2C or C2C type of firms) than those that cater to other business firms. Although marketing and distribution alliances are coded separately because of the inherent theoretical differences in the objectives of the two types and also from the point of view of further studies, they are used together as a measure to support a particular hypothesis. The proportion of firm i's alliances of type m, out of the total number of alliances is denoted as p_{im} and given by $p_{im} = n_{im} / n_i$. The proportion of firm i's alliances of type d, out of the total number of alliances, is denoted as p_{id} and given by $p_{id} = n_{id} / n_i$. The proportion of technological alliances captures a firm's potential to coordinate with a large number of other firms in order to compete as a forming system. The proportion of firm i's alliances of type t, out of the total number of ties, is denoted as p_{it} and given by $p_{it} = n_{it} / n_i$.

Nature of the firm   This is a dummy variable, coded as *consumer*, which takes a value of 1.0 if the firm caters to individual consumers as customers, and 0 otherwise (that is, the firm primarily caters to other business firms as customers).

Legitimacy   I measure legitimacy of the firms in terms of the number of institutional holders that own the shares of each firm in the sample, which is a good measure of the legitimacy of the firm as compared to the percentage of institutional holdings in a firm's outstanding share capital. The institutional investors do not possess any solid financial data as a measure of firm performance on which to base their investment decisions during the early period of the start-ups. They therefore base their investment decisions on subjective measures such as the legitimacy of the firm. A firm whose shares are owned by a larger number of institutional investors can therefore claim to have a higher legitimacy among the potential stakeholders.

Control variables
In predicting the performance of firms, occurrence of alliances, and the diversity of alliances, I explicitly incorporated controls for the *status* of the firm, that is, whether the Internet-based firm existed in some other form before it started transaction over the Internet and whether it is a joint venture between two already existing firms. In doing so, I indirectly controlled for any prior alliances. I therefore created a dummy variable *status*. Status takes on a value of 1.0 if the sample firm existed in any form before starting its transaction on the Internet or is a subsidiary of an existing business firm, and 0 otherwise. I also controlled for alternative explanations that involve firm age or size as predictors, rather than as outcomes, of network behaviour. Researchers in the area of ecological and life cycle theories of organization have used age as a predictor, while greater size, indicating a more extensive hierarchy, is seen as an alternative to alliances in the transaction cost literature (Powell et al., 1996). *Age of the firm*: age was computed for each firm as the

period between the firms going public to the latest completed financial year-end, December 2000 in most of the cases. *Size of the firm:* I used the number of employees at the end of the last financial year before the commencement of the study (FY 2000) to incorporate firm size as a control variable. *Diversity index:* the range of alliances that a firm develops reflects its portfolio of collaborative activities. Diversity index is computed for each firm as follows: for firm i the number of ties of type j is denoted as n_{ij} and the total number of ties aggregated over all types ($j = 1 \ldots \ldots J$; $J=8$) as n_i. The proportion of firm i's ties of type j, out of the total number of ties, is denoted as p_{ij} and given by $p_{ij} = n_{ij} / n_i$. Each p_{ij} is squared and then the sum is taken over all j and subtracted from 1, resulting in the diversity index, $y_i = 1 - \Sigma p^2_{ij}$. This is equivalent to Blau's index of heterogeneity (Blau, 1977). Diversity can be treated as a continuous random variable, though bounded in the interval [0, 7/8]. I use this as a control variable, to test for the effect of virtual (technological) alliances, to control for the diversity of alliances in determining the variance in compounded annual growth rate of technological firms. I assume that technology firms or firms that sell to other firms as customers would have less diverse portfolio of alliances as compared to marketing firms or firms that sell to individual consumers. *Stock growth*: I used the growth in the market value of the shares from the first day of trading of each share to the cut-off period of the study (December 2000) to control for the hype-effect of the market sentiments to the sales of the start-up firms. The firms in the sample being start-ups and the growth of sales recorded on a very small base and for a relatively smaller period, I wanted to control for the effects of spurious stock market effects on start-up firms generating spiked sales for a brief period.

Statistical Methods

The data consist of the virtual alliances formed by 89 pure Internet-based firms during their lifetime within a seven-year period (1994–2000). The variables are measured at both the dyadic alliance level and the firm level. I used SPSS 10.0, a statistical software system, to analyse the data and perform various statistical calculations.

I tested the first and second hypotheses at the dyadic alliance level, and the third and fourth hypotheses at the firm level. All models associated with the predictions are static, for two reasons. This being a pioneering study to establish virtual alliances as a form of organization structure, I felt that the primary objective of analysing the evidence that supports their existence and effects would be adequately served by adopting a cross-sectional approach. I therefore objectively analysed the evidence to examine the necessary conditions that enable their formation and their effects on the behaviour and performance of firms rather than predict the issues involved with their evolution, by using dynamic evolutionary models. Aware of the criticism that cross-section studies very rarely yield consistent estimates of explanatory variables, I have the objective of at the very least contributing stylized facts to guide theory construction in this area of study in future (Schmalensee, 1989). I do recognize that any further study that builds on this research needs to have a descriptive focus and therefore be built on panel data. This study comprises two sets of predictions, enabling conditions and effects of virtual alliances, each of which is discussed below separately.

As regards enabling conditions, to test the predictions concerning formation of virtual alliances, I used a logistic regression model. The selection of this technique involves a primary theoretical consideration and the need to address statistical issues that stem from this concern. The theoretical consideration is that virtual alliances are a sort of a pre-alliance and hence, while they may later be converted into an alliance in the conventional mould, at present they need not satisfy all the antecedent conditions required of a conventional alliance. I argue that the likelihood of any two firms forming a virtual alliance is greater if their respective products are compatible and complementary. This presents some statistical concerns.

The sample size (N = 144 509) of the potential dyadic alliances (by matching the 89 Internet-based firms with each of the 1624 partner firms, they have actually formed either marketing or distribution, or technological alliances) to analyse the effects of the hypothesized enabling variables (compatibility and complementarity) on the probability of forming an alliance should ideally be infinite, because the 89 Internet-based firms selected in this study could form a virtual alliance with any firm present in the universe. I overcome this problem by considering the set of all potential partners of the 89 Internet-based firms in this study as comprising only those firms with which they actually formed virtual alliances during the period of the study (1994–2000). This is based on two simple assumptions: the cost of forming virtual alliances being negligible, the 89 Internet-based firms would have formed the maximum number of virtual alliances possible. Any constraint that would have prevented them from forming an alliance or would have manifested itself as differential ability of the firms to form virtual alliances (unobserved heterogeneity) has been taken care of by a carefully thought out sampling plan and measure of the variables that represent the enabling conditions. All the 89 firms in this study are pure Internet-based firms – they generate their entire revenue online – and not a random sample.

Another important statistical concern is that, out of the 144 509 dyads analysed there are only 2126 alliances (1.47 per cent). I am therefore aware that the estimated coefficients would be overly reliant on the characteristics of those 2126 alliances that actually take place out of the maximum possible 144 509 alliances. The possibility of multiple alliances between a dyad is, however, taken care of by the assumption that the firms in a dyad form either of the two basic types of virtual alliances: marketing/distribution or technological. A better statistical technique would have been to draw a much smaller random sample from the 144 509 dyads and disproportionately sample from those dyads that have an alliance; using different sampling rates for subgroups within the sample of dyads does not cause bias in the slope coefficients of a logit model (Studenmund, 1997).

I used logistic regression to regress *probability of alliance* – a dichotomous dependent variable with values 1.0 if there is an alliance between the two matched dyads, and 0 otherwise – on the two categorical variables *level of compatibility* = {*incompatible, low compatibility, medium compatibility, high compatibility*} and *level of complementarity* = {*low complementarity, medium complementarity, high complementarity*}. I used SPSS that has an inbuilt feature that replaces the categorical independent variables by sets of contrast variables, with each set entering and leaving the model in a single step.

I started by fitting a model containing main effects for all the predictors determined in the theoretical model and found that each of them had high statistical significance. I then added the interaction terms and found none of them to be statistically significant. Since there was high correlation between two predictor variables, *low complementarity* and *medium complementarity*, I fitted different logistic regression models by removing each of the predictor variables, one at a time. I found no difference in the direction of the effects of the predictors and not much difference in their magnitudes. I therefore estimated the final model using all the hypothesized predictors.

As regards effects of virtual alliances, to test the predictions that they affect a firm's behaviour and performance by contributing to their legitimacy and thereby higher compounded growth (hypothesis 3 and 4), I used ordinary least square (OLS) regression model. The mediating variable (legitimacy) is the number of institutional investors that hold stocks of the firm and the dependent variable is the compounded annual growth rate of the firms. The selection of the OLS technique involved a primary theoretical consideration and consequently the need to address statistical issues that stem from this concern. The theoretical consideration is that virtual alliances enable a firm to influence its market outcome. I propose that virtual alliances influence market outcome by two means. First, they enable a firm to achieve a higher compounded annual growth rate by influencing the demand and enabling it to exploit demand-side economies of scale. Second, they provide legitimacy to the firm itself by enabling it to form associations with (large or successful) incumbent firms. It is common logic that a firm that exhibits a high compounded annual growth rate has a better chance of surviving than its rivals who do not. I therefore study the influence of virtual alliances on compounded annual growth rate. Profitability and other accounting rates of returns would not have been appropriate for the simple reason that, in a nascent industry with new firms, the market structure itself is in flux. Prices would not have stabilized, firms would not have developed a cost structure, the share prices would not have reached their optimum level, and so forth. The only objective measure of performance is whether a firm is growing fast enough in terms of its revenues.

The primary theoretical concern may stem from all the variables being endogenous and the absence of any theoretically exogenous variable as an instrumental variable. I address this concern by arguing that the aim of this study is not to establish the explanatory variable (virtual alliances) as a predictor of high compounded annual growth rates of firms. Rather it is merely to test for its effect on the firms' compounded annual growth rates, by controlling for some important variables, which I feel would also affect the compounded annual growth rates. I apply the same logic to explain the effect of virtual alliances on the legitimacy of the firm.

The rationale for choosing OLS was that least square estimation of the models would yield approximately consistent estimates of the coefficients of the explanatory variables and hence satisfy the modest primary objective of this study if I achieved statistically significant coefficients in the direction hypothesized. The basic interest therefore lay not so much in the magnitude of the estimated coefficients but in the verification of the contribution of particular independent variables in explaining the variance of the dependent variable. A criticism of data on endogenous variables is that they cannot be handled by commonly employed estimation techniques and hence require a good deal of prior information. I address this concern by fulfilling the condition of prior information by drawing heavily on existing theory and empirical works in designing the study. Existing empirical works (for example Powell, Koput and Smith-Doerr, 1996; Gulati and Gargiulo, 1999) have heavily influenced the choice of variables, the template for coding the variables and measures of the variables. I have tried to stick as close as possible to the spirit of the theoretical construct in coding novel predictor variables that have not been used in any previous research.

Results

I carried out the study at two levels of analysis. First, at the dyadic alliance level, I analysed the effects of the two hypothesized enabling conditions (complementarity and compatibility) on the probability of alliance formation. Second, at the firm level, I analysed the effect of the virtual alliances on the behaviour and performance of a firm. I consider the two analyses separately.

Table 13.5(a) provides the descriptive statistics and correlations between the dyadic level explanatory and dependent variables that explain the enabling conditions for the formation of virtual alliances. Table 13.6(a) provides the maximum likelihood estimates of the coefficients of the parameters in the logistic regression model fitted to the data. Hypotheses 1 and 2 predicted the positive effects of the two categorical variables, levels of complementarity and compatibility, on the probability of alliance formation between two firms. Level of compatibility had four categories: incompatibility, low compatibility, medium compatibility and high compatibility. I used three dummy variables to represent the four categories. Level of complementarity had three categories: low complementarity, medium complementarity and high complementarity. I did not create a category of 'no complementarity' to reduce subjectivity in coding the data, as theoretically no two differentiated products can be non-complementary. The constructs complementarity and compatibility are highly abstract and coming up with a measure was a Herculean exercise, as it required a delicate balancing act between objectivity and accuracy of the measure. I also assumed a lack of interaction between compatibility and complementarity in the theoretical model. However, I tested for interaction and found no significant effects of the interaction terms. Results in Table 13.6(a) show significant positive effects of the predictor variables and the hypothesized model was fully supported by the results.

The coefficients from the logit model are expressed in terms of the log of odds ratio. I transformed the coefficients of the logit model from the predicted value of the log of the odds ratio into probabilities. To do so, I plugged the mean values of the predictor variables in the estimated equation, with the exception of one variable, which I allowed to take on the two values of 0 and 1. This produced Lhat (logit of alliance for the particular value of a single variable as 0 and 1 and feeding the mean values of other variables into the estimated equation) and the process was repeated for all the predictor variables one by one. I then converted Lhat into probabilities of alliance formation. I then examined the probabilities for percentage change between two consecutive Lhats.

Tables 13.5(b) and 13.5(c) provide the descriptive statistics and correlations between the firm-level explanatory and dependent variables that explain the effects of virtual alliances. Table 13.6(b) provides the ordinary least square estimates of the coefficients of firm-level variables in the data. The two models in Table 13.6(b) predict the effect of virtual (marketing) alliances and virtual (technological) alliances on the compounded annual growth rate of the firms. All the predictions receive support, as shown in Table 13.6(b).

Hypothesis 3 predicted the positive effects of the proportion of virtual (technological) alliances on the compounded annual growth rate of the firms that sell to other firms. The interaction term between consumer and proportion of technological alliances significantly affects the dependent variable, compounded annual growth rate, after controlling for *size, age, status, stock growth and diversity index.*

Table 13.5(a) Mean, standard deviations, and correlations (dyad-level variables)

	N	Mean	Std deviation	Alliance	Incompatible	Low compatibility	Medium compatibility	Low complementarity
Alliance	144 509	1.47E-02	0.1204					
Incompatible	144 509	9.18E-02	0.2887	-0.008**				
Low compatibility	144 509	6.05E-02	0.2385	-0.002	-0.081**			
Medium compatibility	144 509	0.3477	0.4762	-0.015**	-0.232**	-0.185**		
Low complementarity	144 509	0.1898	0.3922	-0.008**	0.487**	0.125	0.005	
Medium complementarity	144 509	0.5184	0.4997	-0.015**	-0.211**	-0.081**	0.232**	-0.502**
Valid N (listwise)	144 509							

Note: ** Correlation is significant at the 0.01 level (2-tailed).

Table 13.5(b)   Descriptive statistics (firm-level variables)

Variables	N	Mean	S.D.
cagr (compounded annual growth rate)	89	483.8447	1171.0706
number of institutional investors	72	114.9722	145.2999
status	89	0.2472	0.4338
age	89	1782.6517	5420.0039
size	89	735.4494	1272.6212
stock growth	86	−70.4043	35.8229
Internet distribution	89	0.7416	0.4403
diversity index	89	0.4042	0.232
consumer	89	0.5955	0.4936
Number of marketing alliances	89	5.764	11.6414
Number of distribution alliances	89	13.236	16.9833
Number of technological alliances	89	5.0899	8.3959
total alliances	89	27.5843	26.0824
proportion of marketing alliances	89	0.1764	0.2151
proportion of distribution alliances	89	0.4533	0.3262
proportion of technological alliances	89	0.1959	0.3033

Table 13.5(c)   Correlations between explanatory, control and dependent variables (firm-level variables)

		1 cagr	2 status	3 size	4 age	5 stockgro
1	cagr (compounded annual growth rate)					
2	status	−0.1280				
3	size	−0.0660	0.1520			
4	age	0.0320	−0.0750	−0.0100		
5	stock growth	−0.1370	0.1270	0.501**	0.47**	
6	number of institutional investors	−0.0080	−0.0660	0.653**	0.0240	0.612**
7	diversity index	0.1430	−0.271*	0.0180	0.1440	−0.0470
8	consumer	0.1190	0.0480	0.0410	0.1310	0.0120
9	Internet distribution	−0.2340	−0.1970	−0.2050	0.0860	0.0610
10	proportion of marketing alliances	0.1480	−0.1870	0.0680	0.0950	0.1680
11	proportion of distribution alliances	−0.0010	0.1610	−0.0130	0.0250	−0.0330
12	proportion of technological alliances	−0.1000	−0.0350	0.1000	−0.0200	0.0650

Notes: ***$p<0.01$, **$p<0.05$, *$p<0.1$.

Hypothesis 4 predicted the positive effects of the proportion of virtual (marketing and distribution) alliances on the compounded annual growth rate of firms that sell to individual customers. As hypothesized, the interaction term between consumer and proportion of marketing alliances significantly affects compounded annual growth rate after controlling for *size, age, status, stock growth, diversity index and number of institutional investors*. However, I did not find any support for the interaction term between consumer and proportion of distribution alliances as hypothesized.

The overall pattern of results is quite consistent with the existing theories in network economics. I stress three general findings. First, the probability of formation of virtual alliances between two firms depends upon the level of compatibility and complementarity of their products. Second, marketing alliances have greater effect on firm performance for all firms while technological alliances have greater effect on firm performance for firms that sell to other business firms (commonly referred to as B2B or business to business). Third, both types of alliances affect the legitimacy of the firm.

Discussion and Conclusion

I find in the results ample support for my argument that demand-side considerations may facilitate the formation of virtual alliances, which do not conform to the yardstick applied

6 noinsinv	7 divindex	8 consumer	9 intdist	10 propmktg	11 propdist
−0.0840					
0.0000	0.1680				
−0.0430	−0.0840	−0.487**			
0.1900	0.354**	0.396**	−0.2070		
−0.0190	−0.0920	0.422**	−0.229*	−0.2050	
0.0700	−0.231*	−0.593***	0.278*	−0.343**	−0.578**

to conventional alliances. I further argue that virtual alliances be viewed as an option to be developed into conventional alliances by fulfilling the supply-side criterion that is required of a strategic alliance: commitment to invest, duration and exclusivity. I am guided by theory development to make two implicit assumptions concerning identification of an alliance between two firms as a virtual alliance. First, such an alliance would be promptly reported or advertised by the firm in the media to ensure that the signal reaches

Table 13.6(a)   Enabling conditions of virtual alliances: results of logistic regression

Dependent variable	Model 1a alliance	Model 1b alliance	Model 1c alliance
Independent variables			
constant	−4.976	−4.735	−5.14****
incompatible	0.378**		0.284***
low compatibility	0.206****		0.163*
medium compatibility	0.340****		0.242****
low complementarity		0.405****	0.24***
medium complementarity		0.386****	0.311****

Notes: **** $p<0.001$, *** $p<0.01$, ** $p<0.05$, * $p<0.1$.

Table 13.6(b)   Effects of virtual alliances: results of ordinary linear regression

	Performance effects of technological alliances		
	cagr model 2a	cagr model 2b	cagr model 2c
cagr (compounded annual growth rate)			
status	−155.354	−177.295	−141.321
size	0.01702	0.02883	0.03039
age	−0.0694	−0.124	−0.198
stock growth	−1.836	−2.409	−2.799
number of institutional investors	0.321	0.616	0.613
diversity index	200.006	246.094	221.198
consumer		95.581	−173.801
proportion of marketing alliances			−676.120
proportion of distribution alliances			98.154
proportion of technological alliances		47.232	71.791
consumer * proportion of marketing alliances			1335.586
consumer * proportion of distribution alliances			91.039
consumer * proportion of technological alliances		−2621.923*	−2017.240
R-squared	**0.087**	**0.139**	**0.180**

Notes: *** $p<0.01$, ** $p<0.05$, * $p<0.10$.

its intended audiences. Second, the signal would be ambiguous about the exact duration, investments by either partners or exclusivity of the arrangement.

My logic was vindicated when I analysed the content of the websites and press releases of the 89 Internet-based firms. Except for the 'external investor' type of alliances, most of the press releases concerning the alliances were silent on the above-mentioned issues. The three types of alliances (marketing, distribution, and technological) constitute 87.33 per cent of the total alliances formed by the firms in this study. I was amazed by the striking similarity of the nature of alliances and the press release that provided the information, especially those that dealt with marketing, distribution and technological alliances. I also recorded other types of alliances such as R&D agreements, e-commerce agreements, external investment agreements, outsourcing agreements and sundry other alliances whose description in the press release did not seem to match any of the objective coding criterion developed by us before commencing the exercise. I coded all such unidentifiable patterns into a miscellaneous category (Table 13.3). However, the proportion of these agreements, taken together, is negligible (12.67 per cent of the total alliances formed). In light of the absence of any relevant theoretical explanation and the findings of this study, I would like to propose the consideration of two types of alliances found in this dataset as virtual alliances: marketing and technological.

Although I initially considered distribution alliances also as virtual alliances in my theory building efforts, I am not confident in categorizing them as virtual alliances *post analysis*, mainly for two reasons. First, I found that distribution alliances did not make

Performance effects of marketing alliances		
logcagr model 3a	logcagr model 3b	logcagr model 3c
−0.330*	**−0.291***	**−0.308***
0.00003148	0.00004467	0.00004858
−0.0001161	−0.0001901	−0.0002067
−0.002472	**−0.0032**	**−0.003363**
0.0007717	0.0007567	**0.0008832*
0.214	0.164	0.224
	−0.426*	−0.449
	−0.594	−0.579
	−0.07984	0.24
	0.294	−0.07111
	**1.533*	**1.502*
		0.161
		−1.252
0.273	**0.389**	**0.402**

any significant contribution to the variance of either the compounded growth rate of the firm or the legitimacy of the firm. Second, distribution alliances may not meet the criterion of 'lack of investment specificity' because a firm, by agreeing to distribute its partners' products or services, does actually incur, if not procurement costs, at least opportunity costs by forgoing the distribution of some other products. Distribution alliances could be of 'virtual types' in the case of distribution of digital products where the marginal cost of producing an extra unit is almost zero and a firm could thus agree to distribute digital products of other producers at no cost to the latter. But, even if a distributor with multiple distribution alliances does not incur any cost in procuring the intermediate title to the goods, s/he might lose out on the consumers' attention to a more focused distributor. On the other hand, I would like to justify the inclusion of marketing and technological alliances in the category of virtual alliances.

A well-entrenched consumer products firm with a considerable market share in its product category would not be interested to incur an additional expense to be a part of any marketing campaign carried out by a start-up that produces complementary products. But it would not object to its goods or services being marketed or promoted gratis, provided the marketing campaign of the start-up, by including a reference to the established firm, does not harm the latter's reputation or goodwill in any form. The two firms can resort to a quasi-discriminatory pricing without actually forcing the consumers to buy the two products together by physically bundling the complementary products together. They merely recommend to the consumers that he will maximize his value if he uses the two products together.

In a rapidly changing technological environment, firms do not have all the internal capabilities necessary for success because the research breakthroughs are broadly distributed (Powell et al., 1996) and they need to rely upon a market-based virtual system for systemic innovation. A well-entrenched technology firm would not hesitate to coordinate with a start-up technology firm that is its licensee provided it can visualize some potential in the latter's new technology. A well-established technology firm, by forming a virtual alliance with a start-up, sends out a signal that today's licensee could be tomorrow's development partner. Virtual technological alliances therefore play a significant role in information sharing and coordinating adjustment between potential partners and at the same time acting as options to develop strategic alliance in the future.

Virtual alliance is a strong phenomenon and could possibly evolve into a standard business practice across a wide spectrum of industries. Each passing day more and more corporations are adopting it. I, as a lay person, am no longer surprised to see a 'strategic alliance' reported between AOL and Burger King in the popular press, to the consternation of scholars in the area of strategic alliances. On the contrary I, as a consumer, find value in such alliances that provide joint offerings.

Acknowledgment

This research was partially supported by a CITI Sloan PhD Fellowship in Telecommunications Research, 2002, granted to Lalit Manral by Columbia Institute of Tele-information, Columbia University.

Bibliography

Journals

Ahuja, G. (2000), 'Collaboration networks, structural holes and innovation: a longitudinal study', *Administrative Science Quarterly*, **45**, 425–55.

Arthur, W.B. (1989), 'Competing technologies, increasing returns, and lock-in by historical events', *The Economic Journal*, **99**, 116–31.

Baker, W. (1990), 'Market networks and corporate behavior', *American Journal of Sociology*, **96**, 589–625.

Baum, J.A.C., T. Calabrese and B.S. Silverman (2000), 'Don't go it alone: alliance networks and startups' performance in Canadian biotechnology', *Strategic Management Journal*, special issue, **21**, 267–94.

Besen, S.M. and J. Farrell (1994), 'Choosing how to compete: strategies and tactics in standardization', *Journal of Economic Perspectives*, **8**(2), 117–31.

Bettis, R., S. Bradley and G. Hamel (1992), 'Outsourcing and industrial decline', *Academy of Management Executive*, **6**, 7–21.

Burt, R.S. and M. Knez (1995), 'Kinds of third-party effects on trust', *Rationality and Society*, **7**, 255–92.

Carroll, G.R. and M.T. Hannan (1989), 'Density dependence in the evolution of populations of newspaper organizations', *American Sociological Review*, **54**, 524–48.

Caves, R.E. (1981), 'Diversification and seller concentration: evidence from changes', *Review of Economics and Statistics*, **63**, 289–93.

Chang, S.J. (1995), 'International expansion strategy of Japanese firms: capability building through sequential entry', *Academy of Management Journal*, **38**(2), 383–407.

Chesbrough, H.W. and D.J. Teece (1996), 'When is virtual virtuous? Organizing for innovation', *Harvard Business Review*, January–February, 65–73.

Cook, K. (1977), 'Exchange and power in networks' interorganizational relations', *Sociological Quarterly*, **18**, 62–82.

Cook, K.S. and R.M. Emerson (1978), 'Power, equity, and commitment in the exchange networks', *American Sociological Review*, **43**, 721–39.

Dixit, A. and J. Stiglitz (1977), 'Monopolistic competition and optimal product diversity', *American Economic Review*, **67**, 297–308.

Doz, Y.L. (1996), 'The evolution of cooperation in strategic alliances: initial conditions or learning process?', *Strategic Management Journal*, **17**, 55–83.

Dyer, J.H. and H. Singh (1998), 'The relational view: cooperative strategy and sources of interorganizational competitive advantage', *Academy of Management Review*, **23**, 660–79.

Economides, N. (1988), 'Desirability of compatibility in the absence of network externalities', *American Economic Review*, **79**, 1165–81.

Economides, N. and L.W. White (1994), 'Networks and compatibility: implications for antitrust', *European Economic Review*, **38**, 651–62.

Eisenhardt, K.M. and C.B. Schoonhoven (1996), 'Resource-based view of strategic alliance formation: strategic and social effects in entrepreneurial firms', *Organization Science*, **7**, 136–50.

Galaskiewicz, J. (1985), 'Interorganizational relations', *Annual Review of Sociology*, **11**, 281–304, Palo Alto, CA: Annual Reviews.

Galaskiewicz, J. and A. Zaheer (1999), 'Networks of competitive advantage', *Research in the Sociology of Organizations*, **16**, 237–61.

Grover, V. and P.K. Ramanlal (1999), 'Six myths of information and markets: information technology networks, electronic commerce and the battle for consumer surplus', *MIS Quarterly*, **23**(4).

Gulati, R. (1995a), 'Familiarity breeds trust? The implications of repeated ties on contractual choice in alliances', *Academy of Management Journal*, **38**, 85–112.

Gulati, R. (1995b), 'Social structure and alliance formation pattern: a longitudinal analysis', *Administrative Science Quarterly*, **40**, 619–52.

Gulati, R. (1999), 'Network location and learning: the influence of network resources and firm capabilities on alliance formation', *Strategic Management Journal*, **20**(5), 397–420.

Gulati, R. and M. Gargiulo (1999), 'Where do interorganizational networks come from?', *American Journal of Sociology*, **104**(5), 1439–93.

Hagedoorn, J. (1993), 'Understanding the rationale of strategic technology partnering: interorganizational modes of cooperation and sectoral differences', *Strategic Management Journal*, **14**, 371–85.

Hagedoorn, J. and J. Schakenraad (1994), 'The effect of strategic technology alliances on company performance', *Strategic Management Journal*, **15**(4), 291–309.

Han, S. (1994), 'Mimetic isomorphism and its effects on the audit service market', *Social Forces*, **73**, 637–63.

Harrigan, K.R. (1985), 'Vertical integration and corporate strategy', *Academy of Management Journal*, **28**(2), 397–425.

Harrigan, K.R. (1988), 'Joint ventures and competitive strategy', *Strategic Management Journal*, **9**, 141–158.
Henderson, R.M. and K.B. Clark (1990), 'Architectural innovation: the reconfiguration of existing product technologies and the failure of established firms', *Administrative Science Quarterly*, **35**, 9–30.
Hennart, J.F. (1988), 'A transaction costs theory of equity joint ventures', *Strategic Management Journal*, **9**, 361–74.
Jonas, N. (1985), 'The hollow corporation', *Business Week*, 3 March, pp. 56–8.
Katz, M.L. and C. Shapiro (1985), 'Network externalities, competition and compatibility', *The American Economic Review*, **75**(3).
Katz, M.L. and C. Shapiro (1986), 'Technology adoption in the presence of network externalities', *Journal of Political Economy*, **94**(4).
Katz, M.L. and C. Shapiro (1992), 'Product introduction with network externalities', *The Journal of Industrial Economics*, **XL**(1).
Katz, M.L. and C. Shapiro (1994), 'Systems competition and network effects', *Journal of Economic Perspectives*, **8**(2), 93–115.
Kleinknecht, A. and J.O.N. Reijnen (1992), 'Why do firms cooperate on R&D? An empirical study', *Research Policy*, **21**, 347–60.
Kogut, B. (1988), 'Joint ventures: theoretical and empirical perspectives', *Strategic Management Journal*, **9**, 319–32.
Kogut, B. (1989), 'The stability of joint ventures: reciprocity and competitive rivalry', *Journal of Industrial Economics*, **38**, 183–98.
Levinthal, D.A. and M. Fichman (1988), 'Dynamics of interorganizational attachments: auditor–client relationships', *Administrative Science Quarterly*, **33**, 345–69.
Maggio, P.J. and W. Powell (1983), 'The iron cage revisited: institutional isomorphism and collective rationality in organizational fields', *American Sociological Review*, **48**, 147–60.
Matutes, C. and P. Regibeau (1988), 'Mix and match: product compatibility without network externalities', *Rand Journal of Economics*, **19**, 221–34.
Meyer, J.W. and B. Rowan (1977), 'Institutionalized organizations: formal structure as myth and ceremony', *American Journal of Sociology*, **83**(2), 340–63.
Milgrom, P., Y. Qian and J. Roberts (1991), 'Complementarities, momentum and the evolution of modern manufacturing', *American Economic Association, Area Proceedings*, **81**(2), 84–8.
Oliver, C. (1990), 'Determinants of interorganizational relationships: integration and future directions', *Academy of Management Review*, **15**, 241–65.
Podolny, J.M. (1993), 'A status-based model of market competition', *American Journal of Sociology*, **98**, 829–72.
Podolny, J.M. (1994), 'Market uncertainty and the social character of economic exchange', *Administrative Science Quarterly*, **39**, 458–83.
Podolny, J.M. and T.E. Stuart (1995), 'A role-based ecology of technological change', *American Journal of Sociology*, **100**, 1224–60.
Powell, W.W., K.W. Koput and L. Smith-Doerr (1996), 'Interorganizational collaboration and the locus of innovation: networks of learning in biotechnology', *Administrative Science Quarterly*, **41**, 116–45.
Ring, P.S. and A.H. Van de Ven (1992), 'Structuring cooperative relationships between organizations', *Strategic Management Journal*, **13**, 483–98.
Ruttan, V.W. (1997), 'Induced innovation, evolutionary theory and path dependence: sources of technical change', *The Economic Journal*, **107**, 1520–29.
Shan, W., G. Walker and B. Kogut (1994), 'Inter-firm cooperation and startup innovation in the biotechnology industry', *Strategic Management Journal*, **15**, 387–94.
Singh, K. and W. Mitchell (1996), 'Precarious collaboration: business survival after partners shut down or form new partnerships', *Strategic Management Journal*, Summer Special Issue, **17**, 99–115.
Spence, M.A. (1976), 'Product selection, fixed costs, and monopolistic competition', *Review of Economic Studies*, **43**, 217–35.
Stuart, T.E. (1998), 'Network positions and propensities to collaborate: an investigation of strategic alliance formation in a high-technology industry', *Administrative Science Quarterly*, **43**(3), 668–98.
Teece, D.J. (1986), 'Profiting from technological innovation: implications for integration, collaboration, licensing and public policy', *Research Policy*, **15**, 785–805.
Walker, G., B. Kogut and W. Shan (1997), 'Social capital, structural holes, and the formation of an industry network', *Organization Science*, **8**, 109–25.
Wernerfelt, B. (1984), 'A resource-based view of the firm', *Strategic Management Journal*, **5**, 171–80.
Williamson, O.E. (1991), 'Comparative economic organization: the analysis of discrete structural alternatives', *Administrative Science Quarterly*, **36**, 269–96.

Books

Bell, D. (1973), *The Coming of Post-industrial Society*, New York: Basic Books.
Berger, P.L. and T. Luckman (1967), *The Social Construction of Reality*, New York: Doubleday Anchor.
Blau, P. (1964), *Exchange and Power in Social Life*, New York: Wiley.
Blau, P. (1977), *Inequality and Heterogeneity: A Primitive Theory of Social Structure*, New York: Free Press.
Bovet, D. and J. Martha (2000), *Value Nets: Breaking the Supply Chain to Unlock Hidden Profits*, New York: John Wiley & Sons.
Burt, R.S. (1983), *Corporate Profits and Cooptation: Networks of Market Constraints and Directorate Ties in the American Economy*, New York: Academic Press.
Burt, R.S. (1992), *Structural Holes: the Social Structure of Competition*, Cambridge, MA: Harvard University Press.
Dunning, J.H. (1993), *Multinational Enterprises and the Global Economy*, Wokingham, England: Addison-Wesley.
Hannan, M.T. and J. Freeman (1989), *Organizational Ecology*, Cambridge, MA: Harvard University Press.
Harrigan, K.R. (1985), *Strategies for Joint Ventures*, Lexington, MA: Lexington Books.
Nelson, R.R. and S. Winter (1982), *An Evolutionary Theory of Economic Change*, Cambridge, MA: Harvard University Press.
Pfeffer, J. and G. Salancik (1978), *The External Control of Organizations: a Resource Dependence Perspective*, New York: Harper & Row.
Scott, W.R. (1995), *Institutions and Organizations*, London: Sage.
Selznick, P. (1957), *Leadership in Administration*, New York: Harper & Row.
Shapiro, C. and H.R. Varian (1999), *Information Rules*, Boston, MA: Harvard Business School Press.
Studenmund, A.H. (1997), *Using Econometrics*, Reading, MA: Addison-Wesley.
Williamson, O.E. (1975), *Markets and Hierarchies*, New York: Free Press.

Chapters in an edited volume

Amburgey, T.L., T. Dacin and J.V. Singh (1996), 'Learning races, patent races, and capital races: strategic interaction and embeddedness within organizational fields', in J.A.C. Baum and J. Dutton (eds), *The Embeddedness of Strategy*, Greenwich, CT: JAI Press.
Buckley, P.J. and M. Casson (1989), 'A theory of cooperation in international business', in F.J. Contractor and P. Lorange (eds), *Cooperative Strategies in International Business*. Lexington, MA: Lexington Books.
Harrigan, K.R. (2001), 'Strategic flexibility in the old and new economies', in M.A. Hitt, R.E. Freeman and J.S. Harrison (eds), *Handbook of Strategic Management*, New York: Basil Blackwell.
Kogut, B., W. Shan and G. Walker (1992), 'Competitive cooperation in biotechnology: learning through networks?' in N. Nohria and R. Eccles (eds), *Networks and Organizations: Structure, Form, and Action*, Boston, MA: Harvard Business School Press.
Levinthal, D.A. (2000), 'Organizational capabilities in complex worlds', in G. Dosi, R. Nelson and S. Winter (eds), *The Nature and Dynamics of Organizational Capabilities*, Oxford: Oxford University Press.
Lyles, M.A. (1988), 'Learning among joint venture sophisticated firms', in F.K. Contractor and P. Lorange (eds), *Cooperative Strategies in International Business*, Lexington, MA: Lexington Books.
Manral, L. and K.R. Harrigan (2005), 'Alliances in the new economy', in Oded Shenkar and Jeff Reuer (eds), *Handbook of Strategic Alliances*, Newbury Park, CA: Sage Publications.
Mowery, D.C. (1988), 'Conclusions and policy implications', in D.C. Mowery (ed.), *International Collaborative Ventures in U.S. Manufacturing*, Cambridge, MA: Ballinger.
Schmalensee, R. (1989), 'Inter-industry studies of structure and performance', in R. Schmalensee and R. Willig (eds), *Handbook of Industrial Organization*, Amsterdam: Elsevier.
Scott, W.R. (1994), 'Institutions and organizations: towards a theoretical synthesis', in W. Richard Scott and John W. Meyer (eds), *Institutional Environments and Organizations: Structural Complexity and Individualism*, Thousand Oaks, CA: Sage.
Starbuck, W.H. (1976), 'Organizations and their environments', in Marvin D. Dunnette (ed.), *Handbook of Industrial and Organizational Psychology*, New York: Rand McNally.
Szulanski, G. (2000), 'Appropriability and the challenge of scope: Banc One routinizes replication', in G. Dosi, R. Nelson and S. Winter (eds), *The Nature and Dynamics of Organizational Capabilities*, Oxford: Oxford University Press.
Winter, S.G. (1995), 'Four Rs of profitability: rents, resources, routines and replication', in C.A. Montgomery (ed.), *Resource-based and Evolutionary Theories of the Firm: towards a Synthesis*, Boston, MA: Kluwer Academic Publishers.

Conference proceedings

Arregle, J.L., T. Amburgey and T. Dacin (1997), 'Strategic alliances and firm capabilities: strategy and structure', paper presented at the Strategic Management Society Conference, Phoenix, Arizona.

Gulati, R. and P. Lawrence (1999), 'Organizing vertical networks: a design perspective', paper presented at the SMJ special issue conference on strategic networks.

Unpublished doctoral dissertation, research reports etc.

Anand, B.N. and T. Khanna (1997), 'Do firms learn to create value?', working paper, Harvard Business School.

Barua, A., J. Pennell, J. Shutter and A.B. Winston (2000), 'Measuring the Internet economy: an exploratory study', Working Paper, Center for Research in Electronic Commerce.

Berg, S. (1984), 'Market augmentation and collective decisions on compatibility standards', unpublished draft, Public Utility Research Center, University of Florida.

Mowery, D.C. and D.J. Teece (1993), 'Strategic alliances and industry research', unpublished manuscript, Haas School of Business, University of California, Berkeley.

PART 5

INDUSTRY SPECIFICS: BIOTECHNOLOGIES

14 The St Louis BioBelt – centre for plant and life sciences: a triumph of converging individual efforts

Edward L. Bayham, Jerome A. Katz, Robert Calcaterra and Joseph Zahner

Introduction

When building a technopolis amid existing institutions, the greatest challenge is arguably integrating often disparate individual efforts and ambitions into the superordinate goal. While classical economists may still believe the magic hand explains how the pursuit of individual optimization can achieve collective optimization, the timeframe, unintended consequences and unexpected costs of relying on this approach can leave much to be desired from a public policy standpoint. Alternatively, economic development and entrepreneurship experts have argued and shown that there are best practices of focused activity which can bring about the integration of individual efforts toward collective goals, in a manner which is more predictable, more controllable, and less likely to yield unexpected or negative results.[1]

This chapter outlines one such best practice example, in which regional development of a technopolis-style high-technology cluster in the plant and life sciences occurred as a planned effort of government, academia, industry and non-government organizations (NGOs). The area was centred on St Louis, Missouri, USA, and involved both local and national experts. The St Louis story is potentially useful for many communities which see themselves as somewhat established economically but in need of change, and possessing a strong local network as a key characteristic of the region. Because of this, the example of St Louis' BioBelt can be instructive for small and medium-sized regions, which often pride themselves on the social integration of their economic network members (Capello, 2002; Benneworth, 2004; Laukkanen and Niittykangas, 2003).

This chapter will start with a consideration of the technopolis model of regional economic development, and the impact of a dense or integrated social network on economic development and entrepreneurship. With these conceptual foundations laid, the case of the St Louis development effort, called the BioBelt, is given in detail, with an eye toward the identification of the network interrelations and dependencies that led to the integration of individual institutional efforts into the larger regional goal of creating the BioBelt technopolis. A discussion of the case and its findings follows, with a concluding section focusing on the potential for policy makers intent on leveraging local networks to promote regional development and for researchers considering social network approach studies of economic development.

Conceptual Background

Technopolis
Imported from Japan (Bass, 1998; Suzuki, 2003), the concept of the technopolis, literally a 'science city', describes a regional development model which seeks to create collections

Table 14.1 Three regional development models²

	Technopolis	Cluster	Innovation milieu
Core idea	Science–technology innovation linkages that represent global technological expertise	Dynamic transactions between synergistic firms and within value chains that create competitive advantage	Interorganizational trust and collective learning in specialized regional environments
Linear innovation chain for new technologies	Yes	No	No
Key existing source for new technologies	Academic/ government research	Firms developing or using similar technologies	Learning processes among firms in the network
Policy aims	Creating the linkages that result in successful commercialization of technology	Creating and leveraging synergies between firms and other actors	Creating learning environments
Policy instruments	Science and technology research programmes Venture capital initiatives Consulting on business development, intellectual property rights and internationalization	Network and cluster programmes	Building and stimulating knowledge flows Enhancing innovation capabilities Encouraging and facilitating firm networks
Challenges/ problems	Failure in the commercialization of the scientific knowledge base Missing links in the linear innovation chain	Failure to bring firms and other actors together Failure to recognize potential synergies	Failure in service providers' credibility Problems with changing from a low-trust culture

of high-technology activities with a common purpose, to commercialize technology in order to create wealth and jobs, preferably high-paying ones (O'Gorman and Kautonen, 2004). The technopolis approach is one of three major technology-focused economic development models suggested by O'Gorman and Kautonen (2004). The other two are called the cluster approach and innovation milieu, and all three types are compared in Table 14.1, above.

The St Louis BioBelt example appears to have been built around a technopolis model. In creating the BioBelt, the major new initiatives included venture capital, new research programmes and improving local support services. These elements represent characteristics most often associated with technopolis development. At the core of the BioBelt were academic and research institutions generating new technologies, and who faced in turn intense pressures to commercialize the technologies they developed. These drives in the case of universities in the United States are based in part in law.

In 1980, the US government passed the Bayh–Dole Act, which ordered universities receiving Federal funds for research to offer the results of the research for commercialization and licensing as a condition for receiving future funds. In support of this, the Act formally granted ownership of the intellectual property developed using government grants to the university where the technology was developed. This clarified what had been a hurdle preventing patenting or commercialization of technology. The Bayh–Dole Act stimulated a tremendous growth in university-based technology transfer, for example the creation of some 2200 firms from 1980 to 1997 based on new university developed technologies, with products such as recombinant DNA and Citracal calcium supplement among the best known examples[3]. St Louis, with major research institutions such as Missouri Botanical Garden, Washington University and Saint Louis University, benefited by having an internal drive to commercialize the life and plant science technologies developed locally.

However, government imperatives alone are not enough to explain the creation of a technopolis (Laukkanen and Niittykangas, 2003) and most technopolis models also include a focus on the nature and interaction of institutional and individual level actors (Abetti, 1992; Botkin, 1988; Smilor, Gibson and Kozmetsky, 1988, 1989; Roberts, 1991; Suzuki, 2003; Wiggins and Gibson, 2003). Smilor, Gibson and Kozmetsky (1988) suggested seven types of institutional actors essential to the creation of a technopolis: one or more universities, large technology firms, small technology spin-off firms, the federal, state and local governments, and support groups. Clusters and innovation milieus often occur without a university or even a large technology firm subgroup present or involved (O'Gorman and Kautonen, 2004).

The importance of the research universities to the creation of a technopolis cannot be overstated. Recent research on biotechnology development has repeatedly shown that university-based research is a central element in the creation of clusters of biotechnology firms (Cooke, 2004; Owen-Smith, Riccaboni, Pammolli and Powell, 2002; Sorenson, 2003; Zucker, Darby and Armstrong, 2002). While Zucker, Darby and Armstrong focus primarily on the university presence, Cooke (2004) has argued that it is the presence of research universities *and* large pharmaceutical companies that is essential, with Owen-Smith, Riccaboni, Pammolli and Powell (2002) and Sorenson (2003) arguing for these two elements amid the other regional characteristics similar to those of the Smilor list. St Louis regionally possessed each of the Smilor seven types of actors, including the academic research centres and the major pharmaceutical firms Cooke contended were necessary. That being said, as the story of St Louis' BioBelt unfolds, it becomes apparent that there would still be considerable redirection and elaboration within the institutional classes. That story also hinges on the key role played in the technopolis creation process by the social network which connected the seven types of institutional actors, discussed below.

Social networks in economic development
From its roots in economics (Herbert and Link, 1982) there has been a tendency in economic development and entrepreneurship to focus on the role of individuals in the

creation of firms. The individuals central to the development of a technopolis have been called by several names: Smilor, Gibson and Kozmetsky (1988, 1989) call them 'influencers', while Flynn (1993) calls them 'sponsors', Abetti (1992) 'executive champions' and Donckels and Courtmans (1990) and Stöhr (1990) 'key individuals'. The role of these individuals is to provide expertise (technological, market, political, institutional), social networking connections, and even motivation, often serving as the key integrating factor in the process of moving a region into a technopolis form (Smilor and Feeser, 1991; Wiggins and Gibson, 2003). These individuals and their role in integrating diverse institutions through social networks represent the second major conceptual element of this chapter's analysis of the creation of the BioBelt.

While the focus before the 1970s was on the traits of the entrepreneur, from the mid-1970s on the emphasis changed to considering the individual in their role as a member of one or more social networks. This built on a persuasive argument by Granovetter (1985) that offered a social network approach to industry creation and clustering as an alternative to the pure agglomeration and industrial complex models which preceded it (Gordon and McCann, 2000). In entrepreneurship research, an analogous concept of the importance of the entrepreneur's social network first emerged in the works of Shapero (1975), and was subsequently promoted by researchers on both sides of the Atlantic.

In the United States, the foremost proponent of this approach has been Howard Aldrich (Aldrich and Whetten, 1981; Aldrich and Zimmer, 1986; Aldrich, Rosen and Woodward, 1987; Aldrich, Reese and Dubini, 1989), who has inspired other efforts in which individual entrepreneurs, operating through social networks, develop regions or industries (for example, Larson, 1991; Brown and Butler, 1995). In Europe, the initiator of this approach was Birley (1985; Ostgaard and Birley, 1994) although Aldrich and colleagues have done studies in Italy (Aldrich, Reese and Dubini, 1989; Dubini and Aldrich, 1991) and Japan (Aldrich and Sakano, 1995).

The general idea behind the social network approach to entrepreneurship is that individuals pass information and other resources to others who share the same network. The network can be based on proximity or shared interest, and can vary in its density or intensity of interaction, measured in frequency of contact or amount of sharing or trust (Capello, 2002; Dodd, 1997; Granovetter, 1985; Green, Williams and Katz, 1998; Hite, 2005; Katz and Williams, 1997). Often there are several overlapping networks, such as business networks and civic networks, whose members meet one another in multiple settings, increasing the opportunity to develop trust and share resources (Dubini and Aldrich, 1991; Hite, 2005; Larson, 1991).

Often the individuals participating in social networks do so because they are operating in a boundary-spanning role (Adams, 1976; Granovetter, 1985) between their home organization and the rest of the environment. Being on the boundary or periphery of their home organization can often mean that the boundary spanner has more in common with other boundary spanners than with people in their own organization who have little involvement in or appreciation of the demands of boundary spanning.

This sense of communality with other boundary spanners can be profoundly affected by the institutional or environmental context (Capello, 2002; Specht, 1993). Where the context promotes collaboration, as in the case of a technopolis initiative, these boundary-spanning individuals can become empowered and, through their resource sharing and solicitation of external supports, become essential to their home organizations, and through this process can more tightly integrate the home organization with others, again through the auspices of the network (Hite, 2005; Laukkanen and Niittykangas, 2003).

St Louis represents an unusual example among major metropolitan areas because of the exceptional density of its local networks and its intensity of self-reliance. For example, for much of the latter half of the twentieth century, St Louis was profoundly influenced by a group called Civic Progress, started in 1952 by Mayor Joseph Darst (Smith, 1995, 1997; Civic Progress, 1980) as an NGO. Civic Progress was composed of the CEOs of the 30 largest companies in St Louis, and was originally charged by Mayor Darst with finding ways to make St Louis a leading national urban centre. Civic Progress was not an isolated institutional event, but rather the latest in a continuing series of leadership groups in the city, with the most famous prior group called The Solar Walkers or The Big Cinch, and whose major accomplishment culminated in the 1904 St Louis World's Fair and Olympics.

Civic Progress and The Solar Walkers were not isolated high-profile social networks, but rather a very visible tip of the iceberg for a pattern of social network involvement that was characteristic of the region. Local universities found very high regional retention rates for their graduates and involvement in social, fraternal, civic and religious organizations were unusually high in the St Louis region. For example, St Louis, ranked twenty-first in population, has the largest Girl Scout Council in North America, with over 15 000 volunteers[4] and the third-largest Boy Scout council, with 17 000 volunteers.[5] What these participation levels suggest is an environment where there is substantial involvement by local individuals in a variety of social networks.

For Civic Progress and The Solar Walkers, their potential for effectiveness was in fact due to the intensely self-reliant and densely networked nature of St Louis. By establishing a new social network with members central to existing social networks and charging the new social network with a goal that fits existing goals of the older social networks, it becomes possible to redirect and focus energies of a large number of people and institutions. Because of this, in many ways the example of St Louis could be readily applied to smaller communities, which are often also characterized by a dense social network and intense self-reliance (Benneworth, 2004; Laukkanen and Niittykangas, 2003).

This intense self-reliance had historic roots. From the time of the American Civil War (Adler, 1994) St Louis increasingly tended to rely on its own resources to develop. This pattern was common to frontier cities. Its major rival, Chicago, in a bold move, embraced resources from the American eastern coast, including cities such as Boston, Philadelphia and, especially, New York. With the infusion of capital and ideas from the east, Chicago found more opportunities, and more financing to operationalize opportunities, than St Louis.

Although the population of St Louis was over twice that of Chicago in 1850 (77 860 to 29 963), by 1870 the trend was clearly reversing, and by 1880 Chicago had half-again as many residents as St Louis (503 185 v. 350 518). Historians contend that, by the 1870s, Chicago had in many ways demonstrated it was on a trajectory to be the region's premier city (Adler, 1994; Cronon, 1991). St Louis had declined major eastern investments in its post-Civil War rebuilding effort, preferring to fund for itself, and grew less quickly as a result, as theory would suggest (Specht, 1993). The trend in population provides a general indication of the economic situation. St Louis, twenty-fourth-largest American city in 1840, fourth-largest city in the USA in 1870 and 1900, had slipped back down to twenty-first by 2000.[6] Chicago, which ranked ninety-second in 1840, had grown to be the nation's second-largest city from 1890 until 1990, when it dropped to third place behind Los Angeles.[7]

Therefore in several important respects when competing against large cities, St Louis in the 1970s and 1980s reflected many of the social and financial dynamics usually identified with smaller cities (Benneworth, 2004), despite St Louis' size, age and geographic centrality. Historically, in relying substantially on its internally generated resources, St Louis and its people developed an exceptionally strong network to provide mutual social, financial and political support. This density of networks, coupled with the substantial economic resources the city's institutions generated, made possible occasional historic feats of achievement, such as the presence of a Worlds Fair and Olympics together in St Louis in 1904. This legacy of dense networks, intense self-reliance and episodes of historic achievement were very much in evidence in the effort to build the BioBelt. It stands in contrast to the efforts of the Chicago region which was attempting to develop an entrepreneurial life sciences community during this same period. There the greater physical and cultural distances between the research universities and technology-driven corporations acted as a barrier to collaboration in support of common objectives. Chicago is not even considered a benchmark by Battelle, which instead added Indianapolis, Pittsburgh and Phoenix to its latest update.

St Louis BioBelt Introduction

The BioBelt™ was born in September, 2000, but its conception was many years earlier. And its birth was certainly not assured. There were competing efforts to develop other high-technology industries. Microelectronics was one. St Louis could have become known as the 'Silicon River', or agriculture and food processing could have become the focus of efforts. Some outsiders had already suggested the term 'SiliCorn Valley'. It was becoming clear that something had to be done, but what? And who was going to lead the effort? What strategy would they employ? And why focus on the plant and life sciences?

St Louis' identity is that of a transportation hub and old industrial city. Its leading industries were automobile manufacturing, aerospace development, shoe manufacturing and chemicals. Little known is that healthcare, botanical and horticultural research became well established in St Louis during the nineteenth century. Saint Louis University, created in 1818 as the first college west of the Mississippi, opened its first medical school in 1835, granting the first MD west of the Mississippi in 1839 (Saint Louis University School of Medicine, 2005). The US Congress authorized funds for hospitals to care for sick and disabled rivermen in 1837 (Wayman, early 1970s). The Civil War required the expansion of facilities because St Louis was at the northernmost ice-free point along the Mississippi River in winter. Botanical research was established when Henry Shaw founded the Missouri Botanical Garden in 1851. He also established the Henry Shaw School of Botany at Washington University in 1885 and created the close bond between the two institutions (Hutchison, 1999). Horticultural research began in 1816, when James Hart Stark settled in nearby Louisiana, Missouri and started what became the largest nursery and orchard in the world, Stark Brothers Company. Plant breeding research accelerated in 1893 when the company began a long collaboration with Luther Burbank. It was through their efforts that Congress crafted legislation for patenting plant traits. Stark Brothers was granted the first plant patent, for the Hal-Berta Giant Peach, in 1932 (Dickson, 1966).

By the year 2000, St Louis had the seeds of a biotech cluster. The region ranked fifth in the nation for total academic research and development, led by Washington University's (WUSTL) School of Medicine, with $235 million in plant and life sciences research expenditures, the University of Missouri–Columbia (UMC), with $99 million, and Saint Louis University (SLU) with an additional $46 million. Washington University's Human Genome Sequencing Center was one of the four major centres in the world funded to contribute to the Human Genome Project. Saint Louis University was one of six sites designated for NIH-funded viral clinical trials. The University of Missouri–St Louis (UMSL) was one of the three leading university centres in the United States for tropical ecology. Southern Illinois University Edwardsville (SIUE) contributed specialized research strengths and top-notch education in the plant and life sciences (Battelle, 2000). The Missouri Botanical Garden provided a strong linkage between these universities through a consortium agreement that had been in place since the 1960s. Students enrolled in one of these botanical science programmes could complete their degree requirements at their respective university, but would have full access to the Garden's staff, facilities and research opportunities (Hutchison, 1999).

These academic resources were bolstered by the presence of three global industrial leaders: Monsanto, Mallinckrodt and Sigma-Aldrich. Monsanto began a major effort to apply molecular biology technology in the late 1960s. Their scientists were awarded the 1998 National Medal of Technology for their pioneering work in transferring desirable genes into crop plants (Hutchison, 1999). Monsanto's Posilac® bovine somatotropin for milk production became the first commercialized agrobiotechnology product in 1984. Mallinckrodt was a pioneer in the development of radiopharmaceuticals and imaging contrast media. Sigma-Aldrich was the world's second-largest supplier of speciality research chemicals. St Louis was also home to two new world-class incubators, the Center for Emerging Technologies and the Nidus Center for Scientific Enterprise, which contributed to a growing base of emerging plant and life science companies. Vibrant non-profit research institutions, such as the Missouri Botanical Garden, the St Louis Zoological Society and the new Donald Danforth Plant Sciences Center, played an important role in augmenting the research capabilities of the region and enhancing its global reputation. By aggressively launching the BioBelt brand, the St Louis region was staking a claim on the growth potential for a vital twenty-first century industry. It was also an admission that the competition would be severe and the future not assured. But the effort was initiated and gaining momentum. What follows is an examination of the efforts and the strategies that led to this climatic point. The significant decisions and events are noted on the timeline matrix that is included as a reference. Many related activities occurred concurrently and influenced other organizations' perceptions of progress.

Early years: 1980 to the early 1990s
The enactment of the Bayh–Dole Act in 1980 and its implementation in 1982 was pivotal in the awakening of an entrepreneurial culture in St Louis. This law enabled universities to retain ownership of inventions made under federally funded research and encouraged licensing and commercialization. George Sloan, a technology expert and executive with the St Louis Regional Chamber and Growth Association (RCGA), organized a task force to respond to this opportunity. It was his vision to create an urban science park that was modelled on North Carolina's Research Triangle. Richard Ward was one of the task force

members. His firm, Team Four, prepared a study for the RCGA, which was titled 'St. Louis Technology Center – Summary – Location Analysis and Facility Evaluation – A Proposal for an Urban Science and Innovation Center'. This 1983 study focused on specific recommendations for locating the science centre near the two university medical research campuses and for anchoring the centre with an incubator (TeamFour, 1983, 1984b). The centre was patterned on the University City Science Park in Philadelphia (Fisher, 1984). The RCGA formed a committee comprising the Missouri Botanical Garden, Washington University, Saint Louis University, UMSL and SIUE to support the creation of the incubator. The members contributed $10 000 each for its establishment. The contributing organizations gained *ex officio* seats on the Tech Center Board of Directors. Additional members were recruited from local industry and service providers (St Louis Technology Center, 1985). Michael Turley, a partner with a local law firm, Lewis Rice & Fingersh, contributed many hours of pro bono support and petitioned the Internal Revenue Service to establish the centre as a not-for-profit 501(*c*)3, the first in the country, in 1986. The task force also drafted legislation that was passed in the Missouri Legislature that established the creation of four state-subsidized regional incubators. Gene Boesch, another attorney with Lewis, Rice & Fingersh and a task force member, became the Director (Michael Turley, personal interview, 3 February 2005).

The St Louis Tech Center incubator was handicapped from its beginning. The level of funding was insufficient to support an incubator on its own. There was no support forthcoming from the local governments or the business community. The available funding was only 25 per cent of the amount budgeted. As a result, it was necessary to lease space in an office building that did not have the desired wet lab facilities. In addition, there were no local venture capital firms and no serial entrepreneurs experienced in creating companies. The Tech Center limped along for several years and managed to graduate a few companies, primarily in software and laser development (J.J. Stupp, personal interview, 3 February 2005). But it never attracted the quality of university research clients that it had envisioned.

The University of Missouri System carried out its own agenda and created a technology park just west of St Louis in neighbouring St Charles County in 1985. They obtained rural land along an interstate highway in a swap with the State Department of Resources. The Missouri Research Park attempted to recruit the Tech Center to be its anchor tenant, but at 50 kilometres, it was too far from the three research universities in St Louis. Twenty years later, the park still has only 15 tenant companies, but it did spur additional development along this corridor (Missouri Research Park, 2001).

The Monsanto Company was convinced that university research collaborations would lead to new discoveries for fuelling product development. In 1974, Monsanto committed $23 million in funding to Harvard University over ten years in the first corporate–university research collaboration (Joseph Feder, personal interview, 14 February 2005). But there was little accountability for the use of the funds. In 1979, Monsanto recruited Howard Schneiderman, an accomplished researcher who, at the time, was Dean of the School of Biological Sciences and first Director of the Developmental Biology Center at University of California at Irvine. He realized that Monsanto did not have the research base to be a leader in life sciences. He approached William Danforth, Chancellor of Washington University, to explore a collaborative research partnership. Howard Schneiderman and David Kipnis, at that time a professor and Chairman of the

Department of Internal Medicine, spent considerable time developing the key principles for an innovative relationship that would support the respective missions of each institution: the university to develop ideas and basic science and the company to develop drugs. They were very careful to establish a transparent process with an outside board to review and fund grant proposals from the faculty. Monsanto was granted first right of refusal on inventions. This relationship was presented before the US Congress and became a prototype for future collaborations between higher education and industry. The agreement has withstood corporate mergers and acquisitions and personnel changes and infused more than $100 million into research during its first 18 years (Smith, 2003; Washington University, 2005). It also prepared many notable academic researchers to interact positively with industry and eventually to move into corporate research positions (David Kipnis, personal interview, 10 March 2005).

The early 1970s also witnessed the beginning of venture capital in St Louis. It started with the establishment of Innoven I Fund, formed jointly by Monsanto and Emerson Electric. The initial focus was on microelectronics and associated chemicals. In 1975, Innoven management returned from a national conference and alerted Monsanto to the potential in the new biotechnology industry. From 1976 to 1978, Monsanto coinvested with Innoven in Genentech, Biogen and Collagen Corporation. Monsanto's vice chairman, Lou Fernandez, met Moshe Alafi, an early biotechnology investor in Berkeley, California, through their investments in Biogen and participation on the board of directors. This led to the formation of Alafi Capital, a venture capital partnership between Moshe Alafi and Monsanto Ventures (Costas Anagnostopoulis, personal interview, 15 April 2005).

In 1984, Alafi Capital and Monsanto funded Invitron, a public company that licensed Monsanto's large-scale mammalian cell culture technology (Invitron, 1987). Although Invitron failed in 1992, the facility passed through a succession of hands, and eventually became a core production site for Johnson & Johnson's Centecor subsidiary. A/W, a partnership between Alafi Capital and Washington University, was established in 1986 to encourage the formation of new companies to commercialize innovations discovered at the university. It completed ten deals, but most of the companies were virtual. It achieved a couple of moderate successes. LipoMatrix, founded in 1992, developed a radiolucent breast implant and was sold to Collagen Corporation in 1996. Megan Health, a vaccine developer, was started in 1993 and was acquired by Avant Immunotherapeutics and moved to Massachusetts in 1999. But Megan Health was the last investment by A/W, which closed in 1993. The partners reached the conclusion that the structure was not workable for the future. While the deals were not highly profitable, the experience provided an education for executives who later became involved with new funds created in St Louis during the late 1990s. Brian Clevinger and Greg Johnson, now managing directors of Prolog Ventures, had each served their turns as the head of A/W. (Greg Johnson, personal interview, 7 February 2005; Brian Clevinger, personal interview, 4 January 2005).

Also in 1984, the RCGA commissioned TeamFour to prepare a study on the impact of locally based venture capital firms in other regions. Its most notable finding was that the vast majority of new ventures funded by the surveyed firms were within two hours' travel time (TeamFour, 1984b). Gateway was the first technology-oriented fund started in St Louis in this same year. Co-founder Dick Ford was a local banking executive. He expressed his mission to Monsanto's CEO, Richard Mahoney, and received a commitment for 1:2

matching funds. He then managed to raise $15 million for Gateway I. To-date, the firm has raised a succession of investment funds totalling in excess of $180 million (Gateway Associates, 2000). Their investments have been primarily in healthcare services and information technology. Two Monsanto executives, Costas Anagnostopoulis and Greg Johnson, later served as fund managers in Gateway.

The region's first involvement with the contemporary approach to academic entrepreneurship development also began during this period. Robert Brockhaus, a PhD graduate of Washington University, and an award-winning researcher and advocate for entrepreneurship, began teaching courses at Saint Louis University in 1980 and creating the region's first academic entrepreneurship centre in 1987 (Saint Louis University, 2005). Along these lines, in 1997, Washington University refocused its Olin Cup competition to be the region's first business plan competition, and created its entrepreneurship consulting programme in 1997 and its entrepreneurship centre in 2001 (Olin School of Business, 2005).

The first entrepreneur–university conflict also emerged during the 1980s. Garland Marshall, a professor in Chemistry at Washington University, founded a drug discovery software company, Tripos Associates, in 1979. He functioned as the chief executive while he continued his teaching and research duties at the University. This raised conflict of interest and diversion of effort issues with the administration. He sold off his interests in 1987. Tripos is now a public company in St Louis. Garland Marshall subsequently formed two additional companies, Metaphore in 1993, and Pharmamonde in 2004 (Duke Leahey, personal interview, 14 January 2005).

There were a number of additional studies conducted by various civic and government groups in the early 1990s (Development Strategies, 1993, 1995; Eva Klein & Associates, 1997). The stimulus was the changing nature of employment as manufacturing jobs declined, particularly with defence industry cutbacks at McDonnell Douglas and lay-offs from Monsanto. The focus was on retraining engineers and upgrading small manufacturers' technical capabilities. The studies cited the region's strengths and weaknesses. Capital was limited and the region was very conservative financially. The local press was particularly brutal in its reporting on financial losses at start-up companies. There was limited support for entrepreneurs and limited university–industry partnerships. The universities were still not comfortable with commercializing technology because of the concern over conflicts of interest, diversion of efforts and liability issues (Duke Leahey, personal interview, 14 January 2005). The St Louis Development Corporation, a public–private organization, successfully obtained a government grant to construct a technology incubator building, but could not raise the local matching funds. The region's civic leadership was more focused on building new sports facilities in hopes of regaining professional football and basketball franchises. They were not successful in attracting a basketball team, but they did snag the Rams franchise from Los Angeles and the Super Bowl XXXIV Championship in the process. Meanwhile, no real leadership emerged to support the effort to create a Technopolis urban science park.

Pivotal events: 1993 to 2000
The centre for Emerging Technologies
The landscape changed significantly in 1993. Democratic Governor Mel Carnahan was elected and brought a renewed economic development focus to Missouri. The Missouri Technology Corporation (MTC) was created to spur technology commercialization and

to oversee the four Missouri innovation centres. Now there was an expectation of results. By this time, the original site for the Tech Center had been torn down and been replaced by the expanded Science Museum. The Tech Center had neither clients nor facility. State financial support had also been reduced significantly.

Marcia Mellitz, a microbiologist with FDA experience and a recent MBA, was dispatched as a consultant to the St Louis Tech Center. She researched successful programmes in other areas of the country for the next two years and began to develop plans for a new incubator. At this time, the state also required that the sponsored innovation centres obtain matching funds. Marcia Mellitz was able to enlist a strong champion, Blanche Touhill, Chancellor of UMSL. Dr Touhill had wanted to locate the innovation centre on the university campus, but was faced with opposition from nearby residents, so she agreed to what was essentially a joint venture. As a result, Marcia Mellitz became a university employee and gained access to university support services, such as facilities engineers (Marcia Mellitz, personal interview, 29 December 2004).

This arrangement still did not provide a facility. What ensued was a resourceful search for potential sites and financial support. It was this effort that eventually drew in a number of competing entities, the St Louis (City) Development Corporation (SLDC), the St Louis County Economic Development and the Missouri Department of Economic Development, to work together to secure a facility. It occurred during the first five-year phase of a unified, proactive economic development campaign spearheaded by then RCGA Chairman Earle Harbison, president of an international company headquartered in St Louis (St Louis RCGA, 2004). This revitalization effort led to the creation of the Greater St Louis Economic Development Council to assemble 'regional leaders representing geographic, political, business and labour interests' to 'develop policies, goals and strategies that would pursue economic development on a unified regional basis'.

Marcia Mellitz enlisted Eva Klein, a nationally-known incubator consultant, to assist in the development of a strategic plan for the new centre (Eva Klein & Associates, 1998). Patrick Bannister, a long-term supporter of the Technopolis concept and head of the SLDC, recruited an advisory board which included WUSTL Medical School Dean, William Peck; Dean of SLU's Department of Health Sciences, James Kimmey; UMSL Chancellor, Blanche Touhill; St Louis City alderman, Joseph Roddy; and several industry representatives. SLDC then purchased an empty industrial building near to the Washington University's and Saint Louis University's medical campuses. Pat Bannister also directed a successful effort to obtain a $2.75 million grant from the Department of Commerce's Economic Development Administration for facility renovations. Additional support was obtained via tax credits, loans and donations of equipment and in-kind services. The total cost reached $8 million. The incubator officially opened in 1998 as the Center for Scientific Enterprise (CET). It was rapidly filled with a diverse range of clients, with technologies ranging from magnetically directed interventional catheters, to genome sequencing research, to high-speed communication microprocessors. Most of these clients were connected to some degree with Washington University. In the cases of Orion Genomics and Symbiontics, the physical facility was the reason for locating the companies in St Louis. Both companies also had founding members in New England research institutions (Marcia Mellitz, personal interview, 29 December 2004).

Client demand for additional space caused the CET to eye expansion to a neighbouring building. Historic restoration tax credits and other funding enabled the CET to acquire and renovate it in 2001. The total space had now increased to 92 000 square feet, housing 14 companies (Center for Emerging Technologies, 2005). Its largest client, Stereotaxis, Inc., designs, manufactures and markets a magnetic navigation system for interventional cardiology to treat coronary artery disease and cardiac arrhythmias. It raised $44 million in an IPO in August 2004 (Stereotaxis, 2004).

What should also be noted is that the physical presence of the building provided much more than facilities for the client companies. The management visualized a much broader role for the CET. They realized that the clients required education, advisors, support services, employee recruitment and funding. They organized training seminars in all aspects of operating start-up companies, from grant writing, to intellectual property protection, to personnel administration. For these programmes, they recruited willing volunteers from the local service providers. They also acted as a clearing-house for people dismissed from area companies. The CET also provided tangible evidence to the local business and academic communities that it was possible to commercialize technology developed at the local universities. And, for the first time, it created an environment for informal collaboration and sharing between companies, researchers and prospective entrepreneurs (Edward Bayham, personal observation).

Saint Louis University start-up support
Starting in 1994, Saint Louis University's Biochemistry Department formed a technology transfer office and adopted liberal incubation practices for both internal and external start-up companies. It leased laboratory space to budding entrepreneurs and allowed access to common equipment and research libraries. BioProfile, an analytic instrument developer that is now called Singulex, spent three formative years at SLU before moving into the CET when it opened (Robert Puskas, personal interview, 15 February 2005). GeneProTech and Progen also took up residence at SLU. This role was expanded in 1998 to include all Health Science departments. Four inside technology start-ups, including VirRx, developing an anti-cancer gene therapy, and Mediomics, a drug research tool company, are currently operating within the Health Science Center. Technology Transfer was reorganized as an independent office and assumed campus-wide responsibilities in 2004.

Celeste & Sabety report: strategy shift – clusters
The large concentration of Fortune 500 companies had long been a source of pride in St Louis. Civic morale was being deflated during the mid-90s as companies such as McDonnell-Douglas, Boatmens Bank, Southwestern Bell and General Dynamics were either being acquired or moving their headquarters to other cities. In 1996, the RCGA and the Greater St Louis Economic Development Council commissioned a study by the consulting firm of Celeste & Sabety Ltd to evaluate the area's science and technology-based economic development programmes and to recommend a course of action (Celeste & Sabety, 1997). Celeste & Sabety 'found consistent evidence that St. Louis had not fully capitalized on its science and technology assets'. Even further, they found that St Louis did not have a 'business climate conducive to, and supportive of, starting new businesses'. They cited the conservative capital markets, tight skilled labour market and the difficulty in recruiting workers, low entrepreneurial skills and culture, underdeveloped networking, few successful role models, limited public sector incentives, and other factors. In particular,

they noted that Washington University emphasized technology licensing instead of local business creation. Inside companies, innovation was managed within sophisticated world-wide enterprises, which reduced the local visibility and impact. It was a common view that the efforts operated at a 'sub-critical' level because they were a collection of 'individual, unrelated endeavours'.

Celeste & Sabety pointed out the need for programmes that would build a stronger set of partnerships and alliances among business, universities and governments in the area. They recommended that the RCGA, because of its representation of all parts of the area, was the logical entity to champion the types of initiatives that could raise the programmes to a competitive level. Their key recommendation was to implement a series of industry working groups to define 'Action Agendas' for selected industry clusters. The resulting plans would specify industry-driven initiatives that could be carried out through the RCGA. And, through this process, they expected that individuals and companies would become 'champions' of the initiatives.

In early 1997, the consultant team identified the industry sectors with the most importance to St Louis' future and grouped them into logical clusters. They recommended that the working groups concentrate their efforts on the top three initially. These clusters were (1) advanced manufacturing, (2) computer software and systems integration, and (3) medical, biomedical and healthcare products and services. Working groups began to form and define action plans. Their impact would begin to be felt in 1998 and would gain momentum into 2000.

The Danforth plant life science centre
In 1995, Washington University recruited its fourteenth chancellor, Mark Wrighton, who at the time was a Professor of Chemistry and Provost at the Massachusetts Institute of Technology. He succeeded William Danforth, who had led the university for an unprecedented 24 years. Dr Danforth then devoted more attention to the Danforth Foundation, which was endowed by his grandfather, the founder of Ralston-Purina. The Foundation's focus had been on dispensing grants to foster national education reform. He became actively involved in community revitalization efforts, particularly in the life sciences.

In 1996, Danforth visited San Diego with Peter Raven, Director of the St Louis Botanical Garden, and Virginia Weldon, Vice President for Public Policy at Monsanto, to research the development of the plant and life science industry in that region. Together, they developed a vision of St Louis as the world's centre in plant sciences. They proposed to create an independent plant science centre that would attract hundreds of top scientists from around the world to conduct ground-breaking research to increase the world's food supply (Hutchison, 1999). This project would require funding, which came initially from Monsanto, the Danforth Foundation and the State of Missouri tax credits. It was during this critical period that the Danforth Foundation firmly shifted its focus to funding local plant and life science initiatives and planned to reduce its assets from $355 million at the end of 2001 to about $75 million in 2005, in what was one of the most dramatic funding initiatives ever undertaken by an American philanthropic foundation (Foundation Center, 2003). This 'bet the farm' effort by the Danforth Foundation was an unequivocal bellwether of the commitment of the community to making the life and plant science initiative succeed.

A unique partnership comprising Missouri Botanical Garden, Monsanto, Washington University, University of Missouri–Columbia, Purdue University and University of Illinois at Urbana–Champaign formally unveiled plans in July 1998 to build the world's premier plant science research centre. Roger Beachy, an internationally-renowned scientist, was recruited in early 1999 to become president of the centre. Most recently, he had headed the Division of Plant Biology at The Scripps Research Institute in La Jolla, California. He was previously a biology professor at Washington University and had collaborated with Monsanto in the development of the world's first genetically altered food crop, a tomato with viral resistance. The striking 170 000 square foot facility was officially opened in November 2001. It was named in honour of Donald Danforth, the father of William Danforth, who had led the Ralston-Purina Company for 30 years and built it into an international leader in cereals and pet foods (Yarnell, 2002).

Nidus Center for Scientific Enterprise
By 1997, Monsanto had diversified considerably beyond its roots in chemicals and plastics. It had entered the agricultural herbicide business during the 1960s and committed itself to genetically modified crops during the 1980s (Hertz et al., 2001). Under CEO Richard Mahoney, Monsanto acquired G.D. Searle & Co. in 1986 to enter the pharmaceuticals market. Then, in 1997, it made a strategic decision to spin-off the industrial chemicals and plastics business as a separate company, Solutia, to focus on the life sciences. Upper management, now led by CEO Robert Shapiro, realized that they would need to recruit new talent to the St Louis region and to create an environment that fostered the development of new biologic technologies.

Monsanto had always been a generous supporter of the community's arts and civic organizations. It had recently supported the new $20 million Monsanto Center at the Botanical Garden to house its collection of millions of plant species and extensive library. Monsanto also provided leadership, funding and land for the Donald Danforth Plant Science Center. It foresaw the need for an incubator to complement the Plant Science Center to commercialize these developments. This provided justification for state tax credits for the not-for-profit Danforth Center (James Kearns, personal interview, 9 March 2005). In 1998, Monsanto committed funding for construction of a 40 000 square foot facility with offices and wet labs on a corner of its suburban campus. Monsanto financial executive David Broughton directed the design effort and recruited Robert Calcaterra, who had run two successful incubators in Colorado and Arizona, to become the President and CEO. It also committed itself to providing 100 per cent of shortfalls to its operating funds during its first ten years (Adkins, 2004; Hutchison, 2000). The Nidus Center for Scientific Enterprise opened its doors in 2000 and was rapidly filled with quality clients. Dr Calcaterra also appreciated the clients' need for intangible support services, such as business planning, advisory boards, mentoring, negotiations, management development and funding sources.

St Louis 2004/RCGA/Technology Gateway Alliance: converging efforts
The 1997 Sabety & Celeste Study recommended the life science and information technologies economic development emphasis. It was now up to the community at large to embrace the effort. St Louis 2004 was an organization that was formed in 1997 to celebrate the centennial of the 1904 World's Fair, the largest ever held, and to be a catalyst for regional revitalization by 2004. It was instrumental in developing the 21st Century Technologies Initiative (St Louis 2004, 1997–2004). The St Louis RCGA implemented this

initiative through its Science and Technology Council, known as the Technology Gateway Alliance (TGA). It was composed of technology professionals working on committees that were focused on key needs: capital formation, resources for entrepreneurs, technology transfer, networking and regional branding. It became the catalyst for creating a critical mass of people, ideas and capital to advance the region's technology-based economy. The Entrepreneurship and Technology Transfer Committee published the *1999 Entrepreneur's Resource Guide* in August of that year. The TGA organized a continuing series of events for highlighting emerging technology companies and providing opportunities for net-working and building alliances. One of the most notable early events was the St Louis Tech Fair 2000. The organizing committee was chaired by Dr Andrew Neighbour, Associate Vice Chancellor of the Center of Technology Management at Washington University, and drew volunteers from a wide range of academic research departments, companies, service providers and the community at large. This two-day conference provided a morale-boosting forum for presenting leading edge developments at the universities, large corpor-ations and the emerging start-ups from the two local incubators.

Battelle study: outside validation and a new development model
In 1999, the RCGA retained Battelle Memorial Institute to develop a set of strategies to position St Louis as the international centre for plant sciences and a major international centre in life sciences. The project tasks 'included identification of core competencies, an economic analysis of the region, benchmarking best practices in leading and comparable regions, and a SWOT analysis'. These were followed by the development of strategies and an implementation plan.

The key finding was that the St Louis region had a 'mature, dynamic and wide-ranging set of plant and life science research and development entities that included universities, non-profit organizations, and private sector companies'. It went on to identify core strengths in the following seven areas: genomics and gene sequencing, plant science, neu-roscience, cardiology, virology/microbiology/immunology, tropical botany and biomed-ical engineering (Battelle, 2000).

The benchmarking study pointed out that it was possible to compete in life sciences with target competitors. It also discovered that few regions were concentrating on the plant sciences. Only Saskatoon, Canada was more focused on this field than St Louis. The main lessons learned were the five success factors that characterized successful life science communities. The first was 'high quality life sciences research universities that were actively engaged with industry and skilled at transferring technology'. The second factor was mechanisms for promoting intersectional and business-to-business networking. Third, regional economies require availability of indigenous early-stage, technology-oriented seed capital. Factor four was that the federal government has been a significant anchor in helping to initiate and build an R&D base. Finally, it is necessary to maintain a long-term perspective, given that successful regions were built up over 12 to 25 year periods.

It was against these factors that Battelle assessed St Louis's comparative opportunities and proposed five strategies; (a) establishing a national and international image for St Louis as the leading centre in plant sciences and a major centre in life sciences, (b) build-ing an entrepreneurial culture that supports and nurtures new firms, (c) capturing the com-mercial potential of the region's intellectual capital resources, (d) insuring a progressive business climate to foster and sustain the region's growth, and (e) building, attracting and retaining a quality workforce. These strategies were to be implemented via a set of 20 action plans and requisite resources as described in Table 14.1.

The Battelle study was significant for the St Louis region's aspirations because it provided the first outside validation of the feasibility of becoming a leading plant and life sciences centre and it crystallized a realistic plan. It also replaced the regional cluster development model with one based on the technopolis concept. This model relies on a dense, integrated social network. The Coalition for Plant and Life Sciences was created by the RCGA, along with the Danforth Foundation, Civic Progress and other civic partners, to direct and coordinate the efforts to implement the Battelle action plans. This organization acted as a forum for executive level discussions and acted through the Technology Gateway Alliance and its existing task forces.

Gathering momentum through Battelle plan implementation, 2000 to 2004

BioBelt branding and a global image
The first priority of the action plan was the establishment of a brand name and an image-building campaign. This effort had already begun in late 1999, when Monsanto provided $25 000 in funding to a volunteer task force that had free rein to solicit ideas and conduct focus groups. Paradowski Design, the Standing Partnership and the Bryan Cave law firm contributed significant hours of pro bono time to trademark searches and registration, logo design and graphics, and publicity campaign planning. The St Louis BioBelt brand name and distinctive logo were launched during another significant event in September 2000, the BioDiscovery Symposium. This was a series of St Louis events to commemorate the completion of the map of the human genome, in which Washington University played a significant role. It drew both local and national media coverage. The RCGA provided additional funding to continue the branding campaign with national advertising and coordination of the region's organizations' participation at industry exhibitions (Kathryn Kissam, personal interview, 14 January 2005).

Another action item was the establishment of a state-wide coalition to support the development effort. The Missouri Biotechnology Organization (MOBIO) was established in 2001 and quickly engaged a wider audience to promote the benefits of a plant and life sciences economy. It convened regional summits to garner the political support of the more rural communities of the state. The late governor Mel Carnahan enhanced this effort by personally chairing a Life Sciences Roundtable and declaring this to be Missouri's lead industry (Dennis Roedemeier, personal interview, 4 February 2005). A significant result was the growing collaboration between Kansas City, Columbia, and St Louis business and research institutions along the Interstate 70 Corridor connecting them. Another was the successful lobbying for a share of the Missouri Tobacco Settlement Fund. Legislation was passed which set aside 20 per cent of the annual tax settlement funds starting in 2007.

Seed capital and venture funding: state, local and midwestern efforts
Another immediate action item was the establishment of locally managed, dedicated life sciences venture funds. The few local venture funds, such as Gateway Associates and Oakwood Healthcare Investors, invested primarily in later-stage deals. Chip Cooper, who was running the Missouri Innovation Center in Columbia, began to lobby the Missouri

Legislature for legislation for the creation of local venture capital firms. Because the Columbia Center did not have a facility, the Center for Emerging Technologies hosted politicians to display tangible examples of successful company start-ups. The four state-funded innovation centres secured commitments and developed a joint proposal for $20 million in tax credits to support new venture funds (Andrew Hoyne, personal interview, 14 December 2004). The passage of Missouri's New Enterprise Creation Act in 1999 and implementation in 2000 enabled fundraising for seed-stage investments. Prolog Ventures raised $33 million for its inaugural fund in 2001. RiverVest Partners raised another $89 million, although their investment focus was not limited to St Louis. But the local managers' presence and awareness of investment opportunities brought in additional funding via syndication with venture capital firms from both coasts.

The locally invested funds were still quite limited. From the beginning of 2000 until the end of 2004, venture funds had invested $142 million in medical device companies, but only $33 million in biotechnology companies in Missouri (PriceWaterhouseCoopers, 2004). Robert Calcaterra, working with William Romjue, Executive Director of MOBIO and seven other Midwestern BIO organizations, convinced the national organization to sponsor the first Midwestern Biotechnology Investment Conference in Chicago in 2003. Previously, the conferences were only held on the East and West coasts. The second annual event was held in St Louis in 2004 and drew venture fund participants from throughout the United States.

These funds are continuing to grow with the local funds, raising new rounds and with outside firms, such as Triathlon, based in Cincinnati, Ohio, establishing offices in St Louis. Vectis I, a new $81.5 million fund-of-funds, was capitalized in 2005 and will invest in local and national venture firms. Investors include local foundations, universities, and union and company pension funds (Melcer, 2005).

Seed funds will also be increased with the reincarnation of local angel funding with the inception of the St Louis Arch Angels, a not-for-profit corporation facilitating individual investments (Sybert, 2005). This effort was initiated by Robert Calcaterra and David Broughton from the Nidus Center; and by Robert Coy, Vice President for Entrepreneurial Development at the RCG, and John McDonnell, retired Chairman of the Board of McDonnell Douglas Corporation. Coy is also on the BioGenerator and MOBIO boards and oversees the BioEnergy and BioInformatics networks. McDonnell chairs the BioGenerator board and is also a member of The Coalition for Plant and Life Sciences.

Growing success capturing its share of government funds   Another measure of progress was the growing success in government grant awards to companies. From 1997 to 2002, Missouri's state ranking for Small Business Innovation Research (SBIR) and Small Business Technology Transfer (STTR) awards hovered around thirtieth, well below its population ranking as seventeenth. Through educational workshops and networking discussions companies improved somewhat, particularly with National Science Foundation grants. Isto Technologies received the first NIST Advanced Technology Program award in St Louis' history in 2001. It was worth $2 million and was only the second one in the state during the 11 years that the programme was in effect. Other companies became quite proficient at writing submissions. Apath, for example, was either the recipient, or functioned as a subcontractor, of 16 SBIR grant awards during the 2000–2004 period.

Successful company retention and recruiting: state, local and RCGA efforts   It was critical during this brittle time of mergers and acquisitions to maintain the region's employment base. State and local efforts resulted in the retention and expansion of Pfizer's and Tyco's local operations and the rapid recruitment of Johnson & Johnson's Centecor to acquire Wyeth's biopharmaceutical production facility (St Louis RCGA, 2003). Sigma-Aldrich also made a major commitment by opening a new $55 million research facility in 2001.

The Inventery

As an indication of the need for wet lab space, a privately-funded incubator, the Inventery, was opened in 2002. Wayne Barnes, an Associate Professor in the Department of Biochemistry and Molecular Biophysics at Washington University, founded DNA Polymerase in 1998 to produce proprietary enzymes for PCR research. The company was based in the Center for Emerging Technologies from 1999 to 2002, until moving into a laboratory building near the Saint Louis University Medical School campus that he purchased and refurbished. Since then, three other start-up companies, Primogenix, Luminomics and InVivo Sciences, have leased space in the building.

BioGenerator pre-seed incubator

The establishment of a dedicated pre-seed/seed fund and technology business formation and commercialization centre was a high priority action item that was realized in 2003 (St Louis RCGA, 2003). Tax-supported contributions from the Danforth Foundation, the Monsanto Fund, the McDonnell Foundation and Bunge North America provided more than $12 million for the operation of the BioGenerator for five years. Its mission was to commercialize new technologies out of local research laboratories and to support the resulting companies through to the completion of seed funding milestones. Patricia Snider, its first CEO, recruited a volunteer advisory board of seven midwestern VC firms to review candidate business opportunities and to recommend whether to fund them. It was then able to pay up to $250 000 in expenses for each approved candidate and provide an additional $150 000 in value-added services. Three companies, Akermin, ISW and Venganza, were started in 2004, its first year.

CORTEX accelerator complex

The Center of Research, Technology and Entrepreneurial Expertise (CORTEX) is a joint undertaking of the three main local universities, along with Barnes-Jewish Hospital Foundation and the Missouri Botanical Garden, to develop a biotechnology corridor in St Louis' central core. CORTEX was created to fill a gap in the region for scientific research space to house an academic/medical centre and new and emerging plant and life science companies (Development Strategies, 2001). This was an unprecedented collaborative effort that encompassed the top executives from a wide range of organizations, from universities and hospitals to corporations, city, state and federal government entities, foundations and service providers (Dubinsky, 2004). It was a radically different response from the laissez-faire attitude during the previous decade (Richard Ward, personal interview, 9 March 2005). The founding institutions pledged $29 million over five years. The Missouri Development Finance Board approved $12 million in tax credits that matched investments 1:2. Ground was broken in late 2004 for the first building, a three-storey, 170 000 square foot, wet lab and office facility that will cost $36 million. Its first tenants will include Washington University Medical School and Stereotaxis, Inc., which is currently in the CET. The organization has already purchased a number of additional sites to expand to a minimum of 50 acres to fulfil the first phase of its plan (Sybert, 2004). This public, private and university collaboration will not only provide for companies graduating from the incubators, but will also offer attractive facilities to attract companies from outside the region.

Research Alliance of Missouri
The Research Alliance of Missouri (RAM) is another example of growing collaboration between the universities. It was created by Governor Holden in 2003 to coordinate the activities of Missouri's research universities and to expand industrial access to their technologies. The organization includes academic officials and technology transfer officers and has grown to include 17 public and private universities. It meets quarterly to identify and act on common interests. Early accomplishments include the development of a model licensing agreement and the creation of a matrix to identify research interests in the member schools. RAM is part of the Missouri Technology Corporation (MTC) that oversees the state-supported Missouri Innovation Centers. Local board members, Robert Calcaterra, CEO of the independent Nidus Center, and Frank Stokes, a retired Monsanto public policy executive and an active RCGA volunteer, provide crucial linkage with BioBelt initiatives (Frank Stokes, personal interview, 11 February 2005).

Expanded and efficient networking opportunities   Tying these various development efforts together was an extensive social and corporate network. At one level, there was a committed corps of volunteers who belonged to the Technology Gateway Alliance Life Sciences Network, MOBIO, or both. The Technology Gateway Alliance and its working committees mobilized resources for the branding effort and other initiatives. The Life Sciences Network met monthly in St Louis and provided a forum for promoting successful start-up companies and providing networking opportunities. Together with the Information Technologies Network, they organized an annual conference to highlight the business opportunities that were emerging at the intersection of life sciences and information technologies. MOBIO was a state-wide organization that organized an annual educational and networking summit at a central location. It also held numerous meetings in outlying areas to promote the economic benefits of biotechnology to the rural communities. There is also frequent executive level interaction on both a formal and ad hoc basis. The Coalition of Plant and Life Sciences only has two employees, but comprises the top leaders from the member universities, businesses and civic organizations (Hagaman, 2003). There is considerable overlap with the Technology Gateway Alliance Executive Committee. Other organizations, such as Focus St Louis, Leadership St Louis (Caba, 2005) and the St Louis Academy of Science, and public–private partnerships, such as Forest Park Forever and St Louis 2004, provided considerable interaction across social strata and fostered the development of broad-based community support on key issues.

What is particularly striking, in the context of this analysis, is the very dense networking that has been characteristic of St Louis. William A. Peck, M.D. was a professor, Executive Vice Chancellor for Medical Affairs and Dean of Washington University School of Medicine until his retirement to become the Director of its Center for Health Policy. He is now the chairman of the Technology Gateway Council, and is also on the boards of both life science incubators and the St Louis Science Center. Robert J. Calcaterra is President and CEO of the Nidus Center for Scientific Enterprise. He was very involved with the formation of the BioGenerator and sits on its board. He is also on the board of the Technology Gateway Alliance and participated on the Capital Committee, as well as spearheading the creation of the Arch Angel Network. At the state level, he chairs the Missouri Venture Capital Roundtable and is on the board of the Missouri Technology Corporation and MOBIO. Robert T. Fraley is an Executive Vice President and the Chief Technology Officer of the Monsanto Company. He is on the board of the RCGA and past Chair of the Technology Gateway Alliance and on the board of the National Corn-to-ethanol Research Pilot Plant at SIUE. Marcia Mellitz is the President and CEO of the Center for Emerging Technologies. She also serves on the Executive Committee of the Technology Gateway Alliance and on the boards of the BioGenerator and CORTEX. All of these members recently participated on the St Louis Regional Competitiveness Initiative Advisory Committee. The same level of heavy participation in community and economic development activities could be said about all of the members of the Coalition.

2004 forward: emergence of a plant and life sciences cluster
In late 2004, the Battelle Memorial Institute was again commissioned to conduct a study, this time to assess the progress against the 2000 Action Plan and to benchmark the region against previous and newly emerging competitors. As noted above, considerable progress was made in building an infrastructure to support the continued growth of St Louis' plant and life sciences sector. Nine of the original 20 goals were achieved or saw substantial progress. There was modest progress on another nine goals. Only two action items were not implemented, those dealing with tax policies and incentives at the state and local levels (Battelle, 2005).

The year 2004 also witnessed the first signs of the emergence of a plant and life sciences industry cluster. The evidence was the first collaborations between the leading local corporations and start-up companies. In September 2004, Divergence, a company in the Nidus Center that is dedicated to the discovery of effective and ecologically sound strategies for the control of parasitic nematodes and other pests, announced two corporate collaborations. The first was with Tripos, Inc. to collaborate in small molecule research to enhance genomic targets and leads discovered by Divergence (Divergence, 2004a). The second was with the Monsanto Company to collaborate on the development of nematode-resistant soybeans (Divergence, 2004b). In the next month Chlorogen, another company based in the Nidus Center, announced an agreement with Sigma Aldrich Corporation for the development and supply of four specific proteins in tobacco chloroplasts (Chlorogen, 2004). Working in the other direction, Tripos is supplying compound libraries to Apath for testing as antiviral drug candidates.

In 2005, the new CORTEX facility is already beginning to foster collaboration with companies from outside the St Louis region. One of the start-up companies currently based in the Center for Emerging Technologies is considering relocation to this new building, where it would be joined by an outside collaborator that is considering opening a regional headquarters there. Both companies would be able to benefit from close proximity to each other and to the facilities at Washington University School of Medicine and Barnes Jewish Medical Center. That is where much of the early clinical research will be performed. These events are an indication of the continuing maturation of the plant and life science industry in St Louis and the dual development of a Technopolis and an industrial cluster.

Discussion

The creation of the BioBelt was positioned initially as a potential case of the technopolis form of economic development, grounded in a densely networked population. Having described the historical development of the BioBelt, it is worth re-examining the analysis, to evaluate its fit with the specifics of the case.

Reviewing the history of the BioBelt, it is evident that two development approaches recur, the technopolis model and the cluster model. For example, the 1983 Tech Center Study espoused technopolis-oriented activities, leveraging the universities in the region. Similarly, the 1997 Celeste and Sabety study built from a technopolis model, although at a higher level of abstraction the C&S study considered cluster-based approaches to the broader development of technology in the region. The 2000 Battelle study confirmed the creation of the technopolis in St Louis' BioBelt, and offered suggestions for its growth.

In practice the majority of work in the BioBelt was driven by technopolis approaches, including the creation of the incubators, the centrality of universities, the development of the local venture capital industry and the commercialization focus. Still, throughout this process, there were clearly evident flashes of activity which reflected a clustering approach. Groups such as the Technology Gateway and MoBio realized that the local pharmaceutical and chemical anchors and universities with their strong research infrastructure could give St Louis a competitive advantage as a biotech cluster, but it can be argued that the cluster development efforts failed on the transactional side, largely through the lack of a strong concerted effort to recruit new entrants and grow the cluster. Promising efforts, such as the transfer of technology out of Mallinckrodt and Monsanto through new companies and partnerships, did not reach a critical mass, where successive waves of spin-outs would come from the new firms.

That said, there were cluster-like instances of attracting companies to the region because they saw the possible synergies with this established base of firms as well as the partnering and co-development opportunities. For example, the whole creation of Efficas, a nutrient development company, was based on this concept. Another element of success was the networking effort through Technology Gateway and geographic proximity. Tripos developed partnering relationships with both Divergence and Apath. Divergence has a research agreement with Monsanto and the Danforth Center; Chlorogen has a research agreement with Sigma Aldrich and an informal relationship with the Danforth Plant Science Center; ISW has a research agreement with Washington University; and there are numerous other examples.

Looking over the technopolis and clustering efforts in the 1995–2004 period, it can be argued that, while the area tried and succeeded sporadically with the cluster approach, during the same period the technopolis approach was also being pursued and was succeeding with greater impact in terms of breadth of involvement and size of resulting development effects. Recognizing the necessity for a winning strategy, the region moved increasingly toward embracing and espousing the technopolis model. Describing the current situation in terms that fit the contemporary realities of the BioBelt, the current development effort can be said to have transitioned into a technopolis–cluster hybrid, with technopolis clearly the dominant process. While the technopolis, with the university base and venture capital orientation, is still very evident, there remains a recurring, sporadic effort to build a self-sustaining business-to-business cluster of life science firms in the region.

The role of densely networked individuals (and through them, institutions) cannot be overstated. In reviewing the history of the BioBelt, a reader cannot help but note the frequency with which certain names keep recurring in the story – Peck, Calcaterra, Fraley and Mellitz are given particular attention here for their multiple memberships, but there are literally dozens of others whose repeated involvements mirror this pattern of diverse community, civic and business involvements.

While networking analyses tend to be based on individuals, the creation of the BioBelt involved not only individuals, but institutions, who facilitated, and even specified, particular involvements to support the development of the local biotech industry. Consider the two major universities. Washington University's Michael Douglas (head of the University's Office of Technology Transfer) has been intimately involved with Technology Gateway and for two years actually chaired Tech Connect, the once-a-year Technology Gateway Conference. He has also served on TechConnect's Executive Committee as well as the BioGenerator Executive Committee. Chancellor Mark Wrighton of Washington University has been on the Coalition for Plant and Life Sciences' Board, while RAM was chaired by Ted Cicero, Washington University's Vice Chancellor for Research.

Likewise, Saint Louis University was a founding member of Technology Gateway and RAM. SLU's Office of Innovation and Intellectual Property has been continuously represented on the boards of TEC, CET and BioGenerator, as well as numerous biotech start-up companies in the region. SLU's involvement in the region's life sciences efforts has been more or less focused on delivering innovations via the formation of technology start-up companies. In 2002, the SLU Board of Trustees established the Technology Transfer Endowment, which has been administered by the Office of Innovation and Intellectual Property, to establish technology start-up companies. To date, two life sciences companies have been established through that endowment.

As extensive as the university involvement is, the pattern is hardly limited to the universities. Monsanto also has been an investor in Prolog I and had officers serving on the board of the BioGenerator with the Monsanto Fund active as a participant in funding of the BioGenerator. Similar arrangements could be listed for several of the major corporations in the region.

The result of these patterns of individual and institutional involvement is the modern equivalent of overlapping directorates, with key individuals and institutions repeatedly in contact and in action together in a wide variety of settings. This kind of mutual experience and multiplicity of venues makes it possible to trade favours and support across wide expanses of a community's institutional infrastructure, giving a hand to a colleague in the arts arena for a favourable vote for another issue in the life sciences development effort.

This horse trading across venues is classically American, but also depends for its success on the civic mindedness of the participants (Hastings, 1996; Friedman and Mason, 2004). Where decisions are being made for the good of the larger community, rather than narrow self-interest, the trading becomes a way to move a community along on several fronts at once, doing so with the support of the larger community. The basis for this effort needs to be the mutual belief in the civic mindedness of fellow participants, which in the end is an issue of trust (Green, Williams and Katz, 1998).

Where participants can depend on dense networking, the process offers tremendous advantages. Information about opportunities and activities can be spread quickly. The most recent example is the successful effort to defeat proposed state legislation to criminalize embryonic stem cell research. A non-profit organization was quickly created, the Missouri Coalition for Lifesaving Cures, which secured positive public support throughout Missouri. Partnering situations can be quickly identified and exploited, such as the rapid response to funding solicitation for the construction of the CORTEX facility. Civic action can be quickly mounted and executed, providing a potential speed advantage in responding to opportunities.

Analysis: what else is working? The roles of luck and leadership
The Danforth bet the farm decision
Finally, there is also the element of leadership amid the many plans and horse-trading efforts of the participants in the BioBelt. From the standpoint of symbolic action, there is perhaps no single act more memorable or more indicative of the depth and strength of commitment to the creation of the BioBelt than the decision of the Danforth Foundation to refocus its activities and funding on the BioBelt. The Foundation in effect 'bet the farm' on the BioBelt, investing $196 million of its assets on BioBelt and related programmes from 2003 to 2005, leaving the Foundation with only $75 million in assets, down from nearly $355 million in early 2002 (Foundation Center, 2003). While the amount of funding was significant, the degree of risk involved, cashing in assets to build the BioBelt, was not wasted on others in the region. The Danforth Foundation's action also set in place a timeline for achievement, since the region's first, easiest and hence best source for funding would in effect substantially dry up by the middle of the decade. In a region known for financial probity and fiscal conservatism, such action powerfully served as a wake-up call to the region's leadership that immediate action was needed.

That said, the results of the dramatic gesture are uneven. The Foundation's gesture did not open up floodgates of funding from other local foundations or corporations. However the Danforth funding did support the majority of projects mentioned in this chapter, unquestionably leading to the development and elaboration of the BioBelt. While the bet-the-farm gesture did not lead to the sense of urgency to secure other forms of funding or achieving self-sufficiency that was hoped for in the early stages of the effort, on balance, the Foundation's action had its greatest impact as a symbolic gesture, and as a harbinger of a more concerted and multifaceted approach to regional development in the plant and life sciences.

Conclusion
As noted earlier, this is a story of conception and birth of St Louis' BioBelt. It is a story where universities, as well as corporations and enlightened business and foundation leaders of the community, collaborated over more than two decades to establish a fertile environment for a biotech community.

There are two sets of conclusions to be drawn from this effort. One relates to the prospects for the BioBelt itself. The other relates to the lessons of the BioBelt for other communities with some innate university-based resources, a tight-knit civic and business community, and a comfortable and somewhat risk-averse financial community.

The future of the BioBelt

The Council on Competitiveness met in February 2005 for a summit in Saint Louis to discuss the innovation and entrepreneurial climate of the region. Building on a year-long assessment of the region's efforts, they came to the following conclusions (Kempner, 2005). Saint Louis (the BioBelt) presents itself as having the potential to be an important and competitive innovation centre, thanks in large part to its high-quality higher education, high-quality standard of living and the beginnings of a growing capital market. There are, however, two challenges facing the region: the lack of an entrepreneurial culture and problems around funding new technology-based start-ups.

The problem of a low entrepreneurial culture has two components. One is a result of the intense networking and self-reliance. The region in the Council evaluation garnered low marks for tolerance of women, minorities and outsiders as well as low marks for providing a supportive network for entrepreneurs. St Louis has a lot of successful business-people from the corporate world, as well as a lot of comfortable old wealth (and a strong distrust of unknown – to St Louis – young innovators), but not much new wealth or technology (life science technology) entrepreneurs with a success under their belt. The BioBelt lacks any real entrepreneurial community that is comfortable with the vagaries of technology entrepreneurship, yet the region is replete with service providers, foundations and good-hearted folks who want to help.

This means that, while the creation of the technopolis proceeds, with increasing university and venture capital efforts, the longer-term development of a self-sustaining biotech community faces limitation from cultural factors. In effect a biotech community cannot be vibrant if the larger economy and community is relatively unconcerned with entrepreneurship. It is the problem of being different in a society (Kanter, 1979).

This problem reflects the darker side of the intense self-reliance and dense networking that is so much the hallmark of the region. The Council report indicates that people in St Louis feel it is harder to break into the community than is true for competing regions. It is also true that the existing densely networked community is seen as less accommodating of people with different backgrounds than competing regions. Together these networking hurdles make it more difficult for new entrants to the biotech industry or the region to gain acceptance and assistance. In competition with those already established in the region, newcomers may feel at a considerable disadvantage trying to 'break into' the local networks.

The universities are also beginning to realize the importance of building an entrepreneurial culture on campus as a prelude to diffusing one throughout the region. For example, Washington University (a half billion dollar institution) has the potential to create ten new start-up companies a year. Chancellor Wrighton has gone on the record as saying that this is a top priority for the university. Saint Louis University has made similar commitments and developed similar supporting funds. However, both universities would be the first to admit they are still struggling with the provision of sufficient funds to develop their patent portfolio and to move their tremendous intellectual capital toward commercializable products and companies.

Along these lines, the culture on both the Saint Louis University and Washington University campuses is being stimulated by the new partnerships between faculty entrepreneurs, technology transfer offices, schools of law and business school entrepreneurship programmes. Both universities are responding by encouraging entrepreneurship and developing policies that allow for a more streamlined and professionalized start-up company process.

A $3 million grant from the Kaufmann Foundation to Washington University provided a huge first step to creating a technology entrepreneurial environment across all aspects of the university life on that campus, which portends a significant impact on the creation of more high-quality start-up companies. For a variety of reasons, ranging from a strong Office of the President, to a smaller bureaucracy, to being one of the nation's first academic centres for entrepreneurship, Saint Louis University has tended to attract scientists who are usually quite entrepreneurial and innovative, often pursuing not only grants but business projects and commercialization ventures on their own. This confluence of academic entrepreneurship and entrepreneurship in the sciences has produced naturally many of the same cross-campus collaborations at SLU that the Kauffman grant sponsors at Washington University. Regardless of the institutional basis, the advantage for the region comes from the diffusion of entrepreneurship expertise more broadly across the largest research campuses in the region.

The above-mentioned lack of tolerance for business failures and outsiders places an even greater reliance on universities and incubators as a tool for cultivating technology entrepreneurship. However those environments are artificial and not self-sustaining. Self-sufficiency comes from having a plethora of technology entrepreneurship success stories, to breed the next generation of entrepreneurs, savvy and courageous angels looking for the next new exciting opportunity. Every developing region needs folks with courage, experience and insight, and sufficient capital to make the old money folks comfortable. That comfort is essential if the region is ever to grow the funds needed to build the BioBelt.

The second problem in the region also goes to the core issues of a technopolis: funding. While there has been considerable, one might even say tremendous, concern about venture capital funding, the realities of technology commercialization indicate that a *range* of types of funding is necessary to commercialize technologies successfully. Whether these are university-level supports for 'gap' funding of promising projects, or state support for high-risk, high-return life sciences ventures and funds, the BioBelt needs more variety in and funding for the full range of financing instruments. There are signs that the region is more willing to solicit outsiders' assistance to further its aims. After an unsuccessful attempt to secure a local developer for an eight-acre accelerator campus adjoining the Danforth Plant Science Center, a national search resulted in the recruitment of a full-service developer to take on the project. This particular developer will also enlist national venture capital firms to establish regional offices in the complex.

The Council's 2005 report pointed out that the region still lags other ones in willingness to support risk taking. The example of the general, if genial, non-response of other funding sources to the Danforth Foundation's dramatic bet-the-farm effort reflects this, as does the lack of high-risk funding such as gap funding in the region. The region's experience with growing venture capital offers hope. If the intensity of focus which brought about significant gains in VC monies can be shifted to other forms of funding, perhaps a more balanced financial instrument portfolio can be developed over time.

Once again the universities are the starting point for this sort of activity. The establishment of the Bear Cub fund, which has invested $250 000 per year over the past two years in commercialization-type grants, is a small but important step toward recognizing and rewarding innovation. SLU has instituted a similar programme (actually before the

Bear Cup fund) and has invested $125 000 per year over the past two years in commercialization research.

Using the benchmarks for funding levels and numbers of resulting start-ups, the BioBelt needs an invested capital base of at least $1–2 billion, with half of these local funds. Thought of this way, St Louis is only 25 to 50 per cent of the way there, and arguably one of the greatest stumbling blocks is the lack of investment by Missouri and other public pension funds. The state itself is considerably behind other states in commitment to high-technology firm development, and indications are that the gap will widen as some states, notably California, undertake high-profile efforts to demonstrate their commitment to biotech and high-tech development.

It seems, but is by no means certain, that St Louis has learned from other cities that high-technology development is a long-term proposition and requires a long-term commitment and staying power. It is probably a 20–25 year game, with the BioBelt little more than halfway there, according to the date of its first major efforts. While the area has survived some setbacks, it has done little to promote, support or undertake dramatic and risky activities, the Danforth bet-the-farm effort notwithstanding. The reason that greater risk needs to be taken is that other states are pouring so much money into their biotech efforts, their regions are going to accelerate past St Louis even though they are currently behind. Examples would be Pittsburgh, Philadelphia, Seattle, Michigan and even some cities in Ohio.

Arguably one of the other lessons the region has learned, especially from the Battelle team and their experiences, is that an integrated approach is essential to success. It does not work to concentrate on only one or two factors such as venture capital or research and hope to succeed. Recalling the table at the beginning of the chapter, comparing the major development models, in reality every one of the technopolis factors needs some degree of attention if the overall project is to succeed.

The St Louis BioBelt is on the cusp of its growth curve. It has completed the initial, extremely difficult ramping up of a region-wide biotechnology technopolis initiative. It has put into place virtually all of the key infrastructures needed to create one of the leading biotechnology centres in the world. To grow the BioBelt in the next stage depends, ironically, on developing the cultural supports to leverage the infrastructures created to date.

At issue is whether the St Louis region can move to embrace biotechnology, and by its example all of high-technology business. The problems of the lack of an entrepreneurial culture, the lack of local support for or understanding of funding high-risk, high-tech businesses, and the dense networking which often *seems* to preclude new entrants to the business and civic communities, are the issues that must be dealt with to make the most of the BioBelt's unique collection of resources. In effect, the answers for the next phase of BioBelt growth lie outside the BioBelt community, in the larger community of St Louis.

Technological change has always proceeded faster than cultural change, and this disjunction is the challenge facing the region's leadership. Ironically, if St Louis could revive once again its historic self-image of a frontier town – this time on the frontier of biotechnology – perhaps there would be a model for the way 'St Louisans act' that would embrace the key cultural values of looking to the future, backing risky ventures and helping one another succeed on the frontier. St Louis provides an excellent model in the support of flight. St Louis businessmen provided Lindbergh's historic flight across the Atlantic in

1927. A few generations later, they funded the $10 million Ansari X Prize for the first private flight into space. Somehow, that spirit needs to be adopted for similar breathtaking research and development in biotechnology.

The lessons of the BioBelt for others

While St Louis is one of the nation's 20 largest cities, its story around the BioBelt is actually more instructive for smaller communities than for larger ones. The reason is that St Louis has been able to preserve many of the characteristics of smaller communities while building a population of over two million. It is a metropolitan area made up of more than 130 small communities, who have passionately resisted amalgamation into a larger region-wide political entity. It remains a community where people still evaluate others in part on what neighbourhood they come from, and what high school they went to. While many people come through St Louis working for the major firms operating there, the vast majority of St Louis citizens remain in the area for most of their lives. The region's leadership is remarkably self-regenerating, with leaders moving from one position to another for years, even decades.

St Louis looks like many smaller communities, and consequently the lesson of St Louis can be instructive to smaller communities, particularly those with a local university on which to base technopolis development. St Louis is marked by an intensely networked community of people who come together to work on civic, government and business projects continually. That intense networking means that, where the community members back an idea, it is possible for them to react quickly and collaboratively to take on projects. Interestingly, intensely networked communities are more likely to be the first to respond to opportunities, should they see the opportunity as desirable. In larger localities, or those with a more conglomerated social or civic structure, it takes time to establish and validate the particular coalition that will pursue an opportunity.

The other characteristic of St Louis that may seem familiar in smaller localities is the degree of self-reliance. St Louis historically has relied on itself and its resources, rather than help from elsewhere. Smaller communities often voice similar beliefs. The BioBelt example points out the strengths and weaknesses of this approach. St Louis *was* able to build its BioBelt in somewhat less time than other cities, in part because so many of the civic, university and business leaders saw the value of a biotech centre, and put their efforts behind it. On the other hand, the limitations facing the BioBelt, the fact that the biotechnology community wants a further infusion of capital, greater support in the general public (and hence in the government) for entrepreneurship – especially the high-tech, high-risk kind which biotechnology embodies – and greater willingness to court businesses, expertise and funding sources outside the region, are also the kinds of limitations that are largely cultural in nature, stemming from the intense internal networking of prior decades.

The problem of integrating new ideas, products or services into the larger organization is a recurring problem in areas such as corporate entrepreneurship (Zahra, 1991, 1996), the new plant movement (Mata, Portugal and Guimaraes, 1995; Wardas, Budek, Rybicka, Deeds and Hill, 1996) and new product development (Olson, Walker and Reukert, 1995). The answers from these diverse studies is that the key factors are the staying power of the champions within the new project, and the corresponding longevity of powerful or highly respected backers outside of the project. Until these efforts become self-sustaining, the role of these internal and external champions is central in keeping the pressure on the larger community to achieve the cultural change and acceptance needed for long-term integration and growth.

The St Louis BioBelt example is still too young to provide a clear example of the integration effort, but can help provide an example of how tightly-knit communities can come together to create new industrial centres.

Notes

1. Malecki, Edward J. (1997), 'Entrepreneurs, networks, and economic development: a review of recent research', in Jerome A. Katz (ed.), *Advances in Entrepreneurship, Firm Emergence and Growth, Volume 3*, Greenwich, CT: JAI Press, pp. 57–118.
2. Adapted from Colm O'Gorman and Mika Kautonen (2004), 'Policies to promote new knowledge-intensive industrial agglomerations', *Entrepreneurship & Regional Development*, 16(6), 459–79.
3. Council on Governmental Relations (1999), 'The Bayh–Dole Act: A Guide to the Law and Implementing Regulations', September, 1999, Washington, DC: URL, Council on Governmental Relations (http://www.ucop.edu/ott/bayh.html).
4. Missouri Historical Society (1999), 'Today's Girls, Tomorrow's Women: Girl Scouts in Greater St Louis, 1918 to Today', St Louis: Missouri Historical Society, URL: (http://www.mohistory.org/content/Exhibitions/archived.aspx).
5. Jonathan Schlereth (2003), 'Molding boys into men and leaders', St Louis Commerce Magazine, March, URL: (http://www.stlcommercemagazine.com/archives/march2003/board.html).
6. The 1900 measures were based on cities alone, while the 2000 measure was based on metropolitan statistical areas (MSAs). This change of unit of measure basically follows the conventional wisdom of how to rank cities, because of their becoming increasingly suburbanized.
7. Gibson, Campbell (1998), 'Population of the 100 Largest Cities and Other Urban Places in the United States: 1790 to 1990', Washington, DC: U.S. Bureau of the Census: URL: (http://www.census.gov/population/www/documentation/twps0027.html), U.S. Census Bureau (2001). Census 2000 PHC-T-3. 'Ranking Tables for Metropolitan Areas: 1990 and 2000, Table 5: Metropolitan Areas Ranked by Percent Population Change: 1990 to 2000', Washington, DC: U.S. Census Bureau; URL: (http://www.census.gov/population/cen2000/phc-t3/tab05.xls). Census 2000 PHC-T-29, 'Ranking Tables for Population of Metropolitan Statistical Areas, Combined Statistical Areas, New England City and Town Areas, and Combined New England City and Town Areas: 1990 and 2000', Washington, DC: Census Bureau; URL (http://www.census.gov/population/cen2000/phc-t29/tab03a.xls).

Bibliography

Abetti, P.A. (1992), 'Planning and building the infrastructure for technological entrepreneurship', *International Journal of Technology Management*, 7, 129–39.
Adams, J.S. (1976), 'The structure and dynamics of behavior in organizational boundary roles', in M.D. Dunnette (ed.), *Handbook of Industrial and Organizational Psychology*, Chicago: Rand McNally.
Adkins, D. (2004), 'The Nidus Center – a unique experiment in corporate and regional entrepreneurship support', National Business Incubation Association.
Adler, Jeffrey S. (1994), 'Capital and entrepreneurship in the Great West', *Journal of Interdisciplinary History*, 25(2), 189–209.
Aldrich, H.E. and T. Sakano (1995), 'Is Japan different? The personal networks of Japanese business owners compared to those in four other industrialized nations', *KSU Economic and Business Review*, 22(May), 1–28.
Aldrich, H.E. and D.A. Whetten (1981), 'Organization-sets, action-sets, and networks; making the most of simplicity', in P.C. Nystrom and W.H. Starbuck (eds), *Handbook of Organizational Design*, vol 2, London: Oxford University Press, pp. 385–408.
Aldrich, H.E. and C. Zimmer (1986), 'Entrepreneurship through social networks', in D.L. Sexton and R.W. Smilor (eds), *The Art and Science of Entrepreneurship*, Cambridge, MA: Ballinger, pp. 3–24.
Aldrich, H.E., P.R. Reese and P. Dubini (1989), 'Women on the verge of a breakthrough?: networking among entrepreneurs in the United States and Italy', *Entrepreneurship and Regional Development*, 1(4), 339–56.
Aldrich, H., B. Rosen and W. Woodward (1987), 'The impacts of social networks on business foundings and profit: a longitudinal study', in N.C. Churchill, J.A. Hornaday, B.A. Kirchoff, O.J. Krasner and K.H. Vesper (eds), *Frontiers of Entrepreneurship Research*, Babson Park, MA: Babson College, pp. 154–68.

Bass, Steven J. (1998), 'Japanese research parks: national policy and local development', *Regional Studies*, **32**, 391–403.

Battelle Memorial Institute (2000), 'Plant and life sciences strategies for St Louis: the technology gateway for the 21st century'.

Battelle Memorial Institute (2005), 'St Louis plant and life science strategy update and action plan'.

Benneworth, Paul (2004), 'In what sense "regional development?": entrepreneurship, underdevelopment and strong tradition in the periphery', *Entrepreneurship and Regional Development*, **16**(6), 439–58.

BIO Mid-America Venture Forum (2004), 'Conference Program – Company Profiles'.

Birley, S. (1985), 'The role of networks in the entrepreneurial process', *Journal of Business Venturing*, **1**(1), 107–17.

Botkin, J.W. (1988), 'Route 128: its history and destiny', in R.W. Smilor, G. Kozmetsky and D.V. Gibson (eds), *Creating the Technopolis: Linking Technology, Commercialization, and Economic Development*, Cambridge, MA: Ballinger, pp. 117–24.

Brown, B. and J.E. Butler (1995), 'Competitors as allies: a study of entrepreneurial networks in the US wine industry', *Journal of Small Business Management*, **33**(3), 57–65.

Caba, Susan (2005), 'Leadership 2004 St. Louis', *St. Louis Commerce Magazine*, November, retrieved 18 March (http://www.stlcommercemagazine.com/archives/november 2004/leadership.html).

Capello, Roberta (2002), 'Spatial and sectoral characteristics of relational capital in innovation activity', *European Planning Studies*, **10**(2), 177–200.

Celeste & Sabety Ltd. (1997), 'Opportunities and challenges for science and technology in St. Louis'.

Center for Emerging Technologies (2005), 'Services and facilities', retrieved 24 March, (http://www.emergingtech.org/Services.htm).

Chlorogen, Inc. (2004), 'Chlorogen, Sigma-Aldrich sign joint development agreement to produce first-ever products from chloroplasts', press release, 4 October, retrieved 18 March 2005 (http://www.chlorogen.com/news.htm).

Civic Progress (1980), 'Civic Progress Inc., Records, 1953–1979. Western Historical Manuscript Collection. Folder Sl 153', University of Missouri–St. Louis.

Cooke, Philip (2004), 'Life sciences clusters and regional science policy', *Urban Studies*, **41**(5/6), 1113–1131, May.

Council on Governmental Relations (1999), 'The Bayh–Dole Act: a guide to the Law and implementing regulations', September, Washington, DC: URL: Council on Governmental Relations. (http://www.ucop.edu/ott/bayh.html).

Cronon, William (1991), *Nature's Metropolis: Chicago and the Great West*, New York: W.W. Norton & Co.

Development Strategies, Inc. (formerly TeamFour) (1992), 'Report on the feasibility of a St. Louis biomedical technopolis'.

Development Strategies, Inc., Phillips W. (1993), 'Report of the St. Louis critical technologies task force'.

Development Strategies, Inc. (1995), 'Master plan and implementation strategy for the St. Louis biomedical technopolis'.

Development Strategies, Inc. (2001), 'Real estate lessons learned: the St. Louis region's market for "wet labs"'.

Dickson, T. (1966), 'The Stark story', *The Bulletin*, Missouri Historical Society.

Divergence, Inc. (2004a), 'Tripos to partner with Divergence in agricultural genomics research', Press release, 1 September, retrieved 18 March 2005 (http://www.divergence.com/press/20040902.html).

Divergence, Inc. (2004b), 'Divergence, Monsanto collaborate to develop nematode-resistant soybeans', Press release, 10 September, retrieved 18 March 2005 (http://www.divergence.com/press/20040909.html).

Dodd, S.D. (1997), 'Social network membership and activity rates: some comparative data', *International Small Business Journal*, **15**(4), 80–87.

Donckels, R. and A. Courtmans (1990), 'Big brother is watching over you: the counseling of growing SMEs in Belgium', *Entrepreneurship and Regional Development*, **2**, 211–23.

Dubini, P. and H. Aldrich (1991), 'Personal and extended networks are central to the entrepreneurial process', *Journal of Business Venturing*, **6**(5), 305–13.

Dubinsky, J. (2004), 'Commentary: an investment in the future', *St. Louis Business Journal*, 24–30 December.

Eva Klein & Associates (1997), 'Technology-based economic development in St. Louis – summary of studies, 1991 to 1997'.

Eva Klein & Associates, Ltd. and Marcia Mellitz (1998), 'Regional strategy for technology commercialization'.

Fisher, Harry N.D. (1984), 'Center formed for research and development', *St. Louis Commerce*, March, pp. 24–6.

Flynn, D.M. (1993), 'A critical exploration of sponsorship, infrastructure, and new organizations', *Small Business Economics*, **5**, 129–56.

Foundation Center (2003), 'Danforth Foundation shifts focus, cuts staff', *Philanthropy News Digest*, 31 January, retrieved 5 February 2005 (http://fdncenter.org/pnd/news/story.jhtml?id=23400051).

Friedman Michael T. and Daniel S. Mason (2004), 'A stakeholder approach to understanding economic development decision making: public subsidies for professional sport facilities', *Economic Development Quarterly*, **18**(3), 236–54.

Gateway Associates L.P. (2000), 'A private equity management firm', retrieved 8 February 2005 (http://www. gatewayventures.com/coreMain.htm).

Gordon, I.R. and P. McCann (2000), 'Industrial clusters, complexes, agglomeration and/or social networks?', *Urban Studies*, **37**, 513–32.

Granovetter, M. (1985), 'Economic action and social structure: the problem of embeddedness', *American Journal of Sociology*, **91**(3), 481–510.

Green, R.P., P.M. Williams and J.A. Katz (1998), 'Trust as a defining characteristic of entrepreneurs', Proceedings of the 1998 Conference of the US Association for Small Business and Entrepreneurship, pp. 182–92.

Hagaman, K. (2003), 'Joining forces to build a technology-based economy: the St. Louis coalition for plant and life sciences', *Development Strategies Review*, Summer.

Hastings, Annette (1996), 'Unravelling the process of "partnership" in urban regeneration policy', *Urban Studies*, **33**(2), 253–68.

Herbert, R.F. and A.N. Link (1982), *The Entrepreneur*, New York: Praeger.

Hertz, M., L.P. Magpili and J. Mead (2001), 'Monsanto and the development of genetically modified seeds', Darden Graduate School of Business Administration, University of Virginia, retrieved 14 March 2005 (http://cti.itc.virginia.edu/~meg 3c/200R/Private/E-220_Monsanto-ABC-2%2379853.doc).

Hite, Julie M. (2005), 'Evolutionary processes and paths of relationally embedded network ties in emerging entrepreneurial firms', *Entrepreneurship Theory and Practice*, **29**(1), 113–44.

Hutchison, L. (1999), 'Planting the seeds: the St. Louis region has the potential to become a world center for plant sciences, biotechnology and life sciences', *St. Louis Commerce Magazine*, October, retrieved 18 March 2005 (http://www.stlcommercemagazine.com/archives/october 1999/seeds.html).

Hutchison, L. (2000), 'Hatching new business: area incubators nurture start-up companies into mature businesses', *St Louis Commerce Magazine*, October, retrieved 18 March 2005 (http://www.stlcommercemagazine. com/archives/february2000/cover.html).

Invitron Corporation (1987), 'Prospectus'.

Kanter, Rosabeth Moss (1979), 'Power failure in management circuits', *Harvard Business Review*, **57**(4), 65.

Katz, J.A. and P.M. Williams (1997), 'Gender, self-employment and weak-tie networking through formal organizations: a secondary analysis approach', *Entrepreneurship and Regional Development*, **9**, 183–97.

Kempner, Randall (2005), 'St. Louis regional competitiveness initiative: key findings', 17 February 2005; Washington, DC: Council for Competitiveness; URL (http://www.compete.org/docs/pdf/1_Kempner_St._ Louis_Regional_%20Findings.pdf).

Larson, A. (1991), 'Partner networks: leveraging external ties to improve entrepreneurial performance', *Journal of Business Venturing*, **6**, 173–88.

Laukkanen, Mauri and Hannu Niittykangas (2003), 'Local developers as virtual entrepreneurs – do difficult surroundings need initiating interventions?', *Entrepreneurship and Regional Development*, **15**(4), 309–31.

Malecki, Edward J. (1997), 'Entrepreneurs, networks, and economic development: a review of recent research', in Jerome A. Katz (ed.), *Advances in Entrepreneurship, Firm Emergence and Growth*, vol. 3, Greenwich, CT: JAI Press, pp. 57–118.

Mata, Jose, Pedro Portugal and Paulo Guimaraes (1995), 'The survival of new plants: start-up conditions and post-entry evolution', *International Journal of Industrial Organization*, **13**(4), 459–81.

Melcer, Rachel (2003), 'Foundation gift boosts life sciences research', *St. Louis Post-Dispatch*, 8 January.

Melcer, Rachel (2005), 'New fund would help biotech here', *St. Louis Post-Dispatch*, 20 January.

Missouri Research Park (2001), 'About the Missouri Research Park', retrieved 4 February 2005 (http://www.umtechparks.com/aboutmrp.htm).

O'Gorman, Corm and Mika Kautonen (2004), 'Policies promoting new knowledge intensive agglomerations', *Entrepreneurship & Regional Development*, **16**(6), 459–79.

Olson, E.M., O.C. Walker and R.W. Reukert (1995), 'Organizing for effective new product development: the moderating role of product innovativeness', *Journal of Marketing*, **59**, 48–62.

Ostgaard, T.A. and S. Birley (1994), 'Personal networks and firm competitive strategy – a strategic or coincidental match?', *Journal of Business Venturing*, **9**(4), 281–306.

Owen-Smith, Jason, Massimo Riccaboni, Fabio Pammolli and Walter W. Powell (2002), 'A comparison of U.S. and European university–industry relations in the life sciences', *Management Science*, **48**(1), January, 24–43.

PriceWaterhouseCoopers (2004), 'Global: Insights & Solutions: MoneyTree™ Survey Report', retrieved 27 February 2005 (http://www.pwcmoneytree.com/moneytree/nav.jsp?page=historical).

Roberts, E.B. (1991), *Entrepreneurs in High Technology*, New York: Oxford University Press.

Saint Louis University (2005), 'Jefferson Smurfit Center History', retrieved 24 March 2005 (http://www.slu. edu/centers/jsces/history.html).

Saint Louis University School of Medicine (2005), 'History: the history of Saint Louis University', Edward A. Doisy Department of Biochemistry and Molecular Biology; URL: (http://biochemweb.slu.edu/history.html).

Shapero, A. (1975), 'The displaced, uncomfortable entrepreneur', *Psychology Today*, **9**(November), 83–8.

Smilor, R.W. and H.R. Feeser (1991), 'Chaos and the entrepreneurial process: patterns and policy implications for technology entrepreneurship', *Journal of Business Venturing*, **6**, 165–72.

Smilor, R.W., D.V. Gibson and G. Kozmetsky (eds) (1988), *Creating the Technopolis: Linking Technology Commercialization and Economic Development*, Cambridge, MA: Ballinger.

Smilor, R.W., D.V. Gibson and G. Kozmetsky (1989), 'Creating the technopolis: high-technology development in Austin, Texas', *Journal of Business Venturing*, **4**, 49–67.

Smith, D.L. (2003), 'Business–academic partnerships: creating a curriculum that mirrors the real world', *The Presidency*, Spring, retrieved 14 March 2005 (http://www.findarticles.com/p/articles/mi_qa3839/is_200304/ai_n9202335/print).

Smith, Jeffrey E. (1995, 1997), 'St. Louis Historic Contexts: Business, Commerce & Industry', St. Louis: Janus Applied History Group; URL (http://stlouis.missouri.org/government/heritage/history/intro.htm).

Sorenson, Olav (2003), 'Social networks and industrial geography', *Journal of Evolutionary Economics*, **13**, 513–27.

Specht, P.H. (1993), 'Munificence and carrying capacity of the environment and organization formation', *Entrepreneurship Theory and Practice*, **17**, 77–86.

St. Louis (2004), '(1997–2004), 21st century technologies', retrieved 4 February 2005 (http://www.stlouis2004.org/html/ap_21sttech.html).

St. Louis City Plan Commission (1969), 'History of the physical growth of the city of St. Louis', retrieved 11 March 2005 (http://stlouis.missouri.org/heritage/History69/index.html).

St. Louis Community Development Administration (CDA) and Planning and Urban Design Administration (PDA) (1999), 'St. Louis five-year strategy consolidated plan', retrieved 17 March 2005 (http://www.stlouis.missouri.org/5yearstrategy/ch2.html).

St. Louis Rams (2004), 'The official site of the St. Louis Rams – Championships', retrieved 22 March 2005 (http://www.stlouisrams.com/History/Championships).

St. Louis Regional Chamber & Growth Association (2003), 'The St. Louis Biobelt announces new initiatives to attract, retain and grow start-up biotech companies; Pfizer, Solae & Bio Venture Forum choose St. Louis BioBelt', Press release, retrieved 14 March 2005 (http://www.biobelt.org/pr/pr_062303a.html).

St. Louis Regional Chamber & Growth Association (2004), 'Campaign for a greater St. Louis: progress report to the investors for 2000–2004 period'.

St. Louis Technology Center (1985), 'Development program questionnaire'.

Stereotaxis (2004), 'Stereotaxis announces underwriters' exercise of optional shares', *PRNewswire*, 3 September 2004, retrieved 21 March 2004.

Stöhr, W.B. (1990), 'Synthesis', in W.B. Stöhr (ed.), *Global Challenge and Local Response*, London: Mansell, pp. 1–19.

Suzuki, Shigeru (2003), 'Technopolis: science parks in Japan', *International Journal of Technology Management*, **28**(3–6), 582–601.

Sybert, L. (2004), 'Biotech building begins on Forest Park', *St. Louis Business Journal*, 26 November.

Sybert, L. (2005), 'Arch Angel investor group forming to fund startups', *St. Louis Business Journal*, 10 January.

TeamFour (1983),' Urban Science and Innovation Center for St. Louis'.

TeamFour (1984a), 'Locally based venture capital funds: their importance to local formation and expansion of technology-intensive new business'.

TeamFour (1984b), 'St. Louis Technology Center'.

Wardas, M., L. Budek, E.H. Rybicka, D.L. Deeds and C.W.L. Hill (1996), 'Strategic alliances and the rate of new product development: an empirical study of entrepreneurial biotechnology firms', *Journal of Business Venturing*, January, **11**(1), 41–55.

Washington University in St. Louis (2005), 'Washington University's impact on the St. Louis region', retrieved 14 March (http://impact.wustl.edu/business.html).

Wayman, N. (early 1970s), 'History of St. Louis neighborhoods, St. Louis Community Development Agency', retrieved 11 March 2005 (http://stlouis.missouri.org/neighborhoods/history).

Wiggins, Joel and David V. Gibson (2003), 'Overview of US incubators and the case of the Austin Technology Incubator', *International Journal of Entrepreneurship and Innovation Management*, **3**(1–2), 56–66.

Yarnell, Amanda (2002), A global view of plant science', *Chemical & Engineering News*, **80**(30), 29–34.

Zahra, S. (1991), 'Predictors and financial outcomes of corporate entrepreneurship: an exploratory study', *Journal of Business Venturing*, **6**(4), 259–85.

Zahra, S.A. (1996), 'Governance, ownership and corporate entrepreneurship: the moderating impact of industry technological opportunities', *Academy of Management Journal*, **39**, 1713–35.

Zucker, Lynne G., Michael R. Darby and Jeff S. Armstrong (2002), 'Commercializing knowledge: university science, knowledge capture, and firm performance in biotechnology', *Management Science*, **48**(1), 138–53.

15 Small businesses for high targets: strategies in industrially exploiting the DNA–RNA biomechanisms
Nicola Dellepiane

Entrepreneurship in the DNA–RNA Area

Virtually all pathological processes in animal and vegetal life are associated with under-production or overproduction of proteins or production of wrong proteins. Each process is also characterized by specific complex pathways, at molecular level, very difficult to unravel. The pathological aspects tied to, overproduction or underproduction or wrong production of proteins, instead, have been more easily grasped and research has therefore concentrated its efforts to find ways of correcting them.

Recombinant technologies, the breakthrough that started the biotechnogenetic revolution, have made possible the production of large quantities of proteins with potential uses to correct the pathological imbalances mentioned above. A number of small dedicated biotech firms started the industrial utilization of recombinant DNA (r-DNA) in the late 1970s. Large companies, mainly operating in human and animal pharmaceuticals and diagnostics, and in animal breeding and agriculture, soon entered the game. Their strategies have aimed at ensuring that the new biotech products could not too quickly weaken the standing of their present products, well positioned in the market. At the same time, they have tried to establish an important presence in controlling the speed and direction of exploitation of the new technologies without excessively exposing themselves to risk. It has been relatively easy for them to capitalize on, sometimes only temporary, weak moments of the young biotech firms, to gain positions of strength that have curbed small biofirms' competitive relevance.

Biotech start-ups have been initiated by bioscientists who contributed with their modest financial resources supported by those of venture capitalists. The frequently stated objective of the founders of such firms has almost invariably been to develop as an independent integrated company performing at least a part of manufacturing and marketing of their products, though often in niches. This has been accomplished only in a rather limited number of cases in which it has given rise to high increase of stockholders' value. On the other hand, venture capitalists' objectives have often aimed at getting the quickest and highest remuneration of the capital invested. That means financial instability for start-ups, which are often left at the mercy of the financial markets by the speculative ins and outs of venture capitalists. Especially when developing new technologies and preparing for the approval and launch of new products with long lead times, both high-risk endeavours, small dedicated firms need financial stability. Actually, until 1986, a financial tool called 'limited partnership' could contribute remarkably to such stability by helping firms to cushion somewhat their balance sheets from the effects of possible negative results of their projects. The abolition of the most favourable rules of this tool after 1986 and the constant increase of the number of potential new technologies, all together demanding ever greater financial resources, definitively worsened the competitive position of dedicated biotech start-ups. In spite of the emergence, since the second half of the 1980s, of new and more complex pathways to exploit the DNA–RNA biomechanisms, all requiring large investments but promising outstanding economic results, achievements in terms of products brought to the market and of their economic value have been lagging behind remarkably.

So a first-stage technology such as r-DNA is playing, longer than many foretellers expected, a basic role in the creation of economic value for the biogenetic sector. One should remark, though, that small organic molecules, which can mimic the active part of r-proteins, may give rise to a competing technological alternative to recombinant.

The strategies of representative actors in the r-area are briefly examined in the next section. Subsequently, the endeavours of actors along the new pathways, in industrially exploiting the DNA–RNA biomechanisms, are presented. New start-ups in the DNA–RNA technological area, and firms that want to extend their operations to it, should not disregard certain basic facts that have influenced successes and failures of companies operating in this area. They might help them to better shape their strategies.

Strategic Profiles of Start-ups in the Recombinant Area

The strategic profiles of Amgen, Immunex, Cetus, Chiron, Genzyme, Genetics Institute, Biogen, Genentech, Enzon, Scios and Infigen are presented below.

Amgen

Amgen, founded in 1982, fundamentally operated, from inception, in the r-technologies and succeeded in creating the most successful fully-fledged and independent industrial enterprise in this area. The high standing of its research and its progressively increased financial strength have helped the company subsequently to extend its presence to other biotech areas, as a hedge against changing technological trends, and to continue to maintain a profile of excellent economic performance.

Amgen's success has been based on three recombinant products, Eupogen (epoetin alfa), approved in 1989, Neupogen (granulocyte colony stimulating factor, G-CSF), approved in 1991, and Aranesp (darbepoetin alfa), approved in 2001, that have the potential of a robust world market, because of the needs they can cater for. Such needs are sufficiently concentrated in a number of demand points (hospitals, health care centres) and this makes it easy and profitable to market these products directly with a limited, but well specialized, sales force.

Eupogen, approved for anaemia associated with chronic renal failure of patients undergoing dialysis, caters for the unmet need of a broad market. Neupogen has been approved for induced neutropenia due to myelosuppressive anti-cancer drugs and Aranesp, with the same indications as Eupogen, has also been approved for chemotherapeutic induced anaemia in patients with non-myeloid malignancies. Both products are blockbusters because they enhance the potential use of chemotherapeutics. The competitive danger for both types of products (chemotherapeutics and the above-mentioned types of r-proteins) can come from new products that make chemotherapeutics less attractive.

It should be observed that G-CSF has now (2002) been approved in a pegylated form (Neulasta), that is, with the addition of a flexible strand or of strands of polyethylene glycol to the r-protein, a modification that remarkably improves the characteristics of that product. Also Aranesp is a more advanced version of epoetin alfa designed in glycosylated form, that is with associated sugar moieties, which also remarkably improves the characteristics of that product. Recombinant proteins produced in bacteria and yeast cells lack the biological mechanisms for glycosylation. Mammalian cells, instead, contain these mechanisms, but there may be cost problems in large-volume production of recombinant therapeutics.

Glycosylation and pegylation of r-proteins have been among the brightest advances in r-DNA technology that can give r-proteins a longer life, fewer side-effects and more powerful characteristics. Different approaches have been devised, thereby contributing to increase the number of technological alternatives in the r-DNA area, which are also relative to the type of host cells to be used for cloning, to the ways of identifying and extracting genes and to transferring them to host cells, to the bioprocesses that can manufacture large amounts of r-engineered cells and to the ways of expressing genes in these cells. This has been only the beginning of the increasing proliferation of technologies and of start-ups that characterizes the biotech revolution.

Less relevant r-products have obtained FDA approval. R-interferon alfacon-1, a type 1 of interferon not naturally occurring in human bodies, was approved in 1997 for the treatment of patients with chronic hepatitis C. It has been a niche product that had to compete with other alpha interferons and was licensed to InterMune in 2001. In 2001, an r-nonglycosylated form of the human interleukin-1 receptor antagonist, Kineret, was approved for the treatment of rheumatoid arthritis. Manufactured by Amgen, it has been licensed for marketing to PMP Pharmaceuticals.

A strong point of Amgen's strategy is that it managed to obtain early enough key patents relative to its technologies and to the design of its products and processes. So it could withstand the legal disputes that arose. Such disputes are frequent in almost all biogenetic products. In the biotech area, the number of patents that it may be worth obtaining to defend proprietary rights to a technology, process or product may be considerable. Companies must be extremely careful in defending the property of each component of their technologies, processes and products. In fact, if only one of them had been patented by another company, this company can prevent others from patenting technologies, processes and products that utilize such a component or, as often happens, can be entitled to receive royalties for allowing the use of just one component under dispute.

Immunex

Early in its history, Immunex was engaged in monoclonal antibody production, then split its therapeutics and diagnostics business in the late 1980s (the latter was sold to Sanofi Pasteur), at which time the development of r-products took precedence.

Immunex devoted large investments to the design and experimentation of a broad group of r-proteins called cytokines (some regulating hematopoiesis, others affecting the inflammatory responses, others regulating the immune responses) and also of their receptors. Initially, the objective was to obtain approval of certain cytokines acting as immune system boosters directed to fighting cancer. However, the cytokine approach (often single-type), generically aimed at improving responses of the immune system, soon appeared insufficient, so cytokines were investigated for their potential support to reduce damage from chemotherapy. The first r-protein, approved in 1991, was Leukine (granulocyte-monocyte colony stimulating factor) to treat neutropenia caused by immunosuppressive drugs in bone marrow transplant and after chemotherapy in acute myeloblastic leukaemia. But it was not approved with chemotherapy of solid tumours. A smaller market potential than for Neupogen resulted.

A fruitful area of investigation has involved receptors of cytokines which act on their target cells by binding specific membrane receptors. An important product, Enbrel, the first r-product for rheumatoid arthritis, was finally approved after a very long process. The mode of action of Enbrel involves its binding to tumour necrosis factor (TNF) one of the cytokines which play a pivotal role in the reactions which cause the inflammatory process of rheumatoid arthritis. Enbrel competitively inhibits the binding of TNF to TNF receptor sites.

In order to strengthen its market position, Immunex had licensed chemotherapeutic products from large corporations. In 1992, when Enbrel was still far away from approval, Immunex merged with American Cyanamid's oncology business, Lederle Laboratories, to strengthen its biotechnology skills, potentially addressed to oncology, with the strong presence of American Cyanamid in the oncology market. The merged company retained the name Immunex and received a good infusion of financial resources from American Cyanamid, which obtained 53.5 per cent of the new Immunex common stocks, the remainder being held by Immunex's stockholders who received the same number of old shares plus cash.

Initially the presence of this new majority stockholder did not seem significantly to affect the independence of Immunex's strategy, but, in 1994, American Home Products bought American Cyanamid and Immunex became a subsidiary of AHP. Immunex continued its chemotherapeutic business and cytokine endeavours and research. The latter led to the long awaited approval of Enbrel for rheumatoid arthritis on Monday 8 November 1998. The market performance of this product, though, has been inhibited by side-effects and by delayed and limited approvals for other uses. Progress continued in the development of r-cytokines essentially aimed at reducing the negative effects of chemotherapeutics on hematopoiesis. At the end of 2001, AHP made the complex financial and product-market strategic decision to sell Immunex to Amgen, obtaining a good profit and 8 per cent stake in Amgen's equity.

The potential of immunotherapeutic products present in the early stages of Immunex's research strategy was important. Had the company been in a more financially sound position, such potential probably could have been more broadly and successfully exploited in multiple area applications instead of being preferentially channelled along the strategic lines of the acquiring large companies.

Cetus

Cetus has been another important actor in the r-area. Founded in 1971, it was one of the earliest biotech firms. It first operated privately and presented itself as a highly scientific and technological firm when, in 1981, it made its Initial Public Offering (IPO) that set a new high point for the biotech revolution.

Backed by a solid financial structure, Cetus started the application of a wide variety of cutting-edge biotechnologies to a number of industrial areas, including agriculture in a joint venture with Grace and food industry in joint ventures with Nabisco and Socal. Its core engagement, though, has been in human and animal diagnostics and therapy with endeavours in both the basic technologies, recombinant and monoclonal antibodies, with which the biotechnogenetic revolution started. In the r-area it developed three main products.

R-Macrolin Macrophage-Colony Stimulating Factor (M-CSF) is a protein produced by the body that helps to control the development of precursor cells in the bone marrow into monocytes and macrophages and stimulates their activity, with potential applications in infectious diseases and treatment of cancer. After many years in preclinical, it entered phase I in 1989 and, almost immediately afterwards the company, because of patent problems, had to make a cross-licensing with Genetics Institute covering their respective rights to M-CSF. In 1992, the product was still in phase I/II clinical trials.

R-Interferon beta-1b (Betaseron), that moved a little more quickly than had the previous product to the successive stages of clinical trials, was developed in joint a venture with Berlex, successor to Triton Bioscience a parent of Shell Oil, with which Cetus had an earlier collaboration agreement. The collaboration with Berlex ended in 1991; Cetus obtained royalties from the potential sales effected by Berlex and the right to manufacture the product at a negotiated price. The drug was approved in 1993 for a first use in multiple sclerosis.

R-Interleukin-2 (IL-2) (Proleukin), is a recombinant form of a lymphokine produced in trace amounts by certain types of white blood cells. It appears to play a pivotal role in both of the major arms of the immune system: cellular and antibody-based immunity. It may be useful in treating a number of cancers and infectious diseases and also in restoring immune system functions. After fairly long clinical trials, on May 1989, Cetus managed to obtain approval of Proleukin in Europe for the treatment of metastatic cell carcinoma, a rather limited area with respect to those in which IL-2 was thought to be a potentially useful product (a typical wrong belief in the start-up phase of the biotech revolution, due to a too superficial look at the complexities of pathological mechanisms and the illusion of dominating them with a single drug). Cetus created a subsidiary in Europe. In the attempt to capitalize on the European approval of Interleukin-2 within the much larger American market, Cetus, also with the financial support of limited partnerships, built a manufacturing plant for the molecule in Amsterdam, built a US sales force to generate a rapid increase in sales once IL-2 was approved and created a US marketing joint venture with a marketer of generic chemotherapeutics (Ben Venture) to obtain a foothold in the oncology market place. Cetus also started clinical trials in the attempt to broaden clinical use of Proleukin, including its pegylated form, an endeavour that might have brought results only in the long term, but contributed to increasing the present need for financial resources. In spite of a designation in 1988 as an orphan drug for the same pathology, for which it was then approved in Europe, approval of IL-2, in the US, even for such a specific use, was further delayed.

Instead a remarkable success of the company's research work in the DNA area has been the invention of Polymerase Chain Reaction (PCR), capable of multiplying the number of target DNA sequences in a sample by several million fold. Because detection and characterization of genetic material is essential to molecular biology and biomedical research, PCR has been adopted rapidly in a wide and diverse spectrum of applications and has become a fruitful asset for Cetus.

Further extending its R&D activity to the area of monoclonal antibodies, in contrast, has absorbed financial resources with no perspective of future returns. In fact, this other main technological pathway in the starting phase of the biotech revolution was full of promises but very poor, for about 20 years, in products brought to the market, and it gave particularly negative results in the area of septic shock, to which Cetus had addressed its efforts. Because of unsatisfactory performance of IL-2 in Europe, its delayed approval in the US and the manufacturing and marketing investments made in expectation of such an approval, because of the insufficient contributions of licensed products and too broad engagements in several endeavours with the prevailing strategy of retaining most of the results for itself, and because of costly legal disputes relative to both the biotech products and the generic chemotherapeutics (typical is the dexorubicin case involving Erbamont), the balance of revenues versus burn rate progressively deteriorated. In1990, the company still managed to make another public stock offering on acceptable conditions, but management, particularly in the light of the delayed approval of Proleukin in the US, concluded that future access to funds as an independent company, in the equity, and other, private and public markets, would be severely limited. The company's stock quotation began to show swings and a potential downtrend. Management decided it was necessary to alter the company's strategic course, from retaining most rights to products and developing its own marketing and manufacturing capabilities, in favour of pursuit of thorough integration with well-matched actors in the biotech arena, trying to preserve, at the same time, stockholders' value. In all, 77 potential partners were contacted in the US, Europe and Japan. Only a few expressed interest in partial transactions, among them Roche, which was interested in the acquisition of PCR, that in 1989 had become the object of a collaborative agreement for development and commercialization of diagnostic products and services utilizing this technology.

With the help of good financial advisers, management was clever enough to find eventually a well matching biocompany, Chiron, interested in acquiring Cetus when the stock market was still recognizing a fair potential value to Cetus. Selling to Roche all rights of Cetus to PCR was then considered, by Cetus' management, a fundamental move for defending stockholders' value in the merger deal. In fact, management believed that a satisfactory agreement with Chiron could not be reached without the sale of PCR, because they felt that Chiron was eager not to deteriorate, through the merger, its financial position. This fact tells how critical, for dedicated biotech firms, the availability of financial resources has been in order to defend freedom in their strategic action, and how large pharmaceutical companies are in a position to take advantage of this compelling condition.

Chiron
Chiron, founded in 1981, has set up a particularly bright strategy centred on successful monetization of its broad portfolio of intellectual properties and on a successful approach to partnering, which have made possible a profitable growth of the company and the maintenance of its independence.

Chiron leveraged its knowledge of r-DNA technologies to prepare diagnostic tests based on nucleic acid probes addressed to particularly rich markets mainly in the areas of infectious diseases where such tests were much needed. Its complex and successful approach to partnering has been one of the pillars of the company's success. It has built a joint business with Ortho, a subsidiary of Johnson and Johnson, based largely on the successful worldwide launch of hepatitis C tests and the successive acquisition of Dupont's blood screening business. A competitor, Abbot, used a bead format technology in blood screening, while Chiron used microplate that can be faster and easier to use in situations where a large number of tests are performed, as in large blood banks. To meet the needs of all customers and to expand the market more rapidly, Chiron and Ortho granted Abbot a licence to develop and market its own hepatitis C immunodiagnostic products, using Chiron–Ortho technology. Abbot markets its own tests worldwide and Chiron manufactures hepatitis C antigens used by both Abbot and Ortho in their tests.

A natural extension of the important position that Chiron was attaining in viral testing systems has been the entry into r-vaccine design and manufacture to develop a new generation of vaccines which will provide greater safety and efficacy than conventional vaccines and the creation of vaccines against diseases for which there were no effective means of protection. Chiron licensed to Merck its yeast cell technology, to be used in the manufacture of an r-vaccine against hepatitis B, the first vaccine, developed using recombinant technology, to be approved by FDA for human use. It also formed a joint venture (Biocine) with Ciba-Geigy (then Novartis), a large pharmaceutical company with several product lines and a leader in vaccines, that reached a 49 per cent participation in Chiron's equity. The joint venture started trials of several types of r-vaccines, to treat genital herpes, HIV, hepatitis C, cytomegalovirus and other pathologies. Its solid and profitable business in viral diseases has given Chiron sufficient strength to devote resources to extending its business to other areas.

In biopharmaceuticals, Chiron has performed a number of clinical trials with mixed results; a process for producing r-insulin has provided licensing fees from Novo. In the area of monoclonal antibodies and enzymes Chiron has developed research on anti-tumour necrosis factor (TNF) antibodies and on human superoxide dismutase (SOD). In 1986, Chiron had started operating directly in the ophthalmic market through its fully integrated subsidiary Chiron Ophthalmics with the long-term strategy of expanding the capabilities of the ophthalmic surgeon to treat wound healing problems and visual disorders using innovative devices and novel pharmaceuticals.

In 1988, Chiron organized Protos as a subsidiary to discover, design and develop a new generation of small-molecule therapeutic products with the help of new emerging technologies for the identification and production of drug targets such as unique cell receptors and enzymes associated with specific physiologic effects and for the rapid identification of useful compounds which interact with these targets.

Genzyme

Genzyme was founded in 1981 and implemented from inception the strategy of building a continuously profitable manufacturing business focused on products that can be readily developed in niches where the company has technological advantages and limited competition. Its business has been built around three strategic areas, biotherapeutics and surgical products, diagnostic products and fine chemicals/bulk pharmaceuticals.

The acquisition of Integrated Genetics in 1989 gave Genzyme the ability and facilities to manufacture r-proteins and the expertise in human genetics to carry out important future discoveries and new advanced diagnostic products.

Genzyme started the biotech component of its business as a manufacturer of r-enzymes to treat diseases because of their insufficiency and concentrated on products that could easily obtain orphan drug status. An enzyme lacking in Type I Gaucher's disease, expensively produced from human placenta, was approved in 1991 and then, as an r-protein

(Cerezyme), it was approved in 1994. A lacking enzyme in Fabry's disease was approved as an r-protein (Fabryzyme) in 2000. An r-thyroid stimulating hormone (Thyrogen) was approved in 1998/1999 for use in a much more efficient follow-up screening of patients who have been treated for thyroid cancer. An r-form of a lacking or malfunctioning enzyme (iduronidase) causing mucopolysaccharidosis was approved in early 2003. In 1998, Genzyme started developing the r-form of the enzyme alfa-glucosidase deficient or absent in Pompe's disease, utilizing milk of transgenic rabbits.

The production of r-enzymes is particularly demanding. Genzyme developed several new production and processing solutions to the unique technical and biological challenges involved in Cerezyme production. The company launched its own transgenic r-business in 1992. It has also pioneered the field of cell therapy bringing the first two cell therapies (Epicel and Carticel) to market, and developed extensive manufacturing facilities and logistics expertise in this area.

Through the acquisition of Geltex Pharma in 2000, Genzyme became a global leader in the field of polymer-based medical products. Genzyme and Geltex had already collaborated in the development and approval, in 1998, of Renagel Capsules, for the reduction of serum phosphorus in patients with end-stage renal disease, that represented a major advance in the development of innovative, polymer-based therapeutics.

Genzyme's leadership in surgical biomaterials traces its roots almost back to the company's founding. Since 1984, Genzyme has been a leader in the high-quality production of sodium hyaluronate, a naturally occurring biopolymer, pioneering the development and commercialization of hyaluronic acid-based medical products; subsequently it brought to the market a suite of advanced HA-based products.

In its first ten to 15 years of life, Genzyme set up a strong manufacturing and marketing business in r-DNA-based diagnostics, risk assessment and therapy monitoring, and has become the largest provider of genetic testing services worldwide. It has subsequently broadened its franchise through leading research and development in the fast growing fields of cancer detection and 'rapid test' products.

Summing up, Genzyme, since inception, has operated both as a bright biotech start-up and as a more conventional pharmaceutical company, thereby setting up a strong, profitable business. It had already reached break-even point in 1996, with 75 per cent of revenue generated by product sales. In that year it became public and presented a valuation of $83 million, growing to $13 billion by 2001. This constant positive performance has allowed Genzyme to become progressively an independent and early starter in experimenting in other types of biogenetic technologies (mainly related to gene therapy, into which it had begun research in 1991) and the potential of the small molecule therapeutic approach.

Genetics Institute
Genetics Institute was founded in 1980 by two scientists affiliated with Harvard University. Their initial business concept was to assemble a first-class management and scientific team to develop protein-based therapeutic products via recombinant DNA approaches. For the first few years the company operated as an applied research centre. Early achievements included gene cloning, blood cell growth factors, coagulation factors and clot dissolving agents. In 1984, leveraging its high standing in research, the company decided to develop products on its own with a business focus based on out-licensing and partnering arrangements.

At the end of 1991, only one product, an r-erythropoietin (EPO), had been approved for marketing outside the US and licensed to Chugai in Japan and to Boehringer Mannheim in Europe, with royalties from both sales and manufacture. In fact, in October 1991, the US Supreme Court had invalidated the company's EPO patent and validated that of Amgen. This was a bad blow for Genetics Institute, as well as losing the patent dispute, for tissue plasminogen activator (t-PA), a clot solver, against Genentech and SmithKline Beecham. The company, though, had a strong product pipeline at that time.

An anti-haemophilic factor (AHF), jointly developed with, and licensed worldwide to, Baxter was approved in the US at the end of 1992, becoming the first r-Factor VIII (Recombinate) on the US market. Despite being perceived as safer than the plasma-derived version, it experienced a rather slow market penetration because of its high cost. Genentech's KoGENate version, licensed to the Bayer/Miles' subsidiary Cutter Biologics, was granted approval in February 1993.

Leucomax, an r-granulocyte macrophage colony stimulating factor (GM-CSF), stimulator of the proliferation of white blood cells, licensed to Schering Plough and Sandoz, received its first approval in October 1992 in the UK. In the US it had to compete with Immunex's Leukine as well as Amgen's wildly successful Neupogen.

Somewhat behind in the pipeline were the clinical trials of other r-products, which were also given for test and commercialization to third parties. Most important have been r-interleukin 3 and r-interleukin 6, blood cell growth factors produced by cells of the immune system as part of the body's natural defence against infections, and a novel recombinant plasminogen activator (NPA), an improved form of thrombolitic agent.

For a number of products, though, the company's strategic focus had shifted from out-licensing and partnering arrangements to development and commercialization as proprietary products, at least in certain countries. The most important cases have been macrophage colony stimulating factor (M-CSF), a protein which is being evaluated as an anti-cancer agent, an anti-infective agent and a cholesterol lowering agent, bone morphogenetic protein-2 (BMP-2), with potential uses in bone repair, a niche in which Genetics Institute was attaining a commanding position after many patent setbacks, and interleukin 11 (IL-11) an agent that can raise both neutrophil and platelet counts in patients undergoing chemotherapeutics, radiotherapy and bone marrow transplantation. Schering Plough had obtained first refusal market rights to IL-11 in Europe, Africa and South America, Wyeth-Ayerst in Australia and Asia excluding Japan, while Genetics Institute retained rights in North America as well as exclusive manufacturing rights.

Genetics Institute had a research group of 120 scientists, focused largely on the discovery protein therapeutics, one of the largest and most able of its kind in the world with a track of record, in novel protein discovery and development, ranking in the forefront of the biotechnology field. Among the most interesting research results, candidates to enter pre-clinical tests were r-inhibitors of phospholipase A-2 (cPLA2), a protein which plays a principal role in initiating inflammation cascade, r-Factor IX for the treatment of haemophilia B, and r-interleuking-12 which may be useful in stimulating the body's immune response against cancer and infectious disease.

In order to exploit profitably such a strong scientific and technological potential and its manufacturing capacity, supported by an organization of about 600 persons, thereby maintaining and increasing shareholders' value, it was evident that the company needed a stable availability of consistent financial resources. The generalized out-licensing and partnering strategy of the company, the bad setbacks it suffered in patent disputes that excluded the company from marketing important products in the US, the less than expected performance of certain products and especially the company's new strategic focus, clearly announced in the 1991 annual report, of full in-company development and commercialization of the many new proprietary products in its research pipeline, were making the financial position of Genetics Institute particularly vulnerable and the risk of significant falls in stockholders' value a likely event.

In such circumstances, at the beginning of 1992, shortly after Genetics Institute had lost a fundamental patent suit against Amgen, management convinced stockholders to accept a major transaction according to which American Home Product (AHP) acquired about 60 per cent of Genetics Institute, thereby providing the company's business with substantial financial resources to support proprietary product development and commercialization and to add new dimensions to its research strategy, which was actually done in the area of small-molecule therapeutics and of potential approaches to gene therapy.

It is important to note that, by 1991, 89 per cent of sales and 92 per cent of profits of AHP came from its broad portfolio of healthcare products, but this very satisfactory performance harboured one potential flaw. Over the decades, AHP had developed an impressive capability in production, marketing and in those activities applicable to meeting regulatory requirements, but it had almost no in-house R&D, a particular weak point at a time when the biotech revolution had started to show its outstanding potential. So the acquisition of Genetics Institute was a real opportunity.

The transaction also gave AHP the option to purchase all of the remaining shares of Genetics Institute held by the public at any time over a five-year period ending December 1996, at an escalating purchase price per quarter, an option that AHP exercised.

Biogen

Biogen, founded in1978, started out with sound technology, but with a faltering business strategy. When James Vincent took over the helm, in 1987, from Nobel laureate Walter Gilbert, the company concentrated on r-engineering a limited number of bio-proteins with potentially high market value, staying out of those in which other biotech start-ups were in a more advanced position. Its main successes have been in the area of r-interferons and of much wanted r-vaccines, while other r-proteins have been abandoned: r-bivalirudin (Hirulog), an antithrombotic that entered clinical trials in 1990, was discontinued in 1994 and licensed to the Medicines Company; the r-Mullerian Inhibiting Substance, a protein involved in pre-natal sexual differentiation with potential anti-cancer utilization, was abandoned because of technical and cost problems in manufacturing sufficient quantities to start clinical trials.

The company's strategy has been to obtain broad and defensible patent rights on its r-products as a prerequisite to fully licensing them to major pharmaceutical companies, which was its prevalent initial approach. Biogen has also built a remarkable manufacturing capacity of bulk protein consisting of two facilities that have been fully validated and approved to meet worldwide requirements and it has managed to create a good balance between product development and expansion of physical infrastructure. To get the most from this strategy, the when and how of licensing deals has become the core of the company's decisions.

In 1979, Biogen entered into an exclusive worldwide licence agreement with Schering Plough for alpha interferon and in 1980 for beta interferon. In 1982, Biogen entered into a licence and development agreement with Shionogi for rights to gamma interferon, in Japan, Taiwan and South Korea, as a potential anti-cancer treatment, antiviral agent and immunomodulatory agent. In 1988, it licensed its hepatitis B r-vaccine technology to SmithKline Beecham for use in vaccines and to Abbot for use in hepatitis diagnostics. In 1990, SmithKline sublicensed to Merck its rights to Biogen's hepatitis B r-vaccine technology.

In 1981, alpha interferon entered clinical trials in humans and in 1986 Schering Plough began commercial sales of Intron A (interferon alfa-2b) for treatment of hairy cell leukaemia. The drug was then approved in 1991 for treatment of hepatitis C; it has progressively become a leading product in the $2 billion global alpha interferon market and has been marketed in more than 80 countries for 16 major indications. In 2001, Schering Plough discontinued payment of royalties to Biogen because it interpreted narrowly the scope of Biogen's alpha interferon patent. A settlement took place in 2002. In 1989, SmithKline Beecham had launched Engerix-B (hepatitis B vaccine).

In 1988, Biogen reacquired from Schering Plough its worldwide rights to recombinant beta interferon, opening the way to its more direct presence on the market. In 1996, FDA approved Biogen's Avonex (interferon beta-1a) for treatment of relapsing forms of multiple sclerosis. The product was directly launched from the company 33 hours later, became the US market leader seven months after launch and then was progressively marketed internationally in some 65 countries.

With a satisfactory stream of profits forming a solid financial base, Biogen has built a globally operating biotechnology company with the capabilities to research, develop, manufacture and market its own products. The company's research and development activities have therefore been expanded to other biotechnologies aimed at serving more complex and exacting market needs.

Genentech

Genentech, founded in 1976, was soon recognized as the leader in the field of recombinant DNA technology. In 1977, it could already announce the successful laboratory r-bacterial production of a human brain hormone (somatostatin), which proved for the first time that a useful product could be made by r-DNA techniques. The following year, r-insulin was developed in laboratory. Genentech had become the most promising biofirm in the just starting biotech revolution. It went public in 1980, with an offering that was one of the largest stock run-ups ever, from an offering price of $35 to $89 during the first 20 minutes of trading, basically on expected quick profits from products that were not yet developed, approved or marketed. Certainly, investors were lured by the company's goal to obtain the highest return on its substantial research investments as a consequence of manufacturing and marketing high-potential products capable of early market entry, and by president Swanson's statement that the company would achieve a billion dollars in annual sales by 1990.

But when its first product, r-insulin, was approved in 1982, potentially an outstanding cash cow if exploited directly, its manufacturing and marketing could only be licensed to a large pharmaceutical company, Eli Lilly. The facts concerning the cloning and approval of r-insulin show that a small firm, even with very strong technological potential and a certain financial strength, is not in a position to try directly to exploit a significant part of a very rich and scattered market for which it has made available a potential blockbuster product. It also shows that, for a large company like Eli Lilly (the world's second-largest manufacturers of animal insulin), it has been an easy game to obtain most manufacturing and marketing rights for a product (r-insulin) that could cater better than animal insulin to broad market needs, leaving to Genentech royalties based on Lilly's decisions about how much to push this market. So Lilly managed to reap high profits and, at the same time, to regulate the evolution of its product line towards new products.

Growth hormone, bioengineered in 1979, was approved only in 1985 (Protropin, somatrem for injection), for children with growth hormone deficiency and was awarded Orphan Drug status. It was the first r-product manufactured and marketed directly by a biotechnology company, and the second approved in the US after r-insulin. Genentech marketed it in the US and Canada, basically to hospitals and healthcare centres. A competing growth hormone, with the same number and sequence of amino acids but manufactured by a different process, patented by Lilly, was also approved for sale. In 1987, Lilly filed an action to declare invalid four Genentech patents relative to the manufacture of r-growth hormone. Only in 1995 did the two companies reach a settlement. In 1993, a new form of the product (Nutropin, somatropin for injection) was approved for treating growth failure in children with chronic renal insufficiency before they undergo kidney transplantation. In 1994, the company received permission to market Nutropin for treating children with growth failure due to inadequate levels of the natural hormone in their bodies. At the beginning of 1996, the company received clearance to market Nutropin AQ, the first and only aqueous, ready-to-use, recombinant human growth hormone product available, for the same indications as the already marketed Nutropin. At the end of 1996, after 12 years of research, the company received clearance to market Nutropin for the treatment of growth failure associated with Turner syndrome, a chromosomal disorder that affects females exclusively. In April 1997, Nutropin AQ received clearance to treat the same syndrome. At the end of 1997, Nutropin as well as Nutropin AQ received market clearance for the replacement of endogenous growth hormone in patients with adult growth hormone deficiency.

In 1987, Genentech received approval of its tissue plasminogen activator (Activase) to dissolve blood clots in patients with acute myocardial infarction. The company has retained market rights in the US where the product has been co-promoted with Boehringer Ingelheim, Genentech's licensee for manufacturing and marketing the product in all countries except the US, Canada and Japan.

Approval of Activase for other indications was delayed considerably. In 1990, the product was approved for the management of acute massive pulmonary embolism. In 1995, the accelerated infusion regimen of Activase was approved for the management of acute myocardial infarction and in 1996 for the treatment of acute ischemic stroke within three hours of symptom onset. Actions for infringing other parties' patents were brought against the company. Moreover many users seemed to believe that other competing and cheaper non-biotech products can perform as well as Activase, which also presents a shorter duration of clot solving.

In 1990, r-interferon gamma-1b was approved for the management of chronic granulomatous disease, a rare inherited disorder of the immune system with frequent severe infections. It was the company's second product designated as an Orphan Drug by the FDA. From mid-1998, marketing and development rights to interferon gamma were fully licensed while Genentech retained the supply of bulk material. In 1996, the product had failed for a very important indication, renal cell carcinoma.

Also trials on recombinant tumour necrosis factor (r-TNF), which was supposed to cause the death of some tumour cells without 'measurably' harming normal cells, had no success. An r-interferon alfa-2a (Roferon-A), on which Genetech had started research with Roche in 1980, was licensed, for manufacturing and marketing, to Roche which, in 1986, obtained approval in the US for the treatment of hairy cell leukaemia. Roferon-A was subsequently approved as a contributing treatment in other types of cancer and in viral infections: chronic myelogenous leukaemia, cutaneous T-cell lymphoma, renal cell carcinoma, non-Hodgkin's lymphoma, malignant melanoma, AIDS-related Kaposi sarcoma and for chronic hepatitis B and C. In 1997, Roche and Genentech entered into an agreement under which Genentech will promote Roferon-A in the US for its approved oncology indications.

In 1984, Genentech started developing, with its potential licensee Cutter Biological, r-factor VIII, a blood-clotting protein that is missing or inactive in persons with haemophilia A. Approval was granted in 1992. The product has been the object of complex cross-licensing arrangements between Genetics Institute and its licensee Baxter, on the one hand, and Genentech and its licensee on the other hand. The product was also the object of litigations with the Scripps Research Institute and Rhône-Poulenc Rorer that ended in favour of Genentech. The r-form of factor VIII certainly represents a great improvement with respect to the plasma-derived product, but it still contains, because of certain biotechnical needs, additives derived from human or animal blood. In 1993, a product made by Baxter, without human or animal additives, was approved by the FDA.

In 1990, an r-Hepatitis B vaccine, licensed to SmithKlein Beecham, received FDA approval. In 1992, Genentech and Roche entered an international development and promotion agreement regarding r-dornase alfa (Pulmozyme), an enzyme that can cut the excess of DNA in the thick secretions accumulating in the lungs of individuals with cystic fibrosis, the most fatal genetic disease in Caucasians, thereby helping to extend their lives and improve their condition. Phase III was completed at the end of 1992. The market licence for the treatment of cystic fibrosis was granted at the end of 1993 for individuals over the age of five presenting mild to moderate cystic fibrosis. At the end of 1996, the indication was expanded to include patients with advanced disease. In 1998, it was also approved for patients under the age of five. Clinical trials to test the product for chronic pulmonary diseases had no success.

Genentech had also designed and licensed r-proteins for agriculture (animal vaccines) and industry (enzymes). Several r-proteins, at various early stages of development and in general covered by licensing agreement, filled the company's pipeline at the beginning of the 1990s (most important were insulin growth factor, nerve growth factor, vascular endothelial growth factors, relaxin hormone that helps in childbirth, CD4 receptors potentially acting like synthetic decoys trapping the AIDS virus). These endeavours, in such a wide number of r-products, were supported by great research effort and investments. Many clinical trials would not have been possible without the utilization of limited partnerships.

But the company's research had also started working on other biotech approaches to drug design, mainly monoclonal antibodies, and had started experimenting with the small molecule approach, a pathway to which large pharmaceutical companies were devoting many resources.

Revenues had increased substantially during the 1980s, but less than expected because of various setbacks. Spending on research and development reached 40 per cent of revenues in 1989. Earnings, though fairly steady, were modest, return on equity was fluctuating and rather low. Genentech looked for a partner to strengthen its financial position, but could find none. Then it approached Roche, which proposed a flexible form of acquisition that managed to save, and protect well, in perspective, the still good stockholders' value. In exchange, Roche gained, variable percentagewise, a majority control of Genentech and transformed it into the most outstanding industrial laboratory controlled by a large pharmaceutical company. In February 1990, the biotechnology community was stunned when Roche announced that it was acquiring 60 per cent of Genentech for $2.1 billion. The main benefit for Genentech was an immediate infusion of cash of $492 million. Simultaneously, Genentech gained the capital to finance its long-term development and reduced its worries about volatility in quarterly profits which were harming its ability to conduct its programmes and secure financing. This highly winning move put Roche in the position to exploit selectively the most important trends in biotechnogenetics and push or slow them down, within the objectives of its overall strategy. By also influencing Genentech's collaborations with minor biotech start-ups, Roche indirectly extended its control over their strategies.

Enzon

Enzon has built its initial success by concentrating its endeavours to develop proprietary approaches to modifications of the structure of r-proteins by means of pegylation, addition of polyethylene glycol (PEG), in order to obtain longer life, fewer side-effects and highly increased performance. Different protein modifications, such as various glycosylation patterns or addition of polyethylene glycol, can alter the mechanisms of action and clearance of proteins. Pegylation has represented an effective approach to obtain prolonged plasma circulation and reduced immunogenicity.

Scios

Scios was founded in 1981 and managed to survive until 2001, when it brought to the market an r-form of a protein discovered in its natural form in 1988. It is the B-type natriuretic peptide that the heart secretes as part of the body's normal response to heart failure. It was approved in 2001 for the intravenous treatment of acute decompensated congestive heart failure.

Scios had trained a proprietary force of 188 salesmen that started operating the day after the product approval in the US (rights for Europe were licensed to Glaxo). The market success of this unique niche product and forecast of steadily increasing sales have opened the way to a remarkable improvement of the economic potential of the company. Scios has not particularly insisted, though, on the r-protein approach and has also started investigating the small molecule approach for other products it is trying to develop. Scios' case shows, however, that the area of potential therapeutic r-proteins remains relatively unrestricted for companies capable of devising the right product/market strategy.

Infigen

R-protein production in transgenic animals, whose stem cells have been transfected with the corresponding gene, is another area of potential r-entrepreneurship. Such a process involves keeping herds of animals, maintaining them in a lacrimating state and transfecting new animals as others die or fail to lacrimate. Cost and convenience of r-protein production are in general more favourable in a fermentation system.

Infigen, spun out in 1997 from the large agro-company ARS Global, seems to have implemented satisfactorily transgenic approaches to manufacturing high-value, complex proteins in the strategic context of producing also transgenic animals for other purposes such as xenotransplants and design of animal models of disease.

New Technological Approaches to Enhance Performance in the Recombinant Area

A set of technologies broadly called 'DNA shuffling' (molecular breeding) have opened new horizons in the recombinant area. They were invented in 1993 and developed at the Affymax Research Institute, at that time an independent Zaffaroni's (the Jim Clark in biotech) creation. Genes are cleaved, reassembled and cloned, creating an artificial genetic diversity that can express new and better types of r-proteins. Such technologies have evolved from shuffling a single gene to a family of related, homologous genes (second generation) and to whole genome shuffling (third generation).

Glaxo bought the Affymax Institute in 1995. Maxygen was founded in 1997, as a spin-out from the Affymax Institute, and Glaxo took a major equity position in it. This has been a typical strategic move of a large pharmaceutical company (quite engaged in small molecule research) to gain control of potentially competitive breakthrough technologies. Another start-up, Diversa, founded in 1994, and still operating independently, has also developed DNA shuffling technologies and stresses the importance of beginning the process with the best ingredients. In fact, Diversa harvests, screens, sequences, clones and catalogues microbe DNA from all over the world and has a library with several billions of plant, animal and microbe genes from which it selectively develops its molecular breeding approach.

An alternative technological pathway in competition with recombinant

An emerging strong competitor of r-proteins is small organic molecules designed (by means of complex structure-activity analyses requiring important computer and other technological supports) to provide the same biological responses as the active part of proteins. Inasmuch as research can elucidate the structure of the active parts of macromolecules such as proteins, the potential exists for mimicking these structures with small molecule synthetic organic compounds, thereby replacing the whole proteic molecule. With reference to the human and partly to the animal markets, proteins often make difficult therapeutics because they are large molecules, unstable in physiological systems and present poor pharmacokinetic properties. Hence most protein therapeutics have to be administered intravenously or intraperitoneally and in large quantities to account for their short half-life, while small molecule compounds can be administered orally.

Large pharmaceutical companies are investing heavily in research along such an alternative pathway. Also the most advanced and financially stable dedicated biotech companies have started working in this area. R-proteins, though, are providing, in the first instance, the easiest route for introducing a biopharmaceutical product to the market. Researchers have the greatest experience with this technology which has the largest foundation of database information. On the other hand, biomimetic compound discovery and development rely heavily on the understanding of the structure of the protein involved.

Consequently experience, both scientific and clinical, with r-proteins will contribute to research and development of small organic molecule compounds.

New Pathways in Industrially Exploiting the DNA–RNA Biomechanisms

Both r-proteins and small organic molecules are to be administered in large quantities. In fact, they have to act downstream of defective transcription and translation processes, that is on quite developed pathological processes.

An impressive technological quantum leap, in exploiting the DNA–RNA biomechanisms, has been the attempt to inhibit either the transcription or the translation step, thereby blocking wrong protein production. In fact, protein production takes place because of the transcription of the DNA of a gene to a single strand messenger RNA (mRNA), whose molecule is then translated into a protein. Thus this type of therapeutic approach would act at the early stage of pathological processes. Instead, if pathologies need to be treated by an increase of protein production or more generally a regulation thereof, a similar upstream approach would require the capability of acting, at gene level, with various degrees of intensity, an even more challenging endeavour.

Three issues have to be tackled in blocking transcription and translation (around which a great number of new start-ups is proliferating): (1) which genes to block, (2) how to implement such blocks, (3) by means of which compounds. As to (1), one can observe that, though spotting genes connected with pathologies and blocking their action would be more effective than acting downstream on their wrong product, genes connected with a pathology may be several and the pathology may also result from many slight polymorphic differences in genes.

The mistake made when an r-protein alone (for example IL-2) was believed capable of tackling complex pathologies is even more likely to happen in correlating genes to pathologies. Genomics and functional genomics are starting to contribute significantly to such genetic target finding. This is one of the causes of the increasing proliferation of start-ups which are basically service-oriented. They are bound to increase as the horizons of research are expanded into proteomics, pharmacogenomics and other investigational approaches of wider scope. As to (2), blocks can be implemented at the translation level (mRNA) or at the transcription level (DNA).

The translation approach is the basis of the so-called 'antisense' and 'ribozyme' technologies. In antisense, the sense of the work of the genetic code (mRNA) is blocked by oligonucleotides, short strings of nucleotides that constitute either DNA or RNA, which contain nucleotide sequences that are complementary to specific m-RNA sequences. As a result, such agents block the translation of the m-RNA into protein (small organic molecules can also enter the picture as blocking agents). In ribozyme, particular molecules of RNA, with enzymatic property, are used to bind to specific sequences on m-RNA and cleave them so that they are no longer functional, thus blocking these sequences' translation into subsequent proteins.

The transcription approach is the basis of the triplex technology that aims at inserting a third strand of DNA into the target gene to prevent m-RNA formation. The technological hurdles in implementing this approach have been much more relevant, so this technology, has, for now, been left aside.

As to (3), the basic problem regarding the implementation of antisense and rybozyme is relative to the stability of the compounds, because naked oligonucleotides are easily broken down enzymatically in the body. Specificity of the bound, delivery/targeting capabilities and efficacy often pose additional hurdles. The issue of specificity often arises because it has not yet been possible to demonstrate that antisense compounds work entirely by the theoretical antisense inhibiting mechanism. Critics of antisense often point out that such inhibition can result from non-specific oligonucleotide–protein interactions and other non-specific interactions. As to delivery, topical applications of antisense compounds appear immune to this problem. Restricting compounds to this delivery mechanism, though, would severely limit the potential of the technology.

So research in both antisense and ribozyme has been oriented to modify chemically their structure to reach more stability and not to alter binding properties. Many variants in these oligonucleotides have been designed by start-ups operating in this technological area, thereby increasing their proliferation.

Strategic Profiles of Start-ups Directly Acting on the DNA–RNA Biomechanisms

Isis

Isis, founded in 1989, has been a frontrunner in antisense. It managed to bring to the market (1998 US, 1999 Europe) the first antisense product (Vitravene), an antiviral to treat, by intravitreal injections, cytomegalovirus (CMV) induced retinitis, which is a local disease frequent in AIDS patients. It is a product with a limited market potential that attempts to replace existing drugs (ganciclovir, foscarnet and cidofovir); the last two are to be administered intravenously and all three exhibit toxicities. Isis has kept commercial manufacturing of Vitravene while world market rights have been given to Novartis. So Novartis, which has also obtained a minority stake in Isis, is in a position to regulate Vitravene entrance to the market within its own strategies.

Capitalizing on its expertise in developing antisense inhibitors to specific genes, Isis has developed a gene functionalization and target validation programme called 'GeneTrove Genomics'. These inhibitors rapidly determine the impact of the inhibition of a gene and the role of a gene in disease (gene functionalization) and whether the gene would be a good target for drug development (target validation). Research collaborations have been developed with large pharmaceutical companies, including Astra Zeneca, Aventis, Abbot, Johnson and Johnson, and with the fully-fledged biotech companies Amgen and Chiron, in target evaluation and gene functionalization programmes.

Isis has also worked at improving the chemistry of antisense compounds. Its first-generation drug has a sulphur chemistry modification that makes the drug more resistant to degradation; it increases stability in the blood stream and in tissues and prevents the rapid elimination of the drug from the body. After creating and testing hundreds of chemical modifications, Isis identified proprietary 2'-methoxyethyl (2'-MOE) modifications to be added to the sulphur modification in the second-generation compounds, which present increased resistance to degradation and improved binding affinity, primarily because of their composition with both RNA-like and DNA-like nucleotides, while first-generation are entirely DNA-like; RNA, in fact, hybridizes more tightly to RNA than to DNA, hence these compounds have more affinity to their RNA targets. Chemistry advances have been paralleled by research to expand delivery methods to include oral delivery.

Isis has set up many collaborations with large pharmaceutical companies and other minor ones more specifically involved in the antisense area and has often licensed market rights to its partners. Some examples are the following. An antisense compound, capable of acting as a selective inhibitor of protein kinase C-alpha in non-small cell lung cancer, initially co-developed with Novartis, was licensed to Lilly, which obtained worldwide rights to the potential product as part of a broad strategic collaboration, which also included the purchase by Lilly of an amount of Isis's common stocks.

Collaborations have been started with Elan and Merck for antisense inhibitors of the hepatitis C virus (HCV) and with Merck for an inhibitor of the PTP-1b gene aimed at the treatment of Type II diabetes. In other cases, Isis has attempted to develop products by itself, for example a pancreatic cancer drug, a psoriasis drug and a drug for ulcerative colitis.

Leveraging its RNA deep knowledge, Isis has also focused on designing low molecular weight compounds (orally bioavailable) that work by binding to sites on RNA. RNA structure has been recently identified, contrary to previous beliefs, as surprisingly intricate, with a complexity rivalling proteins rather than simple motifs like DNA. This observation unlocks opportunities to target RNA, as well as proteins, with small molecules, and thus address important RNA–protein interactions and complexes. This approach may be useful when the structure of the target is not well known or when the extreme specificity of antisense compounds may not be desirable, for example in designing antibacterial drugs that require a broad spectrum of activities capable of interrupting RNA/protein interactions, since contacts between RNA and protein are essential to the life cycle of bacteria. Addressing RNA/protein interactions may also open the way to increasing in-cell protein production.

Revenues obtained from licensing well defended scientific and technical property, from corporate partnerships to investigate potential new products, from public stock issues, private placements and the modest royalties from Vitravene, have not provided the equilibrium with running costs and financial resources needed to carry on the development of many products, including those that the company is trying to exploit fully by itself. Most of the potential products are lagging behind, in early phases of clinical trials, and some have failed in a more advanced phase. As to the many partnering deals, partners are in most cases pursuing other technologies or developing other drug candidates, either on their own or in collaboration with others, including Isis's competitors, for treating the same diseases which are the targets of the collaborative programmes with Isis. So competition may affect negatively a partner's focus on and commitment to a drug candidate licensed from Isis and could delay or otherwise negatively affect its commercialization.

All in all, Isis has difficulties in balancing corporate collaborations and equity-based financing, which are evidenced by a certain downtrend in its stock quotation. If the company raises additional funds by issuing equity securities, their price is bound to decline further and funds may soon be available on unacceptable terms. On the other hand, further pushing collaborative partnerships seems somewhat limited and could open the way to an increase in participation of large companies in the Isis's equity and to loss of strategic independence.

Enzo

The strategy of Enzo Biochem in the antisense area has been unique. Since foundation in 1976, Enzo has concentrated on developing enabling technologies for detecting and identifying genes, for modifying gene expression and regulating the immune function.

The development of a strong scientific and market position, in gene identification applied to biomedical and pharmaceutical research and to diagnostics, has allowed Enzo to build up a small but profitable and independent firm. While many biotech start-ups and also large pharmaceutical companies, in the 1980s and into the 1990s, were directing their efforts to cover the diagnostic market with mediocre products based on traditional technologies such as immunoassays and cell culturing, Enzo leveraged its high-level research to the direct production and marketing of over 300 products based on its advanced genetic knowledge. The market and economic position of the company has been further strengthened by the creation of a full service clinical reference laboratory supporting a network of patient service centres offering direct services based on advanced diagnostic products.

Enzo has worked to develop an approach to antisense remarkably different from those of other biotech companies. It involves introducing into the cellular DNA of an organism genes coding for RNA molecules that can bind to m-RNA produced by pathological behaviours of specific genes in the organism. The gene introduced manufactures biologically the therapy on a continual basis. For example, a gene may be inserted coding for a molecule to deactivate either an overactive gene or a gene producing an unwanted protein. The insertion of the gene is effected by means of a retroviral vector technology that can implement an efficient and stable form of genetic modulation. The benefits of this vector are twofold. It can bind to the target cell and effectively deliver or transduce the gene into the cell nucleus; this is obtained by incorporating, into the surface of the vector, proteins with affinity to the surface of the cell types intended to be transduced. It also avoids transduced cells expressing extraneous proteins that trigger an immune response, causing such cells to be cleared from the body before they can produce therapeutic effect. In fact, the vector has been designed to be 'invisible' to the human immune system so as not to trigger an immune response in the patient. Enzo has often stated that the antisense approaches followed by other companies, generally involving the administration of synthetic nucleic acids sequences, have demonstrated limited success because a single cell may contain thousands of strands of RNA and large amounts of 'oligos' must be delivered in multiple treatments, which can be toxic to the body, as well as costly.

A temporary 'clinical hold', though, was placed on such retroviral gene therapies by the FDA, at the beginning of 2003. This hold has affected Enzo's most advanced (phase I/II) antisense product for HIV-1 infection designed to deliver the antisense genes to be incorporated into the DNA of the blood stem cells with consequent production of the anti-HIV-1 antisense RNA, which prevents replication of the virus.

Enzo's technologic approach should also be useful to open the way to gene therapy (about which so much is heard today) that implies the very advanced steps of modifying the genetic structure of an organism, rather than regulating the expression of its genes as this antisense approach does.

Enzo has also started experimenting with a proprietary revolutionary approach to immune regulation. It is based on its researchers' recent findings that immune responses can be regulated by the oral presentation of specific antigens, with the effect of suppressing the immune response towards those particular antigens and also initiating other complementary immune responses. This could open large spaces, for example, to new hepatitis B and hepatitis C therapies, downgrading modestly efficacious and rather toxic existing therapies, including those based on interferons. It might also affect the strategy of vaccine manufacturers. In-depth research has shown that hepatitis B and C viruses (HBV and

HCV) can lead to a pathology in which the body destroys its own liver cells through an immune response. Enzo has designed and is experimenting, as oral compounds, HBV and HCV viral proteins that eliminate the undesirable immune response elicited by the HBV and HCV infections and apparently are also able to enhance a secondary immune response that clears the viral infection.

Enzo has succeeded in remaining self-sufficient in the pursuit of its goals. In fact it has managed to derive sufficient financial resources, from its profitable advanced diagnostic and clinical laboratory business and from licensing of antisense technology, for example to Japan Tobacco, for applications in agriculture, to be in a position to continue autonomously the development of the above-mentioned therapeutic breakthroughs, without jeopardizing its independent growth.

Genta

Genta, an antisense company founded in 1988, says, on the other hand, that, in the 1990s, the technical aspects of the oligonucleotide design had been successfully addressed by its scientists and by others so that this issue is largely resolved. According to Genta, the central remaining issue in antisense is whether the target that is chosen for antisense attack plays a key role in the biology of a complex pathology.

Genta has concentrated its antisense endeavours on an anti-cancer product, Genasense, designed to inhibit production of BcI-2, a protein made by cancer cells that blocks chemotherapy-induced cell death. So the drug is aimed at restoring the integrity of the apoptoptic process that enables cancer cells to be killed with current anti-cancer therapy, thereby enhancing the effect of conventional chemotherapeutic drugs, the cash cows of large pharmaceutical corporations. The company says that the drug synergizes with almost all types of anti-cancer treatment, including chemotherapy, radiation and im-munotherapy. Since BcI-2 is broadly expressed in most common types of cancer, Genta has planned clinical trials in a number of these illnesses, including melanoma, myeloma, acute myeloid leukaemia, chronic lymphocitic leukaemia, prostate cancer and lung cancer. The company summarizes its strategic technological position by stating that Genta is the only company with a fully validated antisense attack on its target (a target which is easily expressed in a markedly larger number of cancer types, and has no com-petition in the clinic) and with an antisense drug that, developed in collaboration with Aventis, is in advanced clinical trials in several types of cancers.

Since 2001, Genta has tried to broaden its pipeline of anti-cancer drugs by leveraging its oligochemistry capabilities. It has started experimenting with a different approach to acting on the mechanism of wrong protein production, by affecting transcription opera-tions, which are ultimately regulated by transcription factors, proteins that normally bind to specific sites in genomic DNA in a cell where they act as regulators of gene transcrip-tion and can exert either a positive or a negative effect on gene expression. The company has designed sequences of oligonucleotides of appropriate structure, named aptamers, comprising short strands of DNA or RNA bases linked together and chemically modi-fied to give them a longer life in the body, that can attach themselves (acting as decoys) to transcription factors as a way to manipulate gene expression and effect gene activation or suppression in a specific fashion. The multiplicity of transcription factors that regulate a given gene and the multiplicity of target genes that are under control of a single tran-scription factor pose challenges that are also posed by the design of efficient means of delivery of short synthetic strands of DNA to target cells. If such hurdles can be overcome, by selectively inactivating transcription factors, the activity of genes can be turned on or off, thus preventing production of proteins that may be critically involved in the cause of progression of cancer.

Genta has recently completed its technological strategy by entering the field of organic small molecules.

Epigenesis

Small, privately owned, Epigenesis, founded in 1995 as a spinoff of East Carolina University School of Medicine, concentrates on diseases of the respiratory organs, such as asthma, that can also be treated by local drug delivery, which has shown to present fewer problems than systemic delivery of antisense products. The company has elaborated proprietary animal models of human respiratory diseases that it uses to identify and validate genetic targets for antisense drugs. The company states that its target validation technology is the only proven technology for target validation in the respiratory tract and that this technology can spot synergies which exist between targets in multifactorial diseases, such as asthma. A library of Multi-target Respirable Antisense Oligonucleotides has been prepared, all of whose members are capable of inhibiting multiple disease mediators. The company states that it can harness the antisense probes used for target validation directly as therapeutics, because of the unique properties of the lung. It also applies its target identification and validation capability to the development of small organic molecule drugs.

Epigenesis has licensed from Genta broad antisense technology patents and has started a collaboration with Hybridon to develop and market up to five antisense drugs for respiratory diseases. No relationship with large pharmaceutical companies seems to exist, except a modest development and licensing agreement with Taisho (Japan).

At the beginning of 2001, Epigenesis had two most advanced respiratory drugs candidates: a respirable antisense oligonucleotide, having the potential to be the first, once a week, preventive asthma drug, and an inhaled small molecule non-glucocorticoid steroid that attacks the inflammatory and airway obstruction cascade in the asthmatic lung.

AviBiopharma

AviBiopharma, founded in 1980, has been critical of the potentialities of the antisense drugs that are being clinically investigated by other companies for systemic delivery, except perhaps the drugs for topic delivery, like those of Epigenesis. The company has expressed its negative opinion on the typical antisense technologies as usually implemented.

Antisense compounds are composed of repeating subunits, linked together to form a polymer called antisense backbone. Each antisense subunit carries a genetic letter that matches with its pair on the gene target. Although genetic letters are common to all antisense compounds, the chemical structure of the subunits and the linkages that string them together vary widely and so do their physical and biological properties. The early antisense compounds had backbones made from natural genetic material and linkages. They performed poorly, were easily degraded or broken down by enzymes in the blood and within cells, and had difficulty crossing cellular membranes to enter the cell containing their genetic target, thereby also causing significant toxicity. Modified backbones have been designed to resist degradation by enzymes and to enter tissues and cells more efficiently. The most common of these second-generation antisense types use natural DNA subunits linked together by a negatively charged backbone somewhat modified to resist degradation and enter tissues more efficiently: for example, the phosphorothioate backbones used by Isis, Genta and others.

AviBiopharma has stated that all the above-mentioned types of antisense compounds can only achieve minimal specificity and raise continuing safety concerns. As a result, in 1988, the company began developing a third-generation technology consisting of a fully synthetic backbone chemistry and of subunits carrying no charge, announcing antisense compounds that are more stable, specific, efficacious and safe than other antisense or gene-targeting agents. They are distinguished by a synthetic (morpholino-type) backbone which replaces the natural or modified backbones of competing technologies. This technology has been named 'NEUGENE' antisense and announced as one that can achieve broad clinical utility.

Leveraging its conviction of having quite a superior technology available to design antisense compounds, Avi has started to investigate potential genetic targets connected with a rather broad spectrum of pathologies and to design antisense approaches to them. Avi's first NEUGENE target is a transcription factor, the c-myc oncogene. The company believes that this target is applicable to a wide range of proliferative diseases, including many types of cancer, certain cardiovascular and inflammatory diseases and certain non-malignant proliferative disorders such as polycystic kidney disease and psoriasis. The above-mentioned transcription factor is a protein produced by the MYC gene which is an important factor for embryonic development. This factor is a regulator of other genes. It binds DNA at specific sites and instructs genes whether or not they should be transcribed into messages for cells to make additional or other new proteins. Since some c-myc genes are regulators of cell growth while others function in cell division pathways, c-myc is apparently poised at the interface of these processes, capable of inducing both cell proliferation and apoptosis. Hence either up-regulation or down-regulation of intracellular c-myc activity has profound consequences for cell cycle progression.

Avi has started embarking upon the complex challenge of using antisense approaches to perform such regulation in cardiovascular restenosis (a frequent complication following balloon angioplasty during which the smooth muscle cells that underlie the blockage may be damaged, resulting in a proliferative response which can lead to a new closure of the artery) and in cancer. It has also started experimental work to develop antisense drugs for a large number of single-stranded RNA viruses. The company has been particularly successful with SARS, by delivering drug candidates to government laboratories for testing within two weeks of genetic sequences being available from the World Health Organization.

Avi plans to bring two to three NEUGENE drugs into clinical development each year for the foreseeable future. The company has an alliance with XTL Pharmaceuticals in preclinical development of hepatitis B and C antisense drugs.

Avi is working on another strategic platform, cancer immunotherapy, leveraging its knowledge in peptides to develop a synthetic peptide, conjugated to diphtheria toxoid, (named Avicine) designed to elicit an anti-hCG immune response that attacks hCG-producing cancer cells. This is based on the finding that human chorionic gonadotropin (hCG), the hormone that fosters the development of a foetus, is also present in high concentrations in the most invasive cancers. Avi has an alliance with Supergen for developing and marketing Avicine.

Avi has also licensed, from Abgenix, xenomouse antibody technology to experiment with mab-drugs in cancer therapy as well as their use as companion products of immuno-vaccines.

Hybridon

Hybridon, founded in 1989, first worked, as other companies did, to develop synthetic oligonucleotides with a backbone that would withstand degeneration. This was mainly obtained by replacing certain oxygen atoms of the backbone with sulphur atoms; such compounds were still defined, by the company, as 'first generation' antisense. Subsequently the company has developed a combination of more advanced chemistries, thereby improving the characteristics of the backbone in products that the company defines as 'second generation'. In particular, Hybridon has designed and created families of advanced synthetic DNA chemistries, including DNA/RNA combinations called 'hybrid or mixed backbone' compounds. They have fewer side-effects and greater stability in the body; hence less frequent dosage is necessary, greater potency, so that lower doses can be prescribed, and also have the potential of multiple routes of administration, including orally. The company believes that its antisense technology is potentially applicable to a wide variety of therapeutic indications from cancer to viral and infectious diseases, to autoimmune and inflammatory diseases, respiratory diseases, cardiovascular diseases and diabetes, because they are all often caused by overproduction of proteins which may be down-regulated by antisense oligonucleotides.

The company has started focusing on cancer and infectious diseases. It has been strategically very active in obtaining patents also covering therapeutic targets and forms of drug delivery, it has licensed its patents to third parties, and has licensed patents from third parties; it has spun out, to controlled smaller companies, the development of certain projects and has made product development agreements with companies interested in the antisense area, mainly specialized biocompanies. It has therefore strengthened its scientific and technological standing by means of active and fruitful interactive strategies. This strong orientation towards antisense has caused Hybridon to decide to stay out of small molecule drug discovery, an area in which the company believes that drug discovery may take years, while Hybridon can design an antisense drug candidate for a gene target in about 90 days, once the target has been identified.

Some examples of implementation of its strategy are mentioned below. A broad cross-licensing agreement programme of mutual intellectual property licences was established with Isis and completed in May 2001. The company has licensed to Isis advanced antisense chemistries and methods of delivery, including oral administration, and has licensed from Isis a suite of patents claiming certain antisense mechanisms of action. The company is convinced that antisense is maturing into a broad technology platform, that its licensing arrangements with Isis allow each company to move forward to exploit opportunities without encumbering the other and that the success of one party will benefit the other. Smaller companies, such as Epigenesis, have licensed from Hybridon and larger ones, such as Genzyme (molecular oncology), have licensed to Hybridon. In 2002, Hybridon further strengthened its patent position in antisense for oral administration, and in novel antisense design; for example, it has designed oligonucleotides which bind to adjacent sites on the messenger RNA and to each other, resulting in the formation of more active antisense complexes, and new structures of oligo consisting of two domains joined by a linker to form a circular shaped body, thereby increasing metabolic stability and decreasing non-specific interactions. The company has also obtained patents in antisense ribozymes, an area in which another biofirm has been a starter and dominates.

Important product development agreements include that with Aegera to develop an antisense drug aimed at down-regulating a protein implicated in the resistance of cancer cells to chemotherapy, and that with Micrologix, a leader in developing anti-infectives, for an antisense drug aimed at the human papillomavirus.

The company is carrying on by itself the clinical development of its flagship antisense compound to inhibit protein kinase A (PKA), a protein that plays a key role in the control of the growth and differentiation of mammalian cells where it has been shown to reach high levels in many human cancers. In the area of infectious diseases the company had started clinical development of an antisense compound, deliverable orally, aimed at a specific region of the genome of the human immunodeficiency virus HIV-1. The study was suspended after successful phase one, while the company still monitors the trials in the area performed by many large and small companies.

Leveraging its advanced DNA chemistry capabilities, Hybridon is attempting to broaden as much as possible the applications of synthetic DNA. The most important achievement is the creation of immunomodulatory oligonucleotides (IMOs) that act to modulate responses of the immune system. Research carried out by the company has shown that oligonucleotides, containing specific nucleotide segments or motifs, mimic in the human body the immune stimulating effects of bacterial DNA and trigger the same type of immune response, so that they have potential therapeutic effects in the treatment of cancer, of allergies and of infectious diseases and also have a potential as adjuvants in vaccines and antibodies. The company hopes they can be used to treat various diseases by activating the immune system and is developing a portfolio of IMOs.

The impressive technological and business strategies of this small biostart-up have were publicly recognized in November 2002, when Hybridon was named (twenty-second) in the 50 top ranking most innovative companies in entrepreneurial America.

Ribozyme Pharmaceuticals

The main start-up company practising the ribozyme approach to 'silence' genes is Ribozyme Pharmaceuticals, founded in 1992, that presents itself as a world leader in nucleic acid technology. Its intellectual property and core competencies encompass three key areas: selective nucleic acid-based therapeutic products, a proprietary diagnostic technology platform and unique and enabling capabilities in nucleic acid process development and manufacturing.

The starting clinical focus of the company has been on developing ribozymes as novel therapeutics for a variety of large-market applications and unmet medical needs. The clinical focus has led to advancing three product candidates into the clinic: two in cancer and the third addressing hepatitis C.

Ribozyme collaborates with Chiron for the development and commercialization of Angiozyme, a ribozyme that the high affinity receptor for Vascular Endothelian Growth Factor and is designed to decrease the growth of new blood vessels to tumours, preventing the spread of cancer. Phase 2 evaluation was started in 2001 as the first part of a programme aimed at evaluating its potential in the treatment of metastatic breast and colorectal cancers; trials should then be extended to lung, renal and melanoma cancers.

The evaluation of the joint ribozyme and chemotherapeutical treatment has also been started. The two companies share development costs and potential profits equally. Ribozyme has retained the right to manufacture the drug. Moreover, Ribozyme has partnered with Elan, which contributes, mainly for subcutaneous delivery systems, the development of Herzyme, a ribozyme against the epidermal growth factor receptor, aimed at the treatment of breast and ovarian cancer, as well as of a broad spectrum of solid tumours.

As to viral infections, Ribozyme, at the beginning of 2001, started clinical experimentation of a drug named Heptazyme that attacks the conserved region of the hepatitis C virus, the part that is not subject to the typical continuous mutations of this virus. Also a product candidate for chronic hepatitis B, HepBzyme, is being considered as a fourth product candidate.

In the second half of 2002, though, the company, confronted by a significantly deteriorated financial situation, decided to refocus research and development activities on the most promising programmes to improve substantially its prospects for commercial success and significantly reduce operating expense.

As a matter of fact, despite the improvements made in the ribozyme technology, their potency is still an issue in vivo. Technologies aimed at endogenous mechanisms of gene regulation could be a definite response to such problems. That is why the company, leveraging its outstanding position in nucleic acid technology, has expanded its research and development activity in the field of an exciting and newly discovered endogenous cellular mechanism, known as RNA interference (RNAi), that regulates the expression of genes and the replication of viruses. It provides a faster and more effective way to turn off genes than other known methods because it takes advantage of a natural cellular process. In the RNAi-based therapy, a double-stranded short interfering RNA (siRNA) molecule is engineered to match precisely the protein-encoding nucleotide sequence of the target mRNA to be 'silenced'. Following administration, the siRNA molecule associates with a group of proteins termed the RNA-induced silencing complex (RISC) and directs the RISC to the target mRNA. The siRNA-associated RISC binds to the target mRNA through a base-pairing interaction and degrades it. The RISC is then capable of degrading additional copies of the target mRNA.

In order not to miss important commercial opportunities that could contribute to improving its financial position, Ribozyme has leveraged its broad knowledge in oligonucleotide chemistry to become a leader in process development and scale-up and in designing new diagnostic tools. It has assisted Geron in process development and in manufacturing a short oligonucleotide designed as a telomerase template antagonist and has also won an important position in advanced diagnostics by means of its allosteric ribozymes that can be activated by specific target nucleic acids or proteins. This approach, capable of detecting and quantifying a wide range of nucleic acids, proteins and small molecules, can provide an opportunity for the company to generate revenue through partnerships with major diagnostic companies.

Entrepreneurship in the DNA–RNA Area: Concluding Comments

There has been a great quantum leap from the r-technologies utilized in the industrial production of large quantities of proteins (to be used for replacing those insufficient or missing in an organism or for antagonizing pathological ones) and the subsequent generation of DNA–RNA technologies that aim at interfering directly with the DNA–RNA mechanisms of protein production within living organisms.

The contribution of small dedicated biofirms to the successful industrial implementation of r-technologies has been fundamental. Had this implementation been left to large companies, the rate of progress would have been much slower, basically conditioned by their technology/product/market strategies. Small biofirms, though, have sustained the main part of the risk of industrially implementing such an innovative approach, while large companies have tightly monitored it to defend their position and strengthen it with the help of the new technologies.

Strategies of emerging dedicated biofirms in this, for them, unfavourable scenario have been varied, some successful, others failing. All have been somewhat conditioned by large companies interested in keeping under their control the impact of r-technologies. Even for the biocompanies that have been able to grow up, times for attaining success in the exploitation of r-DNA technologies have been somewhat longer than expected. Nevertheless, the potential for birth of new biostart-ups in the r-area should be relatively unrestricted. In fact, r-technologies are developing with many variants and improvements that open new entrepreneurial spaces in this area. Moreover, in therapeutics, in agro-chemicals and in industrial enzymatic processes, research should be in a position to evidence progressively proteins of relevance not yet perceived.

A hurdle that could curb potential entries of small biofirms into the recombinant area is the emergence of small organic molecules that mimic the active part of proteins, on which many large companies are working from a privileged position. The progressive orientation of many, more recently born, biostart-ups has been prevalently towards technologies of more advanced generation, such as those related to the advancement of knowledge in the DNA–RNA biomechanisms. This orientation may be due to the perception that, in the r-area, large companies are more actively and dangerously exerting their competitive control and also work on small molecule products as an alternative. It may also stem from the hope that riding more advanced learning curves will build increased added value for small biofirms, which they could exploit when large companies decide to enter such areas. Not least, it may also be due to the behaviour of venture capital that can speculatively promote, because of its position as main financing source, the proliferation of start-ups, taking advantage of the proliferation of biogenetic technologies. Unfortunately venture capital can then easily take advantage of contingent results or even of rumours, perceived as positive by financial markets, and decide exits when it can get the best financial gains deriving from its early and often cheap entry. This means depriving start-ups of the minimum financial stability they need to achieve their advanced technological goals and abandoning them to the vagaries of the stock market that can quickly react negatively to the hurdles that these start-ups often encounter in carrying out projects of great complexity. Some such small firms are destined to collapse and in general their progress is much slower than expected.

While research is increasing the number of technological approaches to exploiting the DNA–RNA biomechanisms, the number of start-ups following such new technological pathways also increases remarkably and feeds a scenario in which technological progress is likely to be accompanied by longer delays in obtaining economic reward for the increasing amounts of financial resources required.

This trend has become more evident since the beginning of this century and can help large companies to remain the arbiters of the ifs and whens of the progress of the biotech revolution.

Note

An earlier and shorter version of this chapter was presented at the 12th International Conference on Management of Technology, IAMOT 2003 (track 7: small businesses and entrepreneurship), May 2003, Nancy, France. Facts cited in this chapter do not, in general, go beyond 2002, as in the former version.

References

Annual reports on form 10-K, quarterly reports and news releases of the companies mentioned in the text.
Dellepiane, N. (2003), 'The role of the small dedicated firms in the starting phase of the biotechnogenetic revolution', in M. von Zedtwitz, G. Haour, T.M. Khalil and L.A. Lefebvre (eds), *Management of Technology: Growth through Business Innovation and Entrepreneurship*, Oxford: Pergamon Press, pp. 107–24.
Gibson, I. (ed.) (1997), *Antisense and Ribozyme Methodology*, Weinheim: Chapman and Hall.
Li Kim Lee and C.M. Roth (2003), 'Antisense technology in molecular and cellular bioengineering', *Current Opinion in Biotechnology*, **14**, 505–11.
Mann, M.J. and V.J. Dzau (2000), 'Therapeutic applications of transcription factor decoy oligonucleotides', *Journal of Clinical Investigation*, November, **106**(9), 1071–75.
Pelengaris, S., B. Rudolph and T. Littlewood (2000), 'Action of Myc in vivo-proliferation and apoptosis', *Current Opinion in Genetic Development*, February, **10**(1), 100–105.
Schmidt, E.V. (1999), 'The role of c-myc in cellular growth control', *Oncogene*, 13 May, **18**(19), 2988–96.
Tidol, D.M. and R.V. Giles (2000), 'Mechanisms of action of antisense oligonucleotides', in P. Couvreur and C. Malvy (eds), *Pharmaceutical Aspects in Oligonucleotides*, London: Taylor and Francis.

Index